RELIGION ONLINE

RELIGION ONLINE

Finding Faith on the Internet

Edited by
Lorne L. Dawson and Douglas E. Cowan

ROUTLEDGE
NEW YORK AND LONDON

Published in 2004 by
Routledge
29 West 35th Street
New York, NY 10001
www.routledge-ny.com

Published in Great Britain by
Routledge
11 New Fetter Lane
London EC4P 4EE
www.routledge.co.uk

Routledge is an imprint of the Taylor & Francis Group.
Printed in the United States of America on acid free paper.

#53287606

10 9 8 7 6 5 4 3 2 1

Library of Congress Cataloging-in-Publication Data

Religion online : finding faith on the Internet / edited by Lorne L. Dawson and Douglas E.
Cowan.
        p. cm.
Includes bibliographical references and index.
    ISBN 0-415-97021-0 (alk. paper) — ISBN 0-415-97022-9 (pbk. : alk. paper)
    1. Religion—Computer network resources.   I. Dawson, Lorne L., 1954–   II. Cowan,
Douglas E.
    BL37.R46 2004
    025.06′2—dc22

                                                            2003022731

Contents

Part III: New Religions in Cyberspace

Part IV: Religious Quests and Contests in Cyberspace

Acknowledgments

The editors would like to express their appreciation to several publications and publishers for permission to reprint edited versions of the following materials in this book. "Cyberfaith: How Americans Pursue Religion Online," by Elena Larsen and the Pew Internet and American Life Project, is available as a report at www.pewinternet.org. "Cyberspace as Sacred Space: Communicating Religion on Computer Networks" by Stephen D. O'Leary is a slightly edited version of an article that first appeared in the *Journal of the American Academy of Religion* 64, 1996: 781–808. "New Religions and the Internet: Recruiting in a New Public Space" by Lorne L. Dawson and Jenna Hennebry is a slightly edited version of an article that first appeared in the *Journal of Contemporary Religion* 14, 1999: 17–39, www.tandf.co.uk/journals/carfax/13537903.html. Chapter 10, "The Cybersangha: Buddhism on the Internet" by Charles S. Prebish, is a modified version of Chapter 5 of Prebish's book *Luminous Passage: The Practice and Study of Buddhism in America* (Berkeley, CA: University of California Press). Chapter 15, "Virtual Pilgrimage to Ireland's Croagh Patrick" by Mark MacWilliams, modifies and extends material that first appeared in "Virtual Pilgrimages on the Internet," *Religion* 32, 2002: 315–335, published by Elsevier.

Finally, as always, Douglas Cowan would like to thank his wife Joie for her endless patience and unfailing support. Lorne Dawson would like to thank his wife Dianne for providing the loving support that makes everything possible, including this book.

1
Introduction

LORNE L. DAWSON AND DOUGLAS E. COWAN

The Weird, the Wonderful, and What's Next

The Internet is changing the face of religion worldwide. This is a simple but very important claim, one that this book is beginning to document in part to urge others to pay closer attention in the future. The Internet has suffered from an excessively effusive press—it has been hyped and demonized in the popular media to a point where fewer and fewer people may care to pay attention. But the rapidly expanding social-scientific literature on the Internet is discovering the truth behind the hyperbole. Cyberspace is not quite as unusual a place as sometimes predicted. Life in cyberspace is in continuity with so-called "real life," and this holds true for religion as well. People are doing online pretty much what they do offline, but they are doing it differently. Activity is being mediated electronically, and this mediation allows things to be done in ways that are somewhat new and sometimes entirely innovative. We are just beginning to grasp some of the consequences of these changes—which are often rather subtle—for the social life of users. The consequences for religion are as yet largely unknown. Will this new way of being religious make a difference in how religion is conceived and practiced in the future? A brief look at some instances of religion online helps indicate how the Internet is indeed making a difference.

In the rapidly expanding world of Neopagan belief and practice, people belong to covens, not churches, and the term "coven" has a very distinct meaning in this tradition. Gerald Gardner, considered by many the father of modern Wicca, declared that a model coven consisted of "six 'perfect couples' of men and women, plus a leader. Ideally, the couples would be married or be lovers, in order to produce the best harmony and results in magic" (Guiley 1999: 68). Janet and Stewart Farrar, whose own books have popularized Wicca far beyond the British Isles, concur, opining that larger covens tend to become too depersonalized (Farrar and Farrar 1984: 180). Among other popular writers on Wicca and Witchcraft, similar definitions obtain (e.g., Buckland 1987: 53; RavenWolf 1993: 20; Guiley 1999: 68). These definitions are marked by two important consistencies: (a) the small size of the group, which ideally leads to (b) a level of trust and intimacy usually possible only after extended interpersonal association (cf. Berger 1999).

Something mysterious happens, though, when covens go online—when they become "cybercovens." Older, established definitions are traded in for newer, often less precise understandings of what a Wiccan working group is or can become. Traditionally led by a High Priestess initiated into a particular lineage and heir to the office by dint of long training and preparation, covens often carefully screen potential members, and participation is by invitation only. Online, however, the notion of a coven has become considerably more elastic. Lisa McSherry, for example, who as Lady Ma'at is High Priestess of the cybercoven JaguarMoon, defines a "cybercoven" simply as "a group of people of an earth-based religious faith or belief system who interact primarily, if not solely, through the Internet and/or the World Wide Web" (www.jaguarmoon.org/whatis.htm). Here, though, she says little about what that interaction entails or how large the group should be. Moonglade (www.angelfire.com/wizard/moonglade) also calls itself an online coven, though at this point it is comprised of only two members: the High Priestess, "Serenity," a fifteen-year-old who has been practicing Wicca since she was thirteen, and "Amethyst Moon," whose online profile is no longer active. The Coven of the Silver Unicorn (www.geocities.com/Athens/Styx/5357) exists principally online but hopes to make the transition offline. "The coven accepts one & all," its membership policy states, "regardless of background." Finally, consider the Bella Luna Cyber Coven, which has operated as a discussion group through the Yahoo portal since March 2000 and at the time of this writing posts an average of just under sixty messages per month. At this point, Bella Luna has ninety-five members listed, the vast majority of whom, however (including Bella Luna herself, the list owner), have chosen to disclose no personal information beyond their gender in the available group profile folders. Indeed, nearly one quarter of Bella Luna members chose not to disclose even so much as their gender.

This illustration of the shift from the offline world to the online indicates two very important social consequences of the Internet: a crisis of authority and a crisis of authenticity (cf. Cowan forthcoming; Dawson 2000: 43–44; Dawson 2001: 6–7). First, because there is no mechanism by which information posted to or claims made on the Internet may be vetted beforehand, the World Wide Web produces what some have either lauded or deplored as the phenomenon of "instant experts" (cf. Berger and Ezzy, this volume; Hadden and Cowan 2000b; Wright 2000). One wonders, for example, just how a fifteen-year-old girl with only two years experience in the Craft could legitimately promote herself as a High Priestess. Second, has the meaning of the concept not been irretrievably compromised if in the online world a "coven" can be created by anyone regardless of experience, can include as many people as wish to join, regardless of the interpersonal dynamics that emerge in covens offline, and can exist (in many cases) as little more than chatty discussion lists rather than serious religious working groups? If a coven can mean anything its online users want it to mean, has it not ceased to mean anything at all? While we are not suggesting that this is a necessary consequence of religious participation on the Internet, this shift in sensibilities happened online because of unique features of the Internet as a way of bringing people together. The existence, nature, and use of the medium made a difference.

The substitution of a cyberspace for a real place, of a virtual community for a physically present one, often has a strange leveling effect on religions (Beaudoin 1998: 56–58). The obviously constructed and pluralistic character of religious expressions online tends to have a relativizing effect on the truth claims of any one religion or its authorities. Rather than appearing unreal, with enough exposure to the Internet religious people may come "to doubt the absolute claims of sacredness and permanence that a religious site can make in the 'real world'" in light of the obvious "ephemerality and heightened access [to] religion in cyberspace" (Beaudoin 1998: 58) Moreover, the easy coexistence of so many different and openly heterodox views in cyberspace exposes the Net surfer to a more fluid doctrinal environment, one that has the potential to encourage individual religious and spiritual experimentation. Ironically, it would appear, this holds equally true for religious traditions like contemporary Neopaganism, which is only a few decades old, as it does for traditions that have flourished for millennia. A few other examples of the new face of religion/spirituality in cyberspace will help to indicate other aspects of the quiet revolution in religious sensibilities that may be taking place with the aid of the Internet.

In India, when a woman is warned of impending bad luck by an astrologer, she seeks, as is common in her culture, to avert the cruel fate by appealing to the gods. "In the old days, [she] might have taken her astrologer's advice literally and made the 1,450 kilometer (900 mile) journey to a temple on the southern tip of India to pay respects to Shani—the Hindu god she was said to have angered" (Srinivasan 2002). Today she turns to the Web page www.prarthana.com, where, with the click of a mouse and a credit card charge, she can choose from a list of four hundred temples and arrange for an appropriate *puja* (ceremony) to be performed on her behalf. In this way, millions of Hindus living in diaspora outside India can arrange for various religious rites: marking a birth or a death, help in securing a job, or aid in averting illness. In return they receive a package in the mail from the temple, certifying that the ceremony has been performed and providing a sample of the food blessed and placed on the altar as a sacrifice to the god or gods. Likewise, the devotees of different gurus, temples, and religious organizations in India can go online to participate virtually in a variety of festivities and rites. When traveling they can even continue a lively discourse with their guru, meditate, or experience *satsang* (a group meeting for guidance and support) through the use of e-mail, Internet Relay Chat, and Webcasts (*The Times of India* 2003).

What are we to make of these new possibilities? Is the Hindu tradition being trivialized or strengthened by such cyber-rites and services? We should not scoff and rush to judge these developments. Seeing them and other cyber-religious acts for what they are will require a careful consideration of the nature and history of the traditions involved and an assessment of the thoughts and feelings of those using such services. Indirectly, the Internet may be changing many of the basic religious/spiritual sensibilities of users, but sometimes in ways that actually mark a return to an historically earlier understanding of religious experiences and life (see O'Leary, this volume; and Dawson, this volume). While there are changes, more often than not there are also important continuities with traditional practices—if these practices are fairly and honestly perceived.

In Canada a young, ordinary boy named Adam has discovered an extraordinary talent. He can heal people at a distance using the Internet (Gill 2003). People with inoperable or untreatable terminal illnesses contact his Web site at www.distanthealing.com. If they are selected for help, he requests a color picture of them. Then a time is arranged for both parties to sit quietly in their homes, whether across the country or just blocks away. At these times, Adam concentrates on the picture and claims that he can see, layer by layer, into the very physical being of the sick person. He sees more as well: "I can see a physical layer: the heart beating, guts moving, that sort of stuff. Then there's a layer that's just like a hollow image of the person and there are green dots where there are problems—or green bulges, depending on the problem" (Gill 2003: F7). As though he were wearing a set of virtual-reality goggles, he claims he can see the illnesses and by bombarding them with "energy" can destroy them. Sometimes he moves his hands—as in a virtual-reality game—to split or pop cancerous tumors.

The story is incredible, but tales of such miraculous healings are common to religious traditions from around the world and throughout history. Following the example of Jesus, they are frequently part of the grounds for declaring someone a saint in the Catholic Church. But the use of the Internet, while seemingly not essential to the result, allows it to happen much more easily, free from the scrutiny of churches, the state, the medical profession, and simply other people. Moreover, as Adam's parents stress, the Internet allows the healings to happen at all, since they are intent on protecting his identity and his right to live the life of an ordinary teenager. It makes this unusual combination of extraordinary, direct access and nearly complete anonymity possible. With the imitation by others that is sure to come, such so-called "faith healing" is likely to become an increasingly common phenomenon online, precisely because it can be electronically mediated. Of course, some American televangelists have been trying for years to reach out and cure the ills of their TV audiences, crying out through the screen and sending the healing love of God to those afflicted in some way. But television as a broadcast medium lacks the personal touch of the Internet at its best.

In ways illustrated by these few examples and many others raised in the essays collected in this book, the Internet is adding an interesting and important twist to the religious life of a growing number of people. It is intensifying changes already afoot in society and it is broaching entirely new possibilities. But it is also fomenting change simply by helping religious groups to do what they have always done better. It is allowing more people to reach out to more others, in more ways, to a greater extent than ever before in history. The diffusion and clash of religious worldviews has taken a quantum leap forward, but so, it is hoped, has our ability to learn about and from each other and develop ways to live in harmony.

The Internet, Society, and Religion

It has become something of a commonplace in Internet studies, religious or otherwise, to comment on the recent birth and remarkable growth of the computer technology that makes the Internet and its sweeping cultural impact upon us possible. We will not rehash these claims here and urge readers who are interested to consult some of the excellent works on the subject (e.g., Castells 2001; Gillies and Cailliau 2000; Rheingold 1993; Slevin 2000; Wellman and Haythornthwaite 2002). But a few points are in order. First, it is important to note that while the Internet has existed technically since the early 1960s, the application by which it is best known—the World Wide Web—is little more than a decade old. The speed and extent to which the Internet has been embraced by a wide diversity of people in such a short period of time are un-paralleled in human history. The rate of growth is staggering. Worldwide, the number of Internet users is estimated to have been 16 million in 1995, 378 million in 2000 (Castells 2001: 260), and more than 500 million in 2002 (Wellman and Haythornthwaite 2002: 11). If for no other reason, this phenomenal rate of growth assures the importance of continued research into the Internet and its effects on society.

Second, and somewhat paradoxically, it is equally important to realize that the Internet has not grown everywhere. Despite the industry rhetoric and commercial hyperbole about "global connectivity" and the "universalization" of access and meaningful participation, the statistics reveal that a very real "digital divide" exists in the world (cf. Castells 2001; Norris 2001). Any informed discussion of the Internet and its relationship to culture and society must give serious consideration to the division between the Internet haves and have-nots. As Castells points out, for example, "London has more Internet domains than the whole of Africa" (2001: 264) and less than 1 percent of Africa's population are Internet users (2001: 260). This divide, he continues, exists in terms of both access to Internet technology (i.e., who gets to go online) and the production of Internet resources (i.e., who decides what one finds online), and in both regards the asymmetry is growing (Castells 2001: 216). Hence research must be conducted into not only who is using the Internet and for what purpose but also how production of Internet content both reflects other deeply embedded social and cultural divisions and further contributes to them.

Finally, as suggested above, the Internet is both a mirror and a shadow of the offline world. That is, there is very little in the real world that is not electronically reproduced online, and very little online that has no offline foundation or referent. This means that much of today's online activity is rather pedestrian and anticlimactic when compared to the initial hype and rhetoric. According to the Pew Internet and American Life Project, e-mail remains the most common online activity by far (www.pewinternet.org), while searching for information—or what passes for information—comes a distant second. Beyond simply providing information, though—whether it be the current rate of exchange between Indian rupees and Thai bhat, the most direct air connection from Berlin to Bali, or the airspeed velocity of an African swallow—what is significant is how Internet content providers are also seeking to reproduce less tangible aspects of social experience. Online bookstores such as Amazon.com, for example, are trying to recreate the real-life experience of browsing the shelves at a bookshop. When a visitor to the Amazon site pulls up a listing for one book, the software running the online store automatically searches out and displays similar books that other "customers" have either considered or purchased. More than once, we have purchased books other than those we were looking for but which were suggested by this feature—not unlike the experience of finding something on the bookstore shelf right next to the book you were seeking. Likewise, many Web sites that deal with one or another aspect of religious life, belief, or practice are seeking ways to communicate not just information about faith but an experience of that faith as well.

Though its presence on the Internet hardly merits the rhetoric of some of its more enthusiastic observers (e.g., Brasher 2001), few would contest that religion has found a solid home online. As Hadden and Cowan note (2000b: 8):

> There is scarcely a religious tradition, movement, group, or phenomenon absent entirely from the Net. From the Norse neopaganism of Ásatrú to Christian countercult refutations of it, from Tibetan Buddhist prayer bowls and thangka paintings to Wiccan scrying bowls that come with easy-to-follow instructions, from a disenfranchised Catholic bishop exiled to a non-existent North African diocese to a cyber-monastery established exclusively for non-resident students of Zen.

And the online presence of religion is growing daily. One Pew Internet and American Life study reports that, among Americans, "25% of Internet users have gotten religious or spiritual information at one time." Once again, though, this impressive figure must be tempered with other Pew-generated data showing that the number of Internet users who seek online religious information on a *daily basis* is considerably smaller, at just under 5 percent (see Larsen, this volume). As we point out in more detail below, more empirical research, informed by insights from sociological theory, is required before we can say with any certainty just what is going on with religion on the Internet and why. This is not to say, however, that no progress has been made.

One of the most useful conceptual distinctions made about religion on the Internet is that between *religion online* and *online religion*. First proposed by Christopher Helland (2000), this distinction grounds many of the analyses contained in this volume, though others have elaborated and refined it (e.g., Hadden and Cowan 2000b; Cowan forthcoming; Young, this volume). Put simply, on the one hand *religion online* describes the provision of information about and/or services related to various religious groups and traditions. This includes the many thousands of Web sites established by congregations, mosques, temples, and synagogues as well as the larger religious institutions of which these are a part. Commercial sites selling an astounding variety of religious books, products, and supplies fall under the same broad rubric of religion online. *Online religion*, on the other hand, invites Internet visitors to participate in religious practices. These practices may range from online prayer, meditation, ritual observance of Catholic Mass, Hindu *puja*, and the Wiccan Sabbat, to spiritual counselling, online Tarot readings, astrological charts, and runecasts (cf. Cowan forthcoming; Cowan and Hadden forthcoming; Hadden and Cowan 2000b). The distinction, however, is not absolute.

An increasing number of Web sites fall somewhere between these extremes, offering their visitors some combination of the two. So perhaps, as Glenn Young (this volume) argues, we should treat this distinction as identifying the end points of a continuum and not as a dichotomy. Increasingly, congregational Web sites, for example, not only tell visitors when services are held and where the church building is located but also offer online prayer chains, devotional pages, and even electronic confessionals. Likewise, altars from a variety of traditions are available online for perpetual e-adoration, confusing the line between the provision of religious information and the actual practice of religion. Even when the use of the Web appears to be confined to providing various religious texts, more may be at stake. In cases like the Qur'an, Muslims can fulfill their religious duty to propagate the revelations of Allah with the recitation of the sacred verses made available online (Bunt 2000; Bunt, this volume).

It is increasingly difficult to separate the mere provision of information from the practice of religion in cyberspace. While Dawson and Hennebry (this volume; cf. Berger and Ezzy, this volume) challenge the notion that the Internet is a very efficient medium for the recruitment of converts, the Internet is used quite commonly for evangelism and proselytization, which are quintessentially religious activities. Likewise the Internet has proven to be an excellent venue for religious antagonism and countermovement (cf. Cowan, this volume; Introvigne 2000; Mayer 2000). And it has become a unique resource for self-proclaimed religious virtuosi, who have found online a potential audience thousands of times greater than they could have dreamed of even a decade ago. Fuller research into religion on the Internet, then, involves the study of new ways to be religious and not just the description of new ways to convey religious information.

Utopias, Dystopias, and Beyond

The first works published on the nature and social impact of the Internet were highly speculative. Regrettably and yet almost inevitably, before serious study could be undertaken commentators began to sing the praise of the transformative and liberating potentials of the new medium (e.g., Barlow 1995; Rheingold 1993; Rushkoff 1994; Turkle 1995). Drawing primarily on their own experiences with the Internet and limited interviews with heavy users, these rather utopian analyses announced the birth of a new "electronic frontier." A "Wild West" of the imagination fashioned from technology and talk, where people from diverse backgrounds could meet in ways that transcended the physical and social limitations of their daily lives. The first truly global and mass mode of communication, they declared, was vastly expanding the time-and-space parameters of social interaction. With the anonymity of discourse online, people could readily meet individuals from other places, cultures, social classes, ages, and occupations. New and perhaps even multiple identities were possible, as were friendships and conflicts with people of similar and different turns of mind from everywhere in the world. With the rush to go online in the mid-1990s, humankind, we were told, was taking a giant step forward into the "global village" that Marshall McLuhan had predicted in the 1960s.

Other commentators, however, were just as quick to sense the dark side of the Internet. Dystopian texts called for greater caution in embracing the Internet (e.g., Birkerts 1994; Lockhart 1997; Nguyen and Alexander 1996; Slouka 1995; Stoll 1995). The information superhighway, they warned, isolated individuals from real life. It indulged an illusion of sociality that was superficial and furthered the real alienation of modern individuals from themselves, their families, their friends and coworkers, and their neighborhoods. The anonymity of communicating online allowed for deception—men masquerading as women, and teenagers pretending to be professionals ready to offer advice. As popularized by Hollywood technothrillers like *The Net* and *Enemy of the State*, the ever-widening electronic Web gave government agencies unprecedented opportunities to monitor and intervene in the lives of ordinary citizens. The "surveillance" society was coming, and it was largely a creature of the Internet (Lyon 1994). The increasing commercialization of cyberspace also meant that a capitalist agenda would soon dominate this new frontier, stifling true creativity and social protest. Finally, some feared that increased exposure to the Internet, with its growing dependence on images and graphical icons, would lower levels of literacy and the damage the capacity for serious thought as young minds became immersed in the glib, irreverent, and rock video–inspired culture of the new hypertext environment.

The first studies of religion in cyberspace veered towards these utopian and dystopian extremes (e.g., Beckerlegge 2001; Brasher 2001; Brooke 1997; Davis

1998; Lawrence 2000; Ramo 1996; Zaleski 1997). Calling attention to the pervasive presence of religion online, these early investigations tended either to sing the praises of various fascinating possibilities for doing religion in new ways or to condemn the presumed excesses of virtual life, often from the perspective of some more traditional religious commitment. In general, however, the study of religion online has suffered from relative neglect when compared with the burgeoning literature on the political, medical, educational, and even sexual uses and consequences of the Internet.

By the late 1990s things began to change. The first truly empirical studies of life in cyberspace and Internet usage began to appear (see, e.g., the reviews of the literature provided in DiMaggio et al. 2001 and Castells 2001, and the studies collected in Wellman and Haythornthwaite 2002). The consequences of the Internet for religion also began to receive some serious consideration (e.g., Bunt 2000; Hadden and Cowan 2000a; Hojsgaard and Warburg, forthcoming; Larsen 2001). But detailed study of how religion is being practiced online is only just beginning, especially the effort to understand developments online in the context of wider social and cultural conditions changing life in late-modern societies (e.g., Castells 2001; Fornas et al. 2002; Jones 1998; Slevin 2000). This book is part of that new effort.

"The Medium Is the Message"

The Internet has become a part of everyday life for hundreds of millions of people (Wellman and Haythornthwaite 2002). The fact that we have adopted the technology so fast, however, means we are at risk of overlooking its significance. Like the telephone or television, it has become a routine feature of our daily lives. But communications technologies are rarely neutral in their effects (Fischer 1993; Postman 1985). They are not mere media for the transmission of messages. Rather, as McLuhan (1965) argued so successfully long ago, "the medium is the message." The habitat in which we live is always changed by our inventions: from money, clocks, trains, and planes to elevators, ATMs, and shopping malls. The cities and nations in which we live have been radically restructured, for example, by the advent of the automobile, and in ways few anticipated. Communications technologies mold the messages we deliver in unanticipated ways as well, crucially influencing our self-conceptions, notions of human relations and community, and the nature of reality itself (e.g., O'Leary, this volume). From the first written word to the World Wide Web, each technology introduced into our lives has its own unique signature and set of social consequences.

Religious uses of the Internet evoke a comparison with the religious uses of television, most notably televangelism, based in turn on the earlier use of radio by religious groups in America (e.g., Frankel 1987). There are important continuities between the religious uses of these technologies that have yet to be explored. But, there are important differences as well—differences that need to be kept in mind in the search for the signature of the Internet.

At least five crucial differences come to mind: (1) the Internet is an interactive and not simply a broadcast medium; (2) the Internet is truly multimedial; (3) the Internet employs hypertextuality; (4) anyone can launch himself onto the World Wide Web with relative ease and little expense; (5) the Internet is global in its reach. With a comparatively small investment in time, money, and knowledge, Internet users can make their religious views known, at least potentially, to millions of others throughout the world. Television production, on the other hand, is largely the preserve of small cultural elites with the resources required to operate in this expensive medium. While these elites have a vested interest in the status quo, the World Wide Web is open in principle and in practice to almost anyone, no matter how unconventional his opinions. When posting their views online, people are likely to be confronted with alternative opinions posed by people from lands and traditions quite alien to their own (see Lövheim, this volume). Because the flexibility of hypertext allows the Web visitor to select the order of the information presented on a particular site, that information is encountered in a variety of ways simultaneously. Hypertextually speaking, it is entirely possible that no two visitors will view the site in exactly the same way. Both parties to this communication—content provider and Internet visitor—are actively engaged in an interaction that is always unique and largely uncontrolled. These key, qualitative differences in the medium itself have helped to generate the significant quantitative difference in the sheer presence of computer-mediated communication—a difference that in turn magnifies the social and cultural significance of this particular media revolution.

Questions, Questions, Questions . . .

As the social-scientific study of the Internet begins to mature, spawning numerous new empirical studies of how the Internet is being used and with what results, it is becoming increasingly apparent that scholars of religion need to address some basic questions. At least six research concerns spring to mind:

1. We need more and better studies of who is using the Internet for religious purposes, how they are using it, and why. In this regard we need longitudinal studies to detect any changes that are happening with the passage of time and increased experience online.
2. We need studies of the nature and quality of people's experiences doing religious things online. In this regard we need surveys and interviews of users and case studies of groups, Web sites, or particular activities.
3. We need studies of the relationships between people's religious activities online and offline, as well as their religious activities online and offline and other kinds of activities online and offline. We need to gain a better grasp of the overall social context of cyber-religiosity.

4. We need detailed and comparative studies of the specific religious activities online. How is the Internet being used to engage in such things as prayer, meditation, ritual, education, and organizational tasks, and to what effect?

5. We need studies of how the features of the technology itself are being utilized in the service of religious ends and with what consequences for the intrinsic and the social aspects of religious life? What are the actual and potential implications of hypertextuality for religion, for example? Are there special interface issues affecting the religious uses of this technology? How can the technology be changed or improved to facilitate its religious utilization?

6. We need to discern whether the technological and cultural aspects of the Internet are better suited to the advancement of one style or type of religion over another. Is the preponderance of Neopagan activities online, for example, coincidental? Or is the Internet better suited, for instance, to the practices and organizational structure of Hinduism than Catholicism? What is the case, why, and with what implications for the future?

Click to Continue . . .

Successful navigation anywhere is a function of two interrelated processes: orientation and intention—knowing where you are when you begin and having some idea where you want to be when you finish. To that end, we suggest that readers begin their exploration of religion in cyberspace with the executive summary of Elena Larsen's Pew Internet and American Life Project report, "Cyberfaith: How Americans Pursue Religion Online." It helps to establish some of the base facts from which everything else follows, bringing much needed balance to the commercial hyperbole about Internet usage. Following that, the book is divided into four sections, each of which treats a different dimension of religion in the online world.

In Part I, we explore the nature of online religious communication and community. Christopher Helland introduces the Internet as a medium for religious communciation and practice, suggesting that it is "a new space where a freedom of religious expression rules supreme" and that religion online will become more and more a part of everyday life in our technologically mediated world. Following this, we are pleased to be able to reprint Stephen D. O'Leary's pathbreaking essay on "Cyberspace as Sacred Space." O'Leary's essay was the first study to do three things: (1) undertake the serious academic study of religion online; (2) analyze the nature and consequences of performing rituals online; and (3) attempt to understand this new phenomenon in a broader context, that of Walter Ong's theory of the impact of previous communication technologies on human culture. In all three regards it set an example that is still largely unsurpassed.

Douglas Cowan's father bought his first computer at the age of 69 and to this day prefers *Lead Pencil* 1.0, but his son was exposed to computers before entering preschool. This is true for most young people in Western societies today. The Swedish scholar Mia Lövheim investigates how young people—those for whom computers are not an alien technology and who grew up with the Internet as part of daily life—are using the World Wide Web to explore questions of religious identity and community. Since these are questions that are vigorously pursued offline as well, this highlights the important point that the Internet is not a reality separate from "the real world," but an electronic extension of it. How, though, does community happen online, and how would we know it if we saw it? These are some of the questions addressed by Lorne Dawson as necessary considerations for any informed research into religion on the Internet. Religions traditionally happen in communities; they form and inform communities. If "community" looks different online and off, then what are the consequences for religion? How would we know if online communities are different or even if they exist at all? What criteria need we implement to describe online communities, religious or otherwise, and analyze them effectively? Answering these questions will help us understand more fully what it means to be religious in cyberspace.

Part II moves to a consideration of how culturally mainstream religions—those that have long and deeply embedded cultural traditions offline—have adapted to life on the Web. While it is unlikely that online religious observance will ever supplant offline participation in Catholic Mass, Hindu *puja*, or Muslim *salat*, Glenn Young looks at how some mainstream Christian traditions have used the World Wide Web to bridge the gap between the mere provision of information about religion ("religion online") and the more complex experience of religious practice through the Internet ("online religion"). In "This Is My Church," Heidi Campbell discusses how evangelical Christians in Britain have used the Internet as a missionary medium, reaching out to youth in the European club culture. Then, moving from the techno beat of the clubs to the centuries-old call of the *muezzin*, Gary Bunt examines many of the ways in which the Qu'ran has been used online. While the revelation to Muhammed is usually considered the Word of God only when read aloud, Bunt shows how its online presence contributes to the Muslim duty of *da'wa*, the propagation of the faith. Finally, continuing the discussion of the Internet as a site for the creation of religious community, Charles Prebish investigates the emergence of a "cybersangha," an electronic community binding together Buddhists from around the world.

It is likely that the Internet will benefit some religions more than others and in different ways. Because of their inherently innovative character, we include in Part III a number of examples of how new religious movements, particularly emergent Neopagan groups, are using the Web to experiment and extend their own religious communities and understandings. To begin, we reprint another early and influential study, Lorne Dawson's and Jenna Hennebry's essay, "New Religions and the Internet: Recruiting in a New Public Space" (1999). As people first turned their attention to religion and the Internet, popular fears arose, partly in the wake of the Heaven's Gate mass suicide of 1997, that the Internet would become a powerful recruiting tool for dangerous "cults." Examining both the Internet as a communicative space and the literature on recruitment to new religious movements, Dawson and Hennebry challenge this notion while also describing some of the other promises and perils of taking religion online. As Helen Berger and Douglas Ezzy point out, however, the cultural anxiety over Internet recruitment still remains. Addressing this concern, their essay considers teen witches both in the United States and Australia and locates the Internet as only one of an array of sources to which young people turn in their quest for religious identity and commitment. Wendy Griffin looks at the emergence of Goddess spirituality and how the Internet has provided an alternative venue for followers of the Goddess to form communities and to contribute to the globalization of various forms of Neopagan belief and practice. We close this section with Marilyn Krogh and Brooke Pillifant's unique look at the House of Netjer, a revival of ancient Egyptian religion which both began and continues online. Krogh and Pillifant trace the origins and nature of this cyber-religion and its all-important shift to an offline presence. In this, they conclude, "the House of Netjer is not a virtual community, sustained only by electronic communication among members. Instead, the House of Netjer is a blend of offline and online relationships."

Part IV concludes our excursions into cyberspace by considering the Internet as a site for religious quests and contests—the search for enlightenment and fulfillment versus attempts to control the religious experiences of others. Following the path of an online pilgrimage to Ireland's Croagh Patrick, Mark MacWilliams discusses how Internet visitors "can simulate a sacred journey for educational, economic, and spiritual purposes." In "Searching for the Apocalypse in Cyberspace," Robert Campbell discusses another example of the confluence of online and offline worlds, showing once again how the Internet may be changing the basic nature of some religious discourses in subtle yet important ways. Finally, using the often controversial Church of Scientology as an example, Douglas Cowan explores how different social movements have pursued religious conflict in cyberspace and what kinds of movements are best served by the hardware, software, and, indeed, the philosophy of the Internet.

Each of the essays in this book demonstrates that the range of religious experience one can encounter on the Internet is broad and varied. Most of these encounters are likely to mirror real-life events and conflicts. But over and over again the evidence also suggests that subtle transformations are under way as the Internet brings new possibilities and dimensions of experience to almost every aspect of religious life. The key is to detect and delineate the elements of continuity and difference, since the future of the Internet as a medium of religiosity will hinge on the presence, nature, and degree of both elements. If what cyberspace offers is too different from the experience of religion offline, its utility and appeal will be limited; if it is too much the same, it will be limited as well. But small changes of the right type that expand and enhance our religious sensibilities and levels of satisfaction are bound to leave their mark. We offer these exploratory essays in a new field of research to demonstrate the interesting and important ways we can begin to understand the interface of the one of the oldest and one of the newest cultural resources of humanity.

A Final Caution

The Internet is a remarkable resource for information on an almost infinite variety of topics. It provides the quickest way to answer our most basic questions. In some instances it can provide access to documents, statistics, and analyses that would have required extraordinary effort, expense, and expertise to attain even a decade ago. It has become the logical first recourse for anyone doing research on almost any subject. This holds true for religious concerns as well, as the essays in this book demonstrate. The Internet has opened up a truly exciting opportunity to learn about the religious beliefs and practices of peoples scattered across the globe and even more to reach out and actually speak to individuals holding these beliefs. True religious dialogue may still be wanting online, but the sheer possibility of such dialogue has changed the spiritual landscape that humanity inhabits forever. The Internet offers us the opportunity to banish the kinds of religious parochialism based on ignorance that have harmed so many throughout the centuries.

But as the essays in this book also starkly reveal, the Internet must be used with caution when investigating religious concerns. Everything is subject to interpretation but, as common sense suggests, some things are more obviously open to interpretation than others. Religion, like politics and sex, as the old adage asserts, is one of those subjects. Extreme care must be taken in using the Internet as a resource for research on religion to discern the explicit and implicit biases of the people and organizations providing the information. In the unregulated environment of cyberspace extreme opinions can be voiced with little fear of the consequences, and propaganda of one sort or another is pervasive (see Cowan, this volume). What you read may or may not be accurate or even true, and it is wise to exercise some skepticism about claims until you can access multiple sources of information and critically compare them. When the views of a religion and its opponents clash, for example, an ethically responsible researcher, whether a student or eminent scholar, must seek to hear and give voice to both sides of any dispute. Ironically, the very freedom with which ideas can be posted online and the sheer scope and diversity of the opinions offered increase the care with which all information must be approached. The Internet makes getting what appear to be "the facts" of any situation incredibly easy, but at a price. We must work harder than with other media to avoid the lure of fool's gold.

References

Barlow, J. D. (1995). "What Are We Doing Online?" *Harper's* (August): 35–46.

Beaudoin, T. (1998). *Virtual Faith: The Irreverent Spiritual Quest of Generation X*. San Francisco: Jossey-Bass.

Beckerlegge, G., (2001). "Computer-Mediated Religion: Religion on the Internet at the Turn of the Twenty-First Century." *In From Sacred Text to Internet*, ed. G. Beckerlegge. London: Ashgate.

Berger, H. A. (1999). *A Community of Witches: Contemporary Neo-Paganism and Witchcraft in the United States*. Columbia, SC: University of South Carolina Press.

Birkerts, S. (1994). *The Gutenberg Elegies: The Fate of Reading in an Electronic Age*. Winchester, MA: Faber and Faber.

Brasher, B. (2001). *Give Me that Online Religion*. San Francisco: Jossey-Bass.

Brooke, T. (1997). *Virtual Gods: The Seduction of Power and Pleasure in Cyberspace*. Eugene, OR: Harvest House.

Buckland, R. (1987). *Buckland's Complete Book of Witchcraft*. St. Paul, MN: Llewellyn Publications.

Bunt, G. (2000). *Virtually Islamic: Computer-Mediated Communication and Cyber Islamic Environments*. Cardiff: University of Wales Press.

Castells, M. (2001). *The Internet Galaxy: Reflections on the Internet, Business, and Society*. Oxford: Oxford University Press.

Cowan, D. E. (forthcoming). *Cyberhenge: Magic, Metatechnology, and the Neopagan Internet*. New York: Routledge.

Cowan, D. E., and J. K. Hadden, (2004). "Virtually Religious: New Religious Movements and the World Wide Web." In *The Oxford Handbook of New Religious Movements*, ed. J. R. Lewis. New York: Oxford University Press.

Davis, E. (1998). *Techgnosis: Myth, Magic, and Mysticism in the Age of Information*. New York: Three Rivers Press.

Dawson, L. L. (2000). "Researching Religion in Cyberspace: Issues and Strategies." In *Religion on the Internet: Research Prospects and Promises*, ed. J. K. Hadden and D. E. Cowan, 25–54. London: JAI Press/Elsevier Science.

———. (2001). "Doing Religion in Cyberspace: The Promise and the Perils." *Council of Societies for the Study of Religion Bulletin* 30: 3–9.

DiMaggio, P., E. Hargittai, W. R. Neuman, and J. P. Robinson (2001). "Social Implications of the Internet: The Internet's Effect on Society." In *Annual Review of Sociology*, vol. 27, ed. K. S. Cook and J. Hagen. Palo Alto, CA: Annual Reviews.

Farrar, J., and S. Farrar, (1984). *The Witches' Bible: The Complete Witches' Handbook*. Custer, WA: Phoenix Publishing.

Fischer, C. L. (1993). *America Calling: A Social History of the Telephone to 1940*. Berkeley, CA: University of California Press.

Fornas, J., K. Klein, M. Ladendorf, J. Sunden, and M. Sveningsson, eds. (2002). *Digital Borderlands: Cultural Studies of Identity and Interactivity on the Internet*. New York: Peter Lang.

Frankel, R. (1987). *Televangelism: The Marketing of Popular Religion*. Carbondale, IL: Southern Illinois University Press.

Gill, A. (2003). "All about Adam." *Globe and Mail* (May 3): F7.

Gillies, J., and R. Cailliau. (2000). *How the Web Was Born: The Story of the World Wide Web*. Oxford, UK: Oxford University Press.

Guiley, R. E. (1999). *The Encyclopedia of Witches and Witchcraft*, 2nd ed. New York: Facts on File.

Hadden, J. K., and D. E., Cowan, eds. (2000a). *Religion on the Internet: Research Prospects and Promises. Religion and the Social Order*, vol. 8. Greenwich, CT: JAI Press.

———. (2000b). "The Promised Land or Electronic Chaos? Toward Understanding Religion on the Internet." In *Religion on the Internet: Research Prospects and Promises*, ed. J. K. Hadden and D. E. Cowan. London: JAI Press/Elsevier Science.

Helland, C. (2000). "Online Religion/Religion Online and Virtual Communitas." In *Religion on the Internet: Research Prospects and Promises*, ed. J. K. Hadden and D. E. Cowan. London: JAI Press/Elsevier Science.

Hojsgaard, M., and M., Warburg, eds. (forthcoming). *Religion in Cyberspace*. London: Routledge.

Introvigne, M. (2000). "'So Many Evil Things': Anti-Cult Terrorism via the Internet." In J. K. Hadden and D. E. Cowan, eds., *Religion on the Internet: Research Prospects and Promises*. London: JAI Press/Elsevier Science.

Jones, S. (1998). *Cybersociety 2.0: Revisiting Computer-Mediated Communication and Community*. Thousand Oaks, CA: Sage.

Lawrence, B. B. (2000). *The Complete Idiot's Guide to Religions Online.* Indianapolis, IN: Alpha Books.

Lockhart, J. (1997). "Progressive Politics, Electronic Individualism and the Myth of Virtual Community." In *Internet Culture,* ed. David Porter, 219–231. New York: Routledge.

Lyon, D. (1994). *The Electronic Eye: The Rise of the Surveillance Society.* Minneapolis: University of Minnesota Press.

Mayer, J-F. (2000). "Religious Movements and the Internet: The New Frontier of Religious Controversies." In *Religion on the Internet: Research Prospects and Promises,* ed. J. K. Hadden and D. E. Cowan. London: JAI Press/Elsevier Science.

McLuhan, M. (1965). *Understanding Media.* New York: McGraw-Hill.

Nguyen, D. T., and J. Alexander, (1996). "The Coming of Cyberspacetime and the End of the Polity." In *Cultures of Internet,* ed. R. Shields, 99–124. London: Sage.

Norris, P. (2001). *Digital Divide: Civic Engagement, Information Poverty, and the Internet Worldwide.* Cambridge, UK: Cambridge University Press.

Postman, N. (1985). *Amusing Ourselves to Death: Public Discourse in the Age of Show Business.* New York: Penguin Books.

Ramo, J. C. (1996). "Finding God on the Web." *Time.* (Dec.) Reprinted in *Composing Cyberspace: Identity, Community, and Knowledge in the Electronic Age,* ed. R. Holeton, 180–186. Boston: McGraw-Hill

RavenWolf, S. (1993). *To Ride a Silver Broomstick: New Generation Witchcraft.* St. Paul, MN: Llewellyn Publications.

Rheingold, H. (1993). *The Virtual Community: Homesteading on the Electronic Frontier.* Cambridge, MA: MIT Press.

Rushkoff, D. (1994). *Cyberia: Life in the Trenches of Hyperspace.* SanFrancisco: HarperCollins.

Slevin, J. (2000). *The Internet and Society.* Cambridge, UK: Polity Press.

Slouka, M. (1995). *War of the Worlds: Cyberspace and the High-Tech Assault on Reality.* New York: Basic Books.

Smith, M. A., and P., Kollock, eds. (1999). *Communities in Cyberspace.* New York: Routledge.

Srinivasan, S. (2002). "Religion Online: Hindus Turn to the Internet for Prayer." Associated Press (June 27). Retrieved from Worldwide Religion News (www.wwrn.org), June 28, 2003.

Stoll, C. (1995). *Silicon Snake Oil: Second Thoughts on the Information Highway.* New York: Doubleday.

Times of India (2003). "Religion Offers Online 'Satsang'" (July 1). Retrieved from Worldwide Religious News (www.wwrn.org), July 1, 2003.

Turkle, (1995). *Life on the Screen: Identity in the Age of the Internet.* New York: Simon and Schuster.

Wellman, B., and C. Haythornthwaite, eds. (2002), *The Internet in Everyday Life.* Oxford, UK: Blackwell.

Wright, S. (2000). "Instant Genius! Just Add the Net." *.net* (June): 50–58.

Zaleski, J. (1997). *The Soul of Cyberspace.* San Francisco: HarperCollins.

2

Cyberfaith: How Americans Pursue Religion Online

ELENA LARSEN

Some 28 million Americans have used the Internet to get religious and spiritual information and connect with others on their faith journeys. We call them "Religion Surfers."

- 25 percent of Internet users have gotten religious or spiritual information online at one point or another. This is an increase from our survey findings in late 2000, which showed that 21 percent of Internet users—or between 19 million and 20 million people—had gone online to get religious or spiritual material.
- More than 3 million people a day get religious or spiritual material, up from the 2 million that we reported last year.
- For comparison's sake, it is interesting to note that more people have gotten religious or spiritual information online than have gambled online, used Web auction sites, traded stocks online, placed phone calls on the Internet, done online banking, or used Internet-based dating services.

The September 11 terror attacks compelled millions of Internet users to turn to religious issues and concerns online.

- 41 percent of Internet users, many of whom had never considered themselves online spiritual seekers, said they sent or received e-mail prayer requests.
- 23 percent of Internet users turned to online sources to get information about Islam. Presumably most of them considered this to be information-gathering activity rather than spiritual activity.
- 7 percent of Internet users contributed to relief charities online.

The most popular online religious activities are solitary ones. Most Religion Surfers treat the Net as a vast ecclesiastical library and they hunt for general

An executive summary of the Pew Internet and American Life Project (www.pewinternet.org). Used with permission.

spiritual information online. However, they also interact with friends and strangers as they swap advice and prayer support.

- 67 percent of Religion Surfers have accessed information on their own faith.
- 50 percent have sought information on other faiths.
- Religion Surfers appear to be more comfortable offering spiritual advice online than requesting it: 35 percent have used e-mail to offer advice, while 21 percent have sought advice in an e-mail.
- 38 percent of Religion Surfers have used e-mail to send prayer requests. The practice is far more common among congregation members (42 percent) than nonmembers (12 percent).

Within the Religion Surfer population, variations in religious devotion, history, and affiliation play a role in determining what activities attract individuals.

Religion Surfers' online practices can be studied from several viewpoints, based on their offline activities and history. Four patterns of practice highlight different groups: active Religion Surfers use the Internet in different ways from less-active Religion Surfers; religious converts use the Internet in different ways from faith loyalists who remain with the religion in which they were raised; religious outsiders use the Internet in different ways from insiders who consider themselves in the mainstream of their communities; and church or temple members use the Internet in different ways from nonmembers.

- The most active online Religion Surfers (those who go online at least several times a week for spiritual material) are also the most active offline participants in their faiths.
- Those who have converted from the religion in which they were raised are more likely than those who have not to be active Religion Surfers (33 percent vs. 24 percent).
- Religious outsiders are particularly interested in using the Internet to meet others of their own faith and share items of religious interest. Outsiders are those who see themselves as a minority, who say they have few people of the same religion in their local communities, or who say they have faced discrimination due to their beliefs.

For Religion Surfers, the Internet is a useful supplemental tool that enhances their already deep commitment to their beliefs and their churches, synagogues, or mosques. Use of the Internet also seems to be especially helpful to those who feel they are not part of mainstream religious groups. About 27 percent of Religion Surfers attribute to the Internet at least some improvement in their faith lives. Religion Surfers are optimistic about the Web's potential to improve the religious life of others while at the same time they are fearful of the Internet's ability to do harm to others by making heretical or cult-inspired material easily accessible.

Table 2.1 Activities of Online Religious Surfers

The percentage of Religion Surfers who have ever . . .	
Looked for information about their own faith	67%
Looked for information about another faith	50%
E-mailed a prayer request	38%
Downloaded religious music	38%
Given spiritual guidance via e-mail	37%
Bought religious items online	34%
Planned religious activities via e-mail	29%
Gotten idea for religious ceremonies online	28%
Subscribed to a religious Listserv	27%
Downloaded sermons	25%
Gotten ideas for ways to celebrate religious holidays	22%
Sought spiritual guidance via e-mail	21%
Gone online to find a new church	14%
Participated in religious chat rooms	10%
Played spiritual computer games	5%
Participated in online worship	4%
Taken an online religious course	3%
Used a faith-oriented matchmaking service	3%

Source: Pew Internet and American Life Project Religion Surfers. Survey, July 24–August 15, 2001. N = 500; margin of error +/−4%.

- 15 percent of Religion Surfers say their use of the Internet has made them feel more committed to their faith, and 27 percent say it has improved their spiritual life to at least a modest degree.
- 35 percent believe that the Internet has a "mostly positive" effect on the religious life of others. And 62 percent of Religion Surfers say that the availability of material on the Internet encourages religious tolerance.
- 53 percent of Religion Surfers fear that the Internet makes it too easy for fringe groups to promote themselves in ways that can harm people.

Religion Surfers are distinguished from other Americans by their religious devotion rather than conventional demographics. They take their faith seriously in the offline world and use online tools to enrich their knowledge of their faith and to practice their devotions.

- 81 percent of Religion Surfers describe their religious faith as "very strong," compared to 61 percent of the general public, who said in a March 2000 Gallup poll that religion was "very important" in their life.
- 74 percent of Religion Surfers attend religious services at least once a week. Polls such as the General Social Survey, Gallup, and the National

Election Study show that 26 percent to 39 percent of Americans attend religious services every week.

- 86 percent of Religion Surfers pray or meditate at least once a day. By comparison, 54 percent of all Americans say they pray that often, and 23 percent say they meditate every day.

Many Religion Surfers think key spiritual resources are more easily available online than offline.

- 64 percent of Religion Surfers believe that the Internet provides easier access to religious study and educational materials than they can otherwise find offline.
- Nearly half (44 percent) believe that the Internet provides easier access to prayer and other devotional materials than they can otherwise find offline.
- Nonmembers of religious organizations rely on the Internet to find resources that members of actual congregations are likely to find in their faith communities.

I
Being Religious in Cyberspace

3

Popular Religion and the World Wide Web: A Match Made in (Cyber) Heaven

CHRISTOPHER HELLAND

Introduction

With the development and expansion of the Internet and World Wide Web, official religious organizations have flocked to cyberspace, attempting to establish their presence, control, and authority over a growing and developing sphere. Despite this official religious presence, individuals using the Internet for popular or nonofficial religion have embraced this medium as a new environment where freedom of religious expression rules supreme. As a form of computer-mediated communication, the Internet accommodates those individuals and groups who wish to "be" religious outside the control of an organized religious institution. In this way, the Internet has become the ideal medium for communicating religious beliefs and practices in a social context in which syncretism, popular tradition, and religion à la carte are among the most common forms of religious participation.

In the Beginning Was the Word

Owen D. Young was chosen as *Time's* "Man of the Year" in 1929 for several reasons. He was board chairman of General Electric and the Radio Corp., which gave him enormous influence over many of the technological developments occurring in the United States, and he was also a visionary. Indeed, *Time* explained the significance of Young's achievements by noting that although Young himself was not a technician, he had become "obsessed with the idea that some day it may be possible to write a message on a pad at one's desk or bedside and have it instantaneously transmitted to the addressee anywhere on earth" (*Time* 1930: 13).

By the 1960s this vision was becoming a reality. Academics were beginning to use computer networks to share their data and communicate their research, although this was initially a complicated procedure undertaken only by a select few. The first system developed for Intercomputer communication (called ARPANET) linked several computer systems in the United States through telecommunication lines. Although these systems were developed for military, academic, and industrial use, they began to allow for much more personal communications and contact. Having linked this system together, computer technicians developed a software program that allowed users to attach personal messages or electronic mail to the outgoing and incoming data. This extra "add-on" was so popular that the procedure was streamlined and developed so that individuals could send messages to the well-known "certain person@a certain computer system" address. Within a very short period of time e-mail became one of the most popular aspects of computer-mediated communications (Hafner and Lyon 1998). By the 1970s, e-mail was such a significant component of the developing Internet system that many researchers felt they had created simply the most expensive post office in history (Sterling 1993).

In this way, these computer networks developed into social networks (Hampton and Wellman 2001), and with the creation of a program called MODEM in the late 1970s, the public also gained access to this communication technology. Now, using home-based microcomputers, people separated by both time and space could communicate with each other through telephone lines (Kitchin 1998). To better facilitate this communication, electronic discussion forums called "bulletin boards" (BBS) were developed where people could post and respond to messages on a wide variety of topics—including religion.

In some of the earliest research done on this form of computer-based communication, Howard Rheingold found that the religious BBS called ORIGINS "was one of the most intriguing electronic gathering places" (1985). Located on a Santa Cruz BBS called Communitree, ORIGINS promoted a syncretic, open-ended form of religious discourse in which people of varying levels of religious faith, commitment, and practice could post and respond to questions ranging from divination to the afterlife and from the Christian Bible to the Norse Eddas.

> ORIGINS is a movement that started on this computer (Santa Cruz, 408-475-7101). ORIGINS began on the START-A-RELIGION conference, but we don't call it a religion. . . . ORIGINS is partly a religion, partly like a westernized form of yoga society, partly a peace movement. It is a framework for improving your life and improving the world at the same time. . . . The movement centers on "practices"— actions you can use in everyday life to build effective human relationships, strength of community, and self-awareness. All the practices are based on action. None require any special equipment, settings, leaders, theories or social status. The human universals of the ordinary, everyday moment, and the personal relationship, form the basis for this training. . . . ORIGINS has no leaders, no official existence, nothing for sale. Because it started in an open computer conference, no one knows who all the creators are. (Rheingold 1985 and 1993: 134–135)

Using text to communicate in forums like ORIGINS, individuals began using the Internet to express their religious beliefs and concerns, as well as simply to *talk* about religion. In a sense, these Internet bulletin boards became a computer-generated, unofficial, religious environment. Although participants may have been active in official religious organizations or spiritual movements, there was no central authority online to limit the discussion, censor contributors, or set boundaries on the religious participation that was taking place (Helland 2000; see also Dawson and Hennebry, this volume, and O' Leary, this volume). In this way, the Internet became a vehicle for religion, and as the BBS system continued to expand and flourish, religion permeated the medium. Early studies of the development of online community formation indicated that religion had a notable presence and that even religious specialists were using the Internet to "quietly discuss theology and the Bible" (Schwartz 1995: 40).

A contemporary form of Communitree and ORIGINS is the Brainstorms BBS. Within Brainstorms there are hundreds of forum areas, with topics ranging from politics and war to community and life online. There is also a very active area called "Spirituality and Sanctuary," which is set apart specifically for the discussion of religious beliefs and practices. In the introduction to the Spirituality forum, the founder stated, "I would like to see this conference evolve into a place where we can discuss not only traditional religion—but also the role spirituality plays in our lives both online and off." Currently there are ninety three subsections within the spirituality section of the Brainstorms BBS. Although there is a significant amount of *dialogue* about different religious beliefs and practices, actual online rituals are not performed on the BBS. However, people will provide links to such rituals as online Hagaddahs (i.e., Passover rituals; www.orbina.com/StickyNet), online facilitation of the Islamic Qurbani sacrifice (required of affluent Muslims on the occasion of *Eid ul Adhaa*, a festival linked to the *hajj* or pilgrimage to Mecca), or even information concerning online weddings, baptisms, and funerals.

I Link, Therefore I Am

As Internet communication became more popular, home computers became less expensive, and software made the whole process a lot more user-friendly, computer-mediated communication expanded rapidly. By the mid-1990s the World Wide Web had come into existence, and people began to "surf" the Net, to create their own home pages, post their own data, and share information on a scale made possible only by this new technology.

To no one's surprise, religion flourished on the Internet.

As early as 1989 Pope John Paul II saw the potential "opportunities offered by computer telecommunications to fulfill the Church's mission, which he called the 'new evangelization' " (Ramo 1996: 55). Following the Pontiff's vision, in 1995 the Vatican created its own official Web site (www.vatican.va). But with hundreds of thousands of e-mails sent to the Pope, the site was quickly overwhelmed and crashed. By the end of 1996, the Vatican had upgraded its system, using three supercomputers named Raphael, Michael, and Gabriel (Ramo 1996), removing the feature that allowed for e-mail to the

Pope. Since then, while sites like www.vatican.va continue to have a significant presence in cyberspace, it is popular religion that populates the Internet with homegrown, unofficial, religious Web sites.

The conclusion of a 1996 study by Barna Research in California recommended that church organizations quickly establish their presence in cyberspace or they would lose touch with many of their parishioners and risk losing the ability to advise them in an era of rapid technological growth. When the World Wide Web was still relatively new and uncharted, organized religion was urged to establish its presence on the electronic frontier before it was too late. In 1998, Patrick McCormick believed that the massive expansion of religion into cyberspace occurred out of necessity. Believers *had* to make their presence known in the new environment before the influence of the Church would be lost to unofficial religious groups. "Concerned that they not lose touch with their computer-literate congregations," he wrote, "or see the faithful evangelized away from them by more technically adept preachers of the word, more and more pastors and dioceses are building homepages, bulletin boards, and chat rooms" (McCormick 1998).

By 1999, of the 11,000 Web sites focusing upon Christian beliefs and practices in Yahoo's Religion and Spirituality subsection, 7,000 (or 64 percent) represented "official" denominations (Keene 1999). As of August 2002, the categories of Web sites representing Christian beliefs and practices had increased by over 300 percent and showed no signs of abating. These figures demonstrate two important factors. First, that the religious and spirituality sections of the World Wide Web continue to expand at a very rapid rate. In search engine subsections and categories of classification, the religion and spirituality sections have always been among the largest and most dynamic. On Lycos, for example, the section devoted to religiously oriented Web sites increased by almost 70 percent from 57,790 in 2000 to 96,484 in August 2002. No other category—including activism, lifestyle choices, relationships, sexuality, or law—comes close to this level of representation. Secondly, the overall rate of growth suggests that regardless of the increases in official church representation on the Web, it is unlikely that they account for all the new religious and spiritual Web sites coming online on a daily basis.

Drawing upon data from a number of search engines, it is evident that popular religion is flourishing online. One way to demonstrate these online religious demographics is through a Web search environment called the Open Directory Project (OPD). Created in 1998 by Netscape, the OPD was designed to categorize and classify Web sites appearing on the Web. Unlike most other search engines, which use computer software to review and assess Web sites, human beings do the job for the OPD; currently there are 57,135 of these Web editors, all volunteers in the project. Their job is to evaluate and classify all forms of sites appearing on the Internet, separating the commercial from the personal, for example, and then place those sites within a category that best represents them. Currently, within the religion and spirituality section there are sixty six different subsections, representing thousands of different belief systems and denominations in fifty seven different languages (http://dmoz.org/Society/Religion_and_Spirituality).

According to the OPD, Christianity is the largest belief system and constitutes almost 78 percent of all online religious Web sites. Within Christianity, Roman Catholicism is the largest single denomination represented. The majority of these sites are official Catholic sites and include parish and diocesan sites, pages for various church and parachurch organizations, and Catholic religious orders. However, even within the "Catholic" classification there are a number of sites that discuss or present Catholicism from a popular perspective. And when one begins to examine Christian classifications within the ODP outside the Catholic framework, the numbers of these popular sites increase dramatically. They increase again when other belief systems, such as Wicca and the "New Age," are explored.

While all major and most minor Christian denominations are presented online, as well as most Jewish, Muslim, Hindu, and Buddhist traditions, in each case unofficial expressions of these religions along with individuals wishing to communicate their personal religious and spiritual beliefs have permeated the medium. In 1996, *Time*'s Robert Wright wrote that "out on the fringe of the World Wide Web, beyond mainstream religion, storefront preachers and offbeat theologians are springing up like mushrooms" (1996: 60). And, with the turn of the millennium, that trend has become even more prominent, since individuals can now create their own Web sites without having to learn HTML, the programming language in which much of the content on the Web is written.

In the 1990s, those wanting to create their own Web space were often self-taught computer programmers who learned HTML exclusively so that they could create their religious or spiritually based Web sites. Now some, such as Ellie Crystal, who created Crystalinks.com (http://crystalinks.com), contract out their Web design services for extra income. According to her biography, Ellie purchased her first computer in 1989 and used it to transcribe messages she received from an otherworldly entity called "Z," whom she refers to as "the soul of the Egyptian God, Thoth the Scribe" (http://crystalinks.com/bio.html). In 1995 she taught herself HTML specifically so she could create her own Web site. Still in operation today, the site has been extremely successful and is part of a full-time metaphysical endeavor for Ellie. Crystalinks.com often receives in excess of 200,000 visits daily.

Ellie Crystal is not a unique case; a significant number of individuals learned HTML just so that they could create their own religious Web site. Many of those then freely offered their Web design services to others who wished to create similar Web sites. This was a particularly significant trend in the Neopagan community, in which individuals readily shared information about designing and building Web sites through major Neopagan Internet hubs such as the Witches Voice (www.witchvox.com; cf. Hadden and Cowan 2000: 9–10). In 1997, a Pagan Webcrafters' Association was developed specifically for individuals to share their design skills and expertise with other pagans on the World Wide Web. The Pagan Webcrafters' Association (http://thepwa.net) is still active, and members promote each other's Web sites and assist each other with design, artwork, and even content aspects of their Web pages. The resources provided by thepwa.net allow for any person with sufficient motivation to develop a Pagan-based Web environment. To demonstrate this influence, the software *TouchGraph Google Browser* can be used to illustrate the links maintained between Web sites. This shows how individuals who visit sites related to Neopagan beliefs are exposed to a link for thepwa.net—if they follow this link, they will be taken to the site and receive the step-by-step information and the support they need to make their own Neopagan Web page.

Although there is a cost involved in purchasing a Web domain name and hosting the Web site on a server, many religious and spiritual Web designers have been fiscally creative and are online for free. One example is a Web site created in 1996 by Paul Harrison to express his pantheistic religious worldview. Rather than its own domain name, Harrison took advantage of America Online's offer of free Web hosting and posted his site at http://members.aol.com/Heraklit1.

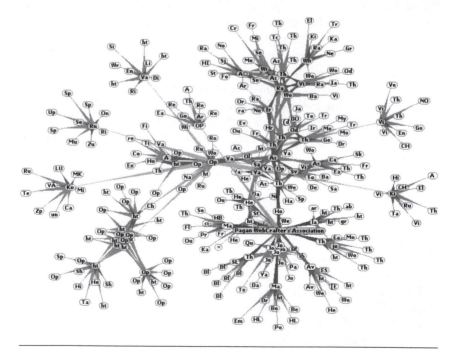

Fig. 3.1 Each node represents a Pagan-related Web site or organization linked directly, or indirectly, to the Webcrafter's Association.

Five months after it began, the site was receiving five hundred visits a day. In an e-mail interview he stated: "There is no other way I could reach those numbers. Imagine touring the backwoods, organizing meetings in echoing community halls. I might if I were lucky, get five or ten people a night, in return for huge expense and effort" (Wright 1996: 61). By the end of March 2000, his site had recorded over a million unique visitors and now receives an average of 43,000 visitors per month.

Sites like Crystalinks.com and Paul Harrison's pantheism Web page are not alone in cyberspace. Sites of similar interest and content are often linked into what Galston calls a "voluntary community" (2000: 195). In this way, small Web pages such as The Dance (www.thedance.com) can become an intrinsic part of a much larger and more active Web environment (Howard 1997). On its own, The Dance contains a relatively small amount of information and has a small group of regular participants. However, once linked to the larger Neopagan community through a cyberspace hub like the Witches Voice (www.witchvox.com), the potential for participation increases dramatically. Much like a small rural community happily engulfed by a rapidly expanding city, now hundreds of thousands (if not millions) of people are exposed to The Dance's Web site, and can easily participate in whatever is being offered—in this case, Wicca 101 information, online divination, chat rooms, and occasional online rituals.

As figure 3.2, created by using *Web Crawler* software, demonstrates, the Witch's Voice has become a massive hub linking thousands of Neopagan and

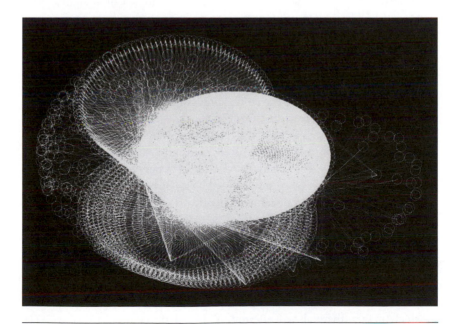

Fig. 3.2 Each circle represents a Pagan-related Web page linked with www.witchvox.com.

Wiccan sites in an online network. While The Dance represents only a few small circles within the much larger group, it is enmeshed and interlinked with hundreds of similar Web sites. As Wellman and Gulia (1999) note, Web surfers do not ride alone, and by linking into these cyberspace megalopoli, individuals who have created their own popular religious Web sites can participate in an ongoing and expanding religious environment.

Popular Religion Online

In many ways, the examples I have just presented pose no challenge to official religious traditions in that they are representative of unofficial, personal, religious beliefs and practices. For these classifications of "official" and "unofficial" religiosity I am using McGuire's framework, which suggests that official religion "is a set of beliefs and practices prescribed, regulated and socialized by orga- nized, specifically religious groups . . . which set norms of belief and action for their members, and . . . establish an official model of what it means to be 'one of us' " (1997: 101). Unofficial or popular religion, on the other hand, "is a set of religious and quasi religious beliefs and practices that is not accepted, recognized, or controlled by official religious groups" (McGuire 1997: 108).

That said, in many ways these Web sites do pose a significant challenge to official religious traditions simply by the very fact that they exist—firmly established and thriving in cyberspace. That a simple, self-created, self-professed psychic's site such as crystalinks.com should receive 250,000 hits on a Sunday is an affront, one would think, to at least some of the official Christian organiza- tions in the United States. But even more problematic are members of such "official" religious organizations as the Roman Catholic Church who establish their own personal religious and spiritual Web sites, the content of which might be seriously at odds with official doctrine and teachings. Although the Internet is in many ways a blessing to religious institutions that use it to their advantage, it can also be an official religion's worst nightmare. Like the printing press, power has shifted through the development of a tool of mass communication. Doctrines and teachings that were once centralized and controlled can now be openly challenged, contradicted, or ignored through a medium that is accessed by hundreds of millions of people every day. With the continued development of computer-mediated communications, we may be witnessing "a potentially radical shift in who is in control of information" (Shapiro 1999: 11, Dawson 2001: 6–7; see also Cowan in this volume).

However, the Internet is more than just the printed word. In a detailed ethnographic study of Internet participation, Markham found that people viewed the Internet as a tool, a place, and a state of being—and each level of perception affected the interactions of the individuals with the Internet envi- ronment (Markham 1998: 87). This has a significant impact upon the manner in which these individuals will attempt to "do" religion online (Helland 2002). As the technology continues to develop and becomes more transparent in the lives of those using the Internet, organized religious Web sites that are using the Internet only as a tool to communicate what we might call "information about" will not have the ability to meet the religious needs of those who want more from the medium. In this case, it is the popular religious sites or the unofficial religious sites that are providing the preferred environment for the online practitioners.

An excellent example of this is the contrast between the official Vatican Web site (www.vatican.va) and one of the most popular nonofficial Catholic sites (www.partenia.net; see also Hadden and Cowan 2000: 10–11). Although the Vatican site offers a wealth of information, it is Partenia that provides the environment for people to talk about their religious beliefs and practices, ask challenging questions concerning their faith, and participate in a safe environment where they can open up and share religious feelings and concerns. Through the Partenia site, even Catholics estranged from their tradition can enter into an open dialogue with other Catholics. There is no hierarchical segregation on the site, and Catholics, both practicing and nonpracticing, as well as individuals who have left the church entirely can be part of an ongoing religious dialogue.

In this way, the Internet has become more than a search tool for many individuals who use it, and some studies indicate "that people who connect to the Internet are more likely to use it for cultivating their social and cultural proclivities" (Matei and Ball-Rokeach 2001: 551). In this, for many people cyberspace is a real space. And for many of them, it is an acceptable medium for religious and spiritual participation. It is becoming an environment—a place—where people can "be" religious if and when they choose to be.

Religious virtuosi, to use Weber's term, now have an inexpensive, mass-communication tool at the end of their telephone lines. With simplified programming, people can now simply point and click their way toward the creation of their own cyberchurch, religious pulpit, or spiritual clearinghouse.

One example of this virtuosi activity on the Web is the Church of the Simple Faith (www.churchofthesimplefaith.org). Founded by "Brother Bill" in 2000, this cyberchurch's motto is "Our mission is to be of spiritual benefit to you . . . because people need Jesus, now!" Their logo, "Church of the Simple Faith . . . Jesus said take care of my sheep" is trademarked and copyrighted. Along with online devotional services, chat rooms and bulletin boards, even baby dedication ceremonies, visitors to the site can get an up-to-date horoscope, local weather forecasts, and even information on the Boy Scouts. Brother Bill takes his online church very seriously and has detailed, specific guidelines for online religious participation. For instance, e-communion is a self-directed ritual for which "almost any bread or cracker could be used," but "I would recommend for the seriousness of the matter that you use a couple of plain white thin crackers." The ceremony requires participants to read several biblical passages off the Web site, to repeat the Lord's Prayer out loud, and then click to play "The Song of Confession" and "The Song of Devotion" in Real Audio files loaded on the Web page. After performing the rituals and reading the liturgy, the e-devotee can then partake in the sacred Eucharist (cf. O' Leary, this volume; Young, this volume).

Although the Web site is reasonably well designed and looks as though it represents some form of official Christian Church, Brother Bill is in fact a middle-aged man with no formal religious training or background. According to information he has posted online, before his epiphany he was an alcoholic with serious marriage and financial problems. In 1999, he became religiously active, attending prayer sessions and taking a Dr. Blackaby's "Experiencing God correspondence workshop." From that foundation he now runs his own cyberchurch. Although it may seem fanciful and insignificant, the Church of the Simple Faith appears successful and even has a section for M2M (Ministry to Ministry services) that includes not only spiritual event planning but also online Internet service support, Web hosting and design, as well as computer and Internet technical assistance.

The cyberculture environment also includes Web-oriented religious organizations. Technosophy (www.technosophy.com) and Digitalism (www.digitalism.org) for example, have been online since the early 1990s. Recently, however, there is has been an increase in the number of more traditional forms of religion establishing an exclusively online presence. In this sense, the e-church is becoming more common. "Virtual Churches" now has its own category within major search engines. Among those sites, for example, is the Alpha Church (www.alphachurch.org), whose only physical address is a post office box in New Mexico. While the Alpha Church site is extremely well designed and features Flash graphics and automatic audio files, there is no information available concerning its denominational affiliation or the credentials of its founder, Patty Walker. The worship section contains a number of Power-Point-type sermons that flash text, graphics, and sound files across the screen. It is never made clear, however, whose denominational vision this church is representing, and the introduction to the e-church simply reads: "Alpha Church is a full on-line Christian global Church. Our Worship Services involve people of every age, race, and ability. You may Worship twenty-four/seven. Take Holy Communion, receive Baptism, be Married and community chat with other people like you who are growing in their faith and understanding of Jesus Christ, our Savior" (www.alphachurch.org/first.htm).

Online Religion in the Wired, Wired West

The examples presented in this chapter demonstrate an important aspect of the religious dimension of the World Wide Web. In its very structure, the Internet has an affinity with the patterns of religious participation in late modern societies in the West. This occurs in two ways. First, those individuals who are highly motivated religiously have an outlet to channel their virtuosi forms of religiosity without having to commit to or affiliate with any official organization or institution. Anyone with sufficient motivation can create their own Web site and express their own personal religious beliefs.

Second, by allowing those people who practice a form of mass religiosity the ability to pick and choose their beliefs and log on when they feel the need, the Web's structure caters to today's preference to choose various levels of religious participation that occur when and only when one wants.

A clear example of this form of mass religiosity occurred in conjunction with the events of September 11, 2001. After the destruction of the World Trade Center towers and the attack upon the Pentagon, hundreds of thousands of people began posting online prayers, lighting virtual candles, and entering into religiously based dialogue in an attempt to cope with the tragedy (Helland 2002). As time went by, many other religious Web sites shifted their content, devoting whole sections to Islam and creating avenues for individuals to learn more about different Islamic traditions and opportunities for dialogue with Muslims about the events of 9/11 and its aftermath. A need arose, and the Web was able to respond quickly and diversely.

It is common to use religious frameworks or paradigms to cope with a situation like the 9/11 attacks. (Bainbridge 1997). In many ways, it is only religiously based language that can give voice to our need for meaning in the face of life's overwhelming events. A large percentage of the Western world maintains religious and spiritual beliefs without belonging to a traditional religious organization and without attending religious services on a regular basis (Bibby 1993, 2002; Davie 1994, 2000). For these, the Internet can constitute an effective medium for nondenominational, nonaffiliated religious participation.

Conclusion

The most recent Canadian census reveals that significant changes in religious participation patterns first noticed in the 1970s are continuing. Mainline Protestant church attendance is in steady decline, falling from a national average of better than 50 percent in the 1950s to 20 percent or less at the beginning of the twenty-first century. While seven out of ten Canadians still claim to be "Christians," many are not affiliated with any specific denomination or church organization, and the percentage of the population who claim to have no religious affiliation has risen from less than 1 percent in the 1960s to 16 percent in 2001 (Statistics Canada 2003). But none of this means that people are abandoning religious and spiritual beliefs entirely. On the contrary, more detailed survey results demonstrate that most Canadians are still interested in the ultimate questions of meaning that various religions seek to answer and wish they could find satisfying answers to these spiritual questions (Bibby 1987, 1993, 2002). But many of these people are now seeking their answers outside the traditional churches and other religious groups. Similar patterns have been documented for Britain and Western Europe (Davie 1994, 2000) as well as the

United States (Roof 1999; Roof and McKinney 1987). While a significant proportion of the massive Baby Boomer generation (i.e., those born between 1946 and 1964) have become secularized, an equally large number have become "seekers" looking for greater spiritual fulfillment. And younger folk—Generations X and Y—seem even more interested in religious and spiritual experimentation (Beaudoin 1998; Dawson and Hennebry, this volume).

As an open and developing religious environment, the Internet caters to people who wish to be religious and spiritual on their own terms. In this environment, by developing and maintaining their own religious Web sites or by searching the tens of thousands of religiously oriented sites available, individuals can either create or simply find what they require religiously. In this way, the expanding religious dimension of the Internet is reinforcing the growing polarization between those who are affiliated to some degree with a traditional religious institution and those who are now expressing their own religious inclinations in a more popular and amorphous way. In some respects, as seekers turn to the Internet for religious purposes and their diverse experiences online reinforce the motivational wellsprings of their seekership, a positive feedback loop is created that will likely accelerate the processes of religious change already happening in the West (see Dawson 2000: 48–49). But since we lack the detailed empirical studies with which to test this supposition, it must remain speculation.

It is clear, however, that the Internet has become a powerful medium for popular religion, one that permits far greater and easier contact between people than was available in the past through books and "old-fashioned" gatherings. It has become the significant environment for a wired generation of religious seekers and spiritual entrepreneurs. And if statistical trends continue in Western societies, it appears that popular religion online will become a significant aspect of the religious environment of the future, creating a new space where a freedom of religious expression rules supreme.

References

Bainbridge, W.s. (1997). *The Sociology of Religious Movements.* New York: Routledge.

Beaudoin, T. (1998). *Virtual Faith: The Irreverent Spiritual Quest of Generation X.* San Francisco: Jossey-Bass.

Bibby, R. (1987). *Fragmented Gods: The Poverty and Potential of Religion in Canada.* Toronto: Irwin.

———. (1993). *Unknown Gods: The Ongoing Story of Religion in Canada.* Toronto: Stoddart.

———. (2002). *Restless Gods: The Renaissance of Religion in Canada.* Toronto: Stoddart.

Davie, G. (1994). *Religion in Britain since 1945: Believing without Belonging.* Oxford, UK: Blackwell.

———. (2000). *Religion in Modern Europe: A Memory Mutates.* Oxford, UK: Oxford University Press.

Dawson, L. L. (2000). "Researching Religion in Cyberspace: Issues and Strategies." In *Religion on the Internet: Research Prospects and Promises,* ed. J. K. Hadden and D. E. Cowan, 25–54. London: JAI Press/Elsevier Science.

———. (2001). "Doing Religion in Cyberspace: The Promise and the Perils." *Council of Societies for the Study of Religion Bulletin* 30 (1): 3–9.

Dawson, L. L., and J. Hennebry (1999). "New Religions and the Internet: Recruiting in a New Public Space." *Journal of Contemporary Religion* 14: 17–39.

Galston, W. A. (2000). "Does the Internet Strengthen Community?" *National Civic Review* 89 (3): 193–202.

Hadden, J. K., and D. E. Cowan (2000). "The Promised Land or Electronic Chaos? Toward Understanding Religion on the Internet." In *Religion on the Internet: Research Prospects and Promises*, ed. J. K. Hadden and D. E. Cowan, 3–21. London: JAI Press/Elsevier Science.

Hafner, K., and M. Lyon (1998). *Where Wizards Stay Up Late: The Origins of the Internet.* New York: Touchstone.

Hampton, K., and B. Wellman (2001). "Long Distance Community in the Network Society." *American Behavioral Scientist* 45 (3): 476–495.

Helland, C. (2000). "Religion Online/Online Religion and Virtual Communitas." In *Religion on the Internet: Research Prospects and Promises*, ed. J. K. Hadden and D. E. Cowan, 205–224. London: JAI Press/Elsevier Science.

———. (2002). "Surfing for Salvation." *Religion* 32 (3): 293–302.

Horsfall, S. (2000). "How Religious Organizations Use the Internet: A Preliminary Inquiry." In *Religion on the Internet: Research Prospects and Promises*, ed. J. K. Hadden and D. E. Cowan, 153–182. London: JAI Press/Elsevier Science.

Howard, T. W. (1997). *A Rhetoric of Electronic Communities.* London: JAI Press.

Keene, M. (1999). "The Church on the Web." *Christian Century* 116 (22): 77–178.

Kitchin, R. (1998). *Cyberspace: The World in the Wires.* New York: John Wiley and Sons.

"Man of the Year." (1930). *Time* 15 (1): 13.

Markham, A (1998). *Life Online: Researching Real Experience in Virtual Space.* Walnut Creek, CA: AltaMira.

Matei, S., and S. J. Ball-Rokeach (2001). "Real and Virtual Social Ties: Connections in the Lives of Seven Ethnic Neighborhoods." *American Behavioral Scientist* 45 (3): 550–564.

McCormick, P. (1998). "Catholic.com: Surfing for Salvation," *U.S. Catholic.* Retrieved from http://www.uscatholic.org/1998/10/featc9810.htm, June 10, 2003.

McGuire, M. (1997). *Religion: The Social Context.* Belmont, CA: Wadsworth.

Ramo, J. C. (1996). "Finding God on the Web." *Time* 149 (1): 52–58.

Rheingold, H. (1985). *Tools for Thought: The People and Ideas behind the Next Computer Revolution.* Available online at http://www.rheingold.com/texts/tft/.

———. (1993). *Homesteading on the Electronic Frontier.* Reading, MA: Addison-Wesley.

Roof, W. C. (1999). *Spiritual Marketplace: Baby Boomers and the Remaking of American Religion.* Princeton, NJ: Princeton University Press.

Roof, W. C., and W. McKinney (1987). *American Mainline Religion: Its Changing Shape and Future.* New Brunswick, NJ: Rutgers University Press.

Schwartz, E. (1995). "Looking for Community on the Internet," *National Civic Review* 84 (1): 37–41.

Shapiro, A. L. (1999). "The Net that Binds: Using Cyberspace to Create Real Communities." *The Nation* (June 21): 11–15.

Statistics Canada (2003). *2001 Census: Analysis Series, Religions in Canada.* Ottawa, Ont.: Statistics Canada.

Sterling, B. (1993). "A Short History of the Internet." *Magazine of Fantasy and Science Fiction* (February). Retrieved from http://w3.aces.uiuc.edu/AIM/scale/nethistory.html, June 15, 2003.

Wellman, B., and M. Gulia (1999). "Virtual Communities as Communities: Net Surfers Don' t Ride Alone." In *Communities in Cyberspace*, ed. M. A. Smith and P. Kollock, 167–194. New York: Routledge.

Wright, R. (1996). "Can Thor Make a Comeback?" *Time* 149 (1): 60–61.

4

Cyberspace as Sacred Space: Communicating Religion on Computer Networks

STEPHEN D. O'LEARY

If the Internet is truly forming a culture, or a complex of cultures, that both reflects and differs from the larger technological and political culture in which it is housed, it should not surprise anyone that as more people come to spend more and more of their time online, they have begun to devise ways to fulfill the religious needs and identities that form such an important part of the fabric of our society. It would indeed be an anomaly if a cultural force of this magnitude were not to find expression in the newly developing world of computer networks.

No less an authority than Pope John Paul II has recognized the crucial importance of this topic. In a 1990 address titled "The Church Must Learn to Cope with Computer Culture," the pontiff noted the revolutionary impact of contemporary developments in communication: "[O]ne no longer thinks or speaks of social communications as mere instruments or technologies. Rather they are now seen as part of a still unfolding culture whose full implications are as yet imperfectly understood and whose potentialities remain for the moment only partially exploited." These implications and potentialities are the focus of this essay. While the Pope appears to celebrate the technological revolution, declaring that "With the advent of computer telecommunications and what are known as computer participation systems, the Church is offered further means for fulfilling her mission," my purpose is to qualify the optimism of technology advocates by exploring potentially troubling questions about the future of religious institutions in an era of computer-mediated communication.

Recent popular and scholarly literature has noted that computer linkages presently provide new forums and new tools for the public advocacy of faith and for participation in public acts of ritual communication that constitute new, virtual congregations (see Kellner [1996]; O'Leary and Brasher [1996]). This paper seeks not to provide a comprehensive map of religious landscapes in cyberspace nor an in-depth analysis of the communicative practices of any particular religious community, but only to speculate on the transformation of religious beliefs and practices as these are mediated by new technologies.

The examples and texts offered here may or may not be typical of current trends in cyber-religion; they were chosen because they raise significant issues about the status of religion on computer networks and, more generally, about the evolution of religion in what some choose to call a "postmodern" age. My intention is to raise these questions rather than to answer them; but in so doing, I will provide qualified support for the claim that something revolutionary is taking place, while peering "through a glass darkly" to see how religious institutions and practices may be affected by the transformation of our communications media.

The theoretical framework for this inquiry is drawn from the work of Walter J. Ong. No one studying the impact on religion of the evolution of communication technologies can afford to ignore the provocative insights of this seminal thinker, who, in a series of brilliant books, has developed an evolutionary theory of culture that focuses attention on the modes of consciousness and forms of communality enabled and promoted by communication technologies and practices, from oral speech to written discourse to printing, radio, television, and computer-mediated communication. While it is the last of these developments that is my primary focus here, I believe that a full understanding of religion in the era of the electronic word is best accomplished by attending to historical contexts and comparisons. Hence my study of contemporary religious discourses will begin with an excursus into historical narrative. After a brief exposition of an Ongian view of communication and culture, I turn to an extended discussion of one of Ong's primary examples of how religious practices may be transformed by a revolution in communication—the Reformation. By investigating the links between changing concepts of the nature and functions of word and symbol in Christian liturgy and the advent of print culture, I hope to demonstrate that contemporary electronic culture can be expected to effect a similar transformation of religious beliefs and practices. The essay closes with an examination of some unusual religious texts that illustrate this transformation, a series of Neopagan rituals conducted online in the electronic "conference rooms" of the CompuServe network.

An Ongian Framework for the Study of Religious Communication

The most succinct theoretical exposition of Ong's evolutionary theory of communication and culture is found in his *Orality and Literacy* [1982]. In less than two hundred pages this book traces the development of communication technology through a series of stages from preliteracy, or in his terms "primary orality," through the eras of chirographic writing, printing, and electronic media ("secondary orality") and offers a provocative analysis of the cultural impacts of technological change. Ong's thesis is that each of the forms of communication utilizes a different complex of the senses and that the particular complex peculiar to the material practices of communication in each culture—the "sensorium"—has profound impact on the formation of individual and cultural identity. For example, sound will play a larger role in the life world of a preliterate culture relying on oral speech for all communication than it does for people whose communication is dominated by print media. It is therefore not surprising that we find speech figuring prominently in the myths and religious practices of primarily oral cultures, which often attach magical significance to the spoken word, or that, lacking the concept of the written record, such cultures rely on expanded powers of memory to preserve their mythic heritage and a record of past events.

As chirographic literacy spread through Western culture, sight and textuality were privileged over sound and speech, and the composition of sacred books transformed ancient oral narratives by fixing them into a text that could be consulted and interpreted in a way that was not possible before the invention of writing. According to Ong, "writing restructures consciousness" (1982: 78) by divorcing the production of a communicative act from its reception. This made it possible to address audiences remote in time and space and turned communication from a public act requiring the presence of others into a private, solipsistic activity of writing and reading. As Ong puts it, writing "makes possible increasingly articulate introspectivity, opening the psyche as never before not only to the external objective world distinct from itself but also to the interior self against whom the objective world is set" (1982: 105). The religious implications of this insight are profound; for if we accept Ong's argument that writing generated a new, interior awareness of the self and a subsequent alienation of this self from the external world, then we may see religions that offer solutions to this alienation as, to some degree, an aftereffect of the psychological changes wrought by literacy.

Since literacy skills were slow to spread in the millennia between the introduction of writing and the invention of the printing press, recitation and memorization still retained a significant role, and the written word could not completely divorce itself from its social contexts or from sounds and images. The communication practices of Western culture in this stage can thus be characterized as a hybrid of different forms which might differ according to the social position of participants. However, the invention of printing privileged sight still more, accelerating the alienation of the word from its aural basis and narrowing the sensorium by focusing on the abstract symbols of typography as the predominant carriers of information and meaning. The consequences of these developments were immense. Among the phenomena that Ong links to the dominance of printing technology are the standardization of vernacular grammars and the subsequent move away from Latin as the lingua franca of Western culture and the rise of science, since printing enabled the replicability and wide dissemination of "exactly worded descriptions of carefully observed complex objects and processes" (1982: 127). The impact on religion was no less fundamental. In the chirographic culture of manuscript writing, the Bible could be controlled by clerics, who preserved the roots of the Word in speech by mediating the sacred writings in public recitations connected with ritual; but the wide distribution of vernacular printed Bibles effectively ended the interpetive monopoly of the institutional church and enabled the reformers to circumvent ecclesiastical authority by proclaiming *sola scriptura* as the ultimate touchstone for authoritative claims. Ultimately, the culture of print gave birth to the unique sensibility of modernism, which bore fruits both in science and in the development of literary genres such as the novel.

The dominance of electronic media in the twentieth century brings us to the present stage of cultural evolution in Ong's scheme, that of "secondary orality." In this stage the sensorium expands again to include first sound and voice (with the advent of radio), and then image and gesture (with film and television). Though print culture is based in the primary sense of sight, its emphasis on typography devalues icons and images in favor of the printed word. The visual emphasis of print is fundamentally different from that of television and film; as any contemporary college instructor will testify, it is extremely difficult to train students saturated in modern visual media to accept the discourse conventions and abstractions of print literacy. Film and television restore the prominence of the visual sense in its full glory and create a much richer feast for the senses than printed text; few of today's students will willingly give up this feast and return to the restricted sensorium of typographic culture. Some critics, such as Jacques Ellul (1985), view the devaluation of the printed and spoken word in favor of the image with alarm, seeing in it a temptation toward the idolatry of consumer culture. Whether we celebrate the revitalization of image and icon (Taylor and Saarinen [1994]) or are nostalgic for the old days of print literacy, there can be little doubt that this development will have profound consequences for religious belief and practice.

The term "secondary orality" refers to the fact that in the new electronic media the divorce between word and image begun by print culture is reversed, so that the total sensorium again includes sight and sound, voice, image, and music. This stage "has striking resemblance to the old [primary oral cultures] in its participatory mystique, its fostering of a communal sense, its concentration on the present moment, and even its use of formulas"; it differs from the old in that it "generates a sense for groups immeasurably larger than those of primary oral culture—McLuhan's 'global village'" (Ong 1982: 136). Modern electronic media change our senses of time and of community by again enabling speech to be shared in the immediacy of real time; but they also retain the self-awareness of print culture, since in most cases media messages, whether political speeches or entertainment, still originate with an act of writing. If, as McLuhan has it, television created the global village, this medium was still a one-way channel from the broadcaster to the audience. In computer networks, the global village has found its public square (the analogy to London's Hyde Park may be apt), whereby media users are transformed from vegetative "couch potatoes" to active participants in dialogues performed before potentially vast publics, linked not by geography but by technology and interests alone. With this new medium, aspects of orality and literacy are combined into a new, hybrid form of communication that, in the words of one networker, "is both talking and writing yet isn't completely either one. It's talking by writing. It's writing because you type it on a keyboard and people read it. But because of the ephemeral nature of luminescent letters on a screen, and because it has such a quick—sometimes instant—turn-around, it's more like talking" (Coate [1992]). . . .

The most significant issue for an inquiry into the implications of computer-mediated religion raised by Ong's theorizing is the potential comparison between the communication revolution that took place concurrently with the Reformation and our current transition into a digital age. Contemporary scholarship has exhaustively documented the crucial role that printing played in the Reformation, the most significant political and religious movement of postmedieval Western culture (see Eisenstein [1979]; Edwards [1994]); we may reasonably anticipate that the digital revolution will be accompanied by similarly massive upheavals in the social sphere in general and in religion in particular. In order to develop this comparison further, it will be useful to linger on an example that Ong uses as paradigmatic of the changes in Christian thought and communicative practice that accompanied the onset of print technology: the evolution of liturgy, the forms and ceremonies of Christian worship, during the Reformation era. Discussion of Protestant liturgical reform is germane to this argument for two reasons: first, as an example of the way theories and practices of language and ritual may be profoundly altered by technological change; and second, because this particular episode in the history of the Christian tradition illuminates the context of contemporary, mediated, ritual practice. The fundamental problem of religious communication is how best to represent and mediate the sacred. By studying the Reformation battles and controversies over this question, over the nature and proper functions of word and image, we may find some historical roots of the ethics and the aesthetics of communication in the cultures influenced by Protestantism and thereby come to a deeper understanding of the significance of ritual in premodern, modern, and postmodern cultures.

Liturgy and Language in the Protestant Reformation

Consider the difference between Catholic and Protestant ritual in terms of Ong's sensorium. It is clear the religious aesthetic and sacramental theology of the Roman Catholic Church has always appealed to the aural and tactile imagination as well as the visual. In the Catholic Mass the spoken word retains the magical efficacy of language that Ong finds characteristic of an earlier stage of primary orality, and ritual action directs attention outward toward the exterior manifestation of the Word in the Eucharist. By contrast, the liturgical and cultural forms of Protestantism direct attention inward; the preaching of the Word, conceived and embodied textually rather than sacramentally, was meant to to induce an interior conviction of sin that was prerequisite to the experience of grace. Believing that the sole legitimate functions of language were education and exhortation, by which members of the congregation were to be taught the message of the Gospel and urged to improve their lives, the Protestant reformers set out to strip away the incantatory functions of language in worship. The most radical of the reformers, such as Zwingli, stripped the churches bare of any ornamentation, banned the use of musical instruments, and banished altogether the whole panoply of ritual elements that had characterized the Latin Mass—vestments, stained glass, iconography of all kinds, incense. This had the deliberate effect of focusing attention upon the purely textual elements of the Christian message.

The differing notions of the symbolic function of language are most evident in the controversy over the nature of the Communion ceremony—the fulcrum of the dispute between Protestant and Catholic theology. In the Catholic Mass, the Communion comes to its symbolic climax in the "words of institution," the scriptural passage that is recited by the priest as he elevates the Communion bread:

> On the day before he suffered death, he took bread into his . . . hands, . . . and giving thanks to thee, he blessed it, broke it, and gave it to his disciples, saying: Take, all of you, and eat of this, for this is my body. (Thompson [1961]: 75)

What is important to stress here is the theory of language that underlies this ritual. For believers, the words of institution, "this is my body," authorized and commanded by Christ himself, were (and are) literally true; when performed by a duly ordained priest, they effected the miracle of transubstantiation by which the bread and wine served as vehicles of the Real Presence. In the terms of J. L. Austin (1970a), the founder of speech-act theory, we can call this a "performative utterance," a speech-act that effects what it describes. Like marriage vows and oaths of office, the words of institution belong to a class of communicative "acts in which saying the words does not merely describe an existing state of things, but rather creates a new relationship, social arrangement, or entitlement in speech-act terms, these are instances when saying is doing" (Danet [1996]). The formula used in Catholic theology to describe this mode of ritual action is to say that the sacrament succeeds *ex opere operato*, that is, that the words (when voiced by the duly ordained, in the right situation, with the right intention) are themselves efficacious as a vehicle of divine grace. Modern speech-act-theorists describe this efficacy in terms of the "illocutionary" force of the utterance (Austin 1970b).

In Catholic theology the visible elements of the sacrament are not signs of the thing, the spiritual reality of salvation through Christ's sacrifice; once transformed by the illocutionary force of the speech act, they *are* the thing, the bread and wine becoming the body and blood of God's saving Word through the power of the words of the liturgy, words that function as the bridge between the visible objects and the spiritual reality, uniting them in a single identity. Thus the sacramental theory of language affirms the *essential* unity of signifier and signified. This theory is hierarchical; the ritual can be enacted only by a duly ordained priest. During the sixteenth century and up until the second Vatican council, the ritual was conducted in Latin, ensuring that the uneducated masses could apprehend it only on the formal and aesthetic levels; and the Church hierarchy jealously guarded their monopoly on scriptural interpretation.

When Luther and the printing press were able to break this monopoly by publishing the first German Bible, interpretation became the prerogative of every believer, and the institutional authority of the Church was weakened. Protestant liturgies further undercut the authority of the priesthood by divesting the liturgy of its mysterious elements. The liturgies devised by Calvin, Zwingli, and other reformers enacted a theory of language that differed radically from the Roman Catholic conception of the relationship of Word and sacrament; they reach their climax, their symbolic payoff not in the Communion but in the sermon, a discourse which is delivered orally but which lacks the supernatural efficacy of the Catholic priest's speech over the Eucharistic elements. In contrast to the Catholic, the Protestant liturgy was enacted in the vernacular tongues; in its most austere forms, it eschewed ornament and visual representation and minimized all sensory input that might lead to idolatry; it focused on the sermon and the words of Scripture to the exclusion of other messages; and it denied the performative character of liturgical speech acts altogether, characterizing the ritual action of the priest as, in Calvin's words, "murmuring and gesticulating in the manner of sorcerers" (quoted in Thompson [1961]; 192).

To minimize the risk of idolatry, Calvin's Communion liturgy placed immediately prior to the distribution of Communion elements the minister's verbal directive to the congregation on how to interpret the sacrament:

> Let us not be fascinated by these earthly and corruptible elements which we see with our eyes and touch with our hands seeking Him there as though He were enclosed in the bread or wine. Then only shall our souls be disposed to be nourished and vivified by His substance when they are lifted up above all earthly things. . . . Therefore let us be content to have the bread and wine as signs and witnesses, seeking the truth spiritually where the Word of God promises that we shall find it. (Calvin 1961[1545]: 207)

The words of the minister were no longer a performative utterance; they simply directed the attention of the congregation. With the aesthetic and formal elements in the liturgy kept to an absolute minimum, this attention was less likely to rest upon external reality as apprehended through the senses and would presumably turn to an interior meditation on salvation characterized by a high degree of abstraction. Whereas the Catholic liturgy presented and represented God's Word in a variety of sensual, formal, and aesthetic embodiments, the Word in Protestant liturgy is desiccated, information-oriented, apprehended through Scripture and sermon but most emphatically not in stained glass, statues, or the taste of bread upon the tongue.

The theology that followed from the devaluation of ritual language, gesture, and performance in favor of preaching thus changed the Communion ceremony from its former status as an actual vehicle of God's presence and grace to a mere reminder or analogy. As Calvin wrote, "For while we refute transubstantiation by other valid arguments, we hold this one to be amply sufficient, that it destroys the analogy between the sign and the thing signified; for if there be not in the sacrament a visible and earthly sign corresponding to the spiritual gift, the nature of a sacrament is lost" (Calvin 1958[1557]: 467). In these statements by Calvin we can see the essential idea of language that lay behind the reform liturgies. Against the concept of identity created through sacramental language Calvin asserted the centrality of the sacrament solely as analogy; in his system, words can only establish the relationship between the sign and the thing signified, a relationship that is analogical, not essential.

Consider the fact that these two conceptions of liturgy were a major cause of a controversy that divided Europe for centuries. From an Ongian perspective, the most significant result of this controversy was that it led to the formation of two communicative cultures, the Catholic and the Protestant. Extending Ong's insight, I argue that the development of two competing cultures grounded in liturgical practice, supported by and elaborated in a whole literature of polemical debate and theorizing about the nature of symbolism and the inter-pretation and embodiment of the Word, was a significant part of the context for the formation of Enlightenment theories of language. If the religious rituals now visible on computer networks seem absurd, bizzare, and entirely without efficacy to those of us in the academy today, it may be because we have been so thoroughly imbued with Lockean, Humean, and Cartesian skepticism that the magical power of sacramental language is entirely foreign to us. As Jonathan Z. Smith notes, the absolute separation between signifier and signified, which was inaugurated by the liturgical reformers and which became a hallmark of Enlightenment thought, meant that "myth or ritual . . . was no longer literally *and* symbolically real and true. . . . The [subsequent] history of the imagination of the categories myth and ritual was sharply divergent. To say myth was false was to recognize it as having content; to declare ritual to be 'empty' was to deny the same" ([1987]: 101). Hence we may measure the progress of the Enlightenment in terms of a gradual shrinking of the space in which the illocutionary force of ritual speech, supported by the social authority of the Church, held sway.

However, the old conception of the ritualistic power of symbolic action (a conception that, whether explicit or implicit, consitutes a theory of lan-guage) is not dead; it survives within the now limited domain of the Church and has a new home in the global communication network.

Though secular culture has long since denied or ignored the claims of Christian dogma, the old traditions are not so easily abandoned; they survive in the communicative cultures to which they gave birth, which may still fairly be labeled as "Catholic" and "Protestant" with regard to their aesthetic conventions and conceptions of language if not to the substantive content of their beliefs. Clearly, innovation is not accomplished only through newly invented forms but by bricolage, as fragments of the old systems are incorporated into the new cultural mosaic. If the past is any guide, the new media of communication will have cultural consequences that we can barely imagine, let alone predict; nevertheless, it is already possible to watch this process of transformation at work and to see how the old forms are taken up into the new. As the introduction of the printing press profoundly altered the symbolic world of Western cultures and forever changed the course of Christian history, so too religious discourse will have to reinvent itself to keep pace with modern technology. As one example of this reinvention, here is a recent text culled from a flood of offerings on the Internet, the "Cyberpunk's Prayer":

Our Sysop,
Who art On-Line,
High be thy clearance level.
Thy System up,
Thy Program executed
Off-line as it is on-line.
Give us this logon our database,
And allow our rants,
As we allow those who flame against us.
And do not access us to garbage,
But deliver us from outage.
For thine is the System and the Software
and the Password forever[1]

However ludicrous or parodic this prayer may seem, it was apparently intended by its author as an expression of sincere devotion. Consider the implications of this symbolic transformation in terms of the political and social impact of representations of deity: as male, as female, as patriarchal king, as benevolent earth mother—and now, as Sysop (systems operator). The divine plan is compared to a computer program ("Thy will be done" = "Thy program executed"); cyberspace itself is equated with heaven ("on earth as it is in heaven" = "Off-line as it is on-line"); the soul's nourishment is equated with information, the bread of the information age ("Give us this logon our database"). Steering a course between those who might regard this poem as blasphemy and those who would dismiss it as inconsequential humor, let us take the "Cyberpunk's Prayer" as a sign of the process of cultural invention and adaptation that is currently under way and ask what this example portends for the future.

As ancient religious formulae are translated into contemporary idioms, their meanings will be profoundly altered along with the mode of their reception. The old symbols will find new functional equivalents in the idioms of technological culture, and some of these will be unrecognizable to today's audiences.

We must anticipate that the propositional content and presentational form of religion in the electronic communities of the future will differ as greatly from their contemporary incarnations as the teachings of Jesus differ from the dialectical theology of the medieval Scholastics or as the eucharistic ceremonies of the earliest Christians differ from the Latin High Mass. With the perspective afforded by an Ongian view of communication and culture, we can be sensitive to true novelty while at the same time retaining awareness of the continuity of tradition, of the manifold ways in which it adapts, mutates, and survives to prosper in a new communicative environment.

Religious Ritual on Computer Networks: Problems of Virtual Ethnography

In 1992 a student who knew of my interest in religious communication brought me a file of messages exchanged in a religion discussion group on the Prodigy computer network. I was intrigued enough to sign up for an e-mail account through my university but went no further than exchanging electronic messages with colleagues. In the spring of 1993 I received a promotional package in the mail that included a free trial account with the CompuServe network. I took the bait and signed on, and spent months reading and occasionally posting to the various message boards in the Religion forum. Most of the traffic that I observed was fairly conventional in nature: there were arguments about the meaning of scriptures, debates over homosexuality in the various denominations, and occasional requests for prayers from forum participants. As my familiarity with the network grew, I began to discover groups meeting at preordained times in electronic "conference rooms" to engage in Scripture study and prayer. A conference or chat room (as they are known on America Online) is a real-time connection in which everyone who enters the "room" may post a message that will be seen immediately by all who occupy that particular corner of cyberspace. What intrigued me about this type of connection to the network was that it allowed for group interaction of a sort not possible through basic e-mail; people were not merely exchanging letters with each other but actually engaged in collective devotion, much as they would at church or in a Bible study group. For some regular participants this activity was a significant part of their spiritual life.

My curiosity was piqued. I explored the network further, looking for the ways in which the new medium was being used by less traditional religious groups, and found that groups stigmatized as "cults" were using the network to present a different face to the public. Practitioners of nontraditional religions can run a considerable risk by publicly declaring their allegiances in communities hostile to non-Christians; the network afforded an opportunity to meet with like-minded others and engage in religious activity without ever leaving one's home or alerting one's neighbors to one's nonconformity. After some months monitoring messages in the New Age section of the Religion forum, I saw an announcement of an online full moon ritual to be held in a CompuServe conference room. The announcement was distributed by the leader of the ritual, a Neopagan priestess who happens to be a registered nurse in Philadelphia; it included a brief statement that the ritual would feature a rite of initiation into the path of Goddess worship for those who desired.

I was fascinated by the idea that a virtual gathering could be an opportunity not just for religious discussion but for an actual rite of passage; unfortunately, I had other committments for the time of the ritual and so was unable to observe. A few days afterward, the group leader posted a message indicating that a full transcript of the ritual was available for downloading from the forum archives. Immediately, I went searching for the document and found not only the one text of the ritual I had missed but dozens of others that had taken place in CompuServe conference rooms over an extended period of time. I downloaded them all and began to study them. From the transcripts it was evident that many of the people whose conversations I had been observing on the network shared a more intimate connection than I had realized. They constituted something close to an actual Neopagan congregation, a community of people who gathered regularly to worship even though they had never seen each other face to face. Though I was convinced that I had stumbled upon something that was both novel and significant, I was unsure how to study or write about the phenomenon; the conventional methods of academic research in religious ethnography seemed of little use in this case. One Lammas ritual that took place in a CompuServe New Age forum conference room on July 25, 1990, typifies the geographic spread of these rituals and the consequent problems of studying them: participants entered from New York, Los Angeles, Illinois, New Haven, Houston, Michigan, Louisiana, and Virginia. How is it possible to understand the religious practices of people one has not met and, even more strikingly, of a group whose participants have not even met each other?

Conventional ethnographic approaches assume that physical presence is prerequisite to study and cultural interaction; in short, that there is no substitute for fieldwork. As Barbara Myerhoff puts it, "Rituals are conspicuously physiological: witness their behavioral basis, the use of repetition and the involvement of the entire human sensorium through dramatic presentations employing costumes, masks, colors, textures, odors, foods, beverages, songs, dances, props, settings, and so forth" (1977: 199). If scholars maintain this understanding of ritual, they can only be led to the conclusion that rituals in cyberspace are simply "unreal," that their significance never transcends the virtual plane. However, one should be cautious of such an easy dismissal. Certainly, important elements of traditional ritual are lost without physical presence; but perhaps we should invert the question. Rather than assuming preemptively that the loss of physical presence produces a ritual that is unreal or "empty," we might ask what ritual *gains* in the virtual environment and what meanings the participants are able to derive from these practices, such that they will gather again and again to perform cyber-rituals together while paying a premium fee for their connect time. Further, some historical and contemporary parallels indicate that the validity of a ritual may not be so easily linked to physical presence or the mode of mediation.

Consider the following: the leader of the Roman Catholic Church celebrates a solemn pontifical Mass which is broadcast on television and announces a plenary indulgence to the faithful who observe the live broadcast from around the world; or a couple decides to get married and arranges a legally valid wedding in which the participants are at remote locations and the vows are typed in via computer keyboards. These ritual events are not fanciful predictions of what is to come; they have already taken place. They are no more or less "unreal" than than the Neopagan gatherings on CompuServe, insofar as the criterion is considered to be physical presence; but their validity, efficacy, and consequences (whether spiritual or legal) have the stamp of institutional approval. In fact, these are not the first instances of new technologies sparking a change in notions of ritual efficacy. In an essay entitled "Speech, Writing, and Performativity: An Evolutionary View of the History of Constituve Ritual," Brenda Danet (1996) brilliantly traces "the transfer of performativity from speech to writing," in periods when writing was in the process of becoming institutionalized, and applies the speech-act theories of Austin and Searle to documents such as Anglo-Saxon wills and modern wills on video, demonstrating yet again that technology can drive changes in our use of language and our concepts of symbolic action. If the creation of a written document can have the illocutionary force of a speech act, then it is not unreasonable to think that this force can be extended to cybercommunication; and if considerable resources in software and system design have already been devoted to making commercial transactions possible on the Internet, who is to say that spiritual goods cannot be peddled there as well?

If the argument based on the "unreality" of virtual reality is set aside, discomforting questions still remain. Anyone who has studied ritual through conventional ethnographic participant observation is likely to ask how ritual criticism (see Grimes [1990]) can be performed on a transcript. In response, I would argue that a departure from traditional ethnography is necessitated by the new technological environment in which these rituals occur. A transcript would certainly be insufficient evidence to support conclusions about a Catholic Mass or a Hopi Kachina dance; lacking the dimensions of intonation, music, image, and gesture, the student of these rituals would clearly be unable to interpret them adequately. However, the rituals in this particular case never had these dimensions to begin with: they are thoroughly and completely textual. The study of cyber-rituals must thus begin with the texts they generate. Ultimately, however, I do believe that academic study of these rituals will require an attempt to interview people in the offline world to see how they interact with their computers in the material realm.

It may seem absurd to compare these rituals to the Catholic Mass or to Protestant worship services; but such objections are likely to rest more on the prestige and influence of established churches than on any objective scholarly considerations. If we recall that the Neopagan movement is large and expanding, with regular gatherings in almost every state of the United States and all over Europe, some of which have brought suit in federal court against local ordinances that allegedly discriminate against their religious practices, and also that many, if not most, of the participants in these online rituals are active members of local groups that practice these rituals (or similar ones) outdoors in real time, we may be inclined to take them more seriously. My purpose in making this comparison is to conclude an earlier train of thought regarding the effect of communication technologies on the conceptions of symbolic action that are illustrated and exemplified in religious performances. Just as Protestant congregations and reformers, influenced by the culture of printing, reformed the liturgy in ways that privileged textuality over gesture and performance as the vehicle of symbolic meaning, so too modern religious practitioners rebel against current religious orthodoxy by devising new rituals that employ new technology to reassert the power of language as performative utterance.

A recent article in *Wired* magazine, a periodical that attempts to keep pace with the cutting edge of cybercommunication, dubs these ritual practitioners "Technopagans" (a description that they seem to embrace willingly) and notes that "a startling number of Pagans work and play in technical fields, as sysops, computer programmers, and network engineers . . . embody[ing] quite a contradiction: they are Dionysian nature worshipers who embrace the Apollonian artifice of logical machines" (Davis [1995]: 128). Refusing to accept any simple dichotomies of nature versus technology, these practitioners view the Internet as a theater of the imagination. The Technopagan community comes to life with the creation of performative rituals that create their virtual reality through text, their participants interacting with keyboards, screens, and modems. This is certainly odd for those who conceive ritual strictly in terms of situated *action*, as a drama involving chant, gesture, and props such as chalices, bread, wine, incense, etc; yet in the online experience, as revealed in archive files at least, such elements are replaced by textual simulations. The ritual objects of fire, bread, salt, and knife are embodied in the words: "fire," "bread," "salt," and "knife." As one Technopagan ritual leader puts it, "Both cyberspace and magical space are purely manifest in the imagination. . . . Both spaces are entirely constructed by your thoughts and beliefs" (Davis 1995: 128).

Here is an example from an undated ritual transcript available in the archives of the CompuServe Religion forum, Pagan/Occult section. In a Neopagan parallel to the Christian Eucharist, the group leader directs the assembly in the breaking of bread:

    | Take a moment to thank the Moon . . .
    | for all she/he means to you . . .
    | Connect deep within the heart of who she/he is—
    | honored by so many, many cultures.

| Take now your bread, muffin, or grain . . .
| (if you don't have such in front of you,
| virtual bread is okay)
| Take it, and split it in half.
| Hold one half in your hands . . .
| Think of the intuitive healing that comes
| through our
| marking of time, one month to the next . . .
| Think of the phases, the changes she/he takes us through . . . the mysteries.
| This half of bread will be libated after ritual outside.
| visualize your thanks into it.
| Place it aside.
| Take up the remaining half.
| See it, study it, sniff it, taste it.
| Eat of it, and think of healing. (ritual.txt)

Interestingly, the transcript is equivocal on the question of whether the bread needs to exist on the physical plane at all. It seems that some practitioners do enact the ritual at home in front of their computers, chanting at the direction of the online leader or High Priestess, manipulating the ritual objects of bread, salt, candles, wands, with gestures that are learned offline in "real time"; nevertheless, the ritual does not require the physical presence of the elements to be effective. Similarly, another ritual called for the placement of three candles in a triangular formation but added that "cyber-candles will do fine." In a final example, participants in a May 1994 full moon ritual kindled a cyber-flame in order to dedicate permanently an electronic conference room on CompuServe for the performance of Neopagan worship. Observe how the introduction to the transcript, authored by the leader of this ritual, characterizes the action performed as using virtual fire to sacralize a portion of cyberspace:

A need for a place of healing, purification and inspiration was identified by several members of Section 15. To meet this need, we decided to call forth a Sacred Flame similar to those in many Holy Temples of the Past and the Present. This flame was to be raised in Conference Room 9, Earth Religions, of the New Age Forum on Compuserve. It was to remain as a site for workings of the Spirit and of Aid for future users of the room. It was to be maintained through the Love and Duty of those that would seek its Majesty and experience its Touch within them. Many were in attendance this night to do this Work. Many Magicks from many Paths converged within the flames. Some of these pathways led to other realms and other times. The Magick of the evening is still here in the pages of transcript that follow. The Flame that was raised still burns! The Circle lives in its people. It is the Spirit of our combined Will! (myfm94.trn)

The evidence of these transcripts indicates that the actual performance of ritual acts using objects in real space is possible but unnecessary; the textual reality of a candle as described on the screen is sufficient to ensure ritual efficacy, while the cyberflame raised in the electronic conference room has *no* embodiment except in text. Signifier and signified are fused in the textual simulation of offline sensory experiences.

A useful perspective on these activities may be gained from the work of one of our most noted theorists of ritual, Jonathan Z. Smith. In his book *To Take Place: Toward Theory in Ritual* (1987), Smith emphasizes the importance of geography and landscape in the history of religion and argues against the traditional view (as articulated by Eliade and others) that myth provides the script that is enacted in ritual. Smith claims that ritual cannot be understood as a mere dramatization of a mythic script; rather, it must be understood on its own terms, as a mode of enactment that is geographically situated in communal space and landscape. With this in mind, what can we say about rituals in cyberspace—a place that is no place, a place that transcends geography in the conventional sense? What is the landscape of this strange world, and how has religion sacralized this landscape?

Cyberspace is without geographic features in the ordinary sense. But there is a kind of geography here, a landscape composed of sites, nodes, systems, and channels between systems. The topography of this landscape is represented by a variety of graphic interfaces that help orient those who explore it; and, as in the "real" world, this landscape has memories attached to it. Electronic archives and libraries store documents and record transactions; threads of conversations persist in groups and in the minds of individual participants; new users are routinely referred to the FAQ (frequently asked questions list). Then, too, the lack of ordinary physical features seems to inspire an attempt to recreate these features textually. This quality of spatial imagination is highly evident in the rituals excerpted here:

(Iuna) To all who have gathered, and to the Harvest King,
(Iuna) I offer and dedicate the cyber Harvest Home,
(Iuna) a Real place in the Virtual,
(Iuna) Named Gallifrey (for the home of the Time Lords).
(Iuna) The Harvest Home rests near the center of our touch,
(Iuna) the place of CompuServe . . .
(Iuna) This is a magic place . . .
(Iuna) and it will serve to link us,
(Iuna) virtual to real,
(Iuna) cyber to the plenty.

As Smith notes:

> Ritual is, above all, an assertion of difference. . . . [It] represents the creation of a controlled environment where the variables . . . of ordinary life may be displaced precisely because they are felt to be so overwhelmingly present and powerful. Ritual is a means of performing the way things ought to be in conscious tension with the way things are. ([1987]: 109)

This is made poignantly clear in an exclamation repeated throughout many of these rituals, a stock phrase in the Neopagan lexicon; when participants pray for blessings or benefits, their utterances are puncutated and given force by the ritual declaration, "so mote [must] it be!" This is perhaps too easily explained with reference to Freud's theory of religion as wish fulfillment. The speech act most characteristic of this assertion of difference in these rituals is not the declaration of wishes but the ritual setting-apart of space within the network.

> (Arianna)We the members of this
> FULL MOON CIRCLE
> CLAIM THIS SPACE.
> WE THE MEMBERS OF THIS
> FULL MOON CIRCLE
> CLAIM THIS SPACE.
> A space set apart.
> A world between worlds.
> Our special place to meet with the Goddess,
> For the purpose of spiritual growth,
> To promote and fellowship/sisterhood
> In the pagan community,
> and to witness the entrance of others
> into the Path of the Goddess of the Craft. (april.txt)

After the space is claimed, the angelic powers that inhabit the four directions of North, South, East, and West are invoked, and a ritual circle is cast. Within this circle a variety of other ritual actions are performed: initiation, investiture, and so forth. But it is the initial declarative act of setting the space apart that sacralizes the acts within that space, which turns further uses of ordinary language into performative speech acts—for those who take the ritual seriously.

If this all seems absurd and unreal to readers, recall again the powerful performative language of the Catholic Mass—which in Western culture virtually invented "virtual reality," a reality supported by a panoply of sensory impressions but created wholly through language and symbolism. From the perspective of the social science of religion, Technopagan rituals are no different in principle, and no less worthy of study than the belief system that underlies the daily utterance of the ancient, fateful, and endlessly contested words, "This is My body," in churches throughout the world. Nevertheless, there is a certain absurdist quality to these rituals: an aura of theatrical performance that calls to mind adolescent games such as Dungeons and Dragons. One notices, for example, the use of pastiche; ritual actors employ elements from many different sources—poems, literature, songs, and textual fragments—in an eclectic mix of numerous religious and aesthetic traditions. The aesthetic of pastiche makes for an astonishing variety of moods, interactions that fluctuate rapidly between reverence, pseudoreverence, and irreverence. Some participants come prepared with a text file and paste in quotations at particular points in the ritual. Prominent is the use of parody and humor, as when one Neopagan prankster concluded a Harvest ritual by virtually "singing" verses of a Neopagan version of an old Christian hymn:

(1-3, Willow) I would like to, while in this sacred space,
(1-3, Willow) thank the divine intervention of Aphrodite!
(1-3, Willow) She introduced Craig and I
(1-2, Shadow Hawk) Willow, do you know her verse in that great pagan classic,
(1-2, Shadow Hawk) Gimme that Old Time Religion?
(1-3, Willow) and, thankfully, my life will never be the same! (toast to Aprodite!)
(1-2, Shadow Hawk) (raising chalice to Aphrodite)
(1-3, Willow) Can you hum a few bars?
(1-2, Shadow Hawk) Hmmmmmmmmmmm . . .
(1-2, Shadow Hawk) We will worship Aphrodite,
(1-2, Shadow Hawk) Tho she seems a little flighty
(1-3, Willow) oh, no
(1-2, Shadow Hawk) Coming naked in her Nightie,
(1-2, Shadow Hawk) And that's Good enough for me! (grin)
(1-3, Willow) Oh, Gods!
(1-2, Shadow Hawk) Yes Goddess?
(1-1, Many Blue Sparks) Hee!
(1-10, Dave) Tis a nice ryme there Shadow Hawk.
(1-2, Shadow Hawk) (pouring more Wine for everyone)
(1-2, Shadow Hawk) Dave, there are about 200 or so verses . . .
(1-3, Willow) Hey, this may be a Spring ritual, but I'm engaged!
(1-2, Shadow Hawk) my favorite is the one that goes . . .
(1-2, Shadow Hawk) We will worship like the Druids
(1-2, Shadow Hawk) Drinking strange fermented fluids
(1-2, Shadow Hawk) Running Naked through the woods
(1-2, Shadow Hawk) and that's good enough for me!
(1-2, Shadow Hawk) (Gimme that old time religion. . . .) (g[rin]) (aprfmn.txt)

But lest we think that the whole thing was an elaborate game, something to take up the time of people who enjoy role-playing, who might otherwise develop an affinity for Morris dancing and the Society for Creative Anachronism, consider that the occult and Neopagan traditions that spawned or inspired these online rituals are, perhaps, second cousins (in their attitudes toward the power of ritual speech, if not in the lineage of their belief) to such New Age groups as the Order of the Solar Temple, the previously obscure sect now notorious for its group murder/suicides in Switzerland, France, and Canada. This brings me to the final issue, the cognitive content of these rituals—which has implications for considering the efficacy of the speech acts, insofar as they fulfill or do not fulfill what John Searle calls the "sincerity condition." If we are to judge the illocutionary force of these verbal actions, the efficacy of the rituals for their participants, it appears that we must first understand the degree to which they actually exhibit sincere belief in the gods they invoke.

What is the actual cognitive status of belief in the Goddess or any pagan deity for those who participate in these rituals? When Technopagans invoke the angels of the four directions, when they declare the circle to be cast so that the Goddess may manifest herself—do they actually "believe" in these entities in the same sense that Catholics believe in the miracle of transubstantiation or in the Trinitarian formula of the Nicene Creed? If we turn to the participants themselves for answers, we find that the question as posed is rejected altogether. By the testimony of some, at least, the cognitive content of Goddess belief, the "truth" of the myth in the conventional, empirical sense of that word, is irrelevant. What counts is the ritual act of invocation, which brings the deities into being or revivifies them. Some, at least, feel perfectly comfortable in viewing the Goddess and the pantheon of Pagan deities as projections of a Jungian collective unconsious—but argue that this renders them no less worthy of worship. As Arianna, a leader of numerous online rituals, writes in a file available in the CompuServe archives:

> What I'd like to say is that these deities are living and real. They are as real as any-thing that has been created. . . . Just as you created [the Goddess], men and women over the centuries have created their deities, and these are real and living. These deities may be seen as friends, as sisters, and brothers. They are alive, they may grant requests, if you so choose to call upon them. They are happy for all the love that you feel for them. . . . [A]ny deity that you choose will become strengthened by the power that you give it. And many still have power, through-out the centuries. The collective unconscious of mankind still recognizes their beauty. They are aspects of the unconscious, but they also live and love. (pagan.txt)

The ritual is seen as primary; belief in the conventional sense of that term is almost beside the point. By participation in the ritual, the actors invoke a goddess who may well be seen as a collective fiction but who nevertheless provides some spiritual sustenance and comfort to her followers. For those who take the ritual practice seriously, the Goddess becomes as real as any other collective fiction—certainly *more* real than the old man sitting on a cloud that many have lost the ability to believe in.

What lessons can be drawn from the ritual transcripts I have examined here? Though this question must await fuller treatment elsewhere, certain apects of computer-mediated Neopagan religious practice can be noted that will be of interest to scholars and perhaps to religious practitioners. In almost all of these transcripts we witness an attempt to recreate or simulate real space in virtual space and to sanctify a portion of this space as a theater in which spirit is manifested; an establishing of difference with the world outside as well as with other territories of cyberspace; and an assertion of the power of language to bring about wish fulfillment through the verbal act of declaring the wish within the ritual circle. To this extent, they appear as attempts to fulfill authentic spiritual needs now unmet by the major institutions of religious tradition. Yet there is an irreverence to these discourses that some will find distasteful; they are ludic and playful, they revel in pastiche and parody, and they make few (if any) cognitive demands upon the participants. This conjunction of reverence and irreverence seems to me to be in some way characteristic of the spiritual situation of postmodern culture, which can neither dismiss religion nor embrace it wholeheartedly but which ultimately leads to its commodification along with every other product and project of the past that is not doomed to be discarded on the ash heap of history.

What, after all, are we to make of a religious ritual that casts itself as a cybernetic reinvention of the ancient Samhain of pre-Christian Europe but includes an invocation of the Oreishas, the deities of Afro-Cuban and Vodou spirituality (whose devotees have their own electronic forums and message boards)? Such practices appear as the religious equivalent of the recent marketing phenomenon of "World Music," which gave us recordings of traditional Gaelic singing against a backdrop of African drums or the music of the medieval mystic Hildegard of Bingen backed up by a jazz combo. The postmodern sensibility of these audiences floats like a hummingbird over the flowers of the world's historical archive, extracting nectar from the offerings of folk culture and high culture alike without distinction, employing the language and the aesthetic conventions of a thousand traditions with allegiance to none. If one defining aspect of the postmodern era is that it is an age when *literally* nothing is sacred, then the options for traditional organized religious bodies in the world of cyber-religion would seem to be limited. They can be dismissed as irrelevant or simply ignored; or they can offer themselves up in the new spiritual marketplace of virtual culture as raw material for playful cyborgs (O'Leary and Brasher 1996) who cut and paste at will through the fragments of our traditions.

I will conclude by invoking again my earlier comparison regarding the similarity of these rituals to those practiced by other esoteric New Religious Movements such as the Order of the Solar Temple. We actually know very little about this particular group's beliefs and practices; there has been much speculation but little hard information reported. But let us suppose a degree of similarity, at least in regard to the belief in the power of ritualistic language. The meeting rooms of the Solar Temple used architecture along with powerful visual and spatial imagery to evoke certain states of acceptance in followers; we may easily imagine ceremonies taking place in these spaces that resemble those enacted by the online Pagans. What the online ritual lacks, in and of itself, is precisely the quality of physical presence that enables ritual actors to become so deeply embedded in the belief system that they will end up in an underground chamber, clutched with each other in a death embrace. By way of illustration, there is an exchange in an online Harvest ritual where one participant is offered cybercakes and cyber-ale in the virtual feast that concludes the ceremony.

She complains about her diet and is reminded that cyberfood has no calories. To put the point somewhat more brutally: unlike the flames of Waco, the ritual flames in these cybertransactions cannot burn.

Rooted in textuality, ritual action in cyberspace is constantly faced with the evidence of its own quality as constructed, as arbitrary, and as artificial, a game played with no material stakes or consequences; but the efficacy of ritual is affirmed time and time again, even in the face of a full, self-conscious awareness of its artificiality. As Ronald Grimes argues, "All ritual, whatever the idiom, is addressed to human participants and uses a technique which attempts to re-structure and integrate the minds and emotions of the actors" (1990: 196). If this is the true aim of all ritual, online as it is offline, then I believe we can say that these cyber-rituals do have efficacy, that they do perform a function of restructuring and reintegrating the minds and emotions of their participants. Toward what end is this restructuring undertaken? And will its integrations be durable? These are questions that must await further investigation, while we all wait to see the nature of the beast now slouching down the information highway to be born.

In a sense the discourses presented here are already obsolete, in that they have been superseded by the superior integration of texts, graphics, video, and even sound afforded to users of the World Wide Web, the fastest growing segment of cyberspace. A clue to the future of religious experiments in cyberspace may be seen in a 1994 Samhain ritual that took place in real time on a Web page housed in San Francisco. The designers of the page used a program called Labyrinth to simulate an altar in three-dimensional space, upon which ritual participants placed offerings of graphic designs and images (see Davis [1995]: 133, 178). As we move from text-based transmissions into an era where the graphic user interface becomes the standard and new generations of programs such as Netscape are developed that allow the transmission of images and music along with words, we can predict that online religion will become more "Catholic," by which I mean that iconography, image, music, and sound—if not taste and smell—will again find a place in ceremony. Surely computer rituals will be devised that exploit the new technologies to maximum symbolic effect. It does not seem too far-fetched to think of cybercommunication as coming to play a major role in the spiritual sustenance of postmodern humans. The possibilities are endless. Online confessions? Eucharistic rituals, more weddings, seders, witches' Sabbats? There will be many such experiments.

The old rituals were enacted by social actors who had to deal with each other outside the church, synagogue, and temple; by their very otherness they both constituted and affirmed the social hierarchies of their culture. In cyberspace we are seeing relationships develop that have no other embodiment but in textual interchange. The transition to online ritual thus allows, even encourages, the self itself to be seen as a textual construction. Ethos is transformed by its appearance in virtual reality, with the assumption of pseudonyms and the option of anonymity allowing a previously unknown freedom to construct an identity divorced from gender, age, or physical appearance (Turkle [1995]: 178–180). This results in new hierarchies that may mirror those of the world offline or depart from them in as yet unknowable ways. It is too soon to tell what the fate of religious community in the digital age will be or, indeed, whether the idea of a "virtual community" will prove to be sustainable. What paradigms will win out in the religious wars of the future we cannot tell; whether this will mean a revival of the Earth religions or reformulation of ancient beliefs and practices in a new guise, or both, or neither, is anyone's guess. It seems safe to predict, however, that we will continue to see old and new religions jostling for attention in the cultural marketplace and using available technology to reach new audiences. If current trends hold, computers and computer networks will play an increasingly significant role in the religions of the future.

Notes

1. Quoted with permission of the author, Bill Scarborough of Austin, Texas. In private e-mail correspondence to this author, Mr. Scarborough wrote: "I had seen a rendition of The Lord's Prayer in the Texas Baptist Standard a few years back. It was done in sports dialect, it could be witnessed in computer dialect. "The Cyberpunk's Prayer" is not copyrighted. Anyone is free to quote, repost, or reprint all or part of it."

References

Austin, J. L. (1970a). *How to Do Things with Words*. Oxford, UK: Oxford University Press.
———.(1970b). *Philosophical Papers*. Oxford, UK: Oxford University Press.
Calvin, John (1958) [1557]. "Last Admonition to Joachim Westphal," trans. Henry Beveridge. In *Tracts and Treatises on Doctrine and Worship of the Church*. Grand Rapids, MI: W. B. Eerdmans.
———.(1961). [1545]. "The Form of Church Prayers and Hymns with the Manner of Administering the Sacraments and Consecrating Marriage According to the Custom of the Ancient Church," trans. Bard Thompson. In *Liturgies of the Western Church*, ed. Bard Thompson. Cleveland: William Collins Publishers.
Coate, John (1992). "Cyberspace Innkeeping: Building Online Community." Reproduced in CRTNET #905 (Communication Research and Theory Network, ed. Tom Benson; back issues available from LISTSERV@PSUVM archives CRTNET).
Danet, Brenda (1996). "Speech, Writing, and Performativity: An Evolutionary View of the History of Constitutive Ritual." In *The Construction of Professional Discourse*, ed. Gunnarson Britt-Lowise, Per Lineell, and Bengt Nordberg. London: Longmans, pp. 13–41.
Davis, Erik (1995). "Technopagans: May the Astral Plane be Reborn in Cyberspace." *Wired* 3.07: 126–133, 174–181.
Eco, Umberto (1994). "Eco on Microcomputers." Available at: http://www.well.com/user/cynsa/engine.html.
Edwards, Mark U. (1994). *Printing, Propaganda, and Martin Luther*. Berkeley, CA: University of California Press.
Eisenstein, Elisabeth (1979). *The Printing Press as an Agent of Change: Communications and Cultural Transformation in Early-Modern Europe*, 2 vols. New York: Cambridge University Press.
Ellul, Jacques (1985). *The Humiliation of the Word*. Grand Rapids, MI: William B. Eerdmans.
Grimes, Ronald (1990). *Ritual Criticism: Case Studies in its Practice, Essays on Its Theory*. Columbia, SC: University of South Carolina Press.
John Paul II (1990). "The Gospel in the Computer Age." *L'Osservatore Romano*. (January 29): 5. Available as "The Church Must Learn to Cope With Computer Culture" at http://listserv.american.edu/catholic/church/papal/jp.ii/computerculture.html.

Jones, Steven, ed. (1994). *Cybersociety: Computer-Mediated Communication and Community.* Thousand Oaks, CA: Sage Publications.

Kellner, Mark A. (1996). *God on the Internet.* Foster City, CA: IDG Books Worldwide.

McDonnell, Kilian (1967). *John Calvin, the Church, and the Eucharist.* Princeton, NJ: Princeton University Press.

McLuhan, Marshall (1964). *Understanding Media: The Extensions of Man,* 2nd. ed. New York: New American Library.

Myerhoff, Barbara G. (1977). "We Don't Wrap Herring in a Printed Page: Fusion, Fictions and Continuity in Secular Ritual." In *Secular Ritual,* ed. Sally Falk Moore and Barbara Myerhoff. Assen, Netherlands: Van Gorcum.

New Age Forum Documents available on Compuserve, New Age Forum Archive, Pagan/Occult section. Filenames: aprfmn. txt, april.txt, pagan.txt, myfm94.trn, ritual.txt

O'Leary, Stephen D., and Brenda Brasher (1996). "The Unknown God of the Internet: Religious Communication from the Ancient Agora to the Virtual Forum." In *Philosophical Approaches to Computer-Mediated Communication,* ed. Charles Ess. Albany, NY: State University of New York Press.

Ong, Walter J. [1967](1981). *The Presence of the Word: Some Prolegomena for Cultural and Religious History.* Minneapolis: University of Minnesota Press.

———.(1982). *Orality and Literacy: The Technologizing of the Word.* London: Methuen.

Rheingold, Howard (1993). *The Virtual Community: Homesteading on the Electronic Frontier.* Reading, MA: Addisson-Wesley.

Smith, Jonathan Z. (1987). *To Take Place: Toward Theory in Ritual.* Chicago: University of Chicago Press.

Taylor, Mark, and Esa Saarinen (1994). *Media Philosophies.* London/New York: Routledge.

Thompson, Bard (1961). *Liturgies of the Western Church.* Cleveland: William Collins Publishers.

Turkle, Sherry (1995). *Life on the Screen: Identity in the Age of the Internet.* New York: Simon and Schuster.

5

Young People, Religious Identity, and the Internet

MIA LÖVHEIM

In 1998, a survey of American teenagers by the Barna Research Group of Oxnard, California, showed that one out of six teens said that within the next five years they expected to use the Internet as a substitute for their current religious practices. The study attracted a lot of attention and contributed to the already high expectations of how the Internet would change our ways of making life meaningful. More than five years later, some of the expectations have waned, but the question of how the Internet will impact the religious development of young people remains.

In this chapter, I will address this question by presenting some findings from a Swedish study of young men and women discussing religion using the Internet. The aim of this study was to examine how online interaction may affect the construction of identity among these young people, giving primary consideration to the role of religion in the identity construction process (e.g., Mol 1976). First I will provide a brief discussion of previous research on the Internet as an arena for the construction of identities. It would be beneficial, I will argue, if this research were set in the context of theories about the problems of identity formation in late-modern societies. Second, I will turn to an examination of some of the experiences of four young men and women discussing religion on the Internet. Third, I will use these findings, with an understanding of the identity challenges discussed in these theories in mind, to highlight the advantages and the disadvantages of working out one's religious identity online.

The Concept of Identity

Finding out who you are, or the construction of identity, is the process by which the individual develops an understanding of herself as a person distinct from others but also related to other people in a certain context (Hewitt 2000: 79f). Identity construction is a reflexive process. A person's experience of her own identity is continuously being formed over time, by forging a biography or story of the self from the lessons learned from different situations that arise in everyday life. A person's identity is being formed as well in the interplay between her presentation of herself in different situations and the responses of others to these presentations (Hewitt 2000: 95; Goffman 1959: 241ff). An individual announces her position relative to a situation. But an individual's possibility to express herself is heavily conditioned by the reactions of others, which confirm or call into question her assumed position. The presentations as well as the responses shaping our identities are based on the meanings and practices upheld in certain contexts. These situational interactions, in the context of culturally given meanings and practices, determine the location of an individual in a group of people as well as how she will relate to different groups in the same context. This location of an individual relative to a social group and system can be termed her ascribed social identity (Hewitt 2000: 97, 111).

Religious beliefs and practices are salient examples of the meanings and practices that have provided a basis for the construction of personal as well as social identities throughout history (Durkheim 1995; McGuire 1987: 27, 48ff). Religious myths, rituals, and symbols create overarching narratives or stories (Ammerman 2003) that give meaning to individual and collective experiences in relation to the struggles of everyday life. In a way similar to other forms of stories, such as political ideologies, religious stories provide a foundation for organizing relations between different groups in society and hence for the formation and reiteration of ascribed social identities. Through relating human life to something "sacred" or transcendent, religion also make sense of existential experiences of a more profound nature, such as confronting death, suffering, and the purpose of life.

Constructing Identity in Online Interaction

The interplay of individual presentations and the responses of other people that shapes identity is influenced not only by the situational meanings and practices of a certain group of people at a certain time in a certain context. It is also influenced by the different means used to make the presentations and experience the interactions. The medium of communication has a role to play in the identity-formation process as well. Following the increased public use of the Internet from the mid-1990s, a growing body of studies looked at how the particular conditions of online interaction might be affecting the process of identity construction (e.g., Kitchin 1999: 78ff). This research focused primarily on the potential to manipulate the presentation of such bodily identity cues as skin color, gender, and appearance in the text-based forms of communication dominant in online interactions. It also looked at the potential of the Internet to provide individuals with a greater diversity of ways of interpreting their personal experiences and relations through access to sets of meanings and practices not readily available in their local time and place. Both of these features seemed to undermine the role played by the conventional cues of ascribed social identity in face-to-face interactions. Hence the identities fashioned in cyberspace would be easier to transform (Goffman 1959; Smith and Kollock 1999: 9). Sherry Turkle's well-known book *Life on the Screen* (1995) is typical of the attention given this seemingly liberating possibility during the first years of research into the social and cultural implications of the Internet, as expressed in experiments with gender-swapping (1995: 220) or the construction of multiple online identities (1995: 180).

Later studies have lamented the dominance of this perspective. The fascination with the potential of the Internet to bracket certain conditions structuring identity formation in face-to-face interaction has meant that many studies have neglected duly to take into account how Internet users are also influenced by their offline context. Castells (1997) and Baym (1998) point to how differences in the offline experiences and positions of users may influence the skills and resources individuals can bring to online interaction. The early studies also took an uncritical approach to the structuring conditions developing within situations of online interaction. Studies by Kendall (1999) and Burkhalter (1999) point to how online interaction might maintain the relations of power based on gender or race found in offline contexts. Quite contrary to the anticipations of early studies, locating people in accordance with stereotyped social identities seemed to be a way of coping with the ambiguity caused by the new possibilities for deception opened up by the disembodied communication online (e.g., Postmes, Spears, and Lea 1998; Kendall 1999).

In sum, previous research into these issues makes it clear that we need to approach the construction of identity in relation to online interaction as a process *situated* in the structuring conditions of the offline as well as the online context. James Slevin (2000) takes such an approach. He has sought to contextualize Internet usage by referring to Anthony Giddens' conception of the changing conditions for identity construction in contemporary society (Giddens 1991; Castells 1997). Giddens describes how the way of organizing life in what can be termed high or late-modern society (1991: 4, 16ff) introduces new elements into the interplay of presentations of self and the responses of others as described above. The development of new means of communication and transportation means that everyday life is being shaped, for a growing number of people, as much by events taking place in distant places as by those in the local community. Hence people become exposed to a variety of sources and types of information that they realize are important but cannot always grasp and control.

Also people are being introduced to opportunities as well as risks that previous generations did not have to face. Thomas Ziehe (1994: 35ff) points to how young people in contemporary society in particular are experiencing these kinds of ambiguous situations. Biologically and socially, young people are situated in a phase of transition from childhood to adult life. In late-modern society, the guidance offered by traditional practices, among them religious beliefs and rites, has been destabilized. Adequate social models for how young people should act are disappearing. At the same time, the fascination of the young with what is "new" and "cool" makes them perfect targets for the life style options and role models marketed by commercial companies and the entertainment industry. Hence, young people find themselves having to negotiate between a diversity of perhaps conflicting values and norms mediated by, on the one hand, authorities such as their parents and the school and, on the other hand, the ever-present messages of films, music, and advertisements. This tension makes the reflexivity of the process of identity construction, in terms of the constant evaluation and reasserting of who I am and how I shall act, all the more explicit in the context of late-modern society (Giddens 1991: 32).

The construction of identity, of a biography or story of the self (Giddens 1991: 53), is increasingly understood as an individual responsibility. On the one hand, this new sense of personal responsibility may enhance a young person's sense of mastery in a time of life characterized by vulnerability and insecurity (Giddens 1991: 149). On the other hand, it might equally increase her insecurity, since it erodes the individual's trust in her capacity to forge a story of self that can integrate her diverse and conflicting experiences in a meaningful way (Ziehe 1994: 133ff; Giddens 1991: 175).

Starting from an understanding of the conditions of life in late-modern society as outlined by Giddens, Slevin (2000: 174, 26) discusses four ways in which the Internet can enhance how individuals handle the project of identity construction. First, use of the Internet can encourage and reinforce the possibilities for individuals to "actively negotiate mediated experience and endow it with structures of relevance to the self" (2000: 175). Second, the Internet as a medium facilitates the reappropriation of knowledge and skills, since it allows ordinary people more readily to access expert information and to compare and assess claims made by different, competing authorities (2000: 177). Third, by bringing people into contact with a greater diversity of cultures and social groups, the Internet compels users to be more articulate about their individual commitments. Also they can find better opportunities to form alliances and enter into social engagements that can be adjusted to changes in the social and material conditions of a person's life offline. Fourth, the Internet can teach users ways of coping with new conflicts and risks that challenge their day-to-day routines, for example through dialogue and the acquisition of better information. In each of these ways, use of the Internet can encourage and reinforce the sense of individual agency crucial to self-development and empower individuals to handle the greater insecurity and ambiguity of life in late-modern society.

When discussing these possibilities, Slevin also emphasizes that using the Internet for this purpose always entails new risks and dilemmas as well, as we will see below. He indicates how these can arise in relation to the online context itself, but his main focus is how the Internet augments or compensates for situations of powerlessness or empowerment relative to the offline situations of Internet users (Slevin 2000: 114ff, 234ff; Haraway 1999). As Slevin's work suggests, studies of the impact of the Internet on identity formation need to consider both the complex and ambivalent implications of the Internet as an arena or tool for identity construction and the analysis of the influence of offline features on the online experiences of individuals.

Identity, Religion, and Contemporary Popular Culture

As Dawson (2000) points out, this kind of contextualization of online interaction has regrettably yet to be explored adequately, especially in relation to the use of religion as a resource for the construction of identity in contemporary society. Studies in the sociology of religion (Woodhead and Heelas 2000: 305ff) have described how the function and plausibility of religion as an overarching story integrating societies and providing a foundation for identity is changing in contemporary society. The influence of organized religion in the everyday life of modern individuals is declining. James Beckford (1989: 170ff) suggests that religion has become a "cultural resource," as symbols and practices once controlled by organized religion increasingly become used for a wide variety of purposes and thus invested with highly diverse meanings. The use of religious symbols in media and popular culture provides salient examples of this development (Hoover 1997).

As described by Nancy Ammerman (2003), individuals in contemporary society are seeking answers to questions about their own stories of self in connection with a possible transcendent source of existential meaning in the intersections between these different approaches to religion. The work of Lynn Schofield Clark (2003: 77ff) illustrates how young men and women construct religious identities by negotiating the different meanings of religious symbols as mediated by contemporary teen popular culture and by organized religion. The new ambiguities of this situation can be discerned in the ambivalent reactions of many young people. Some individuals find successful strategies for integrating different sources of religious meaning into a coherent story of self in relation to the transcendent. Others struggle with how to handle this blurring of the traditional boundaries between different values, norms, and beliefs as prescribed by "proper" religion and presented in popular culture. For some of these young people, a return to the values and norms of very traditional religious organizations provides a way to ensure clear boundaries between different meanings and consistency for their own religious identities (cf. Castells 1997: 26).

Many of these observations and theoretical insights are supported by the findings of a long-term, qualitative study of the experiences of fifteen young Swedish men and women using a Swedish-speaking Web community that I will call the Site. This study was part of a larger research project entitled IT, Community, and Identity that is based at the Theological Faculty, Uppsala University (see also Linderman and Lövheim 2003; Lövheim and Linderman, forthcoming). During the time of the study, the Site was one of Sweden's most frequented Web communities, gathering around 700,000 young members from a range of different contexts. At the Site, individuals present themselves to other users primarily through a chosen alias, but the Site also offers the opportunity to reveal age and gender as well as to construct a personal Web page. Members of the Site have access to different opportunities for interaction, primarily discussion groups on various topics and instant messages. The data used in this paper were collected between February 2000 and February 2001 using a combination of online observations of eight discussion groups focused on religion, offline interviews, and the analysis of individual Web pages and time-use diaries.

Identity, Religion, and Online Interaction: The Possibilities and Problems of Diversity

The plurality and diversity of options for exploring religion offered by the Internet is well documented in previous research (Hadden and Cowan 2000; Larsson 2002). Through its size and diversity of users, the Site holds the potential for increasing the range of religious views to which young people are exposed in seeking to make sense of their own existence. Maria,[1] an eighteen-year-old student brought up in a Reformed Church tradition, explores this potential through taking an active part in several discussion groups that include Christian faith as well as popular culture and scientific research. For her, interaction in the groups represents a new and intriguing experience: "It's like in reality you agree about everything and you read in the Bible and. . .but there you can have more heated discussions and talk to people who are. . .who really hate Christians and Satanists and so on. It's like more fun in some ways and you can be more tough because it's anonymous." The groups, she says, offer a great opportunity to "show what our faith is all about and perhaps get rid of prejudices and so on." In her discussions with other people she tries to create "a bit more understanding between atheists and Christians, I don't want to be aggressive but try to be friends with them, somehow, compromise a little."

Maria's attempts to refute prejudices about Christians, how they are "nerds" and "intolerant," is met most of the time, however, with resistance from others, as can be seen in the following excerpt from one of the discussion groups:

Maria: 2000-06-27

. . .You can choose to follow the rules or ignore them, God does not force anybody, the choice is up to each person. I myself follow them since I think that God know's what's best for me, but respect you if you have chosen to do something else. OK?

Cabined: Maria   2000-07-04

"The choice is up to each person". . . (?!). . . my oh my . . . your God does NOT welcome those who have not accepted him, that is you have your free will, but if you don't choose God then you might not go to hell in today's "modern Christianity"

… but you WON'T go to your heaven … don't claim anything else … then you don't know your bible . . . and you called yourself a Christian, didn't you??? And if you call yourself a Christian then you got to follow your Bible FULLY and not choose certain parts.

Sven: Maria . . .

. . . I guess you were not thinking when you wrote your earlier contribution. . . at least I hope so! The Bible says that ALL of us Christians shall go out into the world and make ALL people disciples. That's like our mission. . . .

Maria's encounter with Cabined and Sven illustrates how interactions online with people with different understandings of one's own religion can be problematic for young people. The problem is further illustrated by the experiences of Hanna, an eighteen-year-old student with an evangelical Christian background. Hanna approached the Site with the intention of being available for people "who maybe won't dare to ask some Christian like straight on, eye to eye, then it's like a good way for those persons to ask something like without anyone knowing who they are." In contrast to Maria, Hanna tends to avoid discussing her faith with other people in the discussion groups. This choice, she explains, is not so much due to a fear of getting into arguments with people who don't share her faith; rather, it is to avoid the ambiguous experience of meeting other Christians who, in her opinion, compromise with the "radical message" of Jesus. For Hanna, being a Christian means "either you buy the whole packet or you just let go of it, because it's just no use to sort of do it half-hearted." As she says: "That's why I have a harder time getting in discussions with Christians who sort of . . . don't believe in the Bible than with non-Christians. 'Cause in the case of the non-Christians there's this wide and great and clear borderline anyway."

The experiences of Hanna, Cabined, and Sven indicate how the diversity of options for relating to religion that the Internet exposes young people to can make their lives more insecure. This insecurity seems to be related to experiences that blur the young peoples' understanding of the conventional boundaries between what belongs to a certain religion and what does not. As Clark's (2003) research suggests, this experience can be handled in different ways. Maria tries to integrate the different meanings into her story of self. She does not find the combination of different ways of relating to religion problematic. As she explains: "Jesus encourages us to question, check our faith, try out if it's correct and so on, you can do that." As Slevin proposes, Maria seems to be able to use these online discussions as a tool to help her negotiate and integrate different ways of approaching religion. The encounters help her to develop an understanding of herself as a Christian but also as someone who "likes questioning things," who "can be cool, too."

The responses by Hanna, Cabined, and Sven indicate how this kind of diversity also can be handled by reinforcing conventional assumptions about, in this case, "radical Christians," "modern Christians," and "non-Christians." A closer analysis of the discussion groups at the Site reveals that people like Maria are in the minority. Most of the exchanges in the groups related to Christianity are structured around stereotyped understandings of "Christians" and "non-Christians," as expressed in the excerpt above. The findings presented hence indicate that the diversity of ways of relating to religion available online must be approached as an ambiguous resource at best for the project of constructing the self. How different individuals use this resource is structured by the conventions and norms about religion that become dominant in the specific online groups.

The Mixed Blessing of Interaction

The significance of the Internet for individuals involved with new religious movements, especially Paganism and Witchcraft, has been aptly described elsewhere (e.g., Dawson and Hennebry, this volume; Berger and Ezzy, this volume; O'Leary, this volume; Fernback 2002). Lugh, a twenty-year-old student and solitary Wiccan, approached the Site to contact and share experiences with like-minded people. Even though Sweden is a highly secularized country, in terms of church attendance and support for basic Christian beliefs, the Christian denominations remain the historically dominant cultural force (Skog 2001). Hence Lugh's opportunities to find information about Paganism and discuss these religious beliefs and practices in his local context are very limited.

Lugh's experiences at the Site illustrate how the very conditions that make the Internet a unique and interesting arena for exploring a new religious identity also introduce certain dilemmas. The discussion groups at the Site aimed at Wicca and other forms of metaphysical and magic belief systems are characterized by a high degree of transience and heterogeneity. This is due in part to the constant inflow of new members asking questions about "how to become a witch/magician" after being exposed to popularized versions of these traditions in films, television, and magazines. It is also a result of the high value placed on the right and responsibility of each individual to construct his own religious story among the young practitioners of these traditions. This individualism produces a notable diversity and inconsistency of answers to such questions.

Lugh, who presents himself as a more "experienced practitioner," is ambivalent about this situation. On the one hand, he finds the transience and heterogeneity difficult to reconcile with his growing urge to move on to a more profound or "serious" discussion of his beliefs. Hence he gets "a little annoyed when people enter like for the seventeenth time and ask about how you learn to fly or stop the time or something." On the other hand, he is critical of the tendency in these groups to ridicule and seek to control the views of new practitioners or "wannabes." He disagrees with the subsequent tendency to impose hierarchies on the tradition: "I become a bit irritated if someone enters and thinks that 'you are not real Wiccans 'cause you don't follow our tradition,' like. This sort of thing, it feels like . . . elitist people and so on . . . I mean there's no possibility for people to, well, become Wiccans if they don't start off by themselves." In Lugh's opinion, the imposition of organization, rules, and hierarchies "doesn't really fit like . . . how do you put it . . . the foundation of the religion . . . it's not really that anyone has any more say than anyone else really."

Lugh's experiences illustrate how an arena like the Site is a mixed blessing for young people out to develop alternative approaches to the transcendent. Above all, this concerns the possibilities and problems of using the Internet in order to share a religious story with other people. As proposed by Slevin, the Site provides a unique opportunity for someone like Lugh to form new relationships with people who share his ideas. At the same time, group interactions online also introduce a heightened awareness of the contingency of religious meanings and religious identities. While this awareness challenges the consistency and continuity of Lugh's Wiccan identity, his attempts to assert a certain consistency online present an additional dilemma. How can he practice tolerance for a diversity of ways of speaking about Witchcraft and magic with his quest for a more "serious" and durable religious identity while also avoiding the establishment of some kind of religious authorities, rules, and dogma?

Lugh's experiences, like Maria's, point to how an individual's use of religion online as a resource for forging a story of self cannot be studied only by looking at how the new opportunities offered online fit or contrast with the offline situation of the individual. We must also analyze the relations that develop between different groups of users in a particular Internet arena and how individuals negotiate these relationships in fashioning their religious identity.

The Ambiguity of Textual Communication

Both Hanna and Maria note how the anonymity of text-based communication opens up alternative ways for the expression of their religion. The different experiences of Hanna and Stirner, an eighteen-year-old student and committed atheist, in the discussion groups at the Site, however, suggest that much depends on the specific form of interaction in a particular Internet arena. The discussion groups at the Site represent a form for multiparty communication, in which contributions are restricted in terms of size and displayed in relation to the time when they were sent. These conditions seem to favor a rhetorical style based on snappy arguments, polarized debates, wit, and theoretical knowledge.

Hanna started a discussion group for Christians to come together and encourage one another. Her experiences of the interaction in the group contradicted these intentions. The group turned into "some kind of intellectual game" in which people use "smart words" and discuss matters on a level that most "people don't get." Hanna's response to this challenge was to avoid the discussion groups and use instant messages instead. Hanna's dissociation from this individualistic, critical, and abstract way of approaching religion as well as relating to other people in the group is shared by most of the young women in the study. In Hanna's opinion, the norms and values emphasized among girls are contradictory to the ones encouraged in the discussion groups:

> **Interviewer:** Do you think that many girls do like you do, write personal messages instead of contributions to the groups?
>
> **Hanna:** Yes I really think so, it's much more like that because . . . girls are more like that on the whole, like . . . more of this personal relations and so on and not so much . . . just this thing that girls hang out in pairs and guys in gangs. Guys are more like "I want people to see me and now I want to say what I think to *everybody.*" Girls are more like "I want to help *her* because she is not feeling well" or something like that.

For Hanna, instant messages provide possibilities more in line with her intentions of communicating her beliefs through kindness and mutual support. As Chandler (1998) suggests, instant messages as well as Web pages represent a form for communication where the individual exercises more control over the process than in discussion groups. This strategy, however, comes with a price. It makes her into an "outsider" in the online groups, which restricts her possibilities to influence the subject of discussions as well as her ascribed social position in these contexts.

Stirner represents the group of members of the Site who have achieved a position as "insiders." This position is partly achieved through frequent contributions in the discussion groups. The crucial aspect of becoming an insider, however, seems to be the ability to take on the "ethos" (Fairclough 1992:166) of the discussion groups. In this case, "ethos" can be seen as the presentation of self and the approach to religion facilitated by the technical means for communication but also by the conventions on religion and the social relations that become dominant in a certain arena. The insiders' ability to use the Site in accordance with these conditions gives them a dominant position in the groups.

In the previous sections, we have seen how certain stereotyped understandings of religion seem to structure the relations between different groups of people in the discussion groups at the Site. In Stirner's words, these are "like stupid atheists, stupid-scientific atheists and us then, and the Satanists, and then we have the religious stupid people, not stupid religious people . . . there are some kind of groups, where everybody pretty much dislikes each other except perhaps . . . well, rational atheists and rational Christians. That's the groups that usually are interesting to talk to." Stirner's description of some people as "stupid" and others as "rational" and hence "interesting to talk to" illustrates how the insiders, through their responses, seek to control interaction in the groups. Stirner identifies himself as a "rational atheist." His intention in using the Site is to challenge "fundamentalist" attitudes to religion and encourage critical, rational, and independent thinking: "I want to create a conflict in their minds in such a way that I want to present new arguments, and I want to question this because I think religious faith is dangerous. . . . It's not like I'm playing atheist crusade . . . it's rather that enlightenment, that's a good thing. If we are to move forward as a society and as individuals we got to . . . see through the illusions and see what's real and what's false."

Hanna's experiences indicate that the mode of communication represented by the discussion groups is well suited for this kind of critical, detached, and rational way of discussing religious beliefs. Stirner's skills and competence in navigating the groups do not protect him, all the same, from misunderstandings resulting from the ambiguities of written messages. His engagement in Christian discussion groups, for example, often results in people identifying him as a Christian. This ambivalent experience is shared by many of the young people, who refer to the difficulties of getting past stereotyped religious identities in a medium where announcements as well as locations of identity are made solely on the basis of textual messages. Presenting oneself as Gods_Servant in the discussion group Radical Belief fails to provide the nuance of meaning that comes from telling someone about your beliefs while standing before them in a T-shirt opposing pornography or from playing in a rock band. But Stirner's skills in using the discussion groups and his favorable access to the Internet during most of the study allowed him to handle these situations in a better way than others: "If you write one single message in say a forum, then the image of you will for good reasons become pretty much without nuances and stereotyped. On the other hand if you spend a lot of time at the same place then I think you have the possibility of forming a more nuanced image of yourself than in many similar 'real' situations."

Stirner has also experienced the dilemma expressed by Lugh of negotiating his own position and approach to religion in the face of the hierarchies created by different participants in the online groups. This tension compels him to be more reflective, recognizing the contradiction between the strategies he must use to maintain his position as an insider and his ideal of being objective, respecting the opinions of even those who fervently disagree with him. Hence he gets disappointed when he lets himself be provoked into an "emotional" response and "uses insults," even though he often manages "in a cowardly fashion to *hide* those behind my objectivity."

Thinking about this dilemma has led Stirner to change his attitudes toward people who have chosen other ways of relating to religion:

> I've also gained more respect for . . . the more secular part of Christianity. For people who have reflected on this and, well, for some reason accept god's existence . . . but that accept other people's opinion about this and do not try to adjust reality in order to fit the bible. I respect these people so much more, and so I don't look upon Christians as a homogeneous group in the same way as before. . . . I guess I know that some were more radical than others, but you don't *think* about it really 'cause it's so much more comfortable to just call them Christians, and then condemn all of them.

In contrast to Hanna, Stirner has been able to use the discussion groups to develop a more complex understanding of himself and the role of religion in his story. In this process, his ability to handle the conditions for discussing religion in the groups plays a crucial role. The different experiences of Hanna and Stirner illustrate how the mode of communication—in this case the written text of contributions and Web pages—may impact these conditions. Also, they illustrate how the possibilities to use discussion groups successfully, for example, require certain skills that might be combined with the individuals' previous experiences of and approach to religion.

Conclusion

The findings presented and discussed briefly in this chapter show that interaction in an online arena like the Site can provide some experiences that enrich young people in their efforts to create their own religious identity. Accessing the Site opens up possibilities for presenting and exploring the nature of one's beliefs in a context that is seemingly free of the structuring conditions of the local context. In the case of Maria it involved new ways of discussing Christian faith. In the case of Lugh, it involved finding his place in a marginal religious group in the Swedish society.

For all of these young people, use of the site also involves encountering a larger number of more diverse and often more direct responses to their presentations of self than they would have to deal with offline. Some of these responses corresponded to their previous understandings of their own religious identity and that of others. Other responses seem to challenge these conceptions, initiating a process of reflection leading to the reassertion of their own way of relating to their religious tradition. But such interactions can also introduce new dilemmas for these young people to handle at the Site.

As Slevin's theoretical analysis suggests, the Internet does seem to assist individuals in their quest for identity by providing unique opportunities for sharing and appropriating new kinds of knowledge and social relationships—in this case, religious ones—and generally shattering the limitations of their local environment and asserting their agency. By negotiating their own path online through the diversity of ways of making their experiences meaningful, the young people begin to develop competencies for forging a satisfactory story of self in the face of the uncertain circumstances of contemporary society. Above all, however, the findings also point to the ambiguity and ambivalence of the Internet as an arena or a tool for identity construction. This ambiguity becomes salient in the dilemmas faced by different individuals, but also in the differences between their ways of using the site to handle those dilemmas. As noted, the site not only provides possibilities to elude structuring conditions in the offline context, it also imposes conditions that structure how religion can be used and by whom. These structuring conditions seem to be formed in the interplay between the previous experiences of individuals that make them approach the site with certain intentions and skills and the approaches to religion that become dominant in the online environments. The approaches that become dominant seem to be structured by the relations that develop between different groups of users in particular forums, for example between "Christians" and "non-Christians" and between "experienced practitioners" and "wannabes." Also, the technical means for communication play a part by favoring approaches that are more cursory than "serious," as experienced by Lugh, and more abstract and critical than emotional and supportive, as experienced by Hanna (Lövheim 2004).

The data presented here are limited but underline the importance of studying the question of the impact of the Internet on the construction of identity among young people and their use of religion in this process in particular. In doing so, attention should be given to the special challenges and dilemmas introduced by the Internet as well as the possibilities. Furthermore, the research clearly shows the importance of situating online interactions in the structuring conditions of interaction both online and offline. It is important not to forget that even though online interaction eludes *some* of the conditions of offline contexts, young people discussing religion in a place like the site also have to relate to circumstances in their lives outside the site. Hanna's experiences indicate that these can be norms and values about gender among young people themselves but also in society at large (cf. Håpnes and Rasmussen 1999). The assumptions about Christians debated by Maria and Stirner indicate the influence of the clash between secularized and traditional Christian ways of approaching religion in contemporary Sweden. Lugh's ambivalence in facing the "wannabe" witches and magicians indicates how he has to deal with the popular mediation of these religious beliefs in the other mass media consumed by his contemporaries.

Finally, tracing the complex intersection between the offline and online experiences of religion of these young people may tell us something about how online interactions are contributing to the broader transformation of religious orientations in contemporary society (Dawson 2000: 45ff). If the ways we think about religion and practice our faith are shifting to meet the changing social conditions of late-modern or postmodern society, then the changes should be evident in the dialogue of young people discussing religion online. Is there a "synergistic" link, as Dawson suggests (2000: 49), between the very character of the Internet and processes of religious change already under way in our societies? It is salient that Maria, Hanna, Lugh, and Stirner have sought not only to embrace the flexibility and blurring of conventional religious boundaries opened up by late-modern society but also to find appropriate boundaries to handle insecurity and contingency of meaning. The reflections of Hanna, but also Lugh, on the need for clear boundaries, authorities, and rules in discussing religion indicate how young people online are becoming involved, at least potentially, in the renegotiation of attitudes toward the doctrines, authorities, and institutionalized beliefs and practices of offline traditions.

Hence, in line with Ammerman (2003), I would argue that the impact of the Internet on religion, at least in terms of its use as a resource for the construction of identity, must involve an examination of the intersection of "embodied" religious experiences offline and "disembodied" experiences online. We need to learn much more about the interplay of these worlds' and contexts in the lives of ordinary Internet users.

Notes

1. The names used in this chapter are chosen in order to protect the confidentiality of the informants. They do not correspond to their birth names, nor to their aliases at the Site.

References

Ammerman, N. (2003). "Religious Identities and Religious Institutions." In *Handbook for the Sociology of Religion*, ed. M. Dillon, 207–224. New York: Cambridge University Press,

Baym, N. K. (1998). "The Emergence of On-line Community." In *CyberSociety 2.0. Revisiting Computer-Mediated Community and Communication*, ed. S. G. Jones, 35–68. Thousand Oaks, CA: Sage.

Beckford, J. A. (1989). *Religion in Advanced Industrial Society*. London: Unwin Hyman.

Burkhalter, B. (1999). "Reading Race On-line. Discovering Racial Identity in Usenet Discussions." In *Communities in Cyberspace*, ed. M. A. Smith and P. Kollock, 60–76. London and New York: Routledge.

Castells, M. (1997). *The Information Age. Economy, Society and Culture. Volume II: The Power of Identity*. Oxford, UK: Blackwell.

Chandler, D. (1998). "Personal Home Pages and the Construction of Identities on the Web." Retrieved from www.aber.ac.uk/media/Documents/short/webident.html, November, 26, 2002.

Clark, L. S. (2003). *From Angels to Aliens. Teenagers, the Media, and the Supernatural*. New York: Oxford University Press.

Dawson, L. L. (2000). "Researching Religion in Cyberspace. Issues and Strategies." In *Religion on the Internet. Research Prospects and Promises*, ed. J. K. Hadden and D. E. Cowan, 25–54. London: JAI Press/Elsevier Science.

Durkheim, E. (1995). *The Elementary Forms of the Religious Life*. New York: Free Press.

Fairclough, N. (1992). *Discourse and Social Change*. Cambridge: Polity Press.

Fernback, J. (2002). "Internet Ritual: A Case Study of the Construction of Computer-Mediated Neopagan Religious Meaning." In *Practicing Religion in the Age of the Media*, ed. S. M. Hoover and L. S. Clark. New York, NY: Columbia University Press.

Giddens, A. (1991). *Modernity and Self-Identity. Self and Society in the Late Modern Age*. Stanford, CA: Stanford University Press.

Goffman, E. (1959). *The Presentation of Self in Everyday Life*. London: Penguin Books.

Hadden, J. K., and D. E., Cowan, eds. (2000). *Religion on the Internet. Research Prospects and Promises*. London: JAI Press/Elsevier Science.

Håpnes, T., and B. Rasmussen, (1999). "Jenteidentitet på Internett." *Sociologisk tidsskrift* 1 (7): 3–21.

Haraway, D. (1999). "A Cyborg Manifesto." In *The Cultural Studies Reader*, ed. S. During, 271–292. London and New York: Routledge.

Hewitt, J. P. (2000). *Self and Society. A Symbolic Interactionist Social Psychology*. Needham Heights, MA: Allyn & Bacon.

Hoover, S. M. (1997). "Media and the Construction of the Religious Public Square." In *Rethinking Media, Religion, and Culture*, ed. S. M. Hoover and K. Lundby, 283–298. Thousand Oaks, CA: Sage.

Kendall, L. (1999). "Recontextualizing 'Cyberspace': Methodological Considerations for On-Line Research." In *Doing Internet Research: Critical Issues and Methods for Examining the Net*, ed. S. G. Jones, 57–74. Thousand Oaks, CA: Sage.

Kitchin, R. (1999). *Cyberspace: the World in Wires*. Chichester: Wiley.

Larsson, G. (2002). *Virtuell Religion*. Lund: Studentlitteratur.

Linderman, A. G., and M. Lövheim, (2003). "Internet, Religion and the Attribution of Social Trust." In *Mediating Religion: Conversations in Media, Religion and Culture*, ed. J. Mitchell and S. Marriage, 257–269. Edinburgh: T&T Clark/Continuum.

Lövheim, M. (2004). "Intersecting Identities: Young People, Religion and Interaction on the Internet." Ph. D. dissertation, Uppsala University, Uppsala, Sweden.

Lövheim, M., and A. G. Linderman, (forthcoming). "Constructing Religious Identity on the Internet." In *Religion in Cyberspace*, ed. M. T. Højsgaard and M. Warburg. London: Routledge.

McGuire, M. (1987). *Religion: The Social Context.* Belmont, CA: Wadsworth.

Mol, H. (1976). *Identity and The Sacred.* New York: Free Press.

Postmes, T., R. Spears, and M. Lea (1998). "Breaching or Building Social Boundaries? Side-effects of CMC." *Communication Research* 25: 689–716.

Skog, M., ed. (2001). *Det religiösa Sverige. Gudstjänst och andaktsliv under ett veckoslut kring millennieskiftet.* Örebro: Libris.

Slevin, J. (2000). *The Internet and Society.* Cambridge, UK: Polity Press.

Smith, M. A., and P. Kollock, eds. (1999). *Communities in Cyberspace.* London and New York, NY: Routledge.

Turkle, S. (1995). *Life on the Screen: Identity in the Age of the Internet.* New York: Simon & Schuster.

Woodhead, L., and P. Heelas, eds. (2000). *Religion in Modern Times. An Interpretative Anthology.* Oxford, UK: Blackwell.

Ziehe, T. (1994). *Kulturanalyser. Ungdom, utbildning, modernitet.* Stockholm/Stehag: Symposion.

6

Religion and the Quest for Virtual Community

LORNE L. DAWSON

Introduction: The Issues

The great sociologist Emile Durkheim defined religion as "a unified system of beliefs and practices relative to sacred things . . . which unite into one single moral community . . . all those who adhere to them" (1965: 62). Religions are, Durkheim insisted, "moral" phenomena. Today we may be reticent to use this term, but Durkheim' s reasons for doing so remain true. On the one hand, being religious involves accepting certain demands and regulations about how we should interact with other people. On the other hand, it means knowing that there are people to whom we can turn in times of need or distress for emotional and material support. Religions are preeminently about the ethical regulation of our social relations and solidarity with a community. This is an intrinsic part of rendering our lives meaningful. In truth there is much "believing" today without really "belonging," without participating very often in the religious activities of a particular group (e.g., Bibby 1987; Davie 1994; Roof 1999). But for most people, being religious still implies being part of a group, even if the affiliation is more symbolic and subjective than real. In the popular mind the notions of religion and community go hand -in- hand.

In his influential theory of religion, Durkheim (1965) goes on to assert that the very sense of power and fulfillment that people experience in the presence of the sacred stems from the impact of sharing the "collective representations" embodied in religious rituals and myths as well as the "collective efferves- cence" ignited by the sheer presence of many people solemnly and sometimes ecstatically joined together in the performance of rites and ceremonies. In his view, if religion has historically been the soul of society, its conscience and guiding force, it is because "society is the soul of religion" (1965: 127). At the core of this relationship is the face-to-face interaction of individuals mediated by their common orientation to what they perceive to be the divine or sacred.

But if this is the case, what are we to make of the possibility of religion in cyberspace? Can individuals communicating by computer from the comfort of their homes practice their religion? We are told that new forms of community are coming into being, "virtual communities" free of any meetings in the flesh in any real place. If these communities exist, can religion happen in them? Stated in this way, the investigation of religion online hinges on the study of communities in cyberspace. Have real communities emerged online? If virtual communities exist, then presumably there can be religions in cyberspace as well. Of course, much depends on what we mean by "community" and "religion," and in the discussion of virtual communities to date the notion of community has been used far too loosely.

This chapter addresses two issues. First, I will provide a brief overview of some of the doubts raised about whether communities, and hence religions, can exist online. Data will be examined that cast a more positive light on the possibilities. Second, I will address a neglected methodological question: How could we know if we were in the presence of community online? We need more precise criteria for determining the degree to which relations online are indicative of the emergence of communities.

Our thinking about religion in cyberspace tends to be distorted by two misconceptions: (1) community is associated too much with a romanticized notion of life in the small towns and villages of the past; and (2) religious life is associated too much with a Western congregational model. Traditional communities are being rapidly replaced today by what the sociologists call "social networks." The primary relevance of the Internet to religious life is its affinity, I will argue, with this new structure of social relations in late-modern societies. If this is the case, then the real research question becomes: Does the Internet offer new ways for religion to happen in the new social context, or is the new social context, as expressed by the Internet, antithetical to being religious? Will religion disappear because the traditional experience of community is in decline? Or will cyberspace give rise to a sufficiently adapted form of communal life capable of sustaining religious experiences? An affirmative answer to the last question requires us to abandon a restrictive congregational model of religious organization.[1]

Are Virtual Communities Possible?[2]

The rise of the Internet led many to claim that a new way exists for overcoming the alienating effects of modern life. Virtual associations could replace the loss of traditional neighborhoods and small personal work environments, and counter the deleterious effects of increasing social and geographic mobility, the impersonal nature of large bureaucratic organizations, and so on. What is more, some argue, the Internet facilitates the formation of entirely new kinds of communities—communities that would be free of such limiting factors as ethnic stereotyping, class distinctions, gender discrimination, and differences in time as well as space. People can reach out to each other twenty-four hours a day from almost anywhere in the world (e.g., Jones 1998; Reid 1991; Rheingold 1993). "Synchronously and asynchronously," as Dave Healy states (1997: 60), "the sun never sets on the virtual community."

But has the sun of communal bliss ever really risen on the Internet in the first place? The substitution of computer-mediated communication for the face-to-face variety may be symptomatic more of the triumph of modern alienation than of its circumvention. It is important to ask whether "most so-called virtual communities [are not] too specialized, largely ideational in content, and too intermittent or transitory to evoke the sense of we-ness commonly associated with the word community" (Dawson 2000: 38). Many observers have suggested that virtual communities are nothing more than pseudocommunities (e.g., Lockard 1997; McLoughlin, Osborne, and Smith 1995; Slouka 1995). But until recently we have lacked the empirical data even to begin adjudicating this dispute. In discussions of groups communicating by computer, it is simply assumed too often that "community" is present, without really specifying why or how (e.g., Jones 1998; Rheingold 1993; Smith and Kollock 1999). As will be discussed below, since community implies more than mere social interaction, not all virtual groups are communities.

The Internet Paradox

At the heart of the debate over virtual communities is a seeming paradox. The Internet allows individuals to reach out globally to form bonds with people of like mind, overcoming the physical barriers and social distinctions that have held them apart, but at the price of reducing the self presented and the social interactions established to text-based and largely asynchronous exchanges between physically isolated individuals. But it is the dialectical interplay of self and other, surely, that forms the basis for true sociality. We tend to presume that greater exposure to real others induces a more sensitive, reflexive, and hence enduring capacity to form communities. How much otherness does one really experience seated alone before a computer screen? Similarly, the Internet facilitates "boundary-breaking" interactions (Kinney 1995: 770). People can enter into conversations with people from the most diverse cultures and subcultures, encountering ideas to which they would never be exposed in the daily routines of their lives. But the technologically limited connection provided inevitably attenuates the experience, and our extraordinary ability to control these contacts may render them more solipsistic than we are willing to admit (Foster 1997; Lockard 1997; Markham 1998; Willson 1997). In her ethnography of Internet users, Annette Markham found that the ability to control communications, limiting undesired self-disclosure, was one of the greatest appeals of communicating by computer (1998: 155–156, 175, 209, 213–215).

The online absence of nonverbal social cues, the ones we normally use to judge the character and trustworthiness of people, draws people into a dependence on stereotypes. Both in interpreting others and presenting themselves, Postmes, Spears, and Lea (1998) found that Internet users are eager to discover and emulate the norms of any group. In exchanges this means they often fall back on stereotypical conceptions to ease and hasten interaction and gain ready acceptance into desired circles. Socially scripted interactions are used to gloss over the interpretive gaps so typical of strictly text-based exchanges (O' Brien 1999 and Kendall 2002 make similar observations). Is such behavior conducive to the formation of viable communities? Perhaps in the short run. But we need to know if, when, and how these communicative shortcuts and preferences will be replaced by more complete and individualized interactions online. Are the technological and cultural biases in favor of quick, witty, truncated, and stereotypical modes of discourse so strong on the Internet that more personal and complex discussions are intrinsically and permanently discouraged? Or is this just a dominant feature of certain types of interactions? What prompts more serious and sustained dialogue between people online, and are these interactions almost always less rich than those undertaken in person or by the phone?

As Wellman and Guila (1999: 170) and DiMaggio and colleagues (2001: 319) lament, the right kind of systematic studies of communal life in cyberspace have yet to be completed. We lack either detailed ethnographies of established communities or survey research into who is using the Internet in this way and how (with the partial exception of Miller and Slater 2000 and Kendall 2002). We need to know more about the qualitative character of online relationships and the actual performance of so-called virtual communities.

The Social Effects of Internet Usage

There are empirical studies available, however, that indicate ways in which real and consequential relationships are forming online (e.g., Blanchard and Horan 1998; Fox and Roberts 1999; Kendall 2002; King 1994; Lea and Spears 1998; Miller and Slater 2000; Parks and Floyd 1996; Parks and Roberts 1998; Rheingold 1993; Turkle 1995). People establish lasting friendships, form business partnerships, provide therapeutic support, and even get married online. The evidence also suggests, though, that online relationships will not become the kind of lasting and more broadly based interactions we associate with community unless they migrate offline—for periods of time, at least.

We also can learn something about the potential of the Internet to support meaningful social relations from studies of the consequences of Internet usage. The advent of television had a deleterious effect on people' s levels of social and civic engagement. In a much publicized study, Kraut and colleagues (1998) reported that higher levels of Internet use were likewise associated with declines in communication with family members, declines in social circles, and increased loneliness and depression. Further study revealed, however, that the negative social and psychological effects dissipated to statistical insignificance with the passage of time (Kraut et al. 2002). The negative impact of the Internet seems to be a temporary side effect of initial inexperience and limited competence. It is quickly rectified as more friends and family members come online.

A series of other comprehensive studies demonstrates that Internet usage is either unrelated or even positively associated with social interaction (e.g., Anderson and Tracey 2001; Anderson et al. 1999; Hampton and Wellman 2000; Howard et al. 2001; Katz, Rice, and Aspden 2001; Robinson and Kestnbaum 1999; Robinson, Barth, and Kohut 1997; Robinson et al. 2000; Wellman et al. 2001; for summary discussions see Castells 2001 and DiMaggio et al. 2001). A controlled comparison of users and nonusers reveals that users are:

- as involved or even more involved with community and political activities
- have wider circles of social contacts
- are as likely to visit friends or call them on the phone
- attend more arts events
- read more literature
- go to more movies
- watch and play more sports

Manuel Castells concludes that there seems to be "a positive feedback effect between on-line and off-line sociability, with Internet usage enhancing and maintaining social ties and social involvements for most users" (2001: 123). In principle, then, the Internet appears to be a highly social medium with a marked potential for community-building.

People use the Internet in ways that are in continuity with or augment their offline social lives (e.g., Anderson et al. 1999; Donath 1999; O' Brien 1999; Anderson and Tracey 2001). Virtual communities, to the extent that they ever become common, are unlikely to operate as substitutes for more traditional forms of social relations. Life online will likely complement life offline, and there is no reason to expect that religious uses of the Internet will differ.

Religious Communities Online

At least some nascent religious communities exist online, and a few direct studies have been undertaken of these social experiments. Davis (1995, 1998), O' Leary ([1996] this volume), and Lövheim and Linderman (1998; Linderman and Lövheim 2001) have looked at the "Technopagans," Schroeder, Heather, and Lee (1998) examine a virtual Pentecostal group, Dawson and Hennebry (1999) discuss a postmodernist cyber-religion, Helland (2000) describes an online UFO religion, and Krogh and Pillifant (2002; this volume) analyze an online revival of ancient Egyptian religion. But these studies are largely exploratory and fragmentary. Sustained and systematic work which lends itself to worthwhile comparative analyses has yet to be undertaken, in part because too few true cyber-religions have come into being.

There is no obvious reason why many of the activities of religious organizations cannot be done on the Internet, from posting announcements, studying scriptures, delivering sermons, and hearing confessions, to providing counseling.

Even rituals have been performed online, but with mixed though very interesting results (Dawson, forthcoming a; O' Leary, this volume). It remains to be seen whether technologically mediated religious experiences are possible, and if so, how. When it comes to the possibilities for religious communities online, we are confronted with a typical "chicken-and-egg" problem. The absence of cases of sufficient scope to study impedes drawing any conclusions, yet the absence of cases may be indicative of the inherent limitation of cyberspace in this regard.

But some measure of true communal life clearly has emerged at some times in cyberspace. It often arises almost accidentally or incidentlly in response to the personal crises of members of an online group (e.g., the collective response of members of the WELL to a participant' s plea for help with a sick child or the suicide of a member, as discussed by Rheingold 1993) or a grievous disruption of the unspoken norms of interaction online (e.g., the cyber-rape discussed by Dibbell 1994). The organized group life born of these circumstances is usually marked by a moderate level of interaction and commitment with regard to a fairly specific set of concerns. But this is in line with long-recognized principles of group formation and solidarity (e.g., Coser 1956), and as Wellman and Guila (1999) argue, most of modern life is marked by social bonds of "intermediate strength" at best. The Internet has facilitated the development of new, true, and sometimes quite unusual personal relationships (e.g., Bruckman 1996; Kendall 2002; Markham 1998; Parks and Roberts 1998).

This situation is a mixed blessing at best, if we consider the formation of religious communities. The anonymity of cyberspace allows religious relationships to be focused squarely on the religious, embodying the age-old ideal of religious fellowship. In relation to the sacred, it should not matter who you are other than your status as a fellow devotee. Consider the following comment made by an Internet user (Lyles 1998: 114):

> Unlike the church, when I am in cyberspace, nobody really knows, unless I tell them, whether I am black, white, red, yellow, or even male or female, whether I am writing from a hovel or a palatial estate.
> Nobody knows my educational background or lack of it, or even my age. That doesn't seem to matter to anybody and this is the way church ought to be. We are a true community of seekers.

But is this communion of cybersouls a sound foundation for religion? Is it conducive to the formation of religious communities? Certainly it flies in the face of the decidedly more social realities of religious life as it has been known for centuries. Striking a Durkheimian note, Chris McGillion (2000) fears that the Internet "encourages people to opt out of the kind of flesh-and-blood relationships that are the indispensable condition of shared religious meanings." If religion becomes detached from real places, real people, and a real sense of shared time and cultural memory, then how can there ever be a significant measure of collective conscience and collective effervescence? Stripped of these embodied elements, McGillion states, the "suprahuman status of the claims of religion meld into all the other claims on the Net and religion's symbolic power is undermined."

In seeking to explore the possibilities for religion online, we need to determine how we would know we were in the presence of community online (religious or otherwise). Resolution of this more foundational question allows us to say whether religious communities exist online, gives us an important way to analyze their comparative operation and sufficiency, and opens the door to investigating the mediation of religious experience online.

How Can We Detect Community Online?

In his groundbreaking book *The Virtual Community*, Rheingold argues that virtual communities "are social aggregations that emerge from the Net when enough people carry on . . . public discussions long enough, with sufficient human feeling, to form webs of personal relationships in cyberspace" (1993: 5). This well-known and often-cited claim is plausible. But how could we measure and compare the relative presence of community using Rheingold's parameters? His terms of reference (i.e., public discussions, long enough, sufficient feeling) are too impressionistic. We need to turn elsewhere to develop more exacting indicators. But in doing so, we must recognize that there is no consensus on a definition of community in sociology, despite over a hundred years of research (e.g., Brint 2001; Hillery 1955). The term is still largely used for groups identified with a specific geographical location. But this traditional consideration is rapidly giving way to an emphasis on other kinds of relational factors. Geographic or residential communities are being replaced by "elective communities" or "communities of choice," and as Castells concludes, there is a growing consensus amongst sociologists of cyberspace "that the study of sociability in/on/with the Internet has to be situated within the context of the transformation of patterns of sociability in our society" (2001: 125).

Communities and Social Networks

Virtual communities are only a subtype of this larger phenomenon—what many are now calling "personalized communities," or "networked individualism" (Castells 1996, 2001: 125–129; Wellman 2001; Wellman and Guila 1999). For decades sociologists engaged in community studies have been tracing the displacement of spatial communities such as neighborhoods by networks of people drawn together by affinities and choices and not mere physical proximity. With the onset of modern forms of mass transportation and mass communication, the physical restructuring of urban centers, and the rise of the information economy, "the pattern of sociability evolved toward a core of sociability built around the nuclear family in the household, from where networks of selective ties were built according to the interests and values of each member of the household" (Castells 2001: 127). People tend to have a far greater range of social relations than in the past and over far greater distances. Ties are weaker and more flexible, yet they are still an important source of social support, stimulation, and material advantage. In fact, people tend to be involved in a series of networks of relations formed on different bases for different durations and at different levels of intensity. These networks either overlap or are totally divergent, happen simultaneously or serially. The sole common denominator is the individual at the hub of each network.

Have networks, then, replaced communities? Or are they actually the antithesis of community? Scholars in the field are disinclined to say yes to either question. The spatial basis of sociability is much reduced. Our friendships and family ties can now be sustained over much greater distances. The ties of most people are weaker in kind and more flexible in operation. We interact with a much greater variety of people for many different reasons and in a diverse array of circumstances. Outside the nuclear family, there are few people with whom we share a common experience of space and daily routine. But these looser ties are still the substance, so to speak, of daily life—the sources of sociability, support, information, and identity.[3]

Detecting the Presence of Community Online

With this larger picture in mind, can we develop analytical tools for determining if communities exist in cyberspace? Helpful leads are provided by the work of Quentin Jones (1997) and Geoffrey Liu (1999). But first we need to consider more broadly the factors influencing whether virtual communities will come into being and what shape they will take.

Modifying the analysis presented in Nancy Baym's excellent essay, "The Emergence of On-Line Community" (1998: 39–49), it can be argued that studies of virtual communities need to give due consideration to four sets of formative factors. First, there are *technical factors*. For example, there is the influence of the system infrastructure of the computer network being used. The pattern of communication will be affected by such variables as the number of computers involved, how they are spatially dispersed, the speed of the system, the flexibility, programmability, and overall user-friendliness of the system. The temporal structure of the computer-mediated communication is also important. Whether it is synchronous or asynchronous influences the content and the style of the interaction and hence the relative sense of community. For instance, in synchronous systems, the duration of time between replies will take on more normative significance. Second, there are *cultural factors*. It is difficult to overstate that even in cyberspace communication is influenced by the cultural backgrounds of participants. We are still the products of quite specific cultures, and "participant perceptions . . . [are] important determinants of communicative outcomes" (Baym 1998: 47). Kyong-Jee and Curtis (2002), for example, found distinct differences in the ways Finnish, American, and Korean students used the Internet to collaborate. Third, there are diverse *social factors*. The features of the participating group itself, for example, will vary with its size, demographic composition, joint interactional history, degree of training in the medium, and organizational structure (e.g., group hierarchies). Likewise, there are questions of relative access to the medium or whether the participants are all employees of the same organization, undergraduate students, or whatever. Fourth and finally, there are *more immediate situational factors*. For example, there is the impact of the assumed purpose of the group interaction (e.g., recreation versus work). It makes a great deal of difference whether a group believes it is required to "generate ideas or plans, choose amongst answers or solutions, negotiate conflicting views or conflicting interests, or execute performances in competition with opponents or external standards" (Baym 1998: 46).

In the end we are dealing with a complicated interaction of many variables and subvariables, and as Baym (1998: 49) concludes, "it may not be possible to specify the specific factors that will combine to affect . . . outcomes in a particular group in advance of actual interaction, let alone what the impact of those factors will be." But "research on [computer-mediated communication] must attend to these factors if the findings are to be comparable with those of other studies and the complexities and differences of on-line communities understood." Few, if any, of these factors has been systematically examined, especially with regard to religious developments on the Internet.

Even if they were, however, Baym's approach would not tell us if we were in the presence of a community. To that end we need to turn to the suggestions of Jones (1997) and Liu (1999). Condensing, modifying, and adding to their analyses, I would propose that a set of communications by computer warrants being considered evidence of the existence of a virtual community to the degree that it displays six elements: (1) interactivity; (2) stability of membership; (3) stability of identity; (4) netizenship and social control; (5) personal concern; (6) occurrence in a public space.

We may be in the presence of a virtual community if the messages posted (including the use of written texts, emoticons, and action-simulating messages) display a significant level of interactivity. As Rafaeli and Sudweeks (1998) argue, computer-mediated communication is a group phenomenon; it is inherently social. But it is actual interactivity that draws people into the social life of the Net and binds them to any ongoing social activity. True interactivity emulates face-to-face conversation, though there is a continuum of interactivity even in face-to-face situations. Unlike most broadcast communication, the Internet has the capacity to draw near to the interactivity of offline relationships. But the actual exchanges initiated in cyberspace may vary greatly. To what extent do the messages typed into cyberspace relate to each other in sequence? To what extent do posted messages display their relatedness to earlier messages in some exchange? To what extent do the turns taken in a cyberspace dialogue constitute a continuous feedback loop fostering the comprehension of a shared interpretive context, one that facilitates the emergence of new jointly produced meanings? Much of the interaction in cyberspace is closer to the reactive or declarative end of some hypothetical continuum of interactivity. Its style is abrupt, instrumental, or impersonal, and even combative at times. Such exchanges are not conducive to building the more multifaceted relationships commonly associated with a sense of community.

We may be in the presence of a virtual community if the participants in the computer-mediated communication post messages relatively frequently and over a reasonably long period of time. These two indicators of stability tell us we are in the presence of something more than a mere exchange of views of some passing topic of common concern. More specifically, Liu (1999) suggests we should look for a significant level of coappearance of participants. Do the members of the group visit the site of the computer-mediated communication at common times and do they tend to dwell there, cognizant of the presence of specific others?

We may be in the presence of a virtual community if the participants in the computer-mediated communication tend to maintain stable identities, as indicated by their nicknames and character displays. Cyberspace is a land of anonymity and multiplicity when it comes to matters of identity. But communities are based on trust, which requires a greater measure of identity stability. Given the technical possibilities and the subcultural proclivities of computer-mediated communication, Liu suggests that statistically it is more likely that communal ties have been forged if at the site in question "the number of nicknames associated with more than one participant is insignificant," and "the number of participants who ever used more than one nickname is insignificant" (Liu 1999: 16).

We may be in the presence of a virtual community if the participants in the computer-mediated communication display a sense of responsibility for sustaining the communication by negotiating and enforcing norms to guide future communications and protect participants from various forms of deviance (e.g., deceptions, harassment, flaming, hijacking people's characters or spaces in MUDS, spamming). Several observers have traced the ways in which commitment to a particular online group is demonstrated by the creation of specific conflict resolution procedures and systems of punishment designed to protect the integrity of various MUDs, chat rooms, and newsgroups (e.g., Dibbell 1994; Du Val 1999; Mnookin 1996; Reid 1999). Such agreements and the will to abide by them certainly add to the durability of any forum for computer-mediated communication. This sense of commitment can also be displayed through various acts of netizenship, like creating and maintaining FAQ pages, helping "newbies" to navigate the new social space successfully, and "gift-giving" (i.e., freely distributing software and other technological information online; see Kollock 1999).

We may be in the presence of a virtual community, as Rheingold (1993) and Wellman and Guila (1999) suggest, if the interactions of the participants in the computer-mediated communication are not exclusively instrumental. The interactions may be largely practical in nature, geared to the sharing of information or the completion of a project. But as Brint (2001: 8) suggests of communities generically, the interactions must also display an "interest in the personalities and life events" of other people. Not everyone has to have an interest in everyone else. But some participants must display this broader level of involvement with some consistency.

Finally, given our commonsense notions of community, it seems reasonable to specify, as both Jones and Lui do, that much of the interaction in question takes place in a context where it is being viewed by others, especially the other potential participants in the group. This need not exclude various additional private communications between participants, but the notion of community implies a shared experience amongst a reasonably large number of people. The members of the community need not all be active participants, at least not all the time. Lurkers may share in a sense of community, but they do little, of course, to sustain it.

This list of considerations is probably not definitive and it leaves much still to the subjective judgment of the analyst. But it does provide us with a gradient of factors with which to assess and compare different situations, and Lui, Rafaeli and Sudweeks, and others have begun demonstrating how we might actually measure the presence of these indicators, given both the special technical advantages and challenges of computer-mediated communication. It would be most interesting to see some of these measures applied systematically to religiously based instances of supposed virtual community.

Conclusion: The Bigger Picture

Will religious uses of the Internet move beyond the instrumental—the positing and retrieval of information and limited e-mail exchanges? It is too early to tell. Clearly, intrinsic features of computer-mediated communication, at least in its present form, pose special problems for the generation and sharing of religious experience *per se* (see O' Leary, this volume; Dawson, forthcoming a). But part of the experience of religion, and if Durkheim is correct, a foundational part of the experience of the sacred, is the sense of community. Comprehensive research now suggests that fears of the antisocial implications of the Internet were mistaken. The Internet is used most often to expand people's social horizons and involvements. People use the Internet to augment and extend their preexisting social lives, not as a substitute or alternative. In general this bodes well for religion, but it must be remembered that the larger framework of our social lives is now the social network more than the community as traditionally conceived. This will have its own consequences for religious practice and the way religious organizations are structured and operate in the future. As a significant material support for the networked structure of society in the twenty-first century, the Internet could play a leading role in the adaptation of religion to the new social reality, but only if the religions seek to explore the possibilities creatively.

One factor that must be taken into account in thinking through these possibilities is whether religious life should be so closely identified with the formation
and maintenance of specific, geographically located, and relatively large
groups. Is it possible, as James Beckford has ingeniously proposed (1989), that
today religion is being reconfigured as a relatively free-floating "cultural
resource" geared to the demands of personal identity more than group life?
At this point there are more questions than answers, but the suggestion is in
line with Anthony Giddens's reading of late-modern societies (see Dawson
2004; Giddens 1990, 1991) as well as the notion of a network society advanced
by Castells (1996) and Wellman (2001). The institutionalized reflexivity so
characteristic of modernity, Giddens argues, is reflected in the societal
preoccupation with the construction of personal identities in an environment
of heightened uncertainty about the choices that must be made to fashion an
identity. In part this is because the local and traditional social order, the source
of identity in the past, is being displaced by global influences and points of
reference, as mediated and fostered by social networks in general and more
specifically the Internet. Religion is coming adrift from its conventional social
moorings, just as our identity constructing processes are, and the Internet
offers one of the few forums for the reflexive construction of identity by means
of the interpenetration of highly personal and more or less global concerns,
issues, and resources.

The resultant interactions may not take on the stable countenance of a "community" if we mistakenly continue to identify religion with the congregational
form of its expression over the last few centuries in the West. Congregations
are modeled on the outdated cultural aspiration for a romantic notion of life
in the small towns of the past. But what would a "church" adapted to a
networked society look like, and how would the Internet play a role? Throughout
human history and in most parts of the world, religious praxis has not been
about an exclusive affiliation to a specific institution or place like a church.
Religion is a more diffuse phenomenon, merged with many of the activities
associated with other social institutions, and the Internet may help us recapture
that possibility in the late-modern societies of the Western world.

But these speculation carry us too far afield for the moment. A more foundational task calls for our attention: we need to find, describe, analyze, and
systematically compare instances of religious life in cyberspace. To that end,
we need to apply the six criteria of community outlined above to religious
groups invested in the Internet to determine if one of the minimal grounds for
experiencing religion is emerging online.

Notes

1. Of course a third option exists. As Durkheim surmised, a new mode of religiosity may be
developing that is better suited to the more individualistic lifestyle of late-modern
societies. Durkheim called this phenomenon the "cult of man," but his analysis remained
rudimentary and speculative (Dawson 1998; Durkheim 1969; Westley 1983). If the nature

of religion is changing in accommodation to a new social reality, then research into the impact of the Internet on religion must investigate how the Internet is related to this change in religiosity (see Dawson 2000: 45–49; Dawson, forthcoming a).

2. This section of the chapter calls upon ideas first presented in Dawson, forthcoming b.

3. Easy grasp of this fact is blocked by a continued and outdated reliance on the sociological conception of *Gemeinschaft* (i.e., community), as popularized by Toennies ([1887] 1957) more than a century ago (see Brint 2001).

References

Anderson, B., and K. Tracey, (2001). "The Significance of Lifestage and Lifecycle Transitions in the Use of Internet Applications and Services." *American Behavioral Scientist* 45: 456–475.

Anderson, B., et al. (1999). "Family Life in the Digital Home: Domestic Telecommunication at the End of the Twentieth Century." *BT Technology Journal* 17: 85–97.

Baym, N. K. (1998) "The Emergence of On-Line Community." In *Cybersociety 2.0: Revisiting Computer-Mediated Communication and Community*, ed. S. Jones, 35–68. Thousand Oaks, CA: Sage.

Beckford, J. A. (1989). *Religion and Advanced Industrial Society*. London: Unwin Hyman.

Bibby, R. (1987). *Fragmented Gods: The Poverty and Potential of Religion in Canada*. Toronto: Irwin.

Blanchard, A., and T. Horan, (1998). "Virtual Communities and Social Capital." *Social Science Computer Review* 16: 293–307.

Brint, S. (2001). "*Gemeinschaft* Revisited: A Critique and Reconstruction of the Community Concept." *Sociological Theory* 19: 1–23.

Bruckman, A. S. (1996). "Gender-Swapping on the Internet." In *High Noon on the Electronic Frontier: Conceptual Issues in Cyberspace*, ed. P. Ludlow, 317–325. Cambridge, MA: MIT Press.

Castells, M. (1996). *The Rise of the Network Society*. Oxford: Blackwell.

———. (2001). *The Internet Galaxy: Reflections on the Internet, Business, and Society*. Oxford, UK: Oxford University Press.

Coser, L. (1956). *The Functions of Social Conflict*. New York: The Free Press.

Davie, G. (1994). *Religion in Britain since 1945: Believing But Not Belonging*. Oxford, UK: Blackwell.

Davis, E. (1995). "Technopagans: May the Astral Plane Be Reborn in Cyberspace." *Wired*. Retrieved from www.wired.com, Jan. 1998.

———. (1998). *Technosis: Myth, Magic and Mysticism in the Age of Information*. New York: Three Rivers Press.

Dawson, L. L. (1998). "Anti-Modernism, Modernism, and Postmodernism: Struggling with the Cultural Significance of New Religious Movements." *Sociology of Religion* 59: 131–156.

———. (2000). "Researching Religion in Cyberspace: Issues and Strategies." In *Religion on the Internet: Research Prospects and Promises*, ed. J. K. Hadden and D. E. Cowan, 25–54. New York: JAI Press.

———. (2004). "The Socio-Cultural Significance of Modern New Religious Movements." In *Oxford Handbook of New Religious Movements*, ed. J. R. Lewis, 68–99. New York: Oxford University Press.

———. (forthcoming a). "The Mediation of Religious Experience in Cyberspace." In *Religion in Cyberspace*, ed. M. Hojsgaard and M. Warburg. London: Routledge. Originally a keynote address delivered to the Religious Encounters in Digital Networks Conference, University of Copenhagen.

———. (forthcoming b). "Religion and the Internet: Presence, Problems, and Prospects." In *New Approaches to the Study of Religion*, ed. P. Antes, A. Geertz, and R. Warne. Berlin: Verlag de Gruyter.

Dawson, L. L., and J. Hennebry, (1999). "New Religions and the Internet: Recruiting in a New Public Space." *Journal of Contemporary Religion* 14: 17–39.

Dibbell, J. (1994). "A Rape in Cyberspace: Or, How an Evil Clown, a Haitian Trickster Spirit, Two Wizards, and a Cast of Dozens Turned a Database into a Society." In *Flame Wars: The Discourse of Cyberculture*, ed. M. Dery, 237–261. Durham, NC: Duke University Press.

DiMaggio, P., et al. (2001). "Social Implications of the Internet." *Annual Review of Sociology* 27: 307–36.

Donath, J. (1999). "Identity and Deception in Virtual Community." In *Communities in Cyberspace*, ed. M. A. Smith and P. Kollock, 29–59. NewYork: Routledge.

Durkheim, E. (1965). *The Elementary Forms of Religious Life*, trans. J. W. Swain. New York: Free Press.

————. (1969). "Individualism and the Intellectuals," trans. S. Lukes and J. Lukes. *Political Studies* 17: 14–30.

Du Val, A. (1999). "Problems of Conflict Management in Virtual Communities." In *Communities in Cyberspace*, ed. M. A. Smith and P. Kollock, 134–163. New York: Routledge.

Foster, D. (1997). "Community and Identity in the Electronic Village." In *Internet Culture*, ed. D. Porter, 23–37. New York: Routledge.

Fox N., and C. Roberts, (1999). "Gps in Cyberspace: The Sociology of a 'Virtual Community.' " *The Sociological Review* 47 (4): 643–671.

Giddens, A. (1990). *The Consequences of Modernity*. Cambridge, UK: Polity Press.

————. (1991). *Modernity and Self-Identity*. Stanford, CA: Stanford University Press.

Hampton, K., and B. Wellman, (2000). "Examining Community in the Digital Neighbourhood: Early Results from Canada's Wired Suburb." In *Digital Cities: Experiences, Technologies and Future Perspectives*, ed. T. Ishida and K. Isbister, 475–492. Heidelberg, Germany: Springer-Verlag.

Healy, D. (1997). "Cyberspace and Place: The Internet as Middle Landscape on the Electronic Frontier." In *Internet Culture*, ed. D. Porter, 55–68. New York: Routledge.

Helland, Chris (2000). "GroundCrew/Planetary Activation Organization." In *Encyclopedia of UFO Folklore and Popular Culture*, ed. J. R. Lewis. Santa Babara, CA: ABC-Clio Pub.

Hillery, G. (1955). "Definitions of Community: Areas of Agreement." *Rural Sociology* 20: 111–123.

Howard, E. N., L., Raine, and S. Jones (2001). "Days and Nights on the Internet: The Impact of a Diffusing Technology." *American Behavioral Scientist* 45: 383–404.

Jones, Q. (1997). "Virtual Communities, Virtual Settlements and Cyber-Archaeology: A Theoretical Outline." *Journal of Computer Mediated Communication* 3 (3). Retrieved from www.ascusc.org/jcmc, January 10, 1998.

Jones, S. G., ed. (1998). *Cybersociety 2.0: Revisiting Computer-Mediated Communication and Community*. Thousand Oaks, CA: Sage.

Katz, J. E., R., Rice, and P. Aspden, (2001). "The Internet, 1995–2000: Access, Civic Involvement and Social Interaction." *American Behavioral Scientist* 45: 405–419.

Kendall, L. (2002). *Hanging Out in the Virtual Pub: Masculinities and Relationships Online*. Berkeley, CA: University of California Press.

King, S. (1994). "Analysis of Electronic Support Groups for Recovering Addicts." *Interpersonal Computing and Technology* 2 (3): 47–56.

Kinney, J. (1995). "Net Worth? Religion, Cyberspace, and the Future." *Futures* 27 (7): 763–776.

Kollock, P. (1999). "The Economies of Online Co-operation: Gifts and Public Goods in Cyberspace." In *Communities in Cyberspace*, ed. M. A. Smith and P. Kollock, 220–239. New York: Routledge.

Kraut, R. et al. (1998). "Internet Paradox: A Social Technology that Reduces Social Involvement and Psychological Well-Being?" *American Psychologist* 53: 1011–1031.

————. (2002). "Internet Paradox Revisited." *Journal of Social Issues* 58: 49–74.

Krogh, M., and B. A. Pillifant, (2002). "Religious Recruitment and Membership on the Web: A Comparison of Kemetic Orthodoxy and Other New Religious Movements." Paper presented to the Association for the Sociology of Religion, Chicago.

Kyong-Jee, K., and J. B. Curtis, (2002). "Cross-Cultural Comparisons of Online Collaboration." *Journal of Computer-Mediated Communication* 8. Retrieved from www.ascusc.org/jcmc, July 7, 2003.

Lea, M., and R. Spears (1998). "Love at First Byte? Building Personal Relationships over Computer Networks." In *Cybersociety 2.0: Revisiting Computer-Mediated Communication and Community*, ed. S. Jones, 197–233. Thousand Oaks, CA: Sage.

Linderman, A. G., and M. Lövheim, (2001). "Young People, Religious Identity and Computer-Mediated Communication: Where Do We Go From Here?" Paper presented to the Religious Encounters in Digital Networks conference, University of Copenhagen.

Liu, G. Z. (1999). "Virtual Community Presence in Internet Relay Chatting." *Journal of Computer-Mediated Communication* 5 (1). Retrieved from www.ascusc.org/jcmc, Feb. 10, 2002.

Lockard, J. (1997). "Progressive Poltics, Electronic Individualism and the Myth of Virtual Community." In *Internet Culture*, ed. D. Porter, 219–231. New York: Routledge.

Lövheim, M., and A. Linderman, (1998). "Internet—a Site for Religious Identity Formation and Religious Communities?" Paper presented to the Society for the Scientific Study of Religion, Montreal.

Markham, A. N. (1998). *Life Online: Researching Real Experience in Virtual Space*. Walnut Creek, CA: AltaMira Press.

McGillion, C. (2000). "Web of Disbelief: Religion Has Staked a Big Claim in Cyberspace, but Has It Done a Faustian Deal?" *Sydney Morning Herald*, December 23. Retrieved from the Worldwide Religious News www.wwrn.org, December 23.

McLoughlin, M. L., K. K., Osborne, and C. B. Smith, (1995). "Standards of Conduct on Usenet." In *Cybersociety: Computer-Mediated Communication and Community*, ed. S. Jones, 90–111. Thousand Oaks, CA: Sage.

Miller, D., and D. Slater, (2000). *The Internet: An Ethnographic Approach*. New York: Berg.

Mnookin, J. (1996). "Virtual(ly) Law: The Emergence of Law in LambdaMOO." *Journal of Computer-Mediated Communication* 2. Retrieved from www.ascusc.org/jcmc, June 30, 2003.

O'Brien, J. (1999). "Writing in the Body: Gender (Re)production in Online Interaction." In *Communities in Cyberspace*, ed. M. A. Smith and P. Kollock, 76–104. New York: Routledge.

O'Leary, S. D. (1996). "Cyberspace as Sacred Space: Communicating Religion on Computer Networks." *Journal of the American Academy of Religion* 64: 781–808.

Parks, M. R., and K. Floyd, (1996). "Making Friends in Cyberspace." *Journal of Communication* 46 (1): 80–97.

Parks, M. R., and L. D. Roberts, (1998). "'Making MOOsic': The Development of Personal Relationships On Line and a Comparison to their Off-Line Counterparts." *Journal of Social and Personal Relationships* 15: 517–537.

Postmes, T., R., Spears, and M. Lea (1998). "Breaching or Building Social Boundaries? Side-effects of CMC." *Communication Research* 25: 689–716.

Rafaeli, S., and F. Sudweeks, (1998). "Interactivity on the Nets." In *Network and Netplay: Virtual Groups on the Internet*, ed. F. Sudweeks, M. McLaughlin, S. Rafaeli, S., 173–189. Menlo Park, CA: AAAI Press/MIT Press.

Reid, E. (1991). "Electropolis: Communication and Community on Internet Relay Chat." Hons. BA thesis, Department of History, University of Melbourne; widely distributed on the Internet.

———. (1999). "Hierarchy and Power: Social Control in Cyberspace." In *Communities in Cyberspace*, ed. M. A. Smith and P. Kollock, 107–133. New York: Routledge.

Rheingold, H. (1993). *The Virtual Community: Homesteading on the Electronic Frontier*. New York: Addison-Wesley.

Robinson, J. P., K., Barth, and A. Kohut, (1997). "Personal Computers, Mass Media, and Use of Time." *Social Science Computer Review* 15: 65–82.

Robinson, J. P., and M. Kestnbaum, (1999). "The Personal Computer, Culture, and Other Uses of Free Time." *Social Science Computer Review* 17: 209–216.

Robinson, J. P., et al. (2000). "IT, the Internet, and Time Displacement." Paper presented to the American Association of Public Opinion Research, Portland, Oregon.

Roof, W. C. (1999). *Spiritual Marketplace: Baby Boomers and the Remaking of American Religion*. Princeton, NJ: Princeton University Press.

Schroeder, R., N. Heather, and R. M. Lee, (1998). "The Sacred and the Virtual: Religion in Multi-User Virtual Reality." *Journal of Computer Mediated Communication* 4 (2). Retrieved from www.ascusc.org/jcmc, March 12, 2002.

Slouka, M. (1995). *War of the Worlds: Cyberspace and the High-Tech Assault on Reality*. New York: Basic Books.

Smith, M. A., and P. Kollock, (1999). *Communities in Cyberspace*. London: Routledge.

Toennies, F. (1957). *Community and Society*. New York: Michigan University Press.

Turkle, S. (1995). *Life on the Screen: Identity in the Age of the Internet*. New York: Simon and Schuster.

Wellman, B. (2001). "Physical Place and Cyberplace: The Rise of Networked Individualism." In *Community Informatics: Shaping Computer-Mediated Social Relations*, ed. L. Keeble and B. D. Loader, 17–42. London: Routledge.

Wellman, B., and M. Guila. (1999). "Virtual Communities as Communities: Net Surfers Don't Ride Alone." In *Communities in Cyberspace*, ed. M. A. Smith and P. Kollock, 167–194. New York: Routledge.

Wellman, B., et al. (2001). "Does the Internet Increase, Decrease, or Supplement Social Capital? Social Networks, Participation, and Community Commitment." *American Behavioral Scientist* 45: 436–455.

Westley, F. (1983). *The Complex Forms of the Religious Life: A Durkheimian View of New Religious Movements*. Chico, CA: Scholars Press.

Willson, M. (1997). "Community in the Abstract: A Political and Ethical Dilemma?" In *Virtual Politics: Identity and Community in Cyberspace*, ed. D. Holmes, 145–162. London: Sage.

II
Mainstream Religions in Cyberspace

7

Reading and Praying Online: The Continuity of Religion Online and Online Religion in Internet Christianity

GLENN YOUNG

Isidore of Seville, a seventh-century bishop popularly venerated by Catholics as the patron saint of the Internet, writes that "Prayer purifies us, reading instructs us. Both are good when both are possible. Otherwise, prayer is better than reading" (www.catholic-forum.com/saints/sainti04.htm). This claim that prayer and reading complement each other also points to an inherent tension between them. What distinguishes these activities from one another? One factor may be that reading involves the reception of information whereas prayer requires some other level of participation from the practitioner. This distinction between information reception and participation in activity is central to the definition of two categories that have been used to describe and interpret religion on the Internet—religion online and online religion (Helland 2000).

This chapter will address the ways in which diverse online manifestations of Christianity call into question the religion online and online religion dichotomy found in previous scholarship on Internet religion. I will suggest that religion online and online religion, rather than being strictly opposed, are two types of religious expression and activity that exist in continuity with one another in Internet Christianity.

Religion Online and Online Religion

For the purposes of this paper, I understand the categories of religion online and online religion to entail two distinctions. These are: (1) the provision of information about religion versus the opportunity for participation in religious activity; and (2) primary reference to offline, preexisting religious traditions versus primary reference to religious activities taking place online.

The first of these distinctions addresses the type of activity that occurs on an Internet site. Modifying Helland's (2000) initial conceptualization, Hadden and Cowan distinguish between those sites that provide information to visitors as opposed to those that offer visitors an opportunity to participate in religious activities. They describe religion online as that which "provides the interested web traveller with *information about* religion: doctrine, polity, organization, and belief; service and opportunities for service; religious books and articles; as well as other paraphernalia related to one's religious tradition or quest" (Hadden and Cowan 2000: 9; cf. Helland 2000). Hadden and Cowan contrast this with online religion, which they describe as that which "invites the visitor to *participate in* the religious dimension of life via the Web; liturgy, prayer, ritual, meditation, and homiletics come together and function with the e-space itself acting as church, temple, synagogue, mosque, and grove" (Hadden and Cowan 2000: 9; cf. Helland 2000). Hence religion on the Internet includes a multiplicity of activities that fall at various places along the spectrum that extends between information and participation.

The second distinction concerns the locus of activity to which an Internet site makes primary reference. While Hadden and Cowan do not explicitly make this distinction, it seems a reasonable inference based upon the definitions they have given. Because it provides information about religion, religion online makes primary reference to offline, preexisting religious traditions and institutions. Online religion, which involves participation in religious activity, refers to the online environment itself as the primary context of that activity.

If religion online and online religion are treated as two theoretical end points, then the issues of information provision versus religious participation and primary reference to offline versus online activity can be understood as two axes which extend between them. We can then ask where specific instances of Internet religion (remembering that the highly fluid nature of this medium lends an ephemeral quality to whatever examples we identify) fall along these axes. Moreover, we can ask if these instances may encompass elements of both religion online and online religion. In this, I am following Cowan's suggestion that "It would be too easy to designate the distinction according to websites which provide one or the other—either religion online or online religion. While there are sites which operate solely in one domain or the other, the vast majority of websites seek to bridge the two" (Cowan 2002). While Cowan is specifically referring here to Neopagan Web sites, I would suggest that his claim is more broadly applicable to other expressions of Internet religion. Assuming this is accurate, this chapter will analyze a number of Christian Web sites in order to demonstrate that religion online and online religion can be seen to coexist within Christianity on the Internet.

What Happens on a Christian Web Site? Information and Participation

The first axis that extends between religion online and online religion concerns provision of information and participation in activity. Even at the relatively simple level of congregational Christian Web sites that deal with an individual church community, there are examples where information and participation conjoin. Consider, for example, www.standrewkc.org, the Web site for

St. Andrew's Episcopal Church in Kansas City, Missouri. The majority of this site is oriented toward providing information, both about this congregation in particular and about the Episcopal Church more generally. At the congregational level, visitors learn about the times of worship services at St. Andrew's. Under the "News & Events" link, there is a monthly list of activities taking place at the church. The Web site also provides information about the Episcopal Church as a tradition and religious institution. The "Episcopal Info" section provides a basic description of the Episcopal Church, explaining that it "is a member of the worldwide Anglican Communion, with 70 million members in 163 countries" (www.standrewkc.org/html/episcopal_info.html). This section of the Web site also describes the basic doctrinal beliefs of the Episcopal Church and includes the texts of the Christian Creeds, brief explanations of the sacraments, and descriptions of Scripture, Tradition, and Reason, the three "Cornerstones of Faith" of the Episcopal Church. These elements all point to this Web site being a clear instance of religion online which informs its visitors about the activities and beliefs of this particular congregation and the denomination to which it belongs.

While the majority of the St. Andrew's site is oriented to religion online, there is also some indication of online religion here. For example, an "Online Prayer Request Form" gives visitors a prepared form that asks for their names and prayer requests to be shared with the church. Those utilizing this form are told that their electronic prayer requests "will be received in confidence by a member of St. Andrew's clergy. An intercessory prayer group meets every Tuesday morning at the church and will pray on your behalf" (www.standrewkc.org/ html/online_prayer_requests.html). While simple, this page represents a significant shift in Internet conceptualization: a Web site largely oriented to the provision of information now invites some level of participation from its visitors. The reception of information has incorporated the activity of prayer. One could, of course, question whether making a prayer request is itself prayer, but this would be difficult to answer without knowing the minds of those who use the prayer request form. What can be noted, however, is that a Web site largely concerned with a one-way flow of information from the church as representative of the Christian faith to the Web site visitor now invites a reciprocal flow of information and perhaps activity in receiving the prayer requests of those who visit the site. If, as Helland suggests (2000: 214, 220), religion online entails a one-way flow of communication while online religion involves reciprocity in information exchange, then this site represents, at least in part, an instance of online religion.

Alive in Christ Lutheran Church's Web site (www.aic.org) also demonstrates this coexistence of information and participation. Although the content is different, the site's basic orientation is similar in many respects to that of St. Andrew's Episcopal Church. The Alive in Christ Web site includes the church's worship schedule and basic doctrinal statements, such as "Alive in

Christ believes . . . Scripture is the inerrant (error-free) word of God . . . Faith in Jesus as your Lord and Savior is the **only** way to salvation (not by works)" (www.aic.org/about.asp). As in the previous example, this site contains a form that visitors can use to share their prayer requests with the church community. On www.aic.org, however, the activity of prayer is taken one step further. A "Prayer Requests" page conveys the prayer requests submitted by others to the church. Here one receives information, but of a special type. This is not simply information about the logistics of parish worship or the doctrine of its members. Here the Web site provides information specifically designed to inspire the activity of prayer in other members of the congregation. Again, while this may not necessarily qualify as an instance of online prayer, it certainly does go some way toward bridging the divide between the provision of religious information and participation in religious activity.

This connection between religion online and online religion in relation to the issue of information and participation is also found on Christian Web sites produced at the denominational level. On www.umc.org, the official denominational Web site of the United Methodist Church (UMC), visitors are offered fairly standard denominational information, including articles, for example, on the annual reappointment of pastors to new congregations, the aging membership of the UMC, and upcoming denominational events such as the John Wesley Tercentenary Celebration and the UMC Youth 2003 meeting.

However, while the UMC home page itself seems oriented toward the simple provision of denominational information—a good example of religion online— links found on this site call this singular orientation into question. "Today's Devotion," for example, takes the visitor out of the UMC denominational home-page and connects to a Daily Devotional site (www.upperroom.org/devotional) produced by Upper Room Ministries, itself a ministry of the United Methodist Church. Here one finds instruction in and content for a short devotional prayer. First, visitors are instructed to read a particular Scripture passage. Next, a meditative reflection is thematically connected to the Scripture passage and the text of a short prayer is included as part of the devotion. Finally, this page includes suggestions for a thought and prayer focus for the day. Clearly, the Daily Devotional page represents a shift away from the simple reception of information to a more complex participation in the activity of prayer.

What is perhaps most noteworthy about this example is the hyperlinked connectivity unique to the World Wide Web. Visitors to www.umc.org are provided with a link that takes them to another, different Web site, moving them from the information-oriented denominational site to the ritual prayer orientation of the Daily Devotional site. This link represents, then, the coexistence of religion online and online religion across these connected Web sites.

The site www.umc.org also includes a "Faith in Action" section that connects to the Web site for the UMC's General Board of Church and Society (www.umc-gbcs.org). This site explains the position of the United Methodist

Church on a variety of social issues. A page describing the proposed Clean Power Act of 2003, for example, includes church statements on the issue of air pollution: "The Social Principles of The United Methodist Church 'support and encourage social policies that serve to reduce and control the creation of industrial byproducts . . . and assist the cleanup of polluted air'" (capwiz.com/gbcs/issues/alert/?alertid=1508616&type=CO). More significantly, visitors can enter their zip codes, which identify their elected senators, and then email them a precomposed letter requesting that they support the Clean Power Act. This page thus includes both information about the United Methodist Church's position on an issue such as environmental protection as well as an invitation to act on that information by contacting one's elected representatives. While this activity is not religious ritual so much as social action based upon religious principles, the fact remains that here one notes the complementary relationship of religion online and online religion in the dynamic of information motivating participation in a religiously informed action.

Considering Christian Web sites with no congregational or denominational affiliation, we note this same coexistence and complementary relationship between religion online and online religion. A particularly clear example of the coupling of information about the Christian faith with opportunities to participate in online religious activities is the Church for All Web site (www.churchforall.org). This site's self-description suggests that it is designed to provide an alternative to more traditional venues of Christian ritual practice: "Church for All is a real church—using the Internet for our communication. . . . We brings God's message to you—instead of demanding you come to our location at our set time."

A central component of this Web site is "Worship Time" (www.churchforall.org/worship.htm), which contains the rubrics and text for a ritual one can perform while online. Here the visitor is invited to "Worship With Us." This ritual begins with a blessing and the text of a short prayer. While there are no specific instructions on how to use these, it is presumed that the person participating would read them to herself. The worship service then continues with a scriptural passage, hymns, which are presented with lyrics and audio files of their melodies, and a biblical reflection delivered in audio file format. The ritual also includes a "Celebration of the Lord's Supper" (www.churchforall.org/lordssup.htm), in which the worshipper is directed to use red grape juice and unleavened bread (if possible), read one of a number of linked Scripture passages, and "partake of the juice and bread in a prayerful, thankful, and happy manner." At the end of the broader ritual, the visitor is invited to "Come back each week and worship our wonderful Father God with us, as we gather from all over the world in the wonderful name of our Lord Jesus Christ" (www.churchforall.org/worship.htm).

As is readily apparent from the description, this part of the Church for All site is oriented toward participation in an online Christian ritual. In the interest of clarity, it might be noted that this ritual worship does not take place in real time with other persons. Rather, it occurs on the worshipper's own schedule, requiring only that one visit the site and follow the instructions and prayers provided. It is in this sense an example of individual rather than communal devotional practice. This being said, the concern here is clearly to provide for an activity of Christian worship.

This orientation of the Church for All Web site toward participation, however, does not mean that instances of information provision are not also present. In fact, this site contains many pages of instruction in Christian doctrine, based largely upon scriptural texts. For example, the page describing the Lord's Supper includes a link, "what Jesus accomplished for us," which makes doctrinal statements such as "Jesus Christ took your place. . . . Because Jesus already paid the price demanded by justice for your sins, you are declared innocent and righteous before God, the supreme Judge, when you are united with Christ Jesus" (www.believers.org/believe/bel141.htm). There is on this site, then, a fundamental complementarity which exists between online ritual in which a visitor can participate and information offered primarily in the form of doctrinal statements, which serves to inform the faith activity that occurs on this site.

The site www.churchforall.org also offers visitors the opportunity to become members of this online church. Doing so requires that the visitor to the site "simply agree with our statement of faith, *Jesus Christ is Lord and God*" (www.churchforall.org). Once the visitor has (presumably) agreed with this statement, he is invited to enter his e-mail address and click a "Join now!" button. Members are then e-mailed a daily scriptural message. But because the Church for All exists solely in cyberspace, the primary significance of becoming a member seems to lie in one's agreement with the statement of faith. Encapsulated in this statement and gesture by visitors to this Web site are both information in the form of a doctrinal proposition and participation in the form of one's assent to the truth of that statement—of religion online and online religion.

One way of interpreting this conjoining of information and participation is with Austin's concept of "performative utterances," in which a person "is *doing* something rather than merely *saying* something" (Austin 1970: 235). Initially, Austin contrasts "performatives" with "statements." While statements are either true or false based upon their correspondence with objective facts, performatives are either felicitous or infelicitous according to their efficacy in performing the actions to which they are linked (1970: 247). Ultimately, however, Austin claims that the distinction between statements and performatives is neither final nor complete. He concludes that when a person makes a statement, she is in fact performing an act; likewise, when a person utters a performative, she is making certain implied claims regarding the relationship of that utterance to the truth (1970: 249–250). Hence relaying information through making a statement and acting via a performative utterance can occur simultaneously.

When one visits the Church for All Web site and decides to become a member by agreeing with the statement proclaiming Jesus' lordship and divinity, both a statement and a performative utterance are taking place. A person making this statement is not only asserting its truth in some abstract or intellectual way; he is also doing something in the sense of declaring his religious faith and in the process joining this online church. At the same time there is an informational aspect to his statement. It would, we can assume, be pointless to make such a declaration if one did not also hold the substance of that declaration to be true and in correspondence with the facts of human existence. Austin's conception highlights the way in which language acts both as an instrument of human "agency" and as a means by which one "maps" reality (Graham 1977: 53–54). Hence to assent to a statement of Christian faith involves one in dynamics of both truth claims and participatory performance. The concept of the performative utterance helps explain how a simple statement of belief and the agreement with this statement through the click of a mouse button are both an exercise of information provision and reception as well as participation in what is ultimately an act of Christian faith.

Sometimes the distinction between what counts as religion online and online religion is not easily discerned. One example of this is the "Catholic Life—Prayers" section of the Catholic Online Web site (www.catholic.org/clife/prayers/), which contains material on the Rosary and the Stations of the Cross, two common forms of popular Catholic piety. The pages discussing the Rosary include step-by-step instructions on how it is prayed, the texts of prayers that are said in this devotion, and a link to which visitors can go if they wish to buy a rosary online. Also included in this section are texts of the Mysteries, reflections upon events in the lives of Jesus and Mary upon which one meditates as the Rosary is prayed. The Mystery of the Resurrection, for example, reflects upon this event from the perspective of Mary: "At dawn of the first day of the week, I was with John and Peter. I was in my room alone. . . . I woke up. There was a light: it was all over the room. There was my Son" (www.catholic.org/clife/prayers/mystery.php?id=3). Taken as a whole, it is not clear how this material on the Rosary should be interpreted. It is certainly information in the sense of being instruction in a technique of Catholic prayer. But the inclusion of the Mystery texts themselves suggests the possibility that these pages could be used for online prayer and meditation as one prays the Rosary. In this case, the line between reception of information and participation in prayer is somewhat blurred.

Similarly, in the pages discussing the Stations of the Cross, a short text is accompanied by an artistic rendering of each of the fourteen stations, which are meditative reflections based upon the events of Jesus' passion and crucifixion. Each meditation is written in the voice of the one performing the devotion. Hence for the First Station, "Jesus is condemned to death," the meditation reads in part, "Jesus, you stand all alone before Pilate. Nobody speaks up for you. . . . As an adult, sometimes I feel abandoned and afraid as well" (www.catholic.org/clife/prayers/station.php?id=1).

The text for the Stations of the Cross, however, is antiphonal—some parts read by a leader with responses provided by a congregation. Hence it is difficult to interpret the intention behind the inclusion of something like this on a Web site. Is the site visitor expected to pray the Stations while online? Initially, this would seem to be the case, given the first-person perspective in which the meditations are written and the visual supports provided on the Web site for reflection. Yet the references to a prayer leader and congregation suggest that this is something more akin to a transcript of the way this devotion is performed in a typical Catholic church, where a priest or other minister leads a congregation in praying the stations. As with the pages on the Rosary, this example demonstrates the indeterminacy that sometimes exists between information about and participation in the activity of prayer. The presentation of the Stations of the Cross here is not strictly informative; it appears to be a text for online prayer. But it is not entirely evident that this is the case either, as the reflections are written in a way that suggests their use by a congregational group in a more traditional sanctuary setting. It is difficult to imagine a group of Catholics gathered around a computer monitor collectively praying the Stations of the Cross while logged on to this Web site. Because we are unable to determine if this is information about the Stations of the Cross or an opportunity to pray them, it is simply not clear where in the spectrum of religion online and online religion this example falls.

Where Does It Happen? The Offline and Online Worlds

The second axis that extends between religion online and online religion concerns whether Internet sites make primary reference to participation in religious activity that occurs offline or that takes place within the online environment itself. A consideration of Christianity on the Internet reveals that often Web sites are not oriented solely to either offline or online practice but actually underscore the interrelationship of these two contexts. One way of interpreting this is with Cowan's distinction between activity that takes place solely online and activity that exists online while still making reference to the offline world in some fashion (Cowan 2002). This distinction is important given that the definitions of religion online and online religion seem to imply that they can be distinguished with regard to the context to which each refers. Whereas religion online is understood to refer to religious traditions that have a locus of activity in the offline world, the description of online religion suggests that it involves participation in an activity that occurs solely (or primarily) online. Cowan states that religion on the Internet in fact almost always makes some reference to the offline world and rarely occurs solely within the online environment (2002).

My discussion of Christian Web sites will suggest that even those that are fairly clear examples of online religion, in the sense that they offer visitors participation in online religious activities, nevertheless retain a characteristic of religion online in that they also connect their visitors in some way to the larger world that exists beyond the borders of their Web browsers.

One of the questions that online religious activity raises is how such activity relates to the embodied state of human existence. Consider Brasher's description of the implications of the Internet for the evolution of religion: "A fantasy universe that stimulates the imagination but ignores the rest of the body, cyberspace is a nonenvironment that sucks attention away from the immediate surroundings in which most traditional religious life occurs" (Brasher 2001: 42). Such a statement is stark, perhaps even foreboding; but it must be asked whether instances of online Christianity really bear out such a characterization of Internet religion as being so utterly disembodied.

A particularly vivid example of Christian online religion is Sacred Space (www.jesuit.ie/prayer), a prayer Web site produced by the Irish Jesuits. That this site is oriented toward participation in online religious activity is clear from the invitation it offers visitors: "We invite you to make a 'Sacred Space' in your day, and spend ten minutes, praying here and now, as you sit at your computer, with the help of on-screen guidance and scripture chosen specially every day." Once one begins, what follows is a guided prayer in which one is instructed—via text that appears and dissolves on the computer screen—to become aware of God's presence, to entrust oneself to that presence, to reflect upon the various relationships within which one exists, to read and meditate upon a scriptural passage, and to imagine oneself engaged in a conversation with Jesus. Because the prayer itself appears online and the person visiting this site is asked to pray while online, this seems a clear example of the participation in religious ritual characteristic of online religion.

This initial impression, however, must be reconciled with some of the suggestions for assistance in prayer which this site offers. These suggestions make explicit reference to an offline, embodied aspect of the online prayer experience. For example, in the stage of prayer that involves cultivating an awareness of the presence of God, one is instructed to accompany the verbal and/or mental prayer with body and breathing exercises. In the body prayer, one adopts a relaxed posture and focuses attention on the various sensations felt throughout the body. In the breathing exercise, the person praying is instructed to focus his attention on the flow of air as he inhales and exhales. This breathing is then explicitly joined with prayer as the inhalation is said to "express all that you long for in life," while the exhalation represents "your surrender of everything to God" (www.jesuit.ie/prayer/eh031028.htm#breathing). This same dynamic occurs at the stage of prayer in which the visitor imagines herself in conversation with Jesus. Here, the Web site offers visual supports to assist the imagination in producing an image of Jesus for this conversation—pop-up windows appear with images of "an icon of Christ, a crucifix or an image of the Risen Christ" (www.jesuit.ie/prayer/eh031028.htm#colhelp). Again, the experience of the body, this time through the sense of sight, is used to assist the online prayer. Hence despite its presentation of an opportunity for online prayer, which is a clear instance of what we can categorize as online religion, this site still makes extensive use of embodied experience as an essential component of this prayer. That is, online religion still makes explicit reference to the offline world.

This appeal to embodied experience is also demonstrated in the New Mercies Community Church Sanctuary (www.new-mercies.org/sanctuary.htm). As with the previous example, the visitor here is offered the opportunity to participate in Christian worship by following a number of Web site screens. The prayers and reflections on these screens rely primarily on the senses of sight (in the form of written texts and illustrations such as crosses and nature scenes) and hearing (in the form of music which plays as one proceeds through the ritual). While in and of itself this is not particularly remarkable, it is noteworthy that at a number of points during the worship experience the visitor is also prompted to perform some ritual gesture that augments what he sees and hears on his computer. For example, the person is directed to worship God, to "Use your mind, use your voice, lift your hands or kneel on the ground before the holy God" (www.new-mercies.org/adoration.html). When the person praying confesses his sins to God, he is told to "Get down on your knees if you want," and is then assured that "This page will still be here when you get back" (www.new-mercies.org/confession.html). Hence while this section of the Web site offers an online worship experience, it clearly relates this to an offline embodied experience.

Examples such as these point to the necessity of clarifying what we mean when we speak of "online religion." While the Sacred Space and New Mercies Community Church Sanctuary sites provide what is essentially a prayer or worship experience taking place entirely online, both make recommendations that refer to the offline world, at least in the sense of an awareness of one's embodied condition. Wilbur writes that "The computer—and particularly the computer as Internet terminal—is an odd sort of vision machine. It involves the user, primarily through vision, in forms of telepresence which may mimic any and all of the senses. It is likely that those who become most immersed in Internet culture develop a sort of synesthesia which allows them to exercise all of the senses through their eyes and fingers" (Wilbur 1997: 10–11). Perhaps this is the case now with some users or will be the case in the future with technology significantly different from what is now available (Cowan 2002). At present, however, examples such as those described here suggest that online religion is not yet ready to forgo appeals to one's ability to sense the state of the body and manipulate it, not only through sight and hearing but also through physical activities such as breathing and the performance of ritual gestures.

These Web sites which provide opportunities for online Christian ritual also connect this to the world outside the online environment in which these rituals have taken place. On the New Mercies Community Church Sanctuary site, for example, the online worship section concludes with an instruction to its visitors: "After you leave this site and shut down your computer I would encourage you to worship with real people in a real church. Whether that's a local congregation or just a group of people meeting in a living room, it's important to fellowship with other Christians who can share your burdens and encourage you along the way" (www.new-mercies.org/benediction.html). Hence this site claims that the experience of offline religious life is as (if not more) important than its online counterpart. This claim is taken a step further on a number of denominational Christian Web sites, such as the Episcopal Church, USA (www.episcopalchurch.org) and the Presbyterian Church (USA) (www.pcusa.org), which include links that allow visitors to locate congregations in their own areas. The assistance these Web sites offer in providing their visitors with information about local churches further emphasizes the connection the online world maintains with offline religious institutions and communities. As Bedell suggests (2000: 193), the reception of information online may empower persons to take some action in their religious lives offline.

Similarly, the Sacred Space Web site contains a section that posts feedback comments submitted by those who have visited the site and participated in its online prayer. These comments frequently make reference not only to the positive experiences visitors have had while practicing the online prayer but also to the ways in which this online activity connects to and informs the participant's offline life. Typical comments include: "Thank you for a wonderful site. I visit it first thing in the morning, and use it as a perfect opening to the day," "I love this site. After a hard day work it is really relaxing and the colour of the screen and even the way it comes on is even relaxing and all the words are peaceful," and "Thank you for an oasis of peace and reflection amid a busy and stressful business day. It really makes all the difference" (www.jesuit.ie/prayer/feedback.htm). Implicit in these and similar comments is the sense that online ritual, no matter how firmly embedded it is in the cyberspace environment, cannot exist without making some reference to the offline lives of those who participate in the ritual. In the case of these comments, it seems that the primary relationship between the experience of online religion and the offline world is one of contrast, in which the solace of the online experience is framed through its opposition to a world that is different and often in need of comfort and inspiration. Hence even those Web sites that seem to be the clearest instances of online religion do not exist wholly online. Even there, the online experience interacts with the offline world.

As with the distinction between information and participation, there are some Christian Web sites that are difficult to interpret in terms of the loci of the religious experiences they offer. An example of this would be Web sites that include video files and/or live video feeds of worship services, such as The Daily Mass (www.themass.com) and the Greek Orthodox Archdiocese in America (www.goarch.org) Web sites. On these sites, visitors have the opportunity to view the entire celebration of a Roman Catholic Mass or Orthodox Christian Divine Liturgy. Sites such as these are somewhat perplexing with regard to questions of participation and embodiment and their relationship to online religion. Here it seems that the visitor acts less as a participant than as a passive viewer, witnessing other persons participate in ritual worship (cf. Helland 2000).

While the only senses engaged in the activity of viewing rituals such as the Mass or Divine Liturgy online are those of sight and hearing, I would suggest that recourse is still being made to the totality of human sensation, if only through the remembrance of one's own past participation in such rituals or through an imaginative participation in what one views while watching the celebration of these rituals online. Speaking personally, while watching the celebration of the Roman Catholic Mass online, the only way in which I found myself able to connect with this ritual in any tangible way was through the relation of what I was viewing to my own previous experiences as a participant in this liturgy. While it is not clear that such activity can really be classified as participation in an online ritual, what can be said is that whatever participation is possible relies to some extent on an embodied experience, in these cases experience that is remembered or imagined. Activities such as viewing the Catholic Mass or Divine Liturgy online seem to fall into a liminal space between reference to the offline and online worlds. In so doing, they call a definitive distinction between religion online and online religion into question.

Further Questions and Conclusions

One issue, which I mention here as a consideration for future discussion, is the extent to which Christianity on the Internet, whether categorized as religion online, online religion, or some combination of the two, actually represents something new in the development of Christianity in particular or religion in general, the extent to which it is "an intriguing site for the study of religious innovation and invention" (Cowan 2002). All of the Web sites discussed in this chapter present information and opportunities for participation that are in themselves not significantly different from what one can access offline. If one can view the Mass or recite the Stations of the Cross online, one can certainly also do these things in a local church. The provision of religious information online is not significantly different from what one might find in a variety of printed catechetical materials or, in the case of information about a particular congregation, in the local telephone book. Qualitative considerations of this sort can be supplemented by quantitative survey data that report that on a given day, only 4 percent of Americans with online access use the Internet to "Look for religious/spiritual information" (Pew Internet & American Life Project 2002). Perhaps the Internet is a medium with the potential for widespread communication of religious information and practice. But how far this extends into the lives of Internet travelers and how different it is from what occurs offline remain very much open and ongoing questions.

What can be said, however, is that religion online and online religion often exist in continuity rather than opposition in Internet Christianity. Christian Web sites that appear to be oriented primarily toward the provision of information also include components that connect that information in some way to religious practice. Similarly, instances of online Christian religious practice do not sever themselves from the offline world. The dichotomy drawn between religion online and online religion, while helpful in distinguishing between two types of religious activity found on the Internet, needs to be conceptualized in such a way that these are understood to coexist in a complementary relationship with one another. To return for a moment to Isidore of Seville, the patron saint of the Internet, while reading and praying—or religion online and online religion—may stand to some degree in tension with each other, in Christianity on the Internet they also underscore and inform one another.

References

Austin, J. L. (1970). "Performative Utterances." In *Philosophical Papers*, 2nd ed., ed. J. O. Urmson and G. J. Warnock, 233–252. London: Oxford University Press.

Bedell, K. (2000). "Dispatches from the Electronic Frontier: Explorations of Mainline Protestant Use of the Internet." In *Religion on the Internet: Research Prospects and Promises*, ed. J. K. Hadden and D. E. Cowan, 183–203. London: JAI Press/Elsevier Science.

Brasher, B. E. (2001). *Give Me That Online Religion*. San Francisco: Jossey-Bass.

Cowan, D. E. (2002). "Online and in the Grove: Ritual and Embodiment in Neopagan E-Space." Retrieved from http://c.faculty.umkc.edu/cowande, April 29, 2003.

Graham, K. (1977). *J. L. Austin: A Critique of Ordinary Language Philosophy*. Sussex, UK: Harvester Press.

Hadden, J. K., and D. E. Cowan. (2000). "The Promised Land or Electronic Chaos? Toward Understanding Religion on the Internet." In *Religion on the Internet: Research Prospects and Promises*, ed. J. K. Hadden and D. E. Cowan, 3–21. London: JAIPress/Elsevier Science.

Helland, C. (2000). "Online Religion/Religion Online and Virtual Communitas." In *Religion on the Internet: Research Prospects and Promises*, ed. J. K. Hadden and D. E. Cowan, 205–223. London: JAIPress/Elsevier Science.

Pew Internet & American Life Project. (2002). "Daily Internet Activities." Retrieved from www.pewinternet.org/reports, June 19, 2003.

Wilbur, S. P. (1997). "An Archaeology of Cyberspaces: Virtuality, Community, Identity." In *Internet Culture*, ed. D. Porter, 5–22. New York: Routledge.

8

"This Is My Church": Seeing the Internet and Club Culture as Spiritual Spaces

HEIDI CAMPBELL

Introduction

The Internet and club culture represent new spaces of technological empowerment and creation. The Internet has become a canvas of personal expression, a place to learn and test new ways of being. This is exemplified by people's attempts to create new spaces of social interaction on Web sites, in chat rooms, and through e-mail. With the rise of contemporary club culture, the DJ, like the Webmaster or list/chat moderator, has also emerged as a new artist/author using technology to create new social spaces. For the DJ, "the true art lies in the 'mix'" (Manovich 2001: 134). As the club track "Last Night A DJ Saved My Life" by Indeep (1982) suggests:

> Hey listen up to your local DJ.
> You better hear what he's got to say—
> There's not a problem that I can't fix
> Cause I can do it in the mix!

Using digital technology to combine preexisting sounds and music, the DJ's role in the club is to create a vibe that transforms the club into a personalized public space of individual and corporate expression. In the hands of the DJ and the Webmaster, new media technology becomes a creative tool, enabling them to form new spaces of communication and experience.

Both club culture and the Internet are technological spheres that use symbols and myths acquired from other sources, mixed and remixed to create new narratives. How people shape these media environments and create these narratives greatly depends on their motivations and interpretations of life. While the clubs are often described as places of entertainment and the Internet as an information tool, some individuals and groups offer an alternative narrative. The Internet and club culture are being interpreted as spiritual spaces. Internet technology is said to offer new images of traditional spiritual concepts, as Wertheim argues in *The Pearly Gates of Cyberspace*: "It (cyberspace) is a repackaging of the old idea of Heaven, but in a secular, technologically sanctioned format. The perfect realm awaits us, we are told, not behind the pearly gates but the electronic gateways labelled .com and .net. and .edu" (1999: 21).

The Internet is increasingly being conceptualized as a spiritual or sacramental space as people transport their spiritual and religious practices online (Campbell 2003). Similarly, club culture is presented as a place of postmodern worship, illustrated by lyrics of the group Faithless (1998):

> This is my church. This is where I heal my hurts.
> Contained in the hum between voice and drum. . . .
> The poetic justice of cause and effect,
> respect, love, compassion.
> This is my church . . . for tonight, god is a DJ.

Aspects of the club scene are laden with religious imagery. The DJ has been likened to the creator or "god" and clubs have been identified as "temples," with communion taking place through consuming "e"-wafers and wine/alcohol (Thompson 2001).

New media technologies offer opportunities for experimentation with methods of interconnection and communication. While many of these explorations have been fuelled by commercial motivations, some innovations have at their heart very different social and even spiritual aims. One such initiative is the Online Missionaries Project, which sought to utilize new media to build a spiritual community tailored to the needs of the contemporary youth culture. The aim of the project was to use the Internet as a tool to connect and communicate with the club culture. Functioning under the presupposition that "clubs are the new church" (BBC Radio 1 slogan), the project perceived club culture as a spiritual sphere and a vital place to engage in Christian outreach. The Online Missionary Project sought to use the Internet and mobile phone technology to create a place for spiritual dialogue online and potentially to facilitate new forms of Christian community.

This chapter explores this unique experiment in connecting new communicative technologies and the tradition of Christian missionary outreach, highlighting the role of the technology in the adaptation of Christianity to new forms of spiritual experience and connection in the youth culture. The analysis of this unusual mission effort has three parts. First, a profile of the technology and strategy of the Online Missionary Project is presented. Second, the reasons for selecting the club scene as a sphere for mission and the spiritual attributes of clubbing and the Internet are explored. Third, examples of how the project shaped new forms of ritual, sacred space, and community are given in order to highlight how new media use can be interpreted as an experiential spiritual practice. This case study exemplifies how a group's religious use of the Internet was informed by their beliefs about popular culture and new communicative technologies.

Information gathered and examples cited are based on four months of research while serving as the project's independent evaluator. This included field observation and interviews with team members in Ibiza, Bristol, and Sheffield, online observation of chat-room interactions, and analysis of a questionnaire distributed to project members and online missionaries.

Case Study: Online Missionaries Project

In 2002 the Online Missionaries Project (OM) was created to develop innovative resources for evangelism and discipleship utilizing the Internet. The project team hoped that "new shapes of church" would emerge from using various technologies to build relationships with clubbers both online and offline. This was a collaborative partnership of three youth-oriented Christian organizations based in the United Kingdom. Spearheaded by NGM, a community of Christian musicians and artists based in Bristol, it also involved 24-7, a youth prayer network based in Chichester that mobilizes week-long twenty-four-hour prayer events, and Tribal Generation, a Sheffield-based Church of England youth network involved in forming new expressions of church. These organizations had the common goals of training and mobilizing Christian youth in sharing their convictions, targeting "spiritual voyagers" or "seekers" for conversion, and attempting to create new "communities of faith." Their aim was to pool resources and expertise to develop technologies that would create new options for building relationships and sharing their beliefs. As stated in a project report: "This unique project will enable missionaries to reach out and to disciple their generation using the Internet as a catalyst."

The OM project involved several components, including the Clubbers Temple Web site (www.clubberstemple.com), training online missionaries to serve in a chat room, a text messaging service used to keep team members informed about the project, and a variety of promotional materials. All of these resources were first tested as part of a "mission outreach" to the clubbers of Ibiza, a popular resort island off the southeast coast of Spain, which was led by 24-7 during the summer of 2002. Together 24-7 prayer teams and NGM DJs, working in the bars and clubs of Ibiza, sought to use the OM technology to cultivate relationships with Ibiza clubbers. Their conviction was that if the Church is to survive "it must continually reinvent itself and adapt its message to the members of each generation, along with their culture and geographical setting" (Online Missionaries Project 2002c). The Online Missionaries Project illustrates how some Christians are trying to adapt their convictions to a new communication culture while retaining their traditional commitment to "making disciples."

The Ibiza Pilot Project

Ibiza was well placed to test this approach. It can be seen as a place both of pilgrimage and of escape. One DJ in San Antonio, a popular tourist town in

Ibiza, described it as "an island of soul searchers" encouraging people to both lose themselves and reflect on the larger questions of life (personal interview, Ibiza, August 2002). Ibiza has long been considered a "holy island," with its earth believed to radiate positive energy (Garratt 1998). In 740 B.C. the island's inhabitants, the Carthaginians, gave the island its own deity, Tanit, a goddess representing love, death, and fertility. Nostradamus prophesied that Ibiza would be the last safe and inhabitable place on earth after a worldwide war. It also became a prime destination for both those on the hippie trail between the West and the East in the 1960s and later New Agers.

Ibiza's first formal dance club, Pacha, opened in 1973. Now the island is home to dozens of clubs including the well-known Space, Café del Mar, and Privilege, the world's largest club, which is able to house eight thousand clubbers on a single night. Several separate communities exist alongside each other within Ibiza. There is the native-island community, foreign club owners and DJs who visit for short bursts, seasonal workers from across Europe who make it their home for the summer, and tourists or clubbers who come for a few days or weeks. It is a young, energetic, frequently changing place. All of these elements make it fertile ground for exploring the creation of new forms of ritual activity and spiritual community.

The Ibiza pilot project was part of 24-7's ten-week summer outreach. A core team of eight people along with four two-week teams of a dozen or more individuals took part in various activities. These included: praying for clubbers on the streets and in a twenty-four-hour prayer room and doing what they described as "servant evangelism" such as volunteer beach cleaning, offering a "taxi" service for clubbers too drunk or stoned to make it home safely, and meeting people while passing out free candy. Their aim was to build relationships that would, they hoped, lead to spiritual conversations. NGM team members also offered free DJ workshops and DJed in local bars.

A focal point of the project was the Clubbers Temple Web site, designed as a "virtual club" using imaginative Flash software, sound, and experiential elements, including a chat room and a prayer wall. Clubbers Temple was built as a connection hub, where spiritual seekers could find information about Christianity and meet with other like-minded clubbers. It was to serve as a "follow-up tool" and "discipleship resource" for the Ibiza team. One 24-7 team member described it as "a tool to keep in touch with new friends we have met here in Ibiza and an accessible way for clubbers to find out about God and us" (Online Missionaries Project 2002a). Promoting the site in Ibiza provided a way to initiate "spiritual conversations" or offer prayer to clubbers.

Back in the United Kingdom online missionaries served as virtual "bar staff" in the Clubbers Temple chat room. They were seen as "online evange-lists" who were commissioned to "befriend users" and "offer pastoral support online," providing follow-up for relationships begun in Ibiza. Based at sites in Bristol and Sheffield, they supported the work of the 24-7 teams during the pilot project by staffing "the bar" during nightly "happy hours." Online missionaries worked the chat room throughout the pilot period and into September 2002.

As well as cultivating friendships online, missionaries were also expected to watch for "one2many" texts (O2M) and respond in prayer. O2M text messaging (texting) functions in similar fashion to an e-mail distribution list, allowing a single text to be sent to numerous phones simultaneously. It was developed by the project team to distribute news and prayer request amongst project members. O2M texting created a prayer and support network, linking online missionaries in the United Kingdom to the team in Ibiza with instantaneous prayer alerts and news. The Online Missionary Project designed and connected new media technology in novel ways in an effort to reach a particular subculture. Their use also involved conceptualizing the Internet and club culture in a unique way as spiritual spaces.

Connecting Club Culture and the Internet as Spiritual Spaces

While proselytizing strategies abound online for various faiths, a creative aspect of the Online Missionaries Project was its targeted audience. The project endeavored to engage with youth by meeting them where they are—in the club scene. Its vision statement also acknowledged a desire to connect with what it identified as the spiritual side of clubbing. "Many people find the clubbing experience offers them a sense of sanctuary, a place to begin and to continue the journey of spiritual enlightenment and the experience of the transcendent" (Online Missionaries Project 2002c). By recognizing the spiritual and experiential components of clubbing, the project's aim was to create a technology that would enable project members to connect with clubbers and inform or influence this perceived spiritual journey.

An underlying aim was to experiment with building new faith communities and creating a church for clubbers. The intention was that these communities or new churches would be sustained long-term online. By "planting relationships and building something of life online" organizers hoped to see "new forms of long term community emerge that will potentially please God" (introduction to OM project, Training Day, June 2002). Throughout the project, "community-building not vacuum-evangelism" remained a central focus (Online Missionaries Project 2002c).

In order to understand the vision of the OM project, it is important to explain how club culture and the Internet were identified as spheres where spirituality can be found and cultivated. Both served as examples of what Stewart Hoover refers to as a "tent where meaning is made," a media-created place to be religious outside the sphere of religious institutions and traditions (Hoover 1997: 294). Researchers of religion and the media have observed that new forms of media practice often provide innovative ways of expressing non-religious forms of spirituality (Clark 2003). The spiritual or spirituality, in this context, refers to the human search for "meaning significance" (Jones, Wainwright, and Arnold 1986: 50). Reading club culture and the Internet as spiritual spaces illustrates how the OM project sought to inform clubber's search for meaning within their culture.

Club Culture as Spiritual Space

The OM Vision Report (Online Missionaries Project 2002c) described club culture as "one of the emerging parishes in 21st century youth culture." Club culture is what is "created by people on the dance floor, reflecting both what they bring with them to a club and what they are trying to escape from in the outside world" (Garratt 1998: 11). Picture a dark, hazy room surrounded by screens of constantly changing computer-generated images, flashing lights, and pulsating beats. Dancing amidst a mass of bodies, a person might experience the equivalent of an altered state of consciousness. Through image, sound, and repetitive movement, the clubber is transported into another dimension. While mass media have primarily treated clubbing as "leisure pursuit," anthropological studies of clubbing practice argue that it is predominately an "experience" (Malbon 1999: 18).

Club culture represents a variety of musical genres: soul, reggae, disco, hip-hop, garage, house, techno, drum and bass, as well as other subgenres such as acid and trance. Each music scene presents a particular lifestyle, represented by styles of dress, attitudes, and experiences sought. While the styles are diverse, the club culture advocates the common values of artistic freedom, cultural diversity, and a "universal spirituality" where "machine rhythms [and] pounding drums are overlaid with a gospel spirituality of peace, love and unity" (Rietveld 2000). Clubbing enables individuals and groups to experience something otherworldly. It is this realm of experience that the OM project team sought to connect with and to inform with their Christian message.

The OM Vision Report (Online Missionaries Project 2002c) also described clubbing as an experience where many young people go to seek "spiritual enlightenment." The connection between clubbing and the spiritual can be noted in names and metaphors that are frequently present in popular club culture. One of the first well-known disco clubs was The Sanctuary (originally called The Church), housed in what used to be called Hell's Kitchen in Manhattan, where DJ decks appeared on the altar and church pews served as seats. Names of clubs often reflect spiritual metaphors: Body and Soul in New York, Heaven & Ministry of Sound in London, Es Paradis in Ibiza, and the Rezerection rave held in Edinburgh.

The often-repeated cliché that "clubs are the churches of the new millenium" in some respects rings true in the icons and vibe of clubbing (Garratt 1998: 305). The role of the DJ has been described as master artist, prophet, superstar, "secular priest," and "god" (Brewster and Broughton 1999). Clubbers can be seen as faithful disciples. Club anthems and records/CDs serve as sacred texts. Clubs are like shrines and their theme nights like quasi-religious festivals. This is seen on Ibiza, the clubbing capital of Europe. Many Ibiza clubs and club nights employ spiritual imagery, including El Divino, which houses a giant Buddha statue and hosts Salvacion night, God's Kitchen, which finds its home in Eden, and DJ Judge Jules, who oversees Judgement Sunday club night. There is a spiritual subtext to much of the club scene on Ibiza, and the OM project sought to target the spiritual seekers drawn to this subculture. The Internet was enlisted as a resource to establish an additional and parallel spiritual space for outreach to these presumed seekers.

Internet as Spiritual Space

The Internet has been described as a communications medium, a computer system, a discourse (Agre 1998) and as a social network (Jones 1997). Yet the Internet not only presents new possibilities for work and communicative tasks; it can also be conceptualized as reconnecting people with the spiritual side of life (Wertheim 1999). Some researchers envision the Internet as a new realm in which to experience the spiritual. Cobb argues that "Cyberspace can aid humanity's spiritual progression" by serving as an "important way station" on humanity's journey towards a greater spiritual evolution (1998: 97). The Internet as a spiritual network that facilitates spiritual experiences and encounters or as sacramental space set apart for "holy use" enables people to describe online activities as part of their spiritual life (Campbell 2001). Seeing the Internet as a spiritual space recognizes the growing phenomenon of people using the Internet as part of their religious practices (Barna Research Group 1998).

One way the Internet has functioned as spiritual space is in the emergence of online spiritual communities. Since the mid-1990s the study of online community has been a primary focus of research into computer-mediated communication, exploring issues such as the impact of the Internet on identity construction, the representation and enactment of gender, the experience of disembodiment, and the creation and maintenance of boundaries in online groups (e.g., Dawson 2000; DiMaggio et al. 2001). Online communities are "social aggregations that emerge from the Net when enough people carry on public discussions long enough, with sufficient human feeling, to form Webs of personal relationships in cyberspace" (Rheingold 1993: 5). Online spiritual communities are intentional groups, which gather around focused issues of faith and allow for two-way interaction through a variety of media (e-mail, Internet Relay Chat, ICQ). Each online spiritual community possesses a unique narrative informing its particular rituals and practices. These narratives, such as being a support network or worship space, bring cohesion and identity to these communities (Campbell 2001). These communities illustrate how individuals consciously set apart Internet technology as a place for spiritual engagement.

The OM training manual (Online Missionaries Project 2002b) highlighted the project's desire to "plant and sustain communities of faith online where people can experience God, discipleship, meaning and belonging." The Internet was seen as a suitable place for "potentially planting an expression of church."

The aim of the project was to proactively cultivate spiritual communities online and offline.

In the OM project, media use for spiritual pursuits is fuelled by a similar desire to that of the club culture itself, a recovery of experience. It has been argued that both the Internet and clubs create spiritual spaces where various forms of ritual can take place. Spiritual pursuits flourish in these environments because of the desire amongst youth for experiences that engage all their senses. Beaudoin describes this as a "pop culture sacramentality," one which "suggests the body and personal experience represent signs of God's grace in this world" (1998: 74). Generations X and Y are experiential spiritual seekers longing for tactile and emotive engagement. They do not just want to see or be told—they want to feel it for themselves (Beaudoin 1998; Sample 1998). The "Net Generation" is comfortable with a religiosity that promotes an integrated spiritual and sensual experience. "They are more spiritual than cognitive, which means that they see no difference between spirit and body, mind and emotion. They prefer personal, raw experience instead of just passively ascribing to other people's thoughts and ideas" (Jensen 2001: 5) The spiritual pursuits of the youth often take them to nontraditional contexts, such as the clubs and the Internet to find the raw materials for fashioning new and more intense experiences.

Ritual, Spiritual Space, and Community in the Online Missionary Project

The purpose of the OM pilot project was to test out "a working model for using modern electronic communication to catalyze mission into the emerging culture" (Online Missionaries Project 2002c). In this process, several interesting forms of spiritual practice and networking took place.

Creating Ritual in Ibiza: Connecting and Clubbing

The goal of 24-7 team members in Ibiza was to connect with the clubbers and young tourists. Team members focused on "building relationships" and trying to instigate "spiritual conversations" with those they met in the clubs, streets, bars, and beaches. Due to regulations about advertising in Ibiza, promotional material for the Clubbers Temple (CT) and NGM DJ gigs had to be treated as "invitations." Inviting people to the Web site and to gigs became a way to explain why Christians were hanging out at the heart of the club scene for the summer. The team cultivated a communal identity as clubbers who happened to be Christians and wanted to offer an alternate image of religion. CT was not only a tool to connect with people; it became an identity marker or "branding" associated with the team.

Team members wore blue T-shirts bearing the CT logo while meeting people in the West End of San Antonio and in the clubs. This brought uniformity to the team throughout the summer. While many people did not realize that it was always different people wearing the shirts, the logo heightened the visibility of the 24-7 team. Specially designed stickers and flyers bearing the Web site address were also distributed and used as conversation starters. These provided the team with instant recognition on the island, as one team member said in an interview: "I got stopped by some girls who recognized the T-shirts and ended up chatting for over an hour about God and even prayed for one." Ibiza is inundated with public relations workers promoting bars, clubs, and special events; and, as is commonly said, "someone is always trying to sell you something in Ibiza." So being seen as the promoters for a Web site gave members a focus and helped them to blend in. Being a CT Web promoter meant that "we have a specific job or role," providing a focus to the outreach and something others could identify the team with (personal interview, Ibiza, August 2002).

The team's presence over the ten weeks, especially in San Antonio, generated much interest among the club and bar workers. Being trailed by a British production team from Channel 4 doing a documentary on their work in Ibiza certainly helped to draw attention as well. The press described them as "20-year-old Christian missionaries bent on saving drunken souls" (Wakefield 2002). But team members emphasized they were not traditional missionaries; instead, they said, "we sow seeds in people's mind's and pray for them." They saw themselves as clubbers with a different purpose, as evidenced in their actions and reputation. They were those "people who pray on the streets" (Wakefield 2002).

Besides being involved in prayer and conversations, team members were regularly seen in many Ibiza clubs. For them, clubbing was an act of prayer and dancing was an expression of worship to God. "Traditional organized religion has nothing to offer most young people," explained an NGM DJ, "but we don't worship in church; we pray when we're clubbing" (Wakefield 2002). In the clubs, team members were always found in groups, often congregating in "dance huddles" on the floor, encouraging each other to be in prayer for those around them. They spoke of consciously creating their own culture on the dance floor by "dancing to a different beat" and "shining God's light" in the way they moved and interacted with others (personal interview, Ibiza, August 2002). In an interview in Ibiza one a 24-7 team member stated: "I find it easier to connect with God through dance music. . . . The culture is very similar to our church culture—often there's a sense of community, belonging and spiritual journey" (personal interview, Ibiza, August 2002).

The idea of consciously creating a space or culture also filtered into the DJ aspects of the outreach. Several DJs on the team managed to secure gigs at well-known beachfront bars such as Mambo and Sugar Sea. DJing, too, was described as an act of worship, through mixing the music in a way that "creates a space that opens people up to the spiritual realm and experiencing God." A team member and DJ from Swansea said: "You listen to a track and you don't play something that is dark or heavy, you pick lyrics and music that bring light when it is played. It's something you sense in your spirit, your gut" (personal interview, Ibiza, August 2002). This touches on Manovich's assertion that DJs are architects of personalized public spaces, engineering and encouraging through their mix a particular form of ritual engagement. By connecting club culture to computer culture, Manovich highlights the acts of "selection and combination," the intentional creation of an atmosphere influenced by the style of the DJ (Manovich 2001: 134). The OM project attempted likewise deliberately to fashion a new space to direct people towards certain beliefs.

Clubbers Temple as Spiritual Space

A central component of the Clubbers Temple Web site is "the temple." According to the project team, it was designed as a "virtual club" to "give people a spiritual experience." Before entering the club, individuals are asked to type their name. In a personalized greeting users are told they are about to enter a church and that if one is to "embark on a spiritual journey, you need to prepare." Individuals are encouraged to "open hands, heart, spirit, mind" and then click on a button confirming they are ready to "receive, feel, experience, learn." As they are transported to the doors of the virtual temple, the voice of the DJ asks a final question: "Are you ready to explore the more of God?" If the answer is yes, with one click users are welcomed into the club. The user then views gyrating dancers and a DJ mixing tracks to the sounds of pounding dance rhythms. In a round screen at the back of the club a stream of changing images are shown, including words such as "life" or "experience" and pictures of Ibiza.

Mixed in with the music, the DJ beckons the clubbers to join in the spiritual journey: "A generation rising, of followers, of lovers, of Jesus . . . open your mind and let Father God take you away. . . . Close your eyes and let the music take you deeper, deeper, deeper into his (God's) presence. . . ."

Three-dimensional navigation allows users to feel as if they are in the club, moving through the dancing crowd towards three "chill-out rooms." These rooms present different spaces for reflection through listening to testimonies while watching a sunset, searching through Bible verses, and taking part in a story about being thirsty for spiritual things. According to its designers, the temple aims at facilitating interaction and "an experience with God" in a club environment (personal interview, Bristol, August 2002). One of the site's designers described their intention of "wanting to flesh out Christ's commission using new technology to communicate God" by offering a "spiritual experience" to clubbers (personal interview, Sheffield, August 2002). The Web site design, the language used, and components included were all geared towards this aim.

It is difficult to assess the effectiveness of such attempts to create a spiritual experience online, but several people associated with the project reported having personal spiritual experiences while using the site. One said: "The first time I logged on and heard the DJ's voice, it was like, 'Wow' I can feel God through this. It's amazing to see how it is possible to have a sense of God through the site. I've seen it and I've experienced it" (personal interview, Bristol, August 2002).

Seeing Clubbers Temple as potentially offering a "real experience of God" was based on a preexisting understanding of how the "spiritual" is encountered. The focus was on the site's ability to prompt an internal, bodily, or emotive reaction, provoked by the sensory stimulation of music, images, words, and "God." Beaudoin writes of Generation X's quest for "transformative spiritual experiences" that are "body oriented" and "religiously branded" (1998: 80). He describes this as the desire to know through feeling and "interpret our experience religiously." Interpreting online experiences through a Christian worldview enabled people to see cyberspace as sphere of sacramental potential. This was illustrated by another project member's account of the temple: "The other night I logged on and heard the tune and felt a shiver go down my spine and could see where God could move through it" (personal interview, Bristol, 2002). For Generation Xers, cyberspace "incarnates" the eternal and the Divine in the here and now (Beaudoin 1998: 87) by presenting it as the "sacramentality of experiences," interpreting online engagement through the lens of grace and mystery. However, the extent to which clubbing and the Internet can lead to authentic experiences of transcendence is in need of further consideration, especially for those without a religious background. Recent research has found that while clubbing cultivates experiences that "can transcend ordinary life," "high levels of stimulation (in clubbing) do not guarantee a religious interpretation" (Savage, Collins, and Mayo 2002).

Through personal contact and conversations with clubbers made by 24-7 team members it was hoped that a particular Christian understanding of the spiritual would shape people's experiences and understanding of the site. Clubbers Temple can be seen as a spiritual space in the way it has been designed. Yet interpretations of the site seemed to be dependent on the meaning people brought to it.

Building Relationships and Community Online

It has been emphasized that an intention of the OM project was to try to "build an online community" through tapping into the community network formed by the 24-7 team in Ibiza. While Clubbers Temple proved effective in helping initiate conversations, there was not a significant take-up by Ibiza contacts afterwards through the Web site. Overall evaluation by team members of the pilot were positive yet dissatisfied. As summarized by one online missionary: "It has loads of potential, but the practicalities of it haven't worked out" (Online Missionaries Project 2002a).

Several reasons were given for the small number of Ibiza clubbers visiting the CT site. Some said it was Ibiza. While people were open to chatting, it was often hard to have in-depth conversations. "Most conversations in Ibiza don't get far enough for the site to be appropriate" claimed one 24-7 team member (personal interview, Ibiza, August 2002). Many clubbers were not in a fit state to remember any conversations or keep ahold of flyers they were given. Another challenge was that when some people logged onto CT, they were looking for specific people they had met in Ibiza. When they did not recognize the online missionaries at the bar, they did not stay long. Several 24-7 team members maintained relationships they had initiated in Ibiza outside the CT Web site, using e-mail or phone contact instead. Also there was no way of knowing how many people logged on to the temple and possibly "met with God," but did not share this experience with others in the chat room or through the message board. The problem may be, it was suggested, that their target audience desired embodied experiences over disembodied interactions. The low uptake raises interesting questions in need of further exploration— about how technology can or should be adapted for use in religious recruitment (see Dawson and Hennebry 1999). While the low number of online visitors frustrated OM missionaries, they remained optimistic about the project's, potential, stating, "it is worth being 'out there' just in case God does send someone along."

Even with few visitors, several interesting and unintentional forms of relationships emerged from the pilot project. Technology used in Ibiza helped sustain and strengthen 24-7 team relationships. Mobile phones were used to keep team members in touch with the activities of others around the island. The team spent many nights in the bar-populated West End of San Antonio chatting to British clubbers and offering prayer. Texting allowed those on the street to send updates to team members in a nearby prayer room and for the prayer room to text encouraging words to those on the streets. A strong supportive family atmosphere was cultivated amongst the team that sustained them through long nights of clubbing, sickness, and even a break-in of their rented home in which most of the team's valuables were stolen.

In cyberspace the online missionaries built a support network amongst the fellow virtual bar workers. The project appointed a "cyber-vicar" to "pastorally oversee" and maintain the flow of information to the missionaries. The cyber-vicar also facilitated "online huddles" in private chat rooms on the CT Web site, allowing space for online missionaries to interact together, keep up-to-date about the project, and disseminate news and stories.

The OM project also helped strengthen relationships within and between the organizations involved by opening new lines of communication. Two or more online missionaries were online each evening in two-hour blocks of time, and many built new friendships with other missionaries online during this time. One missionary based in Bristol commented that his best online session was with another missionary from Sheffield. "We had a good chat, we didn't fulfill the pilot vision as we were waiting for clubbers who didn't come, but it was good for networking." This demonstrated the technology's ability to build supportive links with the "body of Christ" and other Christians involved in similar forms of ministry. As this online missionary observed, it is "easy to get focused on my organization and the work I do, and to interact with similar but separate organizations is positive and healthy. When I at some time bump into this person I conversed with from TG there will be some sort of relationship there" (personal interview, Bristol, August, 2002). In this way the OM pilot offered new potential for creating and sustaining existing relationship networks.

Though the vision to "plant church in club culture" was not realized through the pilot, the Online Missionaries Project did offer some unique ways to "harness the Internet as a tool to reach young people." Its intention to use Internet technology to target a specific segment of youth culture was as much about "equipping a new breed of online missionaries" as it was about creating innovative tools. In *Youthwork* magazine (2002), NGM Assistant Director Phil Ball described CT as a new form of mission work. "It's not just handing out tracks anymore. Missionaries, online or otherwise, need to be connecting with people who are on a spiritual journey." Whether through dancing with hands raised in prayer or in consciously creating space for spiritual encounter online, the project cultivated spiritual space and experiences for both project members and those it sought to influence. The Online Missionary Project offers a unique examination of how a religious group's beliefs about the potential of the Internet as a tool for ministry can shape its use of new media technology.

Conclusions

This chapter has described how the Online Missionary Project utilized new media in unique ways to adapt the Christian message to new social circumstances and address the traditional religious objectives of proselytizing. While using new technology did not achieve the goals of making converts or building new spiritual comminutes, it did have the unanticipated positive consequence of strengthening relationships between team members. It also illustrated how conceiving of a technological sphere such as the Internet or a club as spiritual space allows innovative forms of spiritual practice to emerge. In Ibiza team members were deliberate creators of ritual, whether as DJs trying to generate a spiritual vibe through their "mix" or clubbers altering the club atmosphere by using it as a prayer and worship space. Mobile phones became instruments of connection linking team members in the United Kindom and Ibiza through promoting prayer and support. The Internet symbolized a "new mission field," with the Clubbers Temple "bar" representing a "pioneering" effort to shape a new church.

All of these uses of technology involve conceptualizing the Internet as a potential new space for religious development, one that can be embedded with rituals and symbols to support spiritual practice. Using new technology as a part of one's spiritual practice touches the recognized yearning, especially within Generations X and Y, for the "recovery of experience" (Thompson 2001). This tendency to seek mystical encounters has been described as a new "pop culture sacramentality" (Beaudoin 1998). This pop culture sacramentality "suggests that the body and personal experience represents (*SIC*) signs of God's grace in the world" (Beaudoin 1998: 74). Both the club and Internet cultures promote this sacramentality of experience, whether it is embodied in a club or experienced "virtually" online. The Online Missionary Project addresses this desire for experience by attempting to lead offline spiritual seekers towards online spiritual exploration.

While Clubbers Temple can still be found online offering a club-style worship experience, the OM project has changed its focus from using new media for making converts to using it for sustaining and strengthening existing relationships and communities. NGM is currently adapting the Web site and chat-room formats to create online Christian cell groups. This is to be tested in its work with schoolchildren, building upon previous face-to-face contacts to form online communities. These changes recognize the positive outcome of the OM project of reinforcing existing ties. Other forms of technology from the project have also been adapted to the aim of strengthening relationships. "Take2-2pray," a daily "call to prayer" has been developed by NGM to strengthen its ministry community. This text messaging service sends a short prayer item and a "meditation" to all its members each day, exhorting them to stop for two minutes and pray. The 24-7 group has created "WOW" ("Watchman on the Walls") linking like-minded prayer supporters. Prayer text alerts, news, or Bible verses are sent weekly to subscribers to encourage them to pray (www.24-7prayer.com/wow). These innovations highlight how new technology may serve as a tool for extending and maintaining already existing church-based relationships.

The Online Missionary project raises interesting questions about how religious beliefs motivate new media use and the narratives they employ to shape or justify this use. This project demonstrates how technological innovation, guided by specific Christian beliefs and values, can offer a specific understanding of popular culture and technology. As the Internet is increasingly used as a spiritual sphere and to experiment with new forms of church, there is a need to explore further a Christian understanding of this technology and associated interpretations of new media culture.

References

Agre, P. (1998). "The Internet and Public Discourse." Retrieved from www.firstmonday.dk/issues/issue3_3/agre, June 25, 1998.

Barna Research Group (1998). "The Cyberchurch Is Coming. National Survey of Teenagers Shows Expectation of Substituting Internet for Corner Church." Retrieved from www.barna.org, May 12, 1998.

Beaudoin, T. (1998). *Virtual Faith*. San Francisco: Jossey-Bass.

Brewster, B. and F. Broughton, (1999). *Last Night a DJ Saved My Life: The History of the Disc Jockey*. London: Headline Books.

Campbell, H. (2001). "Connecting to the Spiritual Network: Spiritual Communities within the Online Context." Paper presented at the Religious Encounters in Digital Networks Conference, Copenhagen, Denmark.

————. (2003). "A Review of Religious Computer-Mediated Communication Research." In *Mediating Religion: Conversations in Media, Culture and Religion*, ed. S. Marriage and J. Mitchell, 213–228. Edinburgh: T & T Clark/Continuum.

Clark, L. S. (2003). *From Angels to Aliens: Teenagers, the Media, and the Supernatural.* Oxford, UK: Oxford University Press.

Cobb, J. (1998). *Cybergrace. The Search for God in the Digital World.* New York: Crown Publishers.

Dawson, L. L. (2000). "Researching Religion in Cyberspace: Issues and Strategies." In *Religion on the Internet: Research Prospects and Promises*, ed. J. K. Hadden and D. E. Cowan, 25–54. London: JAI Press/Elsevier Science.

Dawson, L. L., and J. Hennebry, (1999). "New Religions and the Internet: Recruiting in a New Public Space." *Journal of Contemporary Religion* 14: 17–39.

DiMaggio, et al. (2001). "Social Implications of the Internet." *Annual Review of Sociology* 27: 307–336.

Faithless. (1998). "god is a DJ." *Sunday 8pm*. London: Cheeky Records.

Garratt, S. (1998). *Adventure in Wonderland. A Decade of Club Culture.* London: Headline Books.

Hoover, S. (1997). "Media and the Religious Public Sphere." In *Rethinking Media, Religion, and Culture*, ed. S. Hoover and K. Lundby, 293–297. Thousand Oaks, CA: Sage.

Indeep. (1982). "Last Night a DJ Saved My Life." *Last Night a DJ Saved My Life*. New York: Sound of New York Records.

Jensen, C. R. (2001). *A New Digital Generation—A New Postmodern Paradigm.* Paper presented at the Religious Encounters in Digital Networks Conference, Copenhagen, Denmark.

Jones, C., G. Wainwright, and E. Arnold, (1986). *The Study of Spirituality.* London: SPCK.

Jones, S. (1997). "The Internet and Its Social Landscape." In *Virtual Culture*, ed. S. Jones, 7–32. Thousand Oaks, CA: Sage.

Manovich, L. (2001). *The Language of New Media.* Cambridge, MA: MIT Press.

Malbon, B. (1999). *Clubbing: Dancing, Ecstasy and Vitality.* London: Routledge.

Online Missionaries Project. (2002a). "Online Missionaries Project Evaluation Questionnaire". Internal document. Bristol, UK: NGM.

————. (2002b). "Online Missionaries Project Training Manual." Internal document. Bristol, UK: NGM.

————. (2002c). "Online Missionaries Project Vision Report." Internal document. Bristol, UK: NGM.

Rheingold, H. (1993). *The Virtual Community.* New York: HarperPerennial.

Rietveld, H. C. (2000). "The Body and Soul of Club Culture." Retreived from www.unesco.org/courier/2000_07/uk/doss13.htm, April 12, 2003.

Sample, T. (1998). *The Spectacle of Worship in the Wired World: Electronic Culture and the Gathered People of God.* Nashville, TN: Abingdon Press.

Savage, S., S., Collins, and B. Mayo, (2002). "Theology through the Arts for a New Generation." Unpublished research report. Cambridge, UK: University of Cambridge.

Thompson, P. (2001). "Angels in Clubland, Generation E and the Future of Christian Identity." Unpublished M.Th. thesis, Faculty of Divinity, University of Edinburgh.

Wakefield, M. (2002). "Jesus Goes to the Disco." *The Spectator* (October 12). Retrieved from www.spectator.co.uk, October 14, 2002.

Wertheim, M. (1999). *The Pearly Gates of Cyberspace.* London: Virago.

"Web Mission Aims at Clubbers." *Youthwork* (September 2002): 8.

9

"Rip. Burn. Pray.": Islamic Expression Online

GARY R. BUNT

According to Islamic tradition, the Qur'an was received by Muhammad from God via the Angel Gabriel (Jibril) between the years 610 and 632 C.E. Now, nearly fourteen centuries later (according to the Gregorian calendar), there are tens of thousands of references to the Qur'an on the Internet, and hundreds of sites highlighting diverse conceptual, interpretive, and dissemination strategies towards the Revelation (Bunt 2000: 18–33; Robinson 1997: 261–278). Computers have become a significant channel for the dissemination and study of the Qur'an, both in Arabic and in translation, and a number of different interfaces have been introduced to facilitate its digital study. Online Qur'ans feature on a number of different Islamic Web sites, or what I have called elsewhere "cyber Islamic environments" (Bunt 2000). Through studying these qur'anic interfaces, it is possible to develop some insight into the roles digital media play in religious understanding and expression while furthering phenomenological analysis of aspects of contemporary Islamic expression worldwide.

Whether such media engender new identities, insights, and affiliations or simply reflect more "conventional" understandings of Islam is open to question. While online phenomena can be observed, discussed, and recorded—and indeed these are critical activities during this phase of both technological development and (potentially) radical change in the Muslim world(s)—measuring how technologies are applied and whether they have any "real" impact in terms of Muslim networking, community, and individual religious experience introduces a number of factors that are difficult to quantify. They may be "transformational," qualitively affecting relationships and personal and communal worldviews and engendering social change. (Bunt 2000: 132–144; 2003: 124–133; Dawson 2000: 25–54). They could simply "mirror" offline religious expression and experience. Or they could provide new, hypertextual articulations of Islam.

What can be measured is the extent to which the Islamic spectrum is represented on the Internet in terms of its multifaceted religious, cultural, and political complexities. Islam is often categorized into Sunni, Shi'a, and Sufi Islam, although these divisions are not necessarily clear-cut. While, theoretically, core-values of Islam can be shared, they inevitably pass through cultural, linguistic, and interpretative filters and gain specific nuances and understandings. The Internet demonstrates that these divisions are not clear-cut and that there can be substantial common ground in core values of faith, as demonstrated on a variety of Web sites and in chat rooms.

The varieties of Islamic religious expressions and orientations online range from the "orthodox" to the esoteric and the marginalized. This chapter introduces some of the varied ways in which Islam (and specifically the Qur'an) is articulated in cyberspace. The question is whether the translation of Islam and the Qur'an into hypertext facilitates a clearer understanding of the religion in its myriad forms and dimensions, both for Muslims and for other travelers in cyberspace.

One important aspect of this issue is whether searchable interfaces aid understanding of the Qur'an and whether these technological tools might aid in improving understandings of Islam and Muslims in the contemporary world. There are computer-mediated versions of Qur'ans that have acquired substantial audiences; some have a particular "Western" audience (Muslim and non-Muslim) and/or have been generated in "Western" contexts. Various methods have been used to integrate the Qur'an in a digital framework, many of which are designed for specific levels of understanding—readers range from those fluent in classical or qur'anic Arabic through to those who have limited knowledge of Arabic and readers who can approach the Revelation only in a language other than Arabic. Some qur'anic resources clearly have propagation of the faith (*da'wa*) as their mission and seek to engender greater interest in Islam (often from a particular religious perspective) among Muslims or encourage others to "enter" Islam. Others simply seek to develop a sympathetic comprehension of Islam outside the "Muslim world," tied to a specific set of interpretative and cultural values.

Qur'anic content is often integrated into sites with a broad Islamic focus. Two examples of this are

- Authoritative sites, which dispense commentaries, sermons, advice, resources, and/or religious "opinions" or edicts [*fatwas*] that incorporate considerable qur'anic content and which are often associated with a specific Muslim worldview and/or ideologue.
- Portals and platforms for political activism, which apply portions of the qur'anic text in disseminating their agendas. (Bunt 2003)

Not all computer-mediated dissemination of the Qur'an is text-based, however, and Web designers have made good use of other media, specifically the application of multimedia recitations. These take different forms, such as portions of the Qur'an recorded by leading reciters from the significant Muslim locations of Mecca, Medina, and Jerusalem, as well as recordings made at other culturally and religiously important places. Besides possessing an intrinsic ambience and the cachet of "authentic" religious expression and experience, sound files of the Qur'an have an educational value for Muslims. For example, they can be used for teaching recitation or as an aid to the memorization of the Qur'an (one who has memorized the Qur'an has the honorary title of *hafiz*). A *hadith* (saying) of the Prophet Muhammad stresses the importance of acquiring knowledge about the Qur'an: "Narrated 'Uthman: The Prophet said, 'The best among you (Muslims) are those who learn the Qur'an and teach it.'" (al-Bukhari, no. 545). Presumably, this would now apply to the dissemination of the Qur'an through the Internet.

The presence of the Qur'an online can have an evocative effect on the listener, aid in propagation, and provide "immersion" in Islamic religious sources. *Sura al-A'raf*, a chapter from the Qur'an, states: "When the Qur'an is read, listen to it with attention, and hold your peace: that ye may receive Mercy." (*Sura al-A'raf*, 7: 204, Qur'an, Ali trans.). Recitation programs can also be used on the Web. Reciter 2.0 (www.reciter.org) is one example of the growing sophistication of qur'anic interfaces; it allows the reader to follow the qur'anic text in Arabic as the recitation proceeds. Islam Way (http://english.islamway.com) lists approximately 150 reciters and uses a range of recitation styles, featuring extracts from or complete recitations of the Qur'an. Other online forms of religious expression related to recitation include the *adhan* call to prayer in its various forms, as well as "spiritually focused" Islamic music and poetry. Taken together, these indicate something of the diversity of Islamic articulation online. While some of these resources are similar to conventional CD-ROMs of the Qur'an, others have been designed, formatted, or edited specifically with Internet users in mind. This material may be intended as a means to enhance the networking of specific groups of Muslims, whilst other elements may be designed for a "global" audience.

General Web issues relating to application of qur'anic resources include their "searchability," the type and style of recitation, the "user-friendliness" and audiovisual "accessibility" of the interface, and how translations are chosen and approached online. Muslims access and download this material for different reasons: for some, qu'ranic material may be difficult to obtain through other channels; for others, the range of material allows the "consumer" to "mix" specific styles of recitation or to compare and contrast recordings made of similar portions from the Revelation. This activity could extend to "ripping" qur'anic recordings from the Web and "burning" them onto CD-ROM or on to an iPod. For many Muslim surfers, the Web has transcended its novelty phase, and is now a natural source for everyday resources such as the Qur'an.

Given that levels of access to the Internet have increased considerably during the past few years, how are Muslim scholars and religious authorities approaching the Qur'an within the digital age? Scholars and authorities have become aware that in many Muslim cultural and religious contexts an online presence is essential and that a central focus should be the interpretation of the Qur'an.

This can extend to making the text and its interpretation accessible for marginalized or underrepresented groups, such as—in some cultural contexts—Muslim women. During Ramadan 1423/2002, for example, when the scholar Farhat Hashmi addressed an audience of women in Dubai and gave her interpretation of aspects of the Qur'an, her lectures were made available online (Hashmi 2002). The impact of such material is difficult to quantify, but it is interesting that both the scholar and her associates regularly add new content to her Web site.

In Western and Muslim-minority contexts, online representation of the Qur'an can impact understandings of Islam; in Muslim-majority contexts, it can provide significant macro-and micro-channels of networking and understanding. An important question is the extent to which such connectivity is encouraged and enhanced through the development of commentaries and translations of the Qur'an and whether these have an impact on how Muslims interpret Islam and perceive themselves as part of an *umma* or global community.

Muslim Life Online

Many of the elements of Muslim prayer life can be "observed" online. For example, computer programs give the prayer direction and timing; recordings of the *adhan* and the *takbir* (the pronouncement of *Allahu Akbar*—"God is Great"—before prayer); and qur'anic recitation, which comprises a central element of prayer. Multimedia programs demonstrate prayer methods and offer video clips of people praying. Sermons are available online. If these different resources are integrated into a single Web portal, they offer the essential components of a Muslim religious "experience," in some ways mirroring offline religion. Islamic religious life is also represented online through Web sites offering resources for festivals and rites of passage or materials related to specific cultural, religious, political, and/or linguistic interests. It is possible to link up with other members of a religious affiliation online or enter into e-mail or chat-room dialogue with a religious scholar.

Do these, however, represent integral religious experiences in themselves or do they merely supplement more "conventional" religious processes and activities? While it might be possible to engage in religious activity online and lead a virtual "religious life," whether it would be desirable is very much open to question. Individuals might apply aspects of the phenomena presented online in order to enhance their religious lives or knowledge rather than completely live their lives "Islamically" online. I have asked elsewhere if this in itself would engender "the sense of religious essence, the transcendent, the numinous, the Other, what [Rudolf] Otto describes as 'mysterium tremendum et fascinans.'" (Otto 1923, quoted in Bunt 2000). While there have been attempts to engender the essence of Islamic experiences online, their success cannot be quantified. At present, it is possible (especially for impartial observers) to be underwhelmed by supposed technological sophistication in such endeavors, in particular the popular Flash Macromedia shows, while plain qur'anic recitation or text (in Arabic) has the power, particularly for Muslims, to connect its audience to an evocative, sacred experience.

Entering "Islam" into Google yields a list of some of the "market leaders" who have invested time and money developing sophisticated Web sites to present both the Qur'an and Islam on the Internet. Among other things, prominence in a Google search is based on the number of other sites and pages that link to a particular Web site. In relation to Islam, this means that those organizations and individuals who are dominant in nonvirtual contexts are not necessarily those who emerge at the top of a Google listing (see www.google.com/technology). For example, at the time of writing, Al-Azhar University in Cairo—a prominent institution of Muslim learning and source of Islamic authority (especially in some Sunni Muslim contexts)—was not ranked highly in a Google search for "Islam," "Muslims," "Qur'an," or "Islamic." In part this is because the official Al-Azhar site (www.alazhar.org) is poorly resourced and designed in both its Arabic and English incarnations. The reasons for that cannot be discussed here (see Bunt 2000: 127–28), and a scientific analysis of Google and other search engines in Arabic and other "Islamic" languages remains a subject for future research. However, other sites, including a number of "nonofficial" Web pages, have been prominent in the development of Islamic multimedia, especially qur'anic resources.

Islamic Portals and Networking Tools

Islamic portals can stimulate networking and affiliation through provision of regularly updated resources, which encourage frequent return visits by surfers. Information can range from basic materials, such as the Qur'an, through to news provision and areas of specialist Islamic knowledge. There are techniques through which portals may project themselves as central information resources on Islam. In order to enhance their position in the cyber-marketplace, those with appropriate financial and technical resources can apply wide-ranging communication management strategies and utilize specific forms of religious symbolism and language. Loyalty is encouraged through schemes such as membership benefits and through the provision of facilities including chat rooms, Islamic software (such as prayer timetables and Islamic screen savers), Qur'an resources, and free e-mail accounts and Web space. The investment in user-friendly interfaces is intended to encourage readers to develop their interest in Islam, and in some cases converts or "reverts" are a target audience for a portal—whose investors may interpret this as a positive return for its activities. While such objectives are found in a wide range of sites, portal resources often have a depth and sophistication lacking in other sites. The claims of portals to high readership numbers, often expressed on a site's opening page, provide a further indicator to their projected influence and authenticity (although figures can be manipulated or be open to misinterpretation).

IslamiCity (www.islamicity.com) is a prominent example of an Islamic portal, appearing at the top of Google rankings for "Islam." Registered in California to the Saudi Arabian organization Human Assistance and Development International (HADI), this well-organized resource represents an entry point for exploring the Muslim faith on the Internet. Its premium membership channel offers a "Qur'an Memorizer to help learn the Qur'an," an online memorial park, live TV from Mecca, and other multimedia products presented under IslamiCity's specific interpretative ethos. The Devotion section contains a library of information central to Muslim faith, including prayer times, recitations of the Qur'an from noted reciters, and a recitation competition featuring children and young adults. IslamiCity's Mosque section links to accessible material aimed primarily at readers who are not practicing Muslims (a category that could include people who are regarded as Muslims by birth). "Understanding Islam and Muslims," for example, is a succinct series of slides, taking readers through the basic principles of Muslim faith, while "Pillars" discusses the so-called "Five Pillars of Islam" (*al-arkan al-islam*) in a short illustrated essay. Taken from satellite broadcasts such as Saudi Television, "Cyber TV" offers various channels of Islamic content, including live and recorded broadcasts from Mecca and Medina.

The visual imagination is well-catered-to on IslamiCity, which on one level seems to promote accessibility to material rather than dense, text-based equivalents of printed publications. However, since some of these materials have become subscription-only, on another level that accessibility becomes limited. There are many elements of the site that are not subscription-based, however, including an unusual slide show of Virtual Mosques which have been placed in imaginative settings, accompanied by a call to prayer (www.islamicity.com/Video/ch25/ch25_2.ram). While such content could be replicated offline through CD-ROM, that format lacks the elements of immediacy possible on the Web (for example, regularly updated content and responses to contemporary concerns). The possibility exists that neutral surfers who would be unlikely to seek out and purchase an Islamic CD-ROM may casually stumble upon a site such as IslamiCity during a Google search. The phenomenon of converts finding Islam through the Web is increasing and is frequently charted through sites such as IslamiCity.

The Questions and Answers service in IslamiCity allows questions to be submitted to "experts" (based in the Lebanon and the United States) for their learned opinions, and earlier answers can be accessed through the database (www.islamicity.com/qa/). While some of these are specialized in nature, including references to "obscure" *fatwa* sources and legal issues, there is substantial general-interest content, and the database is searchable (e.g., 297 questions relate to the subject of "prayer"). Some of the questions on IslamiCity relate specifically to Internet concerns. For example: "According to my knowledge (I may be wrong) when the Qur'an is being recited, one should listen to it carefully. However, on the ePakistan page, they say hear the recitation of the Qur'an while you browse their Web page. Is this wrong or right?" To which the answer is given: "Dear Br. S. As-salaamu alaykum. You are correct, when the Qur'an is being recited, people should be listening to it and not concentrating on reading other material. Therefore, it is advisable to remind the Pakistani Internet page you are referring to, to remove the Qur'anic recitation in the background. Thank you for asking and God knows best." (IslamiCity, "Qur'an: on the Internet").

Islamic Diversity Online: Shi'a Islam

When discussing the array of Islamic understandings online, there are various examples of how multimedia have been effectively integrated into Muslim "minority" perspectives. Numerically, Shi'a Muslims are in a minority worldwide, but, reflecting Shi'a historical tendencies towards high levels of networking in disparate locations, many in the Shi'a world(s) have used the Internet as an effective networking tool. The Internet has enabled Muslims to access areas of Islamic understanding beyond their cultural-religious frameworks when that information might be limited, censored, or even seen as "dangerous" in other contexts. This can include translations and commentaries on the interpretation of the Qur'an, which vary considerably between and within different Muslim religious environments.

For example, established in 1998 by the Ahlul Bayt Digital Islamic Library Project, the Minnesota-registered Al-Islam (www.al-islam.org) introduces its Shi'a perspective on religious leadership, qur'anic interpretation, as well as advice and commentary on relations with other Muslim worldviews. Al-Islam has devised a substantial set of pages, including "Beginner's Introduction," which discusses the origins of Islam from a Shi'a perspective, and illustrated pages about Shi'a sacred sites—including Karbala and Kufa—as well as those which are "shared" with Sunni Muslims. While some of Al-Islam's content is aimed directly at Shi'a Muslims, there is also much to gain on Al-Islam for general surfers from other religious and/or cultural backgrounds.

The Al-Imam portal (www.al-imam.net), which is registered to an address in Bahrain, is another example of the sophisticated use of the Web in a Shi'a context. Integrating music and images, Al-Imam provides Flash animation clips on religious themes. For example, "The Awaited Saviour" includes references to a key event in Islamic history with particular importance for Shi'a Muslims: the "martyrdom" of Muhammad's grandson, al-Husayn ibn 'Ali, at Karbala in 680. This event features on other areas of al-Imam as well, complete with iconography and recordings of the observance of *muharram* (Islamic New Year and the anniversary of al-Husayn's death) as well as the emotional outpouring of a sermon. "Ya Fatima" asks where the grave of Fatima (the Prophet Muhammad's daughter) is and shows the destruction of various shines and mosques associated with significant Shi'a religious leaders—especially the imams acknowledged as key sources of Islamic authority by (some) Shi'a Muslims (www.al-imam.net/clips.htm). There is a large archive of *Du'aa* (supplication or prayer) on Shi'a themes (www.al-islam.net/duaa1.htm). These materials relate to specific religious and cultural interpretations of Islam and would not be encountered on a Sunni site.

Other resources on Al-Imam include recordings of the *adhan* made at significant Shi'a religious shrines and an opportunity to encounter Shi'a religious practices through an archive of recordings made at ritualized communal meetings. Led by various imams in Bahrain and elsewhere, these incorporate prayers and *nashids* (vocal chants) in Arabic. In July 2003, the site also contained over two hundred *azaas*, ritualized recitations associated with the public mourning of Shi'a martyrs and with the *ta'aziyah* passion plays (www.al-imam.net/azaa.htm). These recordings can either be "ripped" or heard in real time (i.e., without being downloaded).

Away from traditional Shi'a religious material, Al-Imam also has other elements that exploit computer technology for its understanding of Islam. The "Digital Tasbeeh," for example, is a downloadable desktop program that emulates "prayer beads" used in supererogatory prayers—especially the "remembrance" of God (www.al-imam.net/dt.htm). If such remembrance is not enough, Shi'a "Phone Tones" (www.al-imam.net/phonetones.htm) can also be downloaded, ensuring a religious dimension to even the most mundane cell phone calls.

Islamic Diversity Online: Sufism

Reflecting various mystical Muslim approaches to religiosity and prayer, any exploration of Islamic expression online should include those Sufi resources derived and compiled from the Internet. The Naqshbandi Audio Archive, for example, includes a range of *dhikr* recorded by Mawlana Sheikh Nazim al-Haqqani of the Naqshbandi *tariqa* (brotherhood or order). The *Dhikr* is the recitation or "remembrance" of God's name in prayer, often through repetitive incantation (http://videosrv.sunnah.org/naqshb/audio_list.htm). Al-Haqqani also has a page dedicated to his life and work at MP3.com, amidst thousands of other, more conventional recording performers (http://artists.mp3s.com/artists/204/maulana_sheikh_nazim_al_ha.html).

Multimedia notions of Sufi religious experience can also be gleaned from a variety of Web sites in Western contexts. The Garden of the Sufis, for example (www.ibiblio.org/cybersufis), has videos of whirling Dervish activities by the Rifai Marufi Sufi Order. In this case, drumming and *dhikr* were recorded at an event to commemorate the anniversary of the birth of the poet and mystic Jalal al-Din Rumi. Based in Orange County, North Carolina, the Rifai Marufi Sufi Order has recorded other events using multimedia and features them on the site. Featuring "traditional" and other forms of Sufi music, the Garden of the Sufis was developed by Rodrigo Dorfman, a convert to Islam and son of the prominent Chilean writer and activist Ariel Dorfman. Similar sufi recordings are found elsewhere online. For example, the "Hadra" MP_3 is a powerful recording of a communal trance chant activity, but one that gives no obvious indication of context or origins (www.zhikr.org).

The extent to which this kind of material is informative to outsiders is open to question. Although sites like this represent some of the diversity associated with Sufism in Western contexts, the explanations of what is going on in terms of religious activities are limited. There is little in the way of commentary. While this may preserve the essence of the activity from outsiders (emphasizing the secrecy of some religious Sufi concepts), questions emerge of why such a Web site would be produced in the first place. Is it to acquire converts? Or does it encourage cohesion among existing *tariqa* members? There are indications that the Internet may be transforming elements of Sufi expression and understanding, taking its mystical messages beyond traditional borders and confronting the stereotypes often associated with Sufi practices.

Shared Islamic Resources

Looking beyond specific worldviews, the Internet can be a resource for what might be defined as "generic" or shared resources on Islam, those that are not specifically sectarian in nature. Despite the campaigning of some Web sites to promote themselves as central resources and/or to encourage some uniformity and cohesion of belief, arguments still emerge online on central tenets of faith. One example of online discourse is the sighting of the moon during Ramadan, an event integral to the timing of ritual fasting, which commences and concludes according to the moon's waxing and waning. Seeking to bring together conflicting perspectives that are not just inter-Sunni-Shi'a but intra-Sunni and intra-Shi'a, the moon sighting issue has been analyzed on a number of Web sites. Where there are disagreements, these often reflect cultural, historical, and religious patterns and understandings of Islam. They are not necessarily controversial in nature, and differences may be accepted both between and within communities. However, it is a subject that annually generates substantial dialogue on e-mail lists and in chat rooms.

Moonsighting.com (http://moonsighting.com), for example, provides insight into these issues and is one example of a comprehensive resource that details aspects of calendars and prayer calculation. Its main asset is the discussion of the mathematics of such calculations, which are complex but essential for an understanding of the accurate timing of prayers, Ramadan, and such festivals as *Eid-al-Adha*, the feast which marks the conclusion of *hajj*. Moonsighting.com pays attention to the different methodological approaches to calculation, based on varied religious interpretations and traditions. Similar resources include Islamic Finder (www.islamicfinder.org), which offers a facility for Webmasters to paste a Javascript program integrating local prayer time into their sites. Moon calculation and prayer time software is also

available on other Web sites (e.g., MoonCalc, www.starlight.demon.co.uk/
mooncalc; *al-Muezzin*, www.harf.com/software/emuezzin.htm).

The World Wide Web can also offer a digital glimpse into the shared religious
experiences of Muslims. 3-D Kabah (www.3dkabah.co.uk), for example, is a
"virtual" reconstruction of the sacred precincts of Mecca and is also available on
CD-ROM. A similar construction appeared as part of a British TV channel's
coverage of the *hajj* pilgrimage in 2003, including a "virtual *hajj*" using Flash
media (www.channel4.com/life/microsites/H/hajj). Film coverage and day-by-day
reports taken from the pilgrimage were edited together and placed online, forming a resource for further study. Dynamic eyewitness accounts of key elements in
the *hajj* experience are presented from the perspectives of different participants.
This site also includes *hajj* prayers and recitations in English and Arabic audio
formats, basic guides to Islam, and an Ask our Imam page. The site demonstrates
how multimedia could, when intelligently applied, make a contribution to
understanding Islam that goes beyond showy Flash presentations. There are a
number of other examples within the *hajj* genre. For example, the Hajj al-Islam
site (http://hajj.al-islam.com) shows film clips that break the pilgrimage into
sections. *Hajj* Web sites often provide pilgrimage instruction, including related
qur'anic content, both for *hajj* and for the minor *umra* pilgrimage. They may
also have a commercial edge, with links to relevant airline, hotel, and *hajj* package
online bookings (e.g., 21st Century Haj & Umra Services, www.haj-umra.co.uk;
Umra & Hajj Packages, www.umrahtohajj.com).

Islamic Discourse

A more recent phenomena in Islamic cyberspace has been the growing popularity
of Web logs or "blogging": "a personal journal that is frequently updated and
intended for general public consumption. Blogs generally represent the
personality of the author or the Web site and its purpose" (WhatIs, n.d.). A
number of Web sites use this format to present personal views on Islam, while
other individuals and groups have integrated their discourse into magazine
formats. There are thousands of Islamic blogs and magazines in cyberspace,
offering a range of views on Muslim life and the Qur'an.

One important aspect of Muslim blogs is the notion of liberal Islam—
depending, of course, on how "liberal" is used. These seek to represent Islam in
the light of contemporary, often Westernized conditions and can be apologetic
in nature. For example, the lively blog Think Halal (www.thinkhalal.com)
features the slogan "Hug a Muslim Today" and incorporates wry perspectives
on current affairs. In a similar vein, AltMuslim.com (www.altmuslim.com) is
"an interactive Web community dedicated to topical discussion and intellectual
exploration for issues regarding the Muslim community" in a Web log format
and covers such areas such as Art and Culture, Business and Technology, Gender,
Family and Community, and News. Among its slogans are "Ramadan: Not Just
A Diet Plan" (an obvious reference to fasting).

While they are not necessarily hyperlinked, related sites in this category include the *Muslim Wakeup Call* (www.muslimwakeup.com), a Muslim magazine that describes itself as "provocative, opinionated, and sometimes funny," and includes a "Hug-A-Jew" section. The site A Liberal Islamic Web site (www.shobak.org/islam), whose author, Zeeshan Hasan, describes himself as a "theologian at large," has articles on Human Rights, Sexual Ethics, Islam without Islamic Law, and Islam from Patriarchy to Feminism. The extent to which these and related sites challenge conventional discourse and stereotypes about Muslims and Islam—especially post-9 11—is open to question. Blogs have appeared in a variety of Muslim contexts and languages and have a significant following in Farsi and Arabic. It is one thing to be writing a Web site or blog (the lines can get blurred), however, and another altogether to be read by groups outside interested and sympathetic parties. In the future, it will be interesting to observe how this genre of sites presents itself and whether they receive substantial site traffic.

Future Cyber-Islamic Interfaces

In discussing how Islam is articulated in cyberspace, it is possible to locate essential phenomena in multimedia formats, including representations of or information on the primary principles of Islam. While the computer-mediated materials may be produced by computer enthusiasts or professionals and exhibit considerable technological skill, they also synthesize a sense of religious obligation in between the markup code. Their dedication to the task could be in the way qur'anic interfaces are designed according to Islamic sensitivities, the selection and intergration of qur'anic quotes, the separation of symbols and sacred themes from other site content, and the distinctive application of Islamic design and identity markers throughout the Web pages.

As computer technology continues to evolve, Islamic software applications—in particular those incorporating the Qur'an—will further develop in different formats: (personal digital assistants (PDAs), CD-ROMs, web-assisted phones, and specially configured Islamic digital organizers and digital Qur'an readers (e.g., "Pocket Alim," www.intertrama.com/acart/agora.cgi "Complete Holy Quran 1.2 in Arabic," www.ia-intl.com; "Pocket Al-Muhaffiz Digital Quran," www.astrolabepictures.com/ealm.html). These and other interfaces have implications in terms of enhancing accessibility to the Qur'an, especially as information technology becomes cheaper and more accessible. The market for Islamic CD-ROM content, which represents different technological and social issues in terms of user base and access, is also one that requires further research and observations. The development of religious programs on CD can premiere products that evolve into online content (either for subscription or free use), and vice versa. Programs such as Harf Information Technology's dream analysis software, *Mufassir Al-Ahlam*, have been created that fuse Internet interfaces and Islamic elements for offline use (www.harf.com).

The line between offline and online qur'anic content may become blurred, especially when bandwidth becomes less a consideration (for some) and consumer access to the Internet widens. In terms of our observation of religious phenomena, this would herald in some cases a growing sophistication of content beyond Qur'an resources. The increasing integration of the Internet into television and other media (and vice versa) will facilitate growing accessibility to such products. It should become easier for a range of Islamic content to be made available via digital media other than "conventional" computers—hence increasing its audience.

It is difficult to generalize as to whether the Internet is a reflection of conventional understandings of either Islam or the Qur'an. Given the diversity of expression, however, it is clear that many understandings of both Islam and the Qur'an—which are seen by their various proponents as conventional—are represented online. It could also be said that through these resources new insights and affiliations in relation to qur'anic materials are being engineered through the Internet, and that through the translation of Islam into hypertext a clearer understanding of the religion in its myriad forms and dimensions is facilitated, both for Muslims and other travelers in cyberspace. Cheaper, faster, and more accessible technologies make it a straightforward process to obtain digital Islamic media—including Qur'anic content—from the Internet and other sources. Hence the potential to "Rip.Burn.Pray" as a means of approaching the Qur'an and Islamic expression has intensified.

Bibliographical Note and Acknowledgment

URL updates for this chapter can be found on www.virtuallyislamic.com. Locations of sites are based on AllWhois searches (www.allwhois.com). I am grateful to my colleague Neal Robinson and my wife Yvonne Howard-Bunt for discussing aspects of this chapter with me.

References

al-Bukhari, M. b. I. (n.d.). *Sahih Bukhari*, trans. M. M. Khan, vol. 6, Book 61, No. 545. Retrieved from www.usc.edu/dept/MSA/fundamentals/hadithsunnah/bukhari/061.sbt.html, July 7, 2003.

Bunt, G. R. (2000). *Virtually Islamic: Computer-Mediated Communication and Cyber-Islamic Environments*. Cardiff: University of Wales Press.

———. (2003). *Islam in the Digital Age: E-jihad, Online Fatwas and Cyber Islamic Environments*. London: Pluto Press.

Dawson, L. L. (2000). "Researching Religion in Cyberspace: Issues and Strategies." In *Religion on the Internet: Research Prospects and Promises*, ed. J. K. Hadden and D. E. Cowan. Amsterdam and London: JAI Press/Elsevier Science.

Hashmi, F. (2002). "Assorted Lectures." Retrieved from http://www.alhudapk.com/download/assorted/assorted.htm, March 31, 2003.

IslamiCity, (n.d.). "Qur'an: On the Internet." Question 3343, Question Date 6/10/1998, Retrieved from www.islamicity.com/qa, February 4, 2003.

Otto, R. (1923). *The Idea of the Holy: An Inquiry into the Non-Rational Factor in the Idea of the Divine and Its Relation to the Rational*, trans. J. W. Harvey. London: Oxford University Press.

Robinson, N. (1997). "Sectarian and Ideological Bias in Muslim Translations of the Qur'an." *Islam and Christian Muslim Relations*, 8 (3): 261–278.

WhatIs (n.d.). "Internet Acronyms and Lingo: Blog." Retrieved from http://whatis.techtarget.com/definition/0,289893,sid9_gci214616,00.html, July 9, 2003.

10

The Cybersangha: Buddhism on the Internet

CHARLES S. PREBISH

Introduction

This chapter considers a kind of Buddhist community, or *sangha*, never imagined by the Buddha. Nevertheless, this new and unusual *sangha* unites Buddhist practitioners and scholars worldwide into one potentially vast community: the cybersangha. The phrase "cybersangha" was coined in 1991 by Gary Ray as a generic term to describe the entire Buddhist community online. In so doing, Ray established a framework in which the traditional fourfold *sangha* of monks, nuns, laymen, and laywomen might coalesce with and enhance a broader and more pervasive *sangha*: the *sangha* of the four quarters. As such, this chapter seeks to explore some of the ways that Buddhism has made its appearance on the Internet, and to define the organizational structure of the various Buddhist sites that have emerged over the last decade. This organizational pattern is both structural and chronological, highlighting (a) the earliest resources, composed primarily of discussion forums, databases, and electronic journals; (b) the development of specific Buddhist gateways to the World Wide Web; (c) the appearance of online Buddhist religious communities; and (d) a brief look forward toward "completing the *sangha*."

Before exploring the term "cybersangha" in its various applications, we need to examine briefly the way in which the term *sangha* developed in the Buddhist tradition and came to have these several applications to specific Buddhist communities. Despite the fact that the term *sangha* is used today in a more extended and comprehensive fashion than originally, referring to almost any community or group loosely associated with Buddhism, in the time of the Buddha the term was used in a radically different fashion. The Sanskrit word *sangha* simply connotes a society or company or a number of people living together for a certain purpose. The Buddha's followers appropriated the term in a rather distinct fashion, one that gave their fledgling community a clear and unique identity. While outsiders may have referred to the Buddha's first disciples as *Śākyaputrīya-śramaṇas* or "mendicants who follow the Buddha," the original community referred to itself as the *bhikṣu-sangha*. Later, when the order of nuns was founded, they became known as the *bhikṣuṣī-sangha*, and the two units were collectively known as the *ubhayato-sangha*, the "twofold community." Occasionally, in the early literature, the Buddha used the term *cāturdisa-sangha* or the "*sangha* of the four quarters" (see, e.g., Oldenberg 1964, vol. I: 305; vol. II: 147), but it seems clear from his usage that he means the *monastic sangha*.

Eventually, however, as the wandering lifestyle deteriorated in favor of settled monasticism, the term "*sangha* of the four quarters" took on a new meaning. Akira Hirakawa suggested that this new meaning of the *sangha* referred to "a 'universal order' (*cāturdisa-sangha*) and consisted of all the disciples of the Buddha. It transcended time and place and included all the monks of the past, present, and future; it encompassed all geographical areas; it continued forever" (Hirakawa 1990: 64). Despite the fact that Hirakawa's statement greatly expands the temporal and geographic scope of the phrase *cāturdisa-sangha*, it is clear enough that *only* the Buddhist monastic assemblies are its constituent members.

Yet early Buddhist history records that the Buddha also admitted lay members into his community and that they eventually became a vital, symbiotic part of that community. The importance of the role of the laity, or what Reginald Ray (R. A. Ray 1994: 21) calls "the second normative lifestyle" of Indian Buddhism, cannot be minimized. Although the goal of the lay Buddhist is *punya* or "merit," while the monastics' goal is *arhantship* or "liberation," the two communities are clearly interdependent. To think otherwise, and especially so in the West, would be incorrect. It is not hard to see, then, how the fourfold *sangha* of monks, nuns, laymen, and laywomen came to interpenetrate and become coincident with the *sangha* of the four quarters. In other words, it is possible to use the word *sangha*, in the broadest sense, to include all Buddhists. From the above, it does not seem too far an intellectual or pragmatic stretch to suggest that the phrase "*sangha* of the four quarters," once so important for the earliest Buddhist community of monastics in India, now might be usefully applied to the whole of the fourfold Buddhist *sangha*, irrespective of sectarian affiliation, geographic location, or method of practice. What remains is to see just what the "cybersangha" is and how it might play a role in helping to generate or even complete the "harmonious order" (*samagra-sangha*) referred to in Buddhist texts.

For over a quarter-century, the International Association of Buddhist Studies has been the primary professional organization for scholars. It was launched at an international conference on the history of Buddhism held in Madison, Wisconsin, in August 1976. More than thirty scholars of Buddhism from nearly as many countries met together to present scholarly papers and create an ongoing forum and global professional society. During one of the breaks, one of the participants said: "Wouldn't it be great if we could program a computer with all the rules of Sanskrit grammar, the unique grammatical variants of Buddhist Sanskrit, and the totality of the several best Sanskrit dictionaries?

Then we could feed in Sanskrit texts and just sit back as the computer printed out the translations. Maybe we could even do the same for Chinese and Tibetan and Japanese, so we could have multilingual, comparative translations, all nicely cross-referenced." Everyone laughed, and the author of the above statement confessed that he knew he was only dreaming about the impossible. Now, a quarter-century later, everyone who participated in that discussion spends a significant portion of every day sitting in front of a computer terminal, composing electronic mail to share with colleagues around the world and creating scholarship that includes many of the Sanskrit and Chinese and Tibetan and Japanese scripts and characters they had only dreamed of previously. In addition, the International Association of Buddhist Studies now maintains a page on the World Wide Web through which news and information about the society can be shared instantly and globally.

The Earliest Internet Resources: Discussion Forums, Databases, Electronic Journals[1]

In all but the most recent books on Buddhism, not a single word is written about the role of computer technology in the development of the religion. The earliest interest in the application of computer technology to Buddhism occurred when the International Association of Buddhist Studies formed a Committee on Buddhist Studies and Computers at its 1983 meeting in Tokyo (Hubbard 1995: 310). Jamie Hubbard, in his highly significant article "Upping the Ante: budstud@millenium.end.edu," pointed out: "The three major aspects of computer technology that most visibly have taken over older technologies are word processing, electronic communication, and the development of large scale archives of both text and visual materials" (1995: 309). Hubbard went on to relate his experiences with IndraNet, an online discussion forum sponsored by the International Association of Buddhist Studies in the mid-1980s. There was little interest in the forum, and it died a largely unnoticed death within two years. Nonetheless, of the three impact items cited by Hubbard, it was clearly electronic communication that was to have the most important and continuing consequences for the development of Buddhist communities worldwide.

Early in the 1990s, a profusion of online discussion forums began to proliferate and thrive on the Internet. Although these forums were global in scope, the vast majority of subscribers and participants were from North America. One of the very first was Buddhist, founded by Yoshiyuki Kawazoe at Tohoku University in Japan. Although the traffic on the list was often frenetic, it was an exciting beginning. Because the list was unmoderated and most often concerned with various aspects of Buddhist practice and popular issues within modern Buddhism, the number of postings eventually became sufficiently unwieldy that Mr. Kawazoe decided to bequeath the list to a new owner-manager, Paul Bellan-Boyer, and the list was moved to McGill University in Canada.

During one of the periods in which the Buddhist list had broken down, Richard Hayes, a professor on the faculty of Religious Studies at McGill University, surveyed a number of subscribers to the list and discovered that many of these individuals favored beginning a separate list that was restricted to academic discussions of Buddhism and was controlled by a moderator. A new discussion forum called Buddha-L (Buddha-L@listserv.louisville.edu) was created under guidelines composed by Hayes. The forum considered scholarly discussions of virtually all aspects of Buddhism as well issues related to teaching Buddhism at the university level and occasional postings of employment opportunities in academe. Within a year, however, the group had over a thousand subscribers.

In addition to the above groups, a number of other discussion groups built an early but substantial following among Buddhists on the Internet, the best known of which was ZenBuddhism-L, founded in August 1993 at the Australian National University by Dr. T. Matthew Ciolek. This group provided a worldwide forum for the exchange of scholarly information on all aspects of Zen Buddhism. The list was eventually renamed ZenBuddhism and by June 1997 had 370 subscribers.

Lists devoted to discussions of Tibetan Buddhism and to Tibet in general also became active on the Internet. The best known of these was Tibet-L. (Tibet-L@listserv.Indiana.edu) Tibet-L subscribers tended to be academics with a predominantly scholarly interest in Tibet. For discussions of Buddhist practice, one could find Insight-L, started by John Bullitt in 1994 as an open forum, which entertained conversations about Theravāda Buddhist practice and insight meditation. Its subscribers are almost exclusively practitioners of meditation who utilize the forum to discuss their Buddhist practice in a supportive community of online listeners. There are many e-mail discussion forums, and it is not possible to list them all here. I have simply chosen to cite those which I believe, in my own idiosyncratic fashion, are the most important ones. Closely related to the online forums was an extensive network of Usenet newsgroups that provided online discussion on a wide variety of Buddhist topics, and also a series of "chat" opportunities such as Buddhist Chat, or Zen Chat, whereby seekers shared their experiences, questions, and discussions on a more immediate basis.

In February 1992, an Electronic Buddhist Archive was established by the Coombs Computing Unit of the Australian National University.[2] Under the direction of T. Matthew Ciolek, it contained over 320 original documents in ASCII format, including bibliographies, biographies, directories, Buddhist electronic texts, poetry, and the like. It also offered a unique collection of previously unpublished transcripts of teachings and sermons by many famous twentieth-century Zen masters such as Robert Aitken Rōshi, Taizan Maezumi Rōshi, Hakuun Yasutani Rōshi, and others (available at ftp://coombs.anu.edu.au/coombspapers.otherarchives/buddhism-zen/teachings). With the advent of the World Wide Web, much of the above material was consolidated into two new sites: the Buddhist Studies WWW Virtual Library, established in September 1994 and Tibetan Studies WWW Virtual Library, established in January 1995. More on this initiative will be presented in the next section of this chapter.

E-mail discussion forums and Buddhist databases were not the only form of early Buddhist activity on the Internet. As early as 1993, the first electronic Buddhist journal made its appearance. Called *Gassho*, it was edited by its founder, Barry Kapke, who operated it and other enterprises under a broad, umbrella-like organization known as DharmaNet International, founded in 1991. According to Kapke, it was published "as a service to the international Buddhist community, inclusive of all Buddhist traditions." Further, he said: "It was the first e-journal to offer peer-reviewed articles for the Buddhist Studies academic community, in concert with *practice*-oriented articles from both lay and monastic teachers. It combined news shorts with compiled listings of Buddhist resources—sitting groups, publishers, mailing lists, etc." (www.dharmanet.org/gassho.html). Kapke used the past tense in the above description because *Gassho* went on hiatus following the May-June 1994 issue.

The phrase "global online sangha," coined by Kapke, captured precisely the same mood and spirit as Gary Ray's slightly flashier term "cybersangha." Ray noted that: "This rapidly expanding 'cybersangha' provides support and community for Buddhists around the world" (G. A. Ray 1994: 60). The similarity between the projects of Kapke and Ray is no accident. At one time Ray and Kapke were close associates, although they now work separately while continuing to address common goals. It was not long before the term cybersangha began to take on a remarkably expanded meaning. In 1995, Jamie Hubbard wrote: "The network explosion is nowhere more visible than in the growth of the 'cybersangha,' the online communities of Buddhist practitioners. Sometimes representative of one or another traditional communities but more often than not virtual communities existing only in cyberspace, most every sort of discussion group and resource can now be located online" (1995: 313).

Gassho notwithstanding, another online electronic journal would eventually provide the occasion for an immensely rapid and continued growth in the cybersangha by exploiting yet another electronic medium for the dissemination of information: the World Wide Web. The *Journal of Buddhist Ethics* (http://jbe.gold.ac.uk) was born in July 1994. It was originally planned as a traditional, hard-copy scholarly journal by its editors, but they quickly learned that potential publishers had little interest in a highly specialized, purely academic journal that was not likely to turn a profit. One of the coeditors, Damien Keown, suggested publishing the journal online, where there would be no expenses and where the journal could provide a useful service to its constituent community, however tiny that might be. Once a technical editor was added to the staff, plans rapidly moved ahead, making the journal available via the World Wide Web as well as through FTP and Gopher retrieval. The journal went "online" on July 1, 1994, with no articles but with a Web page outlining the aims of the journal and listing its editorial board members. It advertised its presence on a small number of electronic newsgroups, and within a week had a hundred subscribers. By the end of 1994, it had over four hundred subscribers in twentysix countries, managed by a Listserv created by the technical editor. It grew to more than fifteen hundred subscribers in over fifty countries by June 1997 and eventually to 3500 subscribers in sixty countries by 2002. Early in its development, the journal's editorial board recognized what an incredibly potent medium the World Wide Web was for expanding the availability of both scholarly and nonacademic information on Buddhism.

Eventually, the journal began a new section called "Global Resources for Buddhist Studies." The editors discovered rather quickly that many communities of Buddhist practitioners began requesting that links to their own developing Web pages be listed with the *Journal of Buddhist Ethics.* In other words, it became clear that the World Wide Web in general was indeed growing immensely and quickly, furnishing a unique opportunity for communication that Buddhist communities had never known before. Although it was by no means unique in its establishment of a jumping-off point for the exploration of additional Buddhist resources of all kinds on the Web, along with DharmaNet International and the WWW Virtual Libraries at the Australian National Universities, the *Journal of Buddhist Ethics* provided a new way of thinking about Buddhist communities, one that augmented Gary Ray's cybersangha and Barry Kapke's global online sangha.

Buddhist Gateways to the World Wide Web

About the same time as the *Journal of Buddhist Ethics* was implementing its section on "Global Resources in Buddhist Studies," with links to other Buddhist sites and resources on the still-infant Web, Hsuan Peng, a graduate student in Mechanical Engineering at Cornell University, was compiling a similar list of resources to post on Buddha-L. Hsuan Peng's initial list, posted in November 1994, had fewer than twenty entries. By the time of Hsuan Peng's graduation and return to Taiwan in 1996, the file had grown to over 160 listings. One year prior to his departure, Connie Neal created a Web version of the file (in June 1995). It was the most clearly organized and comprehensive record of Buddhist resources on the Web.

Obviously, the growth of the World Wide Web was astronomical in the latter half of the 1990s, and the listings of Buddhist communities and resources were no less dramatic. As such, it has been extremely difficult to keep track of this huge growth in Buddhist Web pages and to organize the various *categories* of pages into a user-friendly environment. In fact, while most groups routinely link to other Buddhist resources on the Web, very few sites make any attempt whatsoever to explain the logic of their own linking procedure or the criteria that govern their choices for inclusion. What follows is a summary of several of the most useful Buddhist resource gateways to the World Wide Web. Of the few sites that do offer an organizational pattern for the presentation of links to various Buddhist resources, five stand out above the rest: DharmaNet International (www.dharmanet.org), created and maintained by Barry Kapke; the Buddhist Studies WWW Virtual Library, created and maintained by Dr. T. Matthew Ciolek; the Buddhist Resource File, (http://sino-sv3.sino.uni-heidelperg.de/ BRF/) created by Hsuan Peng but now operating as a joint project of the National Taiwan University and Chung Hwa Institute of Buddhist Studies; BuddhaNet, (www.buddhanet.net), maintained by the Buddha Dharma Education Association; and H-Buddhism (www.h-net.org/~buddhism), created by Charles Muller of Toyo Gakuen University. Each has a unique approach to managing and presenting Buddhist resources in cyberspace, as will become apparent as we explore each resource.

DharmaNet International

Kapke describes what he calls "Gateways to Buddhism" as "an online clearinghouse for Buddhist Study and practice resources." Gateways to Buddhism is organized around eighteen distinct categories, not structured in a hierarchical framework but rather as "a centralized clearinghouse for Buddhist information, online and offline."[3] The most extensive section of DharmaNet's listings fall under the heading "Buddhist InfoWeb." This section is comprised of two major divisions. First, there is "General Directories: Buddhist Centers and Practice Groups." This is a listing of web links to about thirty various directories and centers, mostly outside the United States, each of which provides further links to the individual groups falling into the domain of that particular topic. The second major division in this section is devoted to "Online Buddhist Centers and Information," and is internally subdivided into separate listings for the Theravāda, Tibetan/Vajrayāna, Zen/Ch'an, Jōdo Shinshū/Pure Land Traditions, and Other Traditions.

An "Interlinks" section on Buddhist Studies Resources is also subdivided into sections on (1) Buddhist Databases and Input Projects, citing such items as the Asian Classics Input Project; (2) Buddhist Studies Academic Resources, including widely diverse resources like the huge complex of materials at the Center for Buddhist Studies at the National Taiwan University and the Numata Center for Buddhist Translation and Research in Berkeley, California; and (3) Non-Academic Buddhist Study Resources, linking to sites such as the *Journal of Buddhist Ethics'* online conference on Buddhism and Human Rights.

The remaining sections deliver essentially just what each section title indicates, but it is worth noting that Kapke cites nearly two dozen online journals of general Buddhist interest and another half-dozen purely academic journals. One can see that DharmaNet International's site is comprehensive, stimulating, and thoroughly infused with the passion and compassion of its founder. It is enormously popular too.

Buddhist Studies–Tibetan Studies WWW Virtual Libraries

As noted above, the Buddhist Studies WWW Virtual Library was established in September 1994 (later also incorporating the Tibetan studies www Virtual Library). Not only are prospective links evaluated prior to inclusion on the main site, but sites that are no longer successful are periodically removed. In other words, the facility maintains rigorous quality control. The Buddhist Studies WWW Virtual Library is organized into twelve primary areas, each of which is further subdivided through additional Web links:

Buddhism Internet Resources: Meta-Register
Buddhism Major WWW Sites
Electronic Resources for the Study of Buddhist Texts
Buddhism Gopher, FTP, Mailing Lists & Chat-Rooms Resources
Buddhism/Buddhist Electronic Newsletters & Journals (including
    Bibliographies)
Buddhist InfoWeb (a link to DharmaNet International's metadirectory)
Buddhist Art
Pure Land Buddhism WWW Virtual Library
Tibetan Studies WWW Virtual Library
Zen Buddhism WWW Virtual Library
Tibet Online Bookstore and Zen Online Bookstore (linked to amazon.com)
Other Religions' Networked Resources

While there is an obvious similarity between this table of contents and that of DharmaNet International, the differing emphases of the two enterprises are almost immediately apparent upon a cursory exploration of the individual areas.

Under Buddhism Major WWW Sites, The WWW Virtual Library offers three major subdivisions: (1) The Academic Study of Buddhism; (2) The Study and Practice of Buddhism; and (3) Introductions to Buddhism. Although the academic servers reveal clearly what their names imply, including the Berkeley Buddhist Research Center, the Buddhist Studies Centre at the University of Bristol, the Center for Buddhist Studies at the National Taiwan University, and a Web Guide to Graduate Studies in Asian Philosophy and Religion (housed at Toyo Gakuen University in Japan), the Buddhism sites are less practitioner-oriented and more scholar-oriented than one might expect. The second major subdivision is broken down into a seemingly tradition-based series of sites, but many of the links in that tradition-based series are to academic or scholarly resources.

The section on Electronic Resources for the Study of Buddhist Texts includes general information sites such as the Classical Sanskrit Fonts Project at the University of Virginia; input projects and online archives, such as the Electronic Buddhist Text Initiative of Hanazono University in Japan; translation projects, such as the WWW Buddhist Canon Translation Project at Ohio State

University; and citations of the many Buddhist texts available online. The above resources are almost certainly the site of choice for scholars and those in the academic community, who will be able to find links to almost every online resource for Buddhist Studies that is available throughout the world.

Buddhist Resource File

If Buddhist Web surfers find DharmaNet International or the Buddhist Studies–Tibetan Studies WWW Virtual Libraries confusing or inconvenient, it can only be because of the sites' chosen perspectives or their somewhat eclectic methods of organizing the immense amount of material collected. The Buddhist Resource File begun by Hsuan Peng in November 1994—and now called the Buddhist Internet Resource—provides the perfect solution to the problems of perspective and organizational methodology. When Connie Neal assumed the responsibility for continually updating the Buddhist Resource File, in 1995, her first efforts involved individually inserting the proper HTML codes in each entry. Eventually, she was able to employ a technology package developed by Bryan O'Sullivan called Bibliography Mode that automatically converted bibliography files to HTML files and allowed keyword searching that would produce highly restricted and stylized returns of the applicable records. The keywords that are available for searching are organized into four main categories: General (including bibliographies, biographies, cartoons, chat, dictionaries, directories, e-magazines, images, Listservs, sound files, texts, information on women's groups, and the like), Traditions, Languages, and Books and Supplies.

Within each main category there is an extensive and alphabetically arranged subdivision, yielding an easy navigational path for any searcher. Each keyword search within any subdivision yields an alphabetical listing for the information requested. Further, each individual listing offers a description of the site, if applicable, its Internet location (either e-mail, Web URL, or both), and the date of the latest update verification. In some cases, contact persons, mailing addresses, and telephone numbers or fax numbers are provided. At the end of each subdivision, a list of references is provided, citing the names of individuals who assisted in the development and updating of that subdivision. The Buddhist Resource File offers an admirable balance between academic or scholarly sites and those of practitioner communities. And because this site presents materials in a variety of foreign languages, computer-literate Buddhiss can also navigate their way to valuable materials in the own language. It has mirror sites at the Ohio State University and Heidelberg University.

BuddhaNet

BuddhaNet identifies itself as a "Buddhist Information and Education Network" and tries to provide a balanced picture of all aspects of Buddhism for the literate practitioner. It is carefully organized into major sections devoted to Buddhist Studies, Meditation, an Archived File Library, a BuddhaZine, BuddhaNet Audio files, a World Buddhist Directory (subdivided by continent), and an eBook Library. The eBook library—subdivided into sections on general Buddhism, meditation methods, Theravāda teachings, and Mahāyāna teachings—is the first Buddhist Internet site to utilize this interesting new approach to online publication. In addition to the major sections, BuddhaNet offers its users a What's New on BuddhaNet link as well as information on the sites special features. The World Buddhist Directory is especially useful to individuals looking for practitioner communities in their vicinity and provides a free alternative to printed locator volumes such as Don Morreale's *The Complete Guide to Buddhist America*. It also offers a section on Buddhism on the Internet, which is very useful to Web surfers. If BuddhaNet is perhaps less exhaustive than the other Buddhist Internet gateways in the volume of resources it presents, it is clearer in its focus on the practitioner rather than academic.

H-Buddhism

H-Buddhism takes the opposite approach, centering almost solely on academic materials and information. The brainchild of Charles Muller, a United States-trained scholar now teaching at Toyo Gakuen University in Tokyo, this resource began as the Buddhist Scholars Information Network, or "budschol" for short. It was designed to link Buddhist Studies scholars worldwide in an academic information network providing almost instant access to specific and sometimes extremely sophisticated information needed by any of its subscribers. To make certain that the focus of the list remained entirely academic rather than practitioner-oriented, Muller required subscribers to have demonstrable academic credentials in Buddhist Studies. Personal rather than professional communication was relegated to off-list pursuit, and in so doing, the volume of messages posted and the integrity of inquiries was maintained. Not long after the beginning of the current millennium, the group moved to the H-Net family of discussion lists hosted by Michigan State University. H-Buddhism's Web home page includes a series of "Buddhist Studies Links Hosted by Members." This section consists of a tidy group of about thirty resources, ranging from Muller's own *Chinese–Japanese–Korean to English Dictionary* to the American Academy of Religion's "Buddhism Section" Web site. Also included are online bibliographies, online academic journals, and a vast amount of resources for the study of East Asian forms of Buddhism. It is the most sophisticated and useful avenue of entry for Buddhist Studies scholarship on the Internet.

Irrespective of which World Wide Web search engine or resource file one uses, including many not mentioned above, the possibility exists for any Internet-linked Buddhist to connect with the enormous richness of the Buddhist tradition throughout the world. By using the ability to navigate through cyberspace, the practitioner can remain an active part of a Buddhist community in which he or she does not reside. Equally important, the scholar of Buddhism can access indispensable research materials on the other side of the globe without ever leaving the computer keyboard. And the scholar-practitioner can do both of the above easily and effortlessly. Yet there is another important application for the technology described in this chapter: it can provide for some practitioners a Buddhist community *without location in real space*, as a means either of intellectual or other kinds of communication or of providing an opportunity for learning and practicing with the pragmatic intention of deepening one's Buddhist practice. It is worth examining some of these landmark efforts aimed at redefining Buddhism in an important new way.

Some Buddhist Cybercommunities

There seem to be at least three major types of online Buddhist practitioner-oriented communities. First, there are Web pages created by many traditional American Buddhist groups as communication tools and conveniences for their members. Some of these latter communities have created enormously complex pages which, if all the linked resources were actually printed in hard copy, would extend to hundreds of pages of documents. Second, there are virtual temples created by traditional *sanghas* as an *addition* to their existing programs. Third, there are a number of communities that exist nowhere except in cyberspace; that is, they have no actual home in geographic space anywhere.

In *Luminous Passage: The Practice and Study of Buddhism in America* (Prebish 1999), I highlighted three cybersanghas (of the third kind): the True Freedom Cyber-Temple, the White Path Temple, and cybersangha: The Buddhist Alternative Journal. It is hard to imagine a Buddhist community with no location in real space: no buildings, no shrine, no supportive lay community of believers, no ritual practices or meditation. Yet in early March 1996 a truly formless community called the True Freedom Cyber-Temple made its debut on the Internet. It no longer exists. Nor does the White Path Temple, a product of the Shin Buddhist community. It was a far more extensive online resource, having links to almost all the online Jōdo Shinshū resources. The *Cybersangha* journal first appeared earlier, in 1995, and despite its ambitious mission dedicated to exploring electronic means of promoting Buddhist practice, within a few years it was gone too. Clearly, Buddhist cyberspace is highly ephemeral, a living personification of Buddha's law of impermanence. That, however, does not mean that new and equally creative online communities and projects have not appeared to fill the void left by now-defunct sites. Nonetheless, there seem to be fewer rather than more of these communities with existence in cyberspace only and with no existence in real geographic space. Presumably, this reflects a renewed acknowledgment of the necessity for face-to-face encounter between teacher and student and between *sangha* members in general.

Virtual temples created by traditional *sanghas* as additions to their existing temples also seem to be on the decline on the Internet. Instead, Buddhist communities worldwide are focusing more energy on creating single but comprehensive Web pages that capture the entirety of their respective *sangha's* programs and emphases. As such, it is not unusual to find links on these communities' Web pages to their programs for adults and children, educational materials, publication efforts, retreats, online lectures, "engaged Buddhism" activities, interfaith dialogues, and the like. In North America alone, there are nearly two thousand Buddhist communities, with as many as half of them hosting Webpages of some form. In *Luminous Passage*, I highlighted Zen Mountain Monastery in Mount Tremper, New York, as one of the most significant Buddhist communities in the United States. Its Web page (www.zen-mtn.org) remains an exemplary model for Buddhist communities on the Internet. I retain fond memories of a day in 1995 when Daido Rōshi, the abbot, told me that for his students his interest in utilizing computer technology and the Internet "kind of blew away their overly romantic image of Zen."

Completing the *Sangha*

At the outset of this chapter, we discussed the traditional meanings of the term *sangha*. We learned that in the initial and strictest use of the term, *sangha* referred to the community of ordained Buddhist monks and nuns, later called the "*sangha* of the four quarters" and extending beyond mere geographic space. Eventually, in using a wider application of the term, *sangha* came to mean the entire fourfold community of monks, nuns, laymen, and laywomen, and we suggested that this latter usage might be subsumed under the former meaning so that the phrase "*sangha* of the four quarters" would truly transcend geographical, temporal, and sectarian boundaries.

Now we have learned that if the "*sangha* of the four quarters" is to be a fully comprehensive term, it must also include the "cybersangha" in its various meanings as the entire Buddhist community online and/or the specific Buddhist *sangha* of a particular, spatially located community. In other words, further considerations of the ongoing development of the Buddhist *sangha* must necessarily include this important aspect of community life. Joachim Steingrubner says as much: "The CyberSangha can be seen as a subset of the all-encompassing Sangha, a community of persons who actively scout their way to truth; who have, as an additional gift, the ability to communicate instantly without regard for their geographical proximities—an ability which would have been considered a siddhi, a magical power, just a couple of decades ago" (Steingrubner 1995). More than fifteen years ago, the 1987 Conference on World Buddhism in North America, held at the University of Michigan, affirmed a "Statement of Consensus:"

(1) To create the conditions necessary for tolerance and understanding among Buddhists and non-Buddhists alike.

(2) To initiate a dialogue among Buddhists in North America in order to further mutual understanding, growth in understanding, and cooperation.

(3) To increase our sense of community by recognizing and understanding our differences as well as our common beliefs and practices.

(4) To cultivate thoughts and actions of friendliness towards others, whether they accept our beliefs or not, and in so doing approach the world as the proper field of Dharma, not as a sphere of conduct irreconcilable with the practice of Dharma. (cited in Rosch 1987: 28)

Certainly it is the inclusion of the cybersangha as a new constituent of the *sangha* of the four quarters that further enables and more deeply enhances the still profound consensus affirmed above. Nor should we lose sight of the fact that it is the *sangha* which completes and empowers the traditional Three Jewels of Buddhism. Yet we should also not lose sight of the fact that it is possible to construe the cybersangha as a true sign of the cold, rational, contemporary world in which communication is faceless and even impersonal. For many, the loss of face-to-face encounter, personal support, and shared practice in real space may be a strong liability that undermines the potential value of the cybersangha. Buddhist practitioners continue to struggle to find a sane balance between their easy access to and personal use of the Internet, and their need for direct human encounter. That sane balance may well be the final expression of Buddhism as the religion of "the middle path."

Notes

1. It must be understood from the outset that the Buddhist resources on the Internet cited in this chapter are not intended to represent a comprehensive listing. Such an attempt is probably not desirable in a book of this nature, nor is it a realistic possibility due to the transient, ephemeral nature of many Internet resources and the occasional changing of Internet addresses. As such, in most cases all but the most stable Internet addresses are excluded. To locate the resources cited in this chapter, one can consult any of the traditional search engines currently used on the World Wide Web.

2. I am deeply indebted to Dr. T. Matthew Ciolek for providing a most lucid account of the development of the vast array of electronic materials devoted to Buddhism at the Australian National University. All information on the Coombs Computing Unit of the Australian National University derives from his kind assistance.

3. E-mail correspondence from Barry Kapke, June 23, 1997.

References

Hirakawa, A. (1990). *A History of Indian Buddhism: From (Sākyamuni to Early Mahāyāna*, trans. and ed. P. Groner. Honolulu: University of Hawaii Press.

Hubbard, J. (1995). "Upping the Ante: budstud@millenium.end.edu." *Journal of the International Association of Buddhist Studies* 18 (2): 309–22.

Oldenberg, H., ed. (1964). *The Vinaya* Pitaka, 5 vols. London: Luzac and Company, reprint.

Prebish, C. S. (1999). *Luminous Passage: The Practice and Study of Buddhism in America*. Berkeley, CA: University of California Press.

Ray, G. A. (1994). "A Resource Roundup for the Cybersangha." *Tricycle: The Buddhist Review* 3 (4): 60–63.

Ray, R. A. (1994). *Buddhist Saints in India: A Study in Buddhist Values and Orientations*. New York: Oxford University Press.

Rosch, E. (1987). "World Buddhism in North America Today." *Vajradhatu Sun* 9 (1).

Steingrubner, J. H. (1995). "CyberSangha: Building Buddhist Community Online." *CyberSangha: The Buddhist Alternative Journal* (Fall). Retrieved from www.worldtrans.org/CyberSangha/steinf95.htm, June 10, 2003.

III
New Religions in Cyberspace

11

New Religions and the Internet: Recruiting in a New Public Space

LORNE L. DAWSON AND JENNA HENNEBRY

Concerns after Heaven's Gate

Twice in 1998 the first author of this paper was asked to speak to groups in our community about the presence of "cults"[1] on the World Wide Web and the threat they might pose. These talks were prompted, undoubtedly, by the tragic death of the thirty nine members of Heaven's Gate at Rancho Sante Fe, California, on March 26, 1997. To the surprise of many, it seems, the media reports of this strange and ceremonious mass suicide revealed a group with its own elaborate Web page. What is more, this new religion designed sophisticated Web pages for other organizations. In fact, it received much of its income from a company called Higher Source, operated by its members. Heaven's Gate had been using the Internet for several years to communicate with some of its followers and to spread its message. This news generated a special measure of curiosity and fear from some elements of the public.[2] This reaction stemmed, we suspect, from the coincidental confluence of the misunderstanding and consequent mistrust of both the new technology and of cults.

Despite the ballyhoo accorded the launch of the "information superhighway" (by the government, the computer industry, and the media), in 1997, the Internet was still used with any regularity by only a relatively small percentage of the population.[3] In the absence of personal experience, the Web was popularly thought to be the creature of those believed to be its primary users: large corporations on the one hand (from Microsoft to Nike), and isolated "computer nerds" on the other. Most certainly, religious organizations are not commonly associated in the public perception with such leading-edge technologies (despite the omnipresence of televangelists on the America airwaves). For most North Americans, in fact, the topic of religion calls to mind churches, and the churches are associated with traditionalism, if not with an element of hostility to the cultural influence of developments in science and technology. New religious movements, in addition, are still rather crudely seen as havens for the socially marginal and perhaps even personally deficient individuals—those least likely or capable of mastering the social and technical demands of a new world order. The image, then, of cultists exploiting the Web seemed incongruous to many. Combined with the established suspicion of "cults" (e.g., Pfeifer 1992; Bromley and Breschel 1992) and the almost mystical power often attributed to the Internet itself, the example set by Heaven's Gate seemed ominous.

When compared with the familiar media used to distribute religious views, such as books, videos, tapes, radio, and television, Internet sites are easily accessible and in many respects more economical to produce and operate. With the appropriate knowledge and minimal computer hardware and software, anyone can sample a wide array of alternative religious views and, if they so choose, just as easily hide their exposure or consumption of such views from the prying eyes of others (e.g., parents, partners, friends, or employers). In fact, the Internet opens surprising new opportunities even to start one's own religion (as will be discussed below).

Have cults found in the Internet, then, a new and more effective means to recruit members? If so, has the World Wide Web changed the playing field, so to speak, allowing quite small and unusual groups unprecedented access to a new and impressionable audience of potential converts and supporters?

Most scholars of new religious movements would be sceptical, we think, that the advent of the World Wide Web offered any reason for renewed concern about the presumed threat posed by "cults" to mainstream society. Within days of the Heaven's Gate deaths, however, several media stories appeared in prominent sources (e.g., *New York Times, Time* magazine, *Newsweek*, and CNN), raising the prospect of "spiritual predators" on the Internet. In the words of George Johnson in *The New York Times*:

> In the public mind—moulded by news reports on the old media, which are still more powerful and pervasive than anything on-line—the Internet is starting to seem like a scary place, a labyrinth of electronic tunnels as disturbing and seedy as anything Thomas Pynchon has dreamed up for the bizarre worlds in such works as *Gravity's Rainbow, V* and *Vineland*. The Heaven's Gate suicides can only amplify fears that, in some quarters, may be already bordering on hysteria. The Internet, it seems, might be used to lure children not only to shopping malls, where some "sicko" waits, but into joining UFO cults. (See the version reprinted in Canada's national newspaper, *The Globe and Mail*, April 5, 1997: C27)

CNN's online newsmagazine carried these suspicions further (http://cnn.com/TECH/9703/27/techno.pagans/index.html), citing comments from presumed experts on the Web, like Erik Davis of *Wired* magazine, and 'experts' on cults, like Margaret T. Singer. The story, posted under the heading "The Internet as a God and Propaganda Tool for Cults," sought to create the impression that "computer nerds" and other compulsive denizens of the Internet, might be particularly susceptible to cult recruitment (and hence eventually to abuse). In Davis's view, "identifying more and more of your life with what's happening on the other side of the [computer] screen . . ." can have a "very dissociative effect," increasing the risk of cult conversion. What is more, Singer assures us, the cults are targeting these very people: "What the cults want to recruit are average, normal, bright people and especially, in recent years, people with technical skills, like computer skills. And often, they haven't become street smart. And they're too gullible."

Wisely, the stories in *The New York Times* and *Time* magazine (April 7, 1997) both seek to cast doubt on such scaremongering. They each seek to do so, however, by defending the integrity of the World Wide Web and not the cults. Their pointed concern is to dissociate the Internet as a neutral means of communication from its use by religions (i.e., do not confuse the medium with the message). No effort is made to even begin to address the realities of cult recruitment in general, let alone their actual use of the Internet.

So what do we know about cult recruitment and the World Wide Web? Do we have reason to believe that the Internet either has or someday could become a significant source of new converts? Is there something to worry about?

This paper examines and compares what we know about the presence of new religious movements on the Internet and how people come to join these groups. The most reliable results of decades of research into religious conversions cast doubt on the special utility of the World Wide Web as a mechanism of recruitment. Face-to-face social interactions and networks of personal relationships play too large a role in the data about conversions collected by scholars. Further, previous studies suggest that such "disembodied appeals" as religious advertisements, radio shows, and televangelism have little significant effect on rates of religious recruitment (Lofland 1966; Shupe 1976; Snow, Zurcher, and Ekland-Olson 1980; Rochford 1982; Hoover 1988). But these are broadcast media and largely under the control of a relatively small elite. Might things be different within the interactive and more democratic—even anarchic—conditions of cyberspace? At present we cannot say, because there is little reliable information and because it is too soon. Discussions of the nature and impact of the new public space opened up by the Internet, however, suggest that the emergence of the World Wide Web may be changing the conditions of new religious life in our societies in significant ways. There are both promise and peril in the new technologies of cyberspace for the future of religion.

Our analysis of these matters is augmented with insights drawn from two surveys: our own survey of the "Web meisters" of several new religious movements, and an online profile of Internet users. In the late spring of 1998, we surveyed the Web page creators of thirty groups by e-mail (see Table 11.1). The brief survey asked twenty three questions, delving into such matters as the origins of their Web pages, whether professional help was used in their design or updating, whether the pages were official or unofficial in status, the primary purposes of the Web pages, their level of satisfaction with the Web pages and what measures of success they used, the mechanisms used for inviting feedback (if at all), the nature of the feedback received and the responses given, any knowledge of whether people had become affiliated with their groups as a

Table 11.1 Survey Sample—New Religious Movements on the Internet (as of May 1998)

Group	Site Name	URL Site Location*
A.R.E.	A.R.E. Inc.	http://www.are-cayce.com
Aumism	Aumism—Universal Religion	http://www.aumisme.org/gb/
BOTA	BOTA Home page (Builders Of The Atydum)	http://www.atanda.com/bota/default.html
Brahma Kumaris	Brahma Kumaris W.S.O.	http://www.rajayoga.com
	Brahma Kumaris W.S.O.	http://www bkwsu.com
Church Universal and Triumphant	Our Church (Church Universal and Triumphant)	http://www.tsl.org/intro/church.html
Churches of Christ	Boston Church of Christ	http://www.bostoncoc.org
	International Churches of Christ	http://www.intlcc.com
Covenant of the Goddess	Covenant of the Goddess	http://www.canjure.com
Eckankar	Eckankar	http://www.eckankar.org
Foundation for Inner	A Course in Miracles—ACIM	http://www.acim.org
Peace (ACIM)	Miracles web site	http://www.miraclesmedia.org
International Society for Krishna Consciousness	ISKON.NET A Hare Krishna Network	http://iskcon.net
Meher Baba Group	Meher Baba Group	http://davey.sunyerie.edu/mb.html
MSIA	MSIA—Movement of Spiritual Inner Awareness	http://www.msia.com
Ordo Templi Orientis	Hodos Chamelionis Camp of the Ordo Templi Orientis	http://pw2.netcom.com/~bry-guy/hcc-oto.html
	Thelema	http://www.crl.com/~thelema.home.html
Osho	Meditation: The Science of the Inner	http://www.osho.org/homepage. html
Raelians	International Raelian Movement	http://www.rael.org
Rosicrucian Order	Rosicrucian Order (English) AMORC Home Page	http://www.rosicrucian.org
	AMORC International	http://www.amorc.org
School of Wisdom	School of Wisdom Home Page	http://ddi.digital.net/~wisdom/school/welcome.html

Group	Site Name	URL Site Location*
Scientology	Scientology: Scientology Home Page	http://www.scientology.org
Shambhala	Welcome to Shambhala	http://www.shambhala.org
Shirdi Sai Baba	Shirdi Sai Baba	http://www.saiml.com
Sikh Dharma (3HO)	International Directory of Kundalini Yoga Centers (3HO)	http://www.sikhnet.com
Soka Gakkai	Soka Gakkai International Public Info Site	http://www.sgi.org
	Soka Gakkai International– USA (SGI-USA)	http://www.sgi-usa.org
Subud	SUBUD: The World Subud Association Website	http://www.subud.org/ english.menu.html
Quest for Utopia (Koufuku no Kagaku)	Quest for Utopia Institute Research Human Happiness (Koufuku no Kagaku)	http://www.quest-utopia.com http://www.quest-utopia.com/ info/irh.html
Temple of Set	Temple's of Set	http://www.xeper.org
	Balanone's Temple of Set Information	http://www.balanone.info
The Family	The Family—An International Christian Fellowship	http://www.thefamily.org
TM	The Transcendental Meditation Program	http://www.TM.org
Unification Church	Unification Church Home Page	http://www.unification.org
Urantia	Urantia Foundation	http://www.urantia.org
Wicca	Wiccan Church of Canada Home Page	http://www.wcc.on.ca
	Welcome to Daughters of the Moon (Dianic Wicca)	http://www.wco.com/ ~moonwmyn/index.html

*URLs may no longer be accurate

result of contact with the Web page, and their views on whether and how the World Wide Web should be regulated. . . .

New Religions on the Net

We do not know much about how surfing the Web may have contributed to anyone joining a new religious movement (NRM). With the exception of the brief forays undertaken by Cottee, Yateman, and Dawson (1996: 459–468) and Bainbridge (1997: 149–155), we know of no specific studies, popular or academic, of this subject. The journalist Jeff Zaleski has written an interesting book about religion and the Internet called *The Soul of Cyberspace* (Zaleski 1997). It contains some fascinating interviews with religious figures from many of the world's religions that have already heavily invested in the Internet as a tool of religious discourse (from the Chabad-Lubavitch Jews of New York, at www.chabad.org, to Zen Buddhists, at www.dharma.net/ dc.shtml). It also contains some equally intriguing conversations with a few of the founding or influential figures of cyberspace and virtual reality about the possible interface of religion and cyberspace. Zaleski's attention, however, is directed to discerning whether anyone thinks that religious services can be performed authentically over the Web, and how. Can the spiritual essence of religion, the subtle energies of *prana*, as he calls it, be adequately conveyed by the media of cyberspace? Or will such hyperreal simulations always be inadequate to the task? The question of recruitment arises in his discussions, but it is never explored in any detail. On the contrary, in his comments on Heaven's Gate and the threat posed by "cults" on the Internet, Zaleski displays a level of prejudice and misunderstanding that is out of keeping with the rest of his book:

> Those most vulnerable to a cult's message—the lonely, the shy, misfits, outcasts—are often attracted to the Net, relishing its power to allow communion with others while maintaining anonymity. While the Net offers an unprecedented menu of choice, it also allows budding fanatics to focus on just one choice—to tune into the same Web site, the same newsgroup, again and again, for hours on end, shut off from all other stimuli—to isolate themselves from conflicting beliefs. Above all, the headiness of cyberspace, its divorce from the body and the body's incarnate wisdom, gives easy rise to fantasy, paranoia, delusions of grandeur. (Zaleski 1997: 249)

In echoing the comments of Davis and Singer, Zaleski is rather unreflexive about his own and others' fascination with religion on the Internet.

Reports on the Web say that Heaven's Gate did contact people by e-mail and through conversations tried to involve them in their activities, even encouraged them to leave home and join the main group in California. One particular conversation between a member of the group and an adolescent in Minnesota has been recorded (we are told), and it does not seem unreasonable to presume that there were more. How many? How successful were these contacts? Who knows? Reports in the news of the past lives of some of the thirtynine people who died indicated that a few of the members first contacted the group through the Internet.[4] But we lack details of how and of what happened. Did these people know of the group before or not? Had they been involved in similar groups before? Did the Internet contact play a significant or a merely peripheral role in the decisions they made about joining Heaven's Gate? There are a lot of important questions that have yet to be answered.

Was the recruiting done over the Internet part of a fully sanctioned and prepared strategy of Heaven's Gate or something simply done by enthusiastic members—like an evangelist in any tradition taking advantage of opportunities as they arise? At present we do not know.

Here we briefly describe the presence of new religions on the Internet. Then we place our discussion in context by looking at the scholarly record about who joins NRMs and how, to see how this data fits with the results of our survey of the creators of Web pages for the NRMs and the survey of the users of the Internet.

Heaven's Gate did have a relatively flashy Web site (for its time) making a lot of information available, although it was of variable quality. The site employed many colourful graphics, but in the main it consisted of programmatic statements of the group's beliefs, focused on the role played by aliens from space in the past, present, and future life of humankind. Undergirding all was the warning that a great change was at hand: "The earth's present 'civilization' is about to be recycled—spaded under. Its inhabitants are refusing to evolve. The 'weeds' have taken over the garden and disturbed its usefulness beyond repair." In the days immediately preceding the mass suicide of the group, the Web page declared: "Red Alert. HALE-BOPP Brings Closure." It was time for the loyal followers of their leader, Do, to abandon their earthy "containers" in preparation for being carried off by a UFO, thought to be accompanying the comet Hale-Bopp, to a new home at "The Evolutionary Level Beyond Human," somewhere else in the galaxy. Few if any people, it now seems clear, were listening or chose to take their warnings seriously—an interesting indicator of the real limits on the vaunted power of the Web as a means of religious "broadcasting".

Apart from the imminent character of its apocalyptic vision, the Heaven's Gate Web site is fairly representative of the presence of NRMs on the Internet. Most of the better-known new religions (e.g., Scientology, Krishna Consciousness, the Unification Church, Soka Gakkai, the Church Universal and Triumphant, Eckankar, Osho, Sri Sai Baba) have had Web sites of some sophistication (in graphics, text, and options) for several years (see Table 11.1). The respondents to our survey said their sites were launched in 1995 or very early in 1996, when the World Wide Web was still more or less in its infancy. In addition, there are literally thousands of other sites for more obscure religious or quasi-religious groups. Most of these sites are official in some sense, although some are privately run by devotees and others, and most simply replicate in appearance and content the kind of material available in other, publications by these groups; the Web materials are often meant to be downloaded as a ready substitute for more conventional publications.

Most of these sites offer ways of establishing further contact to obtain more materials (e.g., pamphlets, books, tapes, and videos) and to access courses, lectures, and other programs by e-mail, telephoanne numbers, or mailing addresses (Table 11.2). All of our respondents indicated that this was an important feature of their sites, most claiming that they respond to several

Table 11.2 Inventory of New Religious Movements on the Internet, Detailed

Group	Keywords	Design	Interactiveness	Special Features	E-mail	Phone	Mail
		Site Characteristics			Communications		
A.R.E.	13	advanced	high	audio, links, books	x	x	x
Aumism	*93	average	med-high	petition	x	x	x
BOTA	*34	advanced	high (Java)	multilanguage, regional, free brochure	x	x	x
Brahma Kumaris	7	advanced	med	books, regional links	x		
Church Universal and Triumphant	*49	average	low	regional links, multilanguage	x	x	x
Churches of Christ (Boston)	–	advanced	med	regional links, directory	x		x
Covenant of the Goddess	5	average	med-low	Web ring, regional links	x		x
Eckankar	*20	advanced	med	free books		x	x
Foundation for Inner Peace (ACIM)	–	basic	low	catalog, mailing list	x	x	x
International Society for Krishna Consciousness	49	advanced	high (Java)	audio, site host, search engine, international	x		x
Meher Baba Group	–	average	low	products, organization links	x		
Movement of Spiritual Inner Awareness	*19	advanced	med	multilanguage	x		
Ordo Templi Orientis	–	basic	low	links to other Thelemic sites	x		
Osho	*14	advanced	high	audio talks, online shopping	x	x	x

Organization	Keywords*	Level	Interactivity	Features		
Quest for Utopia (Koufuku no Kagaku)	–	average	high (Java)	audio, languages (Japanese)	x	
Raelians	–	advanced	low	multilanguage, multigeographical, counter	x	x
Rosicrucian Order	–	basic	med-low	free booklet, counter	x	x
School of Wisdom	11	average	high (Java)	guestbook	x	x
Scientology	*31	advanced	high (Java)	free info, film, search engine, multilanguage	x	x
Shambhala	*32	advanced	med	international server	x	
Sikh Dharma (3HO)	*39	advanced	high	chat room, search engine, international	x	x
Shirdi Sai Baba	–	advanced	high (Java)	multilinks	x	x
Soka Gakkai	–	advanced	med	international	x	x
Subud	15	basic	med	international	x	x
Temple of Set	–	advanced	med	mailing list, language	x	
The Family	*26	advanced	med-high	audio, free info, music	x	x
TM	*78	advanced	med-high	video, links, online books	x	x
Unification Church		advanced	med-high	online bookstore, online newsletter, reading list	x	x
Urantia	4	advanced	med-high	international, online catalog	x	x
Wiccan Church of Canada	–	average	low	regional links	x	x

* Keywords were not specific to organization.

Summary statistics: 47% used detailed keyword searches, with 10 keywords or more; 30% high interactivity; 40% medium interactivity; 63% advanced websites; 97% provided e-mail addresses; 40% provided e-mail, telephone, and mailing addresses.

messages every day and one award-winning site claiming to receive "about 100 messages per day." Similar comments can be found in the conversations Zaleski had with other religious Webmasters. A few of the more elaborate sites (e.g., Scientology, Eckankar) offer virtual tours of the interiors of some of their central facilities and temples. Many offer music and sound bites in Real Audio (e.g. messages from their founders and other inspirational leaders). None of our respondents claimed that their Web sites had been professionally designed or altered. The individuals or groups had done the work themselves. Three of the respondents indicated, however, that they have since become engaged to some extent in the professional creation of Web pages for other groups within their own organization or tradition as well as other clients altogether.

The primary use of the Web is clearly a way to advertise the groups and to deliver information about them cheaply. Most respondents stressed how ideal the medium is for the dissemination of their views (see also Zaleski 1997: 73, 75, 125). To this end, many of the new religions operate multiple pages with slightly different foci, all "hot-linked" to one another, to maximize the chances of a surfer stumbling across one of the pages. Similarly, these pages are often launched with unusually long and diverse lists of keyword search terms, assuring that their address will appear when requests are made through search engines for all kinds of information that may be only tangentially related to the religious beliefs or mission of the group in question (see also Zaleski 1997: 105; see Table 11.2). In these ways, the Web sites act as a new and relatively effective means of outreach to the larger community. They undoubtedly enhance the public profile of each of these religions and add to the revenues obtained by the sale of books, tapes, and other paraphernalia. In fairness, most of the literature available through the Web is offered free of charge—to spread the word.[5]

The Internet and Recruitment

The popular stereotypes of recruits to NRMs are that they are young, naïve, and duped or that they are social losers and marginal types seeking a safe haven from the real world. In an inconsistent manner, some members of the anticult movement (e.g., Singer 1995) have recently claimed that everyone is susceptible to being recruited. The comments of Erik Davis and Margaret Singer in the CNN story on cults and the Internet and those of Zaleski in *The Soul of Cyberspace* manage to combine all three points of view. Heavy users of computers and hence often the World Wide Web are presumed to be "social nerds" and hence more vulnerable to the "loving" outreach of online cult recruiters. Is this the case? The evidence at hand shows that the situation is probably much more complex.

In the first place, the data acquired by sociologists over the last twenty years or more about who joins NRMs and how they join tends not to support the popular supposition (see the summaries and references provided in Dawson 1996, 1998). It is true, as studies reveal, that "cult involvement seems to be strongly correlated with having fewer and weaker extra-cult social ties . . . [as well as] fewer and weaker ideological alignments." In the terms of reference of Rodney Stark and William Sims Bainbridge (1985), the "unchurched" are more likely to join (Dawson 1996: 149; Dawson 1998: 70–71). If heavy users of the Internet are indeed social isolates, then in at least one respect they may appear to be at greater risk of being persuaded to join a NRM.

But there are three other propositions about who joins NRMs and how—with significantly greater empirical substantiation—that offset this impression:

1. "studies of conversion and case studies of specific groups have found that recruitment to NRMs happens primarily through pre-existing social networks and interpersonal bonds. Friends recruit friends, family members each other, and neighbours recruit neighbours" (Dawson 1996: 147; Dawson 1998: 68)
2. "in general, case studies of individuals who joined NRMs or of the groups themselves commonly reveal the crucial role of affective bonds with specific members in leading recruits into deeper involvements" (Dawson 1996: 148; Dawson 1998: 69–70)
3. "equally strongly, from the same studies it is clear that the intensive interaction of recruits with the rest of the existing membership of the group is pivotal to the successful conversion and maintenance of new members" (Dawson 1996: 149; Dawson 1998: 70)

First and foremost, the process of converting to an NRM is a social process. If the denizens of cyberspace tend in fact to be socially isolated, then it is unlikely that they will be recruited through the Web or otherwise. What is more, there is little reason to think that the Internet in itself will ever be a very effective means of recruitment. As the televangelists learned some time ago (Hoover, 1988), the initial provision of information is unlikely to produce any specific commitments unless it is followed up by much more personal and complete forms of interaction by phone and in person. Therefore most of the successful televangelist run quite extensive "parachurch" organizations to which they try to direct all their potential recruits. The religious Webmasters, as Zaleski's interviews reveal (Zaleski 1997: 63, 73, 75, 125), do the same, pressing interested individuals to visit the nearest center or temple. As the creator of one site, Christian Web, states:

> Internet ministries are never meant to be a replacement for the real church. It is impossible for anyone to develop a personal relationship with God without being around His people, His church. These Internet works are nothing more than something to draw in people who may otherwise not want to know anything about Jesus or not want to visit a church for fear of the unknown. For some reason, people find it less intimidating if they can sit at home in the privacy of their own room asking questions about the church and the Bible and God that they have always wanted to ask but never quite feel comfortable enough in the real church to do so. (Zaleski 1997: 125)

Table 11.3 Internet User Statistics (1997–1998)

Age (years)		Sex	
26–30	25.40%	Female	28.40%
22–25	16.50%	Male	71.50%
31–35	13.00%		
41–50	12.90%	**Education**	
19–20	9.10%	College	34.00%
36–40	9.00%	College Graduate	30.10%
51–60	4.60%	Masters Degree	18.20%
13–16	4.00%	Some High School	6.70%
17–18	4.00%	High School Graduate	6.60%
61–70	0.90%	Ph.D. +	4.10%
under 12	0.30%	Ph.D. Student	0.30%
over 71	0.20%		
		Industry	
Occupation		Education/ Student	37.10%
Professional	59.20%	Service	23.60%
Student	34.30%	Publishing	12.20%
Blue-Collar	4.50%	Other/Unemployed	7.10%
Retired	1.90%	Sales	6.30%
		Government	5.10%
Occupation		Manufacturing	5.10%
associated w/		Arts/Creative	3.40%
computers	39.40%		
Primary Use			
of the Internet			
Research	44.50%		
Entertainment	24.50%		
Communication	15.90%		
Sales/Marketing	9.70%		
Education	5.30%		

Source: Inter Commerce Corporation, "SURVEY.NET."

Approaching the same question from another angle, can we learn anything from a comparison of the social profiles that we have of Internet users and the members of NRMs? (See Table 11.3 and Dawson 1996: 152–157; 1998: 74–79.) Both groups tend to be drawn disproportionately from the young-adult population, to be educated better than the general public, and seem to be disproportionately from the middle to upper classes. In the case of the Internet users, the latter conclusion can only be inferred from their levels of education and occupations. But it is fair to say that the fit between this profile and the stereotypes of cult converts is ambiguous at best. By conventional social inferences, it would seem to be inappropriate to view these people as social losers or marginal. Nor, clearly, do they constitute "everybody". Are they more naïve and prone to being duped or manipulated? That would be difficult to determine. But we do not have any reliable evidence to believe such is the case, certainly not for Internet users. On average, they are not as young as most converts to NRMs, are even better educated, and are overwhelmingly from professional occupations (or so they report). Given the extent of their probable involvement in computer technology, surfing the Web, and the real world of their professions, it is plausible to speculate that they will be more skeptical, questioning, and worldly (in at least a cognitive sense) than other segments of the population.

But even if we were to somehow learn that this is not the case, there are other issues to be explored that raise doubts about the soundness of the popular fear of cult recruitment through the Internet. The common complaint of educators, parents, and spouses is that those drawn to the Web for hours on end are simply riding on the surface of things (surfing). They have substituted the vicarious life of the Web for real-life commitments. In this they call to mind certain individuals whom Eileen Barker (1984: 194–198, 203; see also Dawson 1998: 108) noted in her comprehensive study of the Moonies. These are people who seem to fit the profile of potential recruits delineated by the anticult movement yet in fact attend a few lectures with some enthusiasm, only to drop out in pursuit of some other novel interest on the horizon.

On the other hand, following the logic of the argument advanced by Stark and Bainbridge (1996: 235–237) for the involvement of social elites in cults, we can speculate that there are special reasons why a certain percentage of heavy Internet users may be interested in cult activities and why NRMs may have a vested interest in recruiting these people. "In a cosmopolitan society which inflicts few if any punishments for experimentation with novel religious alternatives," Stark and Bainbridge propose, "cults may recruit with special success among the relatively advantaged members of society" (Stark and Bainbridge 1996: 235). Even within elites, they point out, there is an inequality in the division of rewards and room for individuals to be preoccupied with certain relative deprivations (Glock 1964) not adequately compensated for by the power of the elite (e.g., concerns about beauty, health, love, and coping with mortality). In fact, the very material security of this group may well encourage its members' preoccupation with these other less fundamental concerns. People moved by these relative deprivations are unlikely to be drawn to religious sects to alleviate their needs, because the sects are much more likely to be opposed in principle to "the exact rewards the elite possesses as a class" (Stark and Bainbridge 1996: 236). Alternatively, Stark and Bainbridge stipulate:

> an innovative cult ... can offer a set of compensators outside the political antagonisms which divide the elite from other citizens, and focus instead on providing compensators for particular sets of citizens with a shared set of desires that wish to add something to the power of the elite while preserving it. (Stark and Bainbridge 1996: 236)

In addition, "in a cosmopolitan society . . . in which the elite accepts and supports cultural pluralism and thus encourages cultural novelty," certain religious innovations may hold a special appeal because they are emblematic of "progress." Cults are often associated with the transmission of "new culture" and as such may have a certain appeal in terms of the cultural capital of the elite. More mundanely, of course, there is also the fact that the elite are the ones "with both the surplus resources to experiment with new explanations and, through such institutions as higher education, the power to obtain potentially valuable new explanations before others do" (Stark and Bainbridge 1996: 236–237).

From the perspective of the NRMs, members of an elite are particularly attractive candidates for recruitment, not just because of the resources they can donate to the cause but because they are more likely to be involved in the kind of wide-ranging social networks essential for the dissemination of a new cultural phenomenon. "Since networks are composed of interlocking exchange relationships," Stark and Bainbridge reason, "a network will be more extensive, including more kinds of exchanges for more valued rewards, if its members possess the power to obtain the rewards" (Stark and Bainbridge 1996: 236). Recruitment from the elites of society can be instrumental in the success of a new religion.

Whether any of this is relevant in this context is a matter for empirical investigation. The survey of Internet users does suggest, however, that the Web provides a convenient point of access to a seemingly elite segment of our society. Access to computing technology and to the Internet, as well as sufficient time and knowledge to use these resources properly, is still largely a luxury afforded the better-off segments of our society.

The conclusions we can draw about the threat posed by "cults" on Internet are limited yet important. First, while the Internet does make it cheaper for NRMs to disseminate their beliefs over a larger area and to a potentially much larger audience, it is unlikely that it has intrinsically changed the capacity of NRMs to recruit new members. In the first place, Web pages, at present at least, differ little in content or function from more traditional forms of religious publication and broadcasting. Second, we have no real evidence that Internet users are any more prone to convert to a new religion than other young and well-educated people in our society. All the same, there are other reasons for wondering if the World Wide Web is changing the environment in which NRMs operate in fundamental and perhaps even dangerous ways.

The Perils and Promise of the New Public Space

We have been inundated with discussions of the wonders and significance of cyberspace. Much of the dialogue is marked by hyperbole and utopian rhetoric that leaves scholars cold. A few key insights, however, warrant further investigation. Most fundamentally, it is important to realize that it may be best to think of the Internet as a new environment or context in which things happen rather than just another new tool or service. As David Holmes (1997) observes (citing Mark Poster 1997):

> The virtual technologies and agencies . . . cannot be viewed as instruments in the service of pre-given bodies and communities, rather they are themselves contexts which bring about new corporealities and new politics corresponding to space-worlds and time-worlds that have never before existed in human history. (Holmes 1997: 3)

When religion, like anything else, enters these new worlds, there are both anticipated and unanticipated consequences. The new religious "Web meisters" we questioned seemed to approach the Internet simply as a tool and showed little or no appreciation of the potential downside of their efforts. But in thinking about these matters, two disparate sociological observations by Anthony Giddens and James Beckford came to mind, and we began to wonder about a connection.

With the advent of the technologies of modernity, Giddens argues (1990), time has become separated from space and space from place, giving rise to ever more "disembedded social systems." Social relations have been lifted out of local contexts of interaction and restructured across "indefinite spans of time-space" (Giddens 1990: 21). Writing, money, time clocks, cars, freeways, television, computers, ATMs, Walkmans, electronic treadmills for running, shopping malls, theme parks, and so on have all contributed to the transformation of the human habitat, incrementally creating "successive levels of 'new nature'" for humanity (Holmes 1997: 6). As sociologists since Marx (Marx and Engels 1846) have realized, new technologies bring about new forms of social interaction and integration that can change the taken-for-granted conditions of social life. This is especially true of communications technologies. Relative to our ancestors, we have become like gods in our powers of production, reconstruction, and expression. Yet the price may have been high. Even these previrtual technologies have changed our environments in ways that detrimentally standardize, routinize, and instrumentalize our relations with our own bodies and with other people. As we have refashioned our world, we have in turn been remade in the image of technoscience (see, e.g., McLuhan 1964; Ellul 1964; Marcuse 1966; Baudrillard [1970] 1998; Foucault 1979; Postman 1985). Does the advent of the Internet typify or even magnify these and other undesirable social trends? Some keen observers of the sociological implications of the Internet such as Holmes (1997) seem to think it does. If so, what unanticipated consequences might stem from the attempt of religions to take advantage of the disembedded freedom of cyberspace? A clue is provided by an observation by Beckford.

Beckford has intriguingly proposed that it might be better to conceptualize religion in the contemporary Western world as "a cultural resource . . . than as a social institution" (Beckford 1992: 23; see also Beckford 1989: 171). The social structural transformations wrought by the emergence of advanced industrial societies have undermined the communal, familial, and organizational bases of religion. As a consequence, while "religious and spiritual forms of sentiment, belief and action have survived as relatively autonomous resources ... retain[ing] the capacity to symbolize ... ultimate meaning, infinite power, supreme indignation and sublime compassion," they have "come adrift from [their] former points of social anchorage." Now "they can be deployed in the service of virtually any interest-group or ideal: not just organizations with specifically religious objectives" (Beckford 1992: 22–23). Is this an apt description for what the Internet may be doing to religion? Like any "environment," the Web acts back upon its content, modifying the form of its users or inhabitants. Is the "disembedded" social reality of life in cyberspace contributing to the transformation of religion into a "cultural resource" in a postmodern society? If it is, what would be the consequences for the future form and function of religion? Perhaps developments in religion on the Web will provide some initial indications. After examining the pitfalls of life on the Web, we will briefly comment on one such development: the creation of truly "churchless religions".

With these conjectures in mind, we briefly itemize and counterpoise some of the noted benefits and liabilities of life on the Internet.[6] On the positive side, much has been made of the net as an electronic meeting place, a new public space for fashioning new kinds of communities (Shields 1996; Holmes 1997; Zaleski 1997). The defining features of these new communities are the various freedoms allowed by the technology. The Internet allows freedom from "the constraints of the flesh" (Holmes 1997: 7), from the limitations of interaction within Cartesian space and the natural cycles of time. It allows a greater measure of freedom from traditional forms of social control, both formal and informal. It allows for the "breakdown of hierarchies of race, class, and gender." It allows for "the construction of oppositional subjectivities hitherto excluded from the public sphere" (Holmes 1997: 13). It allows people seemingly to "bypass or displace institutional politics" (Holmes 1997: 19). The bottom line, we are told by the hard-core denizens and promoters of the Internet, is that the Internet constitutes a new and freer community of speech, transcending conventional institutional life.

All of these presumed freedoms, each as yet a worthy subject of empirical investigation (see, e.g., Shields 1996; Holmes 1997), rest upon the anonymity and fluidity of identity permitted and sometimes even mandated by life on the Internet. The technology of the Internet allows, and the emergent culture of the Internet fosters, the creative enactment of pluralism at the individual or psychological level as well as the social, cultural, and collective level. This unique foundation of freedom, however, comes at a price that may vitiate the creation of any real communities—of faith or otherwise.

As noted, there is a marked tendency for life on the Internet to be fashioned in the image of the current technoscience, with its new possibilities and clear limitations. This environmental influence on social relations is likely to spill out of the confines of the computer into the stream of everyday life—much like the virtual realities of television that influence the social ontologies of North America, Britain, Japan, and much of Europe. Part of this new standardization, routinization, and instrumentalization of life is the further commodification of human needs and relations. The pitch for the creation of new virtual communities bears the hallmarks of the emergence of "community" as a new commodity of advanced capitalism—a product that is marketed in ways that induce the felt need for a convenient substitute for an increasingly problematic reality.

But do "communities" shaped by the Internet represent real communities any more than shopping malls do? Are the possibilities of interaction and exchange sufficient in kind, number, and quality to replicate and possibly even to replace the social relationships born of more immediate and spatially and temporally uniform kinds of communal involvement? There is good reason to be skeptical, for as Holmes notes:

> technologies of extension [such as the Internet or freeways] . . . characteristically attenuate presence by enabling only disembodied and abstract connections between persons, where the number of means of recognizing another person declines. In the "use" of these technologies . . . the autonomy of the individual is enhanced at the point of use, but the socially "programmed" nature of the technology actually prohibits forming mutual relations of reciprocity outside the operating design of the technological environment. (Holmes 1997: 6–7)

Sharpening the critique, Holmes further cites the views of Michele Willson (1997: 146):

> the presence of the Other in simulated worlds is more and more being emptied out to produce a purely intellectual engagement, and possibilities of commitment to co-operative or collective projects become one-dimensional, or, at best, self-referential. "Community is then produced as an ideal, rather than as a reality, or else it is abandoned altogether." (Holmes 1997: 16)

In like manner, Willson points out (Willson 1997), the Internet seemingly allows us to celebrate and extend social pluralism. But appearances can be deceiving. In the first place, the largely ungrounded and potentially infinite multiplicity of the Internet is often little more than "a play of masks," which serves more to desensitize us to the real and consequential differences between us. Second, the medium simultaneously and paradoxically tends to "compartmentalize populations" and physically isolate individuals while also "homogenizing" them (Holmes 1997: 16–17). As in the rest of our consumer culture, the market of the Internet tends to favor standardization with marginal differentiation. Consequently, with Holmes we find that dialogues on the Internet tend to be "quite transient and directionless, seldom acquiring a substantive enough history to constitute a political [or religious] movement" (Holmes 1997: 18).

To the extent that any of this is true—and speculation far outstrips sound empirical research at this point—it is clear that the side effects of involvement in the Internet could be quite deleterious for religions, new and old. The lauded freedom of the Internet merely compounds the difficulties, since the producers of content have little control over the dissemination and use of their material once launched. Things may be repeated out of context and applied to all manner of ends at odds with the intentions of the original producers. The Internet, as Zaleski says:

> is organized laterally rather than vertically or radially, with no central authority and no chain of command. (Individual Webmasters have power over Web sites, as do . . . system operators . . . over bulletin board systems, and moderators over Usenet groups, but their influence is local and usually extremely responsive to the populations they serve.) (Zaleski 1997: 111)

There is little real regulation of the Internet, and to date, only a few organizations have been able to enforce some of their intellectual property rights (most notably, some software producers and the Church of Scientology—see Frankel 1996; Grossman 1998). The sheer speed and scope of the Internet and the complexity of possible connections can frustrate any attempts to control the flow of information. As several of the Webmasters we surveyed stated, any attempt to regulate the Internet would likely violate the freedom of speech and religion guaranteed by the United States Constitution, and in the process render the Internet itself ineffective.

However, this state of affairs can have a number of other unanticipated consequences for religions venturing onto the Internet that our Webmasters did not seem to realize:

> Because the medium influences the message, it's possible that in the long run the Internet will favour those religions and spiritual teachings that tend toward anarchy and that lack a complex hierarchy. Even now, those who log on to cyberspace may tend to gravitate to religious denominations that emphasize centrifugal rather than centripetal force, just as the medium that is carrying them does. Authority loses its trappings and force on the Net. . . . (Zaleski 1997: 111–112)

This reality of the world of the Internet might well pose serious problems for religions that have historically stressed the role of a strong central authority, like the Roman Catholic Church or Scientology: "As public information sources multiply through the Internet, it's likely that the number of sites claiming to belong to any particular religion but in fact disseminating information that the central authority of that religion deems heretical also will multiply (Zaleski 1997: 108).

When everyone can potentially circumvent the filters of an ecclesial bureaucracy and communicate directly and *en masse* with the leadership in Rome, Los Angeles, or wherever, there will be a shift in power towards the grassroots (Zaleski 1997: 112). The Internet could have a democratizing effect on all religions and work against those religions that resist this consequence.

The elaborate theorizing of Stark and Bainbridge (1996) and their colleagues (e.g., Innaccone 1995) suggests, however, another, somewhat contrary unanticipated consequence of the emergence of the World Wide Web for new religions. As Stark points out in his discussion of the rise of Christianity (1996), the way had been cleared for the phenomenal triumph of Christianity in the Greco-Roman world by the "*excessive* pluralism" (Stark 1996: 197) of Paganism. The massive influx of new cults into the Roman Empire in the first century created "what E.R. Dodds called 'a bewildering mass of alternatives. There were too many cults, too many mysteries, too many philosophies of life to choose from." (Stark 1996: 197) This abundance of choice had at least two consequences with parallel implications for the fate of new religions on the Internet.

In the first place, it assured that only a truly different religion, one that was favored by other circumstances largely beyond its control, was likely to emerge from the crowd. For excessive pluralism, as Stark argues, "inhibits the ability of new religious firms to gain a market share" (Stark 1996: 195), since the pool of potential converts is simply spread too thin. The competition for this pool, moreover, is likely to drive the competing new religions into ever-new radical innovations to secure a market edge.

Secondly, as Stark and Bainbridge argue elsewhere (Stark and Bainbridge 1985; 1996; see also Stark 1996: chap. 8), if many of the religious choices people have are "nonexclusive," as was the case in the Roman Empire and seems to be the case on the Internet—there is no way of demanding or assuring that people hold to only one religion at a time—then, given the inherent risks of religious commitment (i.e., choosing the wrong salvific investment), people "will seek to diversify" (Stark 1996: 204). The most rational strategy in the face of such structurally induced uncertainty will be to maintain a limited involvement in many competitive religions simultaneously—quite possibly to the long-term detriment of all. Stark, Bainbridge, and Innaccone suggest that true religious "movements" are much more likely to emerge from new religions that demand an exclusive commitment. As a medium, however, the Internet carries a reverse bias.

This bias is reflected most clearly in some new religions to which the Internet itself has given birth—communities of belief that exist only, or at least primarily, on the Internet. The ones people most likely to know are intentional jokes, blatant parodies like the Church of the Mighty Gerbil (www.corg.org) or the First Presleyterian Church of Elvis the Divine (www.geocities.com/ presleyterian_church/ home.html). But there are other more problematic instances as well, one of which we have begun to study: Thee Church Ov MOO (http://victoria.tc.ca/~half-mad/moo/). This new religion was invented, almost by accident, by a group of gifted students interacting on an Internet bulletin board in Ottawa, Canada, sometime in the early 1990s. By the late 1990s, many of these same people were operating a sophisticated Web site with over eight hundred pages of fabricated religious documents covering a sweeping range of religious and pseudoreligious subjects. A visit to the Web site reveals an elaborate development of alternative sets of scriptures, commandments, chronicles, mythologies, rituals, and ceremonies. Much of this material reads like a bizarre religious extension of *The Hitchhiker's Guide to the Galaxy*. It is irreverent and playful, verging alternately on the sophomoric and the sophisticated. Many of the texts of the Church ov MOO seem to have been devised with a keen awareness of religious history, comparative beliefs and practices, and some real knowledge of the philosophy, anthropology, and sociology of religion. The site records a great many hits every day, we are told, and about ten thousand people have applied for membership.

Several of the key figures have pursued training or careers in physics, mathematics, computer science, and the other so-called hard sciences. With MOOism they are attempting to devise a self-consciously postmodern, socially constructed, relativist, and self-referenial system of religious ideas purposefully and paradoxically infused with humor, irony, and farce as well as a serious appreciation of the essentially religious or spiritual condition of humanity. In a typically postmodernist manner, the conventions we normally draw between academic reflection and religious thought are flaunted. An unsolicited essay we received from one of the church leaders on "MOOism, Social Constructionism, and the Origins ov Religious Movements" characteristically begins with the following note:

> Thee language ov this essay conforms to TOPY (Thee Temple or Psychical Youth) standards ov language discipline. Thee purpose ov this is twofold: first, to prevent thee reader from forgetting that E am not attempting to separate this sociological comment from religious text; second, to prevent thee writer from forgetting thee same thing. These ideas should be taken neither too lightly nor too seriously.

Similarly, the MOO home page declares:

> Among other things, MOOism has been called the Negativland of religion. Not only does it irreverently (and sometimes irrelevantly) sample innumerable other religious traditions, it uses recontextualization and paradoxical framing techniques to prevent minds from settling into orthodoxy. Paradox and radical self-contradiction are, in the post-modern context, the most reasonable way to approach the Absolute.

MOOIsm is certainly about "having fun" with religion. But the objective does seem to be to encourage and facilitate the rise of a new conceptual framework and language for religious experience suited to the changed environmental conditions of postmodern society. The "religion" seems to be influenced significantly by Neopaganism and is representative of what is coming to be called Technopaganism. (But it is also influenced by such earlier and quite sophisticated joke religions as Discordianism and the Church of the SubGenius.) In line with many aspects of that movement, it is seeking to provide an intellectual and social forum for fostering the kind of human imagination and creativity that empowers people to override the public demise of spiritual life or "realities" in our time (see Luhrmann 1989). But unlike many other forms of Neopaganism, this "religion" is well suited in form and function to life on the Internet, perhaps because it is in many respects the witting and unwitting mirror reflection of the sensibilities of the Internet culture in which it developed. But in truth we do not know as yet whether MOOism is a "religious" movement or just a most elaborate hoax. The Church solicited our attention, and its Web page once carried the disclaimer: "This page is in the progress of being altered to mislead *Lorne Dawson*. It may therefore seem disjointed and confused."

If it is all a joke, then one must marvel at the time and energy invested in its creation and perpetuation. In conversations, however, we have been lead to believe that the originators of MOOism are beginning to have an ambiguous understanding of their creation and are seeking some assistance in thinking through the significance of MOOism as a social phenomenon. One thing is clear: without the Internet, this phenomenon is unlikely to have developed or exercised the influence it undoubtedly has on some people. But is it reflective of the future of religion in some regard? Joke or not, it may be similar to other current or future religious phenomena on the Internet that are of a more serious intent. The Church ov MOO does appear to embody elements of both Beckford's conception of religion as a "cultural resource" and Stark's and Bainbridge's speculations about the special appeal of cult innovations to elites.[7]

At present, most of the virtual communities of the Internet are much less intriguing and problematic. Most new religions seem content to use the Internet in quite limited and conventional ways. But the Webmasters we surveyed are uniformly intent on constantly improving their Web pages in visual, auditory, and interactive technology. So we must be careful not to underestimate what the future may hold. There is merit, we think in the metaphorical conclusion of Zaleski:

> Virtual and physical reality exert a gravitational pull on one another. At present, virtuality is the moon to the real world, bound by its greater mass, but just as the moon influences tides, spiritual work in the virtual communities is influencing and will continue to influence that work in real-world communities. (Zaleski 1997: 254)

The new religious uses of the Internet are likely to exercise an increasingly determinant, if subtle, effect on the development of all religious life in the future (Lövheim and Linderman 1998).

Notes

1. The term "cults" is so strongly associated with negative images in the popular mind that academics have long preferred to use such terms as "new religions" or "new religious movements" (see, e.g., Richardson 1993). The word will be used, nonetheless, at various points in this essay to call to mind the fears giving rise to this discussion in the first place.
2. "Web of Death" was the double entendre used as the headline of a *Newsweek* cover story on the Heaven's Gate suicide.
3. In 1997, Statistics Canada reported that of all the homes in Canada with some type of facility to access the Internet, only 13 percent made use of the opportunity (www.statcan.ca). Reginald Bibby (1995) reported that 31 percent of Canadians had some contact with the Internet, ranging from daily to hardly ever.
4. As Zaleski reports (1997: 249) and we recall from the news: "At least one of the suicides, 39-year-old Yvonne McCurdy-Hill of Cincinnati, a post-office employee and mother of five, initially encountered the cult in cyberspace and decided to join in response to its online message."

5. Of course, the Web has offered new opportunities to the opponents of new religions as well. Entering the term "cults" in any search engine will produce a surfeit of sites dedicated to so-called watchdog organizations or the home pages of disgruntled ex-members (e.g., Operation Clambake—The Fight Against Scientology on the Net, www.xenu.net).
6. These reflections are strongly influenced by the ideas discussed by David Holmes in the introduction to his book on identity and community in cyberspace, *Virtual Politics* (1997).
7. This is not the only Internet-created religion of which we are aware. The Otherkin, for example, is a "religious movement" that, at least in some of its forms, exists largely only on the Internet. The Otherkin believe they are reincarnated elves, dwarfs, and other mythical and mystical creatures (http://kinhost.org/res/Otherfaq.html).

References

Bainbridge, W. (1997). *The Sociology of Religious Movements.* New York: Routledge.
Barker, E. (1984). *The Making of a Moonie: Choice or Brainwashing.* Oxford UK: Basil Blackwell.
Baudrillard, J. (1970). *La societe de consommation.* Paris: Editions Denoel. Trans. and republished as *The Consumer Society.* London: Sage, 1998.
Beckford, J. (1989). *Religion in Advanced Industrial Society.* London: Unwin Hyman.
———. (1992). "Religion, Modernity and Post-Modernity." In Wilson, B. ed. *Religion: Contemporary Issues,* ed. B.Wilson, London: 11–23 Bellew.
Bedell, K. (1998). "Religion and the Internet: Reflections on Research Strategies." Paper presented to the Society for the Scientific Study of Religion, Montreal.
Bibby, R. W. (1995). *The Bibby Report: Social Trends Canadian Style.* Toronto: Stoddart.
Bromley, D. G., and E. Breschel, (1992). "General Population and Institutional Elite Support for Social Control of New Religious Movements: Evidence From National Survey Data." *Behavioral Sciences and the Law* 10: 39–52.
Cottee, T., N., Yateman, and L. Dawson, (1996). "NRMs, the ACM, and the WWW: A Guide for Beginners." In *Cults in Context: Readings in the Study of New Religious Movements,* ed. L. Dawson 453–468. Toronto: Canadian Scholars Press (published in the United States by Transaction Pub.).
Dawson, L. L. (1996). "Who Joins New Religious Movements and Why: Twenty Years of Research and What Have We Learned?" *Studies in Religion* 25(2): 193–213.
———. (1998). *Comprehending Cults: The Sociology of New Religious Movements.* Toronto and New York: Oxford University Press.
Ellul, J. (1964). *The Technological Society.* New York: Alfred A. Knopf.
Foucault, M. (1979). *Discipline and Punish.* New York: Vintage Books.
Frankel, A. (1996). "Making Law, Making Enemies." *American Lawyer* 3 March. Retrieved from www2.thecia.net/users/rnewman/scientology/media/amlawyer-3.36.html, July 1997.
Giddens, A. (1990). *The Consequences of Modernity.* Cambridge, UK: Polity.
Glock, C. Y. (1964). "The Role of Deprivation in the Origin and Evolution of Religious Groups." *In Religion and Social Conflict,* ed. R. Lee, and M. Marty, M., 24–36. New York: Oxford University Press.
Grossman, W. M. (1998). "alt.scientology.war." *Wired* Magazine. Retrieved from www.wired.com/wired/3.12/features/alt.scientology.war.html, Oct. 1998.
Holmes, D. (1997). *Virtual Politics: Identity and Community in Cyberspace.* London: Sage.
Hoover, S. (1988). *Mass Media Religion.* Thousand Oaks, CA: Sage.
Innaccone, L. R. (1995) "Risk, Rationality, and Religious Portfolios." *Economic Inquiry* 33: 285–295.
Lofland J. (1966). *Doomsday Cult.* Englewood Cliffs, NJ: Prentice-Hall.
Lövheim, M., and A. Linderman, (1998). "Internet—A Site for Religious Identity Formation and Religious Communities?" Paper presented to the Society for the Scientific Study of Religion, Montreal.
Luhrmann, T. M. (1989). *Persuasions of the Witch's Craft: Ritual Magic in Contemporary England.* Cambridge, MA: Harvard University Press.
Marcuse, H. (1966). *One-Dimensional Man.* Boston: Beacon Press.
Marx, K., and F. Engels, [1846] (1970). *The German Ideology.* New York: International Pub.
McLuhan, M. (1964). *Understanding Media.* New York: McGraw-Hill.
Miller, J. (1998). "Internet Subcultures." Senior Honours Essay, Department of Sociology, University of Waterloo, Waterloo, Ontario, Canada, April.
Pfeifer, J. E. (1992). "The Psychological Framing of Cults: Schematic Representations and Cult Evaluations." *Journal of Applied Social Psychology* 22(7): 531–544.

Poster, M. (1997). "Cyberdemocracy: The Internet and the Public Sphere." In *Virtual Politics*, ed. D. Holmes, 212–228. London: Sage.

Postman, N. (1985). *Amusing Ourselves to Death*. New York: Penguin Books.

Richardson, J. (1993). "Definitions of Cult: From Sociological-Technical to Popular-Negative." *Review of Religious Research* 34(4): 348–356.

Rochford, E. B. Jr. (1982). "Recruitment Strategies, Ideology and Organization in the Hare Krishna Movement." *Social Problems* 29: 399–410.

Shields, R., ed. (1996). *Cultures of the Internet: Virtual Spaces, Real Histories, Living Bodies*. London: Sage.

Shupe, A. D. (1978). "Disembodied Access' and Technological Constraints on Organizational Development: A Study of Mail-Order Religions." *Journal for the Scientific Study of Religions* 15: 177–185.

Singer, M. T. (1995). *Cults in Our Midst: The Hidden Menace in Our Everyday Lives*. San Francisco: Jossey-Bass.

Snow, D. A., L. A. Zurcher, Jr., and S. Ekland-Olson, (1980). "Social Networks and Social Movements: A Microstructural Approach to Differential Recruitment." *American Sociological Review* 45(5): 787–801.

Stark, R. (1996). *The Rise of Christianity: A Sociologist Reconsiders History*. Princeton, NJ: Princeton University Press.

Stark, R., and W. S. Bainbridge, (1985). *The Future of Religion: Secularization, Revival and Cult Formation*. Berkeley, CA: University of California Press.

———. (1996). *A Theory of Religion*. New Brunswick, NJ: Rutgers University Press. (Originally published by Peter Lang, 1987.)

Willson, M. (1997). "Community in the Abstract: A Political and Ethical Dilemma?" In *Virtual Politics*, ed. d., Holmes 145–162. London: Sage.

Zaleski, J. (1997). *The Soul of Cyberspace: How New Technology is Changing Our Spiritual Lives*. New York: HarperCollins.

12

The Internet as Virtual Spiritual Community: Teen Witches in the United States and Australia

HELEN A. BERGER AND DOUGLAS EZZY

Those of us who have been studying contemporary Witchcraft have noted a significant influx of teenagers into the religion in the last ten years. This phenomenon has also gained the attention of the mass media and of the religious right in the United States and Australia, who view it as one more indication that young people are being seduced into the occult at the risk of their souls. McGrory warns us of the dangers, for example, in an article from *The Times of London* but also reported in Australian media: "Children seduced by Forces of Satanism on the Internet" (2001: 8). The article highlights the "malign influence of satanic cults" that have become "adept at snaring" young people and suggests links between the rise of the occult and youth suicide. Clark (2003) documents the American religious right's frequent equation of the occult with Satanism and the accusation that American youth are being lead astray by the occult, to which they are introduced in all forms of media, including the Internet. Similarly, a recent Australian article reported that "television, the internet, enviornmentalism, and even feminism" have all played a role in encouraging an interest in Paganism that "normalises spiritual evil" (Reuters 2003).

While the hypothesis that the Internet somehow seduces people into new religious movements has been called into question in academic research (Dawson and Hennebry 1999), both mass media and the Christian Right continue to suggest that the Internet is, among other things, seducing young people into new religious movements, including Witchcraft. The idea that young people are being "seduced" into the occult implies a passivity and naïveté among young people that is not empirically supported and bears some similarity to the now-discredited argument that new religious movements "brainwash" their members (Beckford 1985; Dawson 1998; Zablocki and Robbins 2001). The "brainwashing" hypothesis, which was most popular in the 1970s and 1980s, was used by mass media, worried parents, and the secular anticult movement to explain why young people might be attracted to new religious movements (NRMs). It implied that members of these NRMs used mind control techniques on young people to force them to join and remain in the groups. Many sociologists, on the other hand, argued that these young people were in control of their actions and had chosen to explore alternative religions. Both the brainwashing hypothesis and the idea that young people are "seduced" by the Internet fail to take into account the complex set of influences that shape choices about religious beliefs and practices.

Scholars have noted that the Internet has not served as a significant venue for recruitment into new religious movements (Dawson and Hennebry 1999; Introvigne 2000; Mayer 2000). Our research similarly indicates that the Internet is not the primary entry point for most of our respondents. In point of fact, books found primarily at local bookstores and libraries are the medium through which most young people first learn about the religion. However, the Internet is part of a larger process by which teenage Witches explore and participate in Witchcraft.

Unlike many religions, becoming a Witch is less a process of conversion to a particular set of beliefs, such as inviting Jesus into your life, than it is a process of learning about and participating in the practices that make one a Witch— that is, doing the rituals and practicing magic. The Internet serves as one important source in this ongoing process. Similar to the way people often search the Internet to find out about a particular medical condition or a place they intend to visit, the young people in our sample used the Internet to explore their spiritual questions. It is in this context that the Internet serves as one of a variety of cultural resources upon which young people draw when they are exploring Witchcraft and developing their spiritual and magical abilities and personae.

For those young Witches who participate in chat rooms or post notes on bulletin boards, the Internet provides an avenue to meet others who have similar interests. Chat-room participation also allows individuals to become "instant experts," as even those who have only recently started studying the religion can share rituals they have written and teach others about the religion.

Popular books such as Scott Cunningham's works on solitary Wicca (1988; 1994) have helped to create a category of individuals who practice Witchcraft alone and who have been trained (or trained themselves) outside the coven tradition. Particularly for young people who may not know other Witches in their communities and who are restricted in how far they are able to travel, the Internet provides a spiritual community in which they can share their ideas, work on rituals, feel part of a larger spiritual movement, and, as one young Witch in our sample notes, meet other Pagans for dating.

Scholars and social analysts have noted that the Internet has the potential of changing religions by decreasing the importance of hierarchies, increasing individual autonomy, and creating an international community of believers who do not necessarily have face-to-face interactions (Cobb 1998; Helland

2000; O'Leary and Brasher 1996; Zaleski 1997). On the Internet a new type of community can form that reflects the contemporary process that Giddens (1991) refers to as time-space distanciation: the compression of time and space through the development of telephones, movies, television, quick and relatively cheap travel, and, more recently, the Internet. As a religion of late-modernity, Witchcraft lends itself to transmission through the Internet and other forms of mass communication (cf. Berger 1999; Eilberg-Shwartz 1989).

Unlike older religions that have a tradition of face-to-face congregations, a predetermined hierarchy, and set of standardized beliefs and practices, Witchcraft as typically practiced in the United States and Australia is polymorphous. For the majority of Witches, each individual is considered the ultimate authority on her spiritual quest. There is no central authority that can excommunicate or deny an individual the right to claim that she is a Witch. Although there are some traditions that do have established hierarchies and orthodoxies, these tend to be increasingly in the minority, particularly among young people. Celebrations, rituals, and magical workings can be done alone or with others. The Internet, as well as other forms of mass communication such as books and journals, free seekers from finding a coven willing to train them. This is particularly important for underage seekers, as many covens will not train anyone under the age of eighteen because they fear litigation by angry parents (Berger, Leach, and Shaffe 2003; Harrow 1994; K 1998).

Although there are covens that train Witches on a face-to-face basis, for many people spiritual and magical teachings have been removed from this more traditional environment with the increase in popularly available material. In this, at the same time as the Internet works with books and journals to democratize information about Wicca, it is redefining and changing the religion. Knowledge becomes separated from a community within a particular time and place (Ezzy 2001), and for teens there is no need to learn from their "elders"; they are able to create their own form of Witchcraft or Paganism. Although in theory each individual can create her own form of Witchcraft, in reality there is a great deal of similarity, as individuals use the same sources for inspiration and understanding (Berger 1999). However, for these youths there is a tendency to emphasize one aspect of traditional Witchcraft—that is, self-development (Greenwood 1998). Although the focus on the self and its transformation has always been an important element of Witchcraft, it has been embedded in a larger sense of transforming the world—through religious ritual, through direct political action (Crowley 1998), or through life-style choices (Berger 1999). Some young Witches are concerned with political issues, but on the whole they are more interested in using magic and rituals to transform themselves and their lives. In part the focus on self-transformation to the exclusion of larger political issues among young Witches is the result of their life stage. In part, it is also a product of their spiritual quest having been primarily informed by the mass media (Ezzy 2003).

Although Witchcraft, particularly as practiced by teens, provides an excellent case study of the effect of mass media on a religion, it is not unique. Other new religions or religious movements that also do not require regular face-to-face interactions also prospered using the mass media. The success of the Promise Keepers' rallies, for example, depended on coverage in newspapers and television. The Internet is yet another facet of these contemporary mass media.

Our Study

Our research examines teenagers' participation in Witchcraft at "two ends of the earth," the United States and Australia. Our decision to do research in the United States and Australia was in part serendipitous—we each live and work in one of these countries. However, while chosen for pragmatic reasons, it quickly became apparent that looking at this phenomenon in two English-speaking nations that are so geographically separated provides an interesting opportunity to explore the relationship of globalization, teen Witches, the Internet, and mass media. To date, we have interviewed people between the ages of eighteen and twenty three who began practicing Witchcraft while they were in their teens and have defined themselves as Witches for at least one year. Our respondents were found through advertisements in school newspapers, colleagues who placed ads around their own universities, help from the Pagan Alliance in Australia, and our own contacts within the Witchcraft community in Australia and the United States In all instances we have accepted our respondents' self-definition as Witches.

As our interview process is ongoing, this chapter is based on fifty one interviews. In Australia, twenty eight interviews (twenty five female and three male) were conducted in the cities of Hobart, Melbourne, and Sydney between September 2001 and March 2003. In the United States, twenty three (fifteen female and eight male) were conducted in Boston and several towns in New Jersey, New York, Pennsylvania, and Vermont between November 2001 to March 2003. The differences in gender distribution for the two countries probably reflect our different recruiting strategies rather than differences in gendered participation between the two countries. Specifically, in Australia recruiting was conducted through first-year university courses with high proportions of females. Our research into this gender difference is ongoing.

Our primary goal in this study was to do a cross-national comparison of teenage Witches. We had initially hypothesized that although there would be similarities, we would find significant geographic differences in terms of practice and belief. We also anticipated that these teenage Witches would be somewhat frivolous in their religious pursuit, focusing, for example, almost exclusively on magic. We discovered that neither hypothesis was supported. On the whole Witches on both continents were remarkable similar and very serious about their spirituality. Our interview technique was to use open-ended questions about individual practices, beliefs, processes of becoming

Witches, and integration into the larger Neopagan world, and the effects of becoming a Witch on other aspects of their lives. Our study was not focused exclusively on Internet use, nor was our recruitment done primarily on the Internet. We are not, therefore, focused exclusively on "Internet junkies" but are providing a view into the extent that the Internet has permeated the practice of Witchcraft among young people.

Internet usage among our sample varied from participants who had never accessed the Internet to people who spent an average of two hours a day on the Internet, with some days spent almost entirely on the Internet. Since most of our respondents had at least at one point explored Witchcraft sites on the Internet, it is clear that the Web serves a number of different purposes for these young Witches. These can be broadly categorized as: (1) information-seeking about the theory, practice, and history of Witchcraft; (2) information-seeking about events and meetings in a person's local area; (3) informal social engagement with Internet Witchcraft communities through participation in chat rooms and e-mail forums; and (4) formal participation in Internet communities through Internet-based training programs, established Internet covens, and formal mentoring through the Internet. Our research suggests that the most important use of the Internet is seeking information on practice and knowledge; the least important is formal participation in Internet communities.

The remainder of this paper examines two phases of teenage Witchcraft: becoming a teenage Witch, and participation in a virtual spiritual community. In our examination of the process of becoming a teenage Witch, we demonstrate that although only rarely the first avenue of exploration, the Internet is actively used by most teenagers as a resource to facilitate their religious seekership. In the second section, we examine the various ways that the Internet is utilized to facilitate the dispersed and often shifting forms of community in late-modernity among contemporary teenage Witches.

Becoming a Teenage Witch

Only seven of our respondents—three from the United States and four from Australia—told us that they first learned about Witchcraft on the Internet. Two other Australians cited books and the Internet equally as their first introduction. Although the most commonly cited source of initial information about Witchcraft was books, most respondents subsequently combined reading books with "surfing" the Internet. As mentioned earlier, becoming a Witch is less an epiphany than a process through which an individual learns techniques and rituals. As such, the Internet plays a role in the process of individuals developing and practicing Witchcraft, even though it was not the first port of entry into learning about the religion.

None of the teenagers describes any experience that could be classified as being "seduced" into Witchcraft by information or people on the Internet. None noted feeling that particular images or ideas she found on the Internet played on her mind. In fact, several individuals in our sample who initially explored Witchcraft via the Internet now do so rarely or not at all. For example, Koehl,[1] an American Witch who had used the Internet early in her spiritual quest, states in answering a question about whether she currently used the Internet:

> Not really, not since I have gotten into the college really. The last time I used it was, I have to say February [eight months before]. . . . Because then I started buying books, and I thought those books had . . . more insight . . . .And then I started having these Wiccan lessons sort of thing with my friend who I met through class [at the University], so I thought, you know, it is much easier to learn from someone who has the same viewpoint.

Jason, another American who first learned about Witchcraft from the Internet, claims that he now rarely looks at Witchcraft sites. Instead, the two hours a week he is able to spend on the Internet are spent primarily playing Diablo II, a role-playing game. Furthermore, none of our sample describes being pursued or pressured in any way by people on the Internet to join a Witchcraft group or to meet someone in person. The young Witches in our sample appear to be in control of the amount of time they spend on the Internet and whether they continue to use it to further their spiritual quests. While the Internet is a technology that facilitates a particular type of dispersed social relationship, it is the information available online along with the potential for social contact that plays a significant role in many young people's self-identification as a Witch.

Some of the teenagers we interviewed did not make use of the Internet at all, and for them the process of becoming a Witch relied primarily upon personal contacts as well as information gleaned from books and magazines. Further, several of the teens we interviewed were born into Wiccan or Neopagan families. For these young people the primary source of information about Witchcraft was their parents, their parents' friends, and/or covenmates. A few individuals in our study have not read many books about Witchcraft but have learned about the religion through friends and schoolmates.

A substantial proportion of the teenagers we interviewed described the process of becoming a Witch as an outcome of what could be described as "religious seekership" (Roof 1993). Similar to that of other religious adherents, this seekership often grew out of childhood religious experiences, a sense of being different, or an expressed dissatisfaction with their current life or the religion in which they were raised. Although not the only source, the Internet was often an important resource for these people.

As with adult Witches, most teenage converts in our study noted that they had always been inclined toward Witchcraft or that what they read or heard about Wicca resonated with something within them. They also pointed to an experience of "searching" as motivating their exploration of Witchcraft. Dane, a twenty two-year-old American, stated: "I was definitely searching for something the whole time." Jodie, on the other hand, said that she "stumbled" across Witchcraft on the

Internet: "I went searching for nature religions [on the Internet] and that's what popped up. . . . I really wanted to find something that was me—like to do with nature, and I just read through it and I actually felt 'Oh no, not witchcraft. It's evil.' [Laughs] But the more I researched the more [I felt comfortable with it]."

Throughout our interviews we were impressed with the books our respondents claimed they read when they first became interested in Witchcraft. Although some began with *Teen Witch* by Silver RavenWolf (1999), many cited works by Amber K, Vivianne Crowley, Raymond Buckland, Scott Cunningham, and Laurie Cabot. Although these authors differ in their sophistication, they are all serious books that were not written for teens but for a general Wiccan or more educated audience. Furthermore, teens on both continents read many of the same books, suggesting that the movement is truly international. The American youth tended to read more books by American authors, but at least in some instances they noted reading British and Australian works.

Two Witches, one Australian and one American, who said they had initially learned about Witchcraft on the Internet (at the ages of fourteen and fifteen respectively), indicate that their early explorations developed as a result of their peers' interest in the occult. The Australian, Joanne, became interested in the occult from her own participation in Goth culture. Coming across a Satanist site, she states that after looking at this site, and because she knew someone who was a Satanist, she began reading the works of Anton LeVey. "I sort of started reading some of his books," she told us, "and got a little bit into it and one thing that stood out I suppose was in those first few month just reading about what Satanism was about and—I mean I found it sort of selfish . . . like people have got real misconceptions about Satanism, but I didn't think—I'm like sort of studying and looking for something that suited what I believe, but I didn't find that was it, so I went further into the occult and studied Paganism." Joanne's quote underlines that she used the information she found on the Internet to shape the choices she made about her spiritual path. The first site she came upon was about Satanism, a religion she determined did not suit her. She subsequently found Witchcraft sites, which she combined with reading books, particularly those of Dion Fortune, to develop her spiritual practice. Similarly Jason, an American Witch, states:

> Well, somehow in middle school I got this reputation of sort of being a scary kid, just because I was weird and a lot of people thought I was into black magic right off the bat, when I really wasn't. . . . So basically, just out of curiosity . . . I went on the Internet and checked out some Web pages on magic and that is how I sort of got introduced into Wicca. I found out how completely wrong everything that they said was, like there is no real black magic and like, nor white magic or anything . . . it became sort of a hobby of mine.

Like others in our sample who explored the Internet, Joanne and Jason visited several Web sites. They did not accept everything they read on the Internet and were able choose which sites they found most useful.

Some people used the Internet as an equivalent of a library. For example, Jodie, the Australian Witch quoted earlier, told us that she learned about Witchcraft through the Internet. "We looked at a lot of sites," she said:

> I think she [Jodie's friend Alysa] found the word "Wicca" in one of the fantasy books that she was reading and she looked it up on the Internet and came up with a lot of references. Then, of course, we went—I think the first book I bought was Silver RavenWolf's *Teen Witch*, which was definitely really good because it was focused at teenagers and didn't assume that you knew everything beforehand.

Others used the Internet to find information about Wiccan groups in their areas. For example, Clarissa, another Australian, said:

> I met this girl at University and we were attempting to form a Pagan Society at University and I met a few more of those and then decided that they weren't really the kind of Pagans or kind of people I really wanted to hang around with. But later that year I got onto the Internet at the Library and found Pagan Awareness Network and went along to their next full moon and met a few people there and have just been going back ever since.

Similarly, an American Witch, Olivia, noted that her quest for a working group took place on the popular Witchcraft site, Witchvox (www.witchvox.com). She told us that the first group she found she "didn't quite click with." As she notes:

> Although I did meet the leader and he was a very nice guy. . . . I ended up finding the group that was [name of coven] and I really liked the things that they had on there [their Web site], and you know, they were serious, very serious and what-not, and they offered classes and things, so I emailed the high priestess, who's a good friend of mine now . . . we clicked instantly.

The Internet functions as a virtual spiritual community for many teenage Witches. Macha NightMare, a well-known Witch, describes the importance of the Web for Witches and Neopagans of all ages: "On the Web, isolated individuals and groups found one another. On the Web, networks were woven around common concerns and goals. The Web allowed community to be created where none had been. The anonymity of online communications liberated witchen folks to express their thoughts and feelings and experiences in relative safety" (NightMare 2001: 24).

For teenage Witches, the anonymity and convenience of the Internet may be of particular importance. Parents' responses to their children becoming Witches varied substantially. Some of the teenagers were sure that if their parents knew or if one parent in particular was told about their involvement in Witchcraft, they would be upset. The other extreme is an American woman who, when she expressed interest in worshipping the Goddess at the age of twelve, was introduced to a Women's Spirituality group by her father, a Protestant minister. Although Goddess Spirituality is not synonymous with Witchcraft, it was one of the women in this group who subsequently trained and initiated this young woman as a Witch. For young Witches who fear parental hostility toward their religion, the Internet can provide a hidden community away from their parents. Although Witchcraft on the Web is extremely varied, discussion often acrimonious, and online interaction not without disrespect for teenagers, these young people have often found Internet communities in which they are respected for their ideas and spiritual insights and not judged by their age. Although the Internet provides one arena in which young people can explore their interest outside their parent's gaze, it is only one such place. Owners and employees of occult bookstores, for instance, are often willing to share their knowledge with customers.

Our respondents varied in the degree to which they have Internet access and how much they surf the Net. Dane, who began practicing Witchcraft at thirteen, did not have regular access to a computer until he was sixteen. "I first got Internet access in the computer and I was really started getting into it," he told us. "I knew a lot about it before because my friends had computers, but I was really getting into the Internet looking for sites, and finding out about people. Finding out about Wicca more. I was getting into chat rooms and interacting with people." One Australian woman notes that in the year since she became interested in Witchcraft she used the Internet "all the time." When asked what sites she visits she replied:

> Witchvox . . . Wizards' Realm, I think it is. I think that's more of a shop, but they've got some herb definitions and things there. The Esoteric Bookstore has a shop. . . . I printed out the entire herb page, which is very thorough because I didn't know very much about herbs at the time, so I have a list of what all the herbs do—things like that. Umm, yeah, just every now and then I'll bump across a site and I'll cut and paste into Microsoft Word and then print it all out.

When asked "Do you participate in any of the sort of e-mail discussion groups sort of thing?" she noted: "I've never really come across many. I was introduced to one by a guy at school. . . . Louise [her friend] is on it—anyway Louise is on it and it was Pagan something or other and you enter e-mail and a message 'Anyone want to e-mail me back?" I didn't get anyone e-mailing me back, so I thought I'd e-mail the three outer suburban girls that were on there and then they all e-mailed me back and . . . it turned out I knew them all."

Other young Witches regularly participated in chat rooms. Aguina, an American who at nineteen assumed the role of High Priestess of the coven in which she was trained, states that while there are twelve people in her offline coven:

> my coven worldwide is huge. . . . [The] Internet is the most amazing place. . . . We have meetings. For those who live in like Minnesota, California, those I can't get to, they will email me and say can I meet you on line at such and such a time, and I'm like sure, and by that time I am in the room we have, we have private rooms where you can meet, and I'm talking to that one person and I guess another person sees me on, and they come in.

Aguina claims that her Internet coven is composed of about eighty people throughout the world, the most distant being in Australia. Her notion of an Internet coven is one in which people share information about rituals and magic. While she claims she is teaching Wicca on the Internet, the Internet also permits her to see herself as part of an international religious movement.

Jeanette, an Australian, also notes that the Internet made her feel part of a larger movement: "The way I got into it [Witchcraft] I didn't think there were that many people. I thought oh yeah there's probably a few and you read and you read stuff. But [once she found the Internet] yeah you realize that all over the world people are doing this. . . . It makes you feel part of a wider community." The Internet shows these youths that there is a larger world of Witchcraft of which they are part. Chat rooms also help validate the youths' experiences and sometimes provide them with a forum in which they learn to explore ideas about Witchcraft and develop a confidence in their own voice. Dane said that while chat-room conversations were often mundane, every now and then people would have a "real" conversation about rituals or magical ceremonies in which people shared their own ritual scripts and experiences.

Some young people are part of a sophisticated and complex Internet community. Salem, for example, was working through a set of lessons provided as part of an online training course in Witchcraft and on which she spent about one hour per week. The course consisted of a number of levels, each with twelve lessons. Each lesson included specific readings as well as suggested ritual and magical practices. There was a multiple-choice test at the end of each lesson. She is also part of a group of three people that she considers her online coven. She met these people by placing a Web advertisement describing herself and her interests and inviting people to contact her. Finally, she participates in an online "Witch School," which involves answering one question per day and developing a relationship with a mentor. In Salem's case, because she could not find anyone in Australia, her mentor is in America.

It is important to emphasize the centrality of choice and reflexivity to these young people's involvement with Internet communities. This is described clearly by Jenny, an Australian Witch, when she recounts her experience of participating in Witchcraft discussion groups:

> A lot of the time I was a lurker and just reading other people's posts and if I felt that I had something to contribute I would, but I learnt a lot by just watching or least reading what other people do. [I learnt] different ideas mainly. I guess I almost redefined my own beliefs. Before they were hazy, whereas after I'd done that [participated in the chat room] and got different perspectives and different ways of wording things, it was really—OK I believe this. I don't agree with you on that point, but I believe this.

Jenny did not only find information on the Internet, she also learned how to think about her own religious identity. As she watched others questioning and making choices, she came to engage in similar reflexive practices with respect to her own beliefs and practices. She did not accept everything she read, but it gave her a language to reflect on and redefine her religious beliefs and practices.

While some people use the Internet frequently and have developed strong friendships through it, and although it is an increasingly important communication technology, it remains simply that—another form of communication. As such, the Internet facilitates interaction between people who are dispersed geographically, who are sometimes stigmatized within mainstream culture, and who want to meet other people with similar interests. Individuals have the option of entering or leaving these communities at will. Instead of church meetings on Tuesday evenings and Sunday mornings, the Internet permits people to interact at any time and on any day of the week. In contrast to the telephone, small groups can easily meet simultaneously in chat rooms, and it is no more expensive to meet someone on the other side of the world than to meet someone next door. The virtual communities of teenage Witches are no more and probably not that much less seductive than the meetings of a local church congregation. If anything, the ease of leaving is greater because of the more tenuous nature of the relationships formed via the Internet. The use to which the teens in our sample put the Internet—whether seeking information or participating in a worldwide dialogue—varied over time, as did the sheer amount of time they spend on the Internet. However, in almost all instances, the Web was part of these Witches' spiritual community.

Although Internet communities can be supportive and provide important friendships, this does not mean that everything on the Internet is beneficial. Zack, a twenty-year-old American, pointed out: "I have never really put too much stock in chat rooms because I didn't know who I was talking to." The young people we interviewed often displayed considerable caution in who they chose to trust on the Internet. For example, Simone was recruited to participate in our research through an Australia Pagan e-mail discussion group. Her account of why she chose to meet one of the authors in person before participating in the study demonstrates caution in moving from meeting people in virtual space to meeting them in real space. When asked if she had ever encountered any dangerous people on the Internet, she said:

> No. In most of the communities everyone's pretty friendly and if people post messages like "If you really wanna learn more about Wicca come and meet me at this place" everyone else on the list would write back "What are you doing? [Don't do it]" that kind of thing. [For example] when you [Douglas Ezzy] posted to Australian Pagans, people replied saying "Yep, I know this guy. I can vouch for him." But a lot of the other times people couldn't vouch. So it's like the whole community was looking out for each other' cause they didn't want people to be sort of abused.

Dawson (2000) raises the issue that the creation of multiple selves on the Internet may come in conflict with identity integration—something he credits traditional religions with helping to create. But late-modernity may itself be mitigating against the creation of one integrated self (Gergen 1991; Giddens

1991). For some, the reflexive nature of the self in contemporary society is equated with a fragmentation of the self and increased individualism. However, Castells suggests: "But individualism is not social isolation or even alienation, as superficial observers or nostalgic commentators often suggest. It is a social pattern, it is a source of meaning, of meaning constructed about the projects and desires of the individual. And it finds in the Internet the proper technology for its expression and its organization" (2002: xxx).

As Turkle (1995) contends, particularly in terms of MUDs (multiuser domains) and MOOs (multiuser domains that are object-oriented), the Internet provides an arena for the creation of multiple selves. Through its rituals of self, Witchcraft provides its participants with both a forum and the magical techniques to create multiple selves (Berger 1999). Chat rooms and e-mail forums help facilitate this identity experimentation, and information gleaned from Web sites also feeds into the reflexive process. The teenage Witches in our sample are experimenting not only with Witchcraft as a religion but with their own identities (see Lövheim, this volume).

The Internet supports the identities and community of contemporary Witchcraft in a manner similar to the way Internet usage supports and facilitates community and identity in other social groupings. For example, Matei and Ball-Rokeach (2002) found that among ethnic communities in Los Angeles, the more individuals interacted online, the more likely they were also to belong to physical communities. Hampton and Wellman (2002) found that Internet usage in an American suburban neighborhood facilitates ties with people who were previously "just out of reach" geographically.

Similarly, active participation in Witchcraft-related online communities provides young Witches with an important sense of contact with and belonging to a group of people who share similar beliefs and practices but who were perhaps "just out of reach" geographically. A number of respondents reported that some of the people they had met on the Internet they went on to meet in person. These people may live in the next suburb, the next city, overseas, or sometimes in their own community. Rather than causing identity fragmentation, participation in the Internet may actually be facilitating identity integration under the conditions of late-modernity, in which relationships are increasingly dispersed geographically and temporally and identity is always in the process of transformation.

All the teenage Witches we interviewed said that Witchcraft had been a positive experience for them, typically providing them with greater self-confidence and allowing them to deal with a variety of emotionally difficult issues. The Internet sometimes contributed to this process. For example, Clarissa, an Australian Witch, told us:

> I was wearing a pentagram and a girl came up and started chatting to me and it was the first kind of public Pagan I'd really met. I was very shy and very reserved until then and I knew [through magazines] about groups and things that were happening, but I was too scared to go along. I didn't have access to the Internet back then. [But

now] I'm on several e-mail discussion lists. When I first started out I quite enjoyed Witches Voice, which is the U.S.-based site. It was an easy way to get in contact with people [and] I did when I started and then met them at public circles. [Those Internet contacts gave me] a head start. [It was] much easier to meet people and get an idea of chatting to them on line whether you're going to get along in real life as well.

For teenage Witches, cyberspace serves as both an alternative community and as a source of information. Almost all of those we interviewed have used the Internet as an alternative encyclopedia—going to it for information about rituals, healing herbs, or magical practices. Some have also used the Internet as a way to experiment with their identities as Witches. They communicate with others about their rituals and have those rituals and their practices affirmed by others copying down those rituals or contacting them for information or advice.

Some of the Witches in our sample have been trained in covens and have sought others out with whom to practice, while others have remained solitary practitioners. In both cases the Internet remains an important part of their sense of self and of community. Our research is consistent with Dawson's (2001: 2) observation that "the link between the Internet and religion, through experiments in the formation of identity and community, is dialectical and not causal." Young Witches are using the Internet as one of a variety of resources to explore and develop their identities and to create a community. Along with movies, television, books, and magazines, the Internet is only one part of the new and not-so-new information technologies that are profoundly shaping contemporary religious.

Acknowledgments

An earlier version of this paper was presented at the 2002 Association for the Sociology of Religion annual meeting.

Notes

1. Names of teenage Witches used in this paper are pseudonyms.

References

Anthony, D., and T. Robbins, (1994). "Brainwashing and Totalitarian Influence." In *Encyclopedia of Human Behavior*, ed. V. S. Ramachandran, 1: 457–471. San Diego: Academic Press.

Beckford, J. (1985). *Cult Controversies: The Societal Response to the New Religious Movements*. London: Tavistock.

Berger, H. A. (1999). *A Community of Witches: Contemporary Neo-Paganism and Witchcraft in the United States*. Colombia, SC: University of South Carolina Press.

Berger, H. A., E. A., Leach, and L. S. Shaffer, (2003). *Voices from the Pagan Census: A National Survey of Witches and Neo-Pagans in the United States*. Columbia, SC: University of South Carolina Press.

Clark, L. S. (2003). *From Angels to Aliens: Teenagers, the Media, and the Supernatural*. Oxford, UK: Oxford University Press.

Castells, M. (2002). "The Internet and the Network Society." In *The Internet in Everyday Life*, ed. B. Wellman and C. Haythornthwaite. Malden, MA: Blackwell.

Cobb, J. (1998). *Cybergrace: The Search for God in the Digital World*. New York: Crown Press.

Crowley, V. (1998). "Wicca as Nature Religion." In *Nature Religion Today*, ed. J. Pearson, R. Roberts, and G. Samuel. Edinburgh: Edinburgh University Press.

Cunningham, S. (1988). *Wicca: A Guide for the Solitary Practitioner*. St. Paul, MN: Llewellyn Publications.

———. (1994). *Living Wicca: A Further Guide for the Solitary Practitioner*. St. Paul, MN: Llewellyn Publications.

Davis, E (1995). "Technopagans: May the Astral Plane Be Reborn in Cyberspace." *Wired* 3.07: 126–133, 174–181.

Dawson, L. L. (1998). *Comprehending Culte; The Sociology of New Religious Movement.* Toronto: Oxford University Press.

Dawson, L. L. (2000). "Researching Religion in Cyberspace: Issues and Strategies." In *Religion on the Internet: Research Prospects and Promises*, ed. J. K. Hadden and D. E. Cowan. London: JAI Press/Elsevier Science.

———. (2001) "Cyberspace and Religious Life: Conceptualising Concerns and Consequences." Paper presented at the Center for Study on New Religions/INFORM 2001 International Conference, London School of Economics.

Dawson, L. L., and J. Hennebry, (1999). "New Religions and the Internet: Recruiting in a New Public Space." *Journal of Contemporary Religion* 14: 117–139.

Eilberg-Schwatz, H. (1989). "Witches of the West: Neo-Paganism and Goddess Worship as Enlightenment Religions." *Journal of Feminist Studies of Religion* 5: 77–95.

Ezzy, D. (2001). "The Commodification of Witchcraft." *Australian Religion Studies Review* 14: 31–44.

———. (2003). "New Age Witchcraft?" *Culture and Religion* 4 (1): 17–33.

Gergen, K. J. (1991). *The Saturated Self: Dilemmas of Identity in Contemporary Life.* New York: Basic Books.

Giddens, A. (1991). *Modernity and Self-Identity: Self and Society in the Late Modern Age.* Cambridge, UK: Cambridge University Press.

Greenwood, S. (1998). "The Nature of the Goddess: Sexual Identities and Power in Contemporary Witchcraft." In *Nature Religion Today: Paganism in the Modern World*, ed. J. Pearson. Edinburgh: Edinburgh University Press.

Hampton, K., and B. Wellman, (2002). "The Not So Global Village of Netville." In *The Internet in Everyday Life*, ed. B. Wellman and C. Haythornethwaite. Malden, MA: Blackwell.

Harrow, J. (1994). "Other People's Kids: Working with the Underaged Seeker." In *Modern Rites of Passage: Witchcraft Today, Book Two*, ed. C. S. Clifton. St. Paul, MN: Llewellyn Publications.

Helland, C. (2000). "Online Religion/Religion Online and Virtual Communitas." In *Religion on the Internet: Research Prospects and Promises*, ed. J. K. Hadden and D. E. Cowan. London: JAI Press/Elsevier Science.

Introvigne, M. (2000). "'So Many Evil Things': Anti-Cult Terrorism via the Internet." In *Religion on the Internet: Research Prospects and Promises*, ed. J. K. Hadden and D. E. Cowan. London: JAI Press/Elsevier Science.

K, A. (1998). *Covencraft: Witchcraft for Three or More.* St. Paul, MN: Llewellyn Publications.

Matei, S., and S. Ball-Rokeach, (2002). "Belonging in Geographic, Ethnic, and Internet Spaces." In *The Internet in Everyday Life*, ed. B. Wellman and C. Haythornthwaite. Malden MA: Blackwell.

Mayer, J-F. (2000). "Religious Movements and the Internet: The New Frontier of Cult Controversies." In *Religion on the Internet: Research Prospects and Promises*, ed. J. K. Hadden and D. E. Cowan. London: JAI Press/Elsevier Science.

McGrory, D. (2001). "Children Seduced by Forces of Satanism on the Internet." *Times* (London), August 28: 4.

NightMare, M. M. (2001). *Witchcraft and the Web: Weaving Pagan Traditions Online.* Toronto: ECW Press.

O'Leary, S. D., and B. E. Brasher, (1996). "The Unknown God of the Internet: Religious Communications from the Ancient Agora to the Virtual Forum." In *Philosophical Approaches on Computer-Mediated Communications*, ed. C. Ess. Albany, NY: SUNY Press.

RavenWolf, S. (1999). *Teen Witch: Wicca for a New Generation.* St. Paul, MN: Llewellyn Publications.

Reuters. (2003). "Web, Potter Help Paganism." *Sydney Morning Herald* (June 20). Retrieved from www.smh.com.au/1013381511140html, July 15, 2003.

Roof, W. C. (1993). *A Generation of Seekers: The Spiritual Journeys of the Baby Boom Generation.* San Francisco: HarperCollins.

Turkle, S. (1995). *Life on the Screen: Identity in the Age of the Internet.* New York: Simon and Schuster.

Zablocki, B., and T., Robbins, eds. (2001). *Misunderstanding Cults: Searching for Objectivity in a Controversial Field.* Toronto: University of Toronto Press.

Zaleski, J. (1997). *The Soul of Cyberspace: How New Technology Is Changing our Spiritual Lives.* San Francisco: HarperEdge.

13
The Goddess Net

WENDY GRIFFIN

Introduction

Considerable discussion has taken place regarding the inherent democracy of the Internet, where traditional distinctions of social status are less visible than in the flesh-and-blood world and individuals and groups have an opportunity to voice their opinions and to create community among like-minded Web users. Although the nature of these virtual communities as communities has yet to be determined (Dawson 2002; see also Dawson's chapter in this volume), there is no question but that the Web has become a portal to a world of ideas and contacts far beyond what previous generations could have imagined. In great part this is due to the explosive growth the Web has experienced since its introduction in the United States in 1993. Even five years ago, the number of Web sites was doubling every six months (Hadden and Cowan 2000). Another contributing factor is that by 2000, over half of all Americans under the age of sixty had access to the Web from their homes (Arthur 2002), and some 55 million Americans are online on any average day (Pew Research Center 2000).

The significance of so much easily acquired information can be seen in the area of religion. Whereas our grandparents may have had exposure to a few religious traditions, texts, and organizations in their life times, the Internet provides a virtual smorgasbord of choices regarding religious information, from the very traditional faiths to the most contemporary and innovative. Research demonstrates that people are indeed using the Web for this purpose.

Religion has a long history of using new technologies, from Gutenberg's printed Bible to the world's first radio broadcast to television soul-saving and fund-raising (Hadden and Cowan 2000). Brasher (1996: 819) argues that the creative technology of the Web is particularly suited to new religious movements, that "untethered from ancient texts . . . appear most at home." Among the new religions that have taken advantage of this medium are contemporary Paganism and Goddess Spirituality. In fact, it has been reported that the first religious groups active on the World Wide Web were contemporary Pagans (Arthur 2002), a group that is overrepresented among people employed in areas of computer technology (Adler 1986; Berger, Leach and Shaffer 2003; Jorgensen and Russell see 1999).

Today's Pagans are a diverse group that includes Witches, Wiccans, Druids, Goddess worshippers, and more. What they have in common is "an affirmation of interactive and polymorphic sacred relationship by individual or community with the tangible, sentient and nonempirical" (York 2000: 9). The Divine is understood to be immanent in all things and sometimes transcendent as well. There is some debate as to whether women who focus on "the Goddess," practicing what is sometimes referred to as Goddess monotheism, fit this definition (Griffin 2003; Long 1997). Indeed, some of these practitioners would not be totally comfortable with the label of Pagan, although many others claim it. However, British scholar Asphodel Long argues that asking women if the Goddess is one or many is akin to asking if water is one or many (Long 1997). Women believe the Goddess is both. She is seen as polymorphic, and their belief in her immanence emphasizes their relationship with the Divine as it manifests in themselves and all of Nature. While both women and men who identify as Pagans use female symbolism and imagery to represent Deity, the female imagery used is polymorphic, and many Pagans also use male metaphors along with the female ones. Hence although they may have other affiliations as well, all are part of the Goddess community.

Pagans Online

Both scholars and practitioners have asked how the Internet is affecting the Goddess community; there is a general consensus that it is. As one High Priestess of a virtual coven and author of *The Virtual Pagan* explained, the Web's "cutting-edge technology has the ability to weave centuries old magick with hyperlinks and fiberoptics" (McSherry 2002).[1] Removing the barrier of physical distance permits real-time group participation in virtual religious rituals. Virtual shrines and altars provide places for online solitary devotion. There are also active, learning-based environments, Pagan newsletters, newspapers, journals, and 'zines, online radio broadcasting, performance, and the cooperative sale of Pagan music. Webcams trace the path of the sun at ancient monuments on the solstices and the relighting of the Beltane fires in Ireland. Web sites dedicated to archeological digs such as that in Catal Huyuk, one of the first and greatest Neolithic sites, host online discussions on ancient Goddess worship where Pagans leave long, involved postings. Classes abound in everything from Wicca 101, to divination using the Tarot, to Pagan pastoral counseling. There is even a Pagan seminary in Vermont—Cherry Hill Seminary—that offers both on-site and distance learning and provides professional Pagan ministerial training and ordination.

Macha NightMare, an author and a founding member of the Reclaiming Collective of Witches, agrees that the Internet has given Witches a new set of tools with which to direct intent and manipulate energy, which is the most common Pagan definition of magic. She believes that Pagan culture has been radically altered by the Web through Web sites, Listservs, and e-mail, allowing:

Witches to communicate, react, and respond with extraordinary speed and effectiveness. An act of bias is met with swift mobilization—with kindred aid and comfort. Legal assistance, and media efforts. . . . Our connections in cyberspace become connections in terraspace—friendships are made, covens are found or formed, organizations take shape, and goals with plans of action emerge. We are no longer invisible—to one another, or the world. The weaving Witches do on the Web has made us luminously visible. (NightMare 2001: 16)

The Web is an apt metaphor for the Goddess community in general. O'Leary (1996) pointed out that Wiccan rituals, both offline and on, often have elements that focus on reweaving and strengthening the community web. This is especially true of women-only groups, whether or not they are Wiccan, where the community web refers to both the local and global community of women and to the Web of Life itself. Of course, surfing the Internet and being a consumer of information does not mean communicating, nor does simply posting or possessing shared information make a community. It is this potential for community, for being more than a supercolossal digitized library, that makes the Web so exciting and rich for research.

Methodology

This chapter examines two kinds of virtual communities. One is a Community of Action and the other a Community of Discourse. The first, the Goddess 2000 Project, was originally created by an artist who wanted to celebrate the beginning of the new millennium with religious art representing the Divine in female form. This part of the research began with an e-mail received from NightMare in early December 1999, with suggestions for doing a ritual on the Winter Solstice. The research continued with observation of a growing Web site (www.goddess2000.org) for the two years the project was active, with occasional follow-ups until April 2003.

The research on the Community of Discourse covered a twelve-month period ending in July 2003 and consisted of a content analysis of five different online discussion groups: Fea2st, Goddess Scholars (GS), the Temple of Isis Los Angeles (TOI),[2] the Institute for Feminism and Religion Discussion Group (IFR), and the Nature Religions Scholars Network (NRSN).[3] The first three groups were women-only, the fourth may have had males but they did not post during the time of this study, and the last included both sexes. The first three groups were made up exclusively of women practicing Paganism and Goddess *thealogy*, the word commonly used among Goddess scholars and practitioners to denote the study of religion where the Divine is envisioned as female. IFR, although including some Pagan women, was broader in focus and also had members interested in revisionist feminist theology. NRSN focused primarily on contemporary Paganism, although not all members were Pagans. The largest group studied had 271 members; the smallest, seventeen.

All five groups included lay and academic scholars and students. The significance of this distinction may not be immediately apparent. Various studies have noted that practitioners of both Goddess Spirituality and contemporary Paganism tend usually to be well-read and typically have more formal education than average (Berger, Leach, and Shaffer 2003; Griffin 1995). It is clear from online discussions that many of these individuals consider themselves to be scholars, and indeed they may well be. However, academic scholars are systematically trained in critical analysis and their work is subject to continual review by others with similar training. This tends to make them somewhat more cautious in accepting truth claims than lay scholars. As will be discussed later in this chapter, this was especially evident in discussions regarding interpretations of prehistory. All of the groups emphasized their scholarly orientation except TOI, which was more focused on actual spiritual practice.

The Community of Action

As many people prepared for the year 2000 (Y2K) to usher in a wide range of possible cataclysms, others prepared to celebrate the return or "Second Coming" of the Goddess, a phrase reflecting the belief that humanity worshipped a female deity long before male monotheism.[4] On the eve of the new millennium they declared: "The next 1000 belong to the Goddess and Her Wisdom" (Willowroot 1998). This became a rallying cry for Goddess 2000, a grassroots art project that attempted to create a virtual Goddess community. G2K (as Goddess 2000 was called) was the vision of Abby Willowroot, a nationally known artist.

The year-long event began with an opening ritual on the Winter Solstice 1999, called "Dancing the Goddess Home." Willowroot had spent over a year collecting ideas and contributions from well-known Pagan poets, artists, writers, and ritualists and developing a Web site (www.goddess2000.org) that explained the project. From these, she and NightMare spun together a detailed ritual, even to the extent of including recipes for food and drink to be shared. The script was posted online and was widely advertised in the Goddess community for people to use in its entirety or in bits, as they preferred (Willowroot 1999). Willowroot and NightMare envisioned that all participants would perform the Winter Solstice ritual at 8 P.M. in their own time zone, so that "the energy of the ritual would be carried around the Earth, passing from one time zone to the next, all night long" (Nightmare 2001: 194).

But that was just the beginning. The whole year was to be filled with Goddess events and art. By February 2000, people in thirty five countries were participating, and e-mail addresses for area coordinators began to be posted on the official G2K Web site. The page informed people that they did not "have to be an artist to make Goddess Art. If you love the Goddess, you will honor Her with whatever you make." It continued: "Many of the Goddess pieces are for public display and many are being displayed only in people's homes and in their gardens. The point is to create a web of Goddess energy. You don't need to be public with your Goddess art unless you want to. The power is in the

Creation of these pieces of sacred imagery" (Willowroot 1998). Items promoting G2K were offered for sale online: bumper stickers, T-shirts, coffee mugs, decals, jewelry, and canvas bags. The Web site offered suggestions and even instructions for art projects such as mask-making and community labyrinth building. By March, there were twenty Web pages of photographs of Goddess art submitted by participants, as well as discussion boards, e-mail lists for each area, a main e-mail list of three hundred, and page after page of events postings.

Some groups did one event, others had ongoing programs for the year. The busiest group appeared to be in the state of Georgia, with public activities occurring throughout the year. Brazil reported a gathering of seven hundred people dancing in six spiral dances and building a statue of Isis ten meters tall. The G2K Message Board announced events as varied as women making small peat or unfired clay goddesses for their gardens in New Zealand, Ireland, and Germany, to a full year of bimonthly meetings in Toronto to create Goddess art, to the rental of three large public billboards announcing the Goddess's presence in Minneapolis–St. Paul.

By fall of 2000, the focus had shifted—rather than on event organizing, it was on manifesting a "Goddess on every block." Willowroot suggested that this could be done very simply. A chalk outline of a Neolithic female form familiar to the Goddess community would do; the words "Blessed Be" drawn on the sidewalk would tell practitioners that the Goddess was present. As the year wound down and the focus changed, the discussion board was moved to the MSN Groups site and displayed very little traffic. It became clear by the postings that people were more interested in individual art projects than in large-scale communal works and were no longer submitting photographs of their artwork to the G2K site. Nevertheless, the numbers of participants listed on the Web site continued to grow, and at its peak in late 2001, G2K claimed contacts in every state of the United States and in fifty six countries. These included all countries where English is an official language, but also places where one might not expect to find participants, including Argentina, Bosnia and Herzegovina, Finland, Iceland, Israel, Lebanon, Morocco, Serbia, South Africa, Sweden, and Turkey (www.goddess2000.org/Community.html). By the close of the project, there were 547 area coordinators and contact people listed on the community page of the official G2K Web site.

Although the project continued throughout 2001, it grew less active by year's end. By mid-2002 no new postings appeared. By March 2003, the contact people were no longer listed, and the entire Web site was set to expire at the end of July 2003. In October, however, it was still available, at that time, though, the site and project would have been online for four years.

Although G2K did not result in a Goddess on every block, it did succeed in creating a community of sorts. For example, one Los Angeles coven was so inspired that each member committed to drawing a chalk sidewalk goddess on the first day of the month for a full year. Unfortunately, however, not only did they *not* photograph the drawings or post this activity on the G2K Web site, they decided not to use the sidewalks near their own homes for fear of religious persecution. In a project as widespread as G2K, other unreported Goddess art undoubtedly appeared.[5] Bumper stickers and decals are still occasionally sighted, and some of the art, such as cement Goddesses, is obviously more permanent than a spiral dance. The final significance of G2K lies not primarily in the community of action made up of artists and other participants, but in the sense of community created among Pagans who saw the art and the Web site. Although some may still be deep in the "broom closet" and reluctant to have a goddess statue on their front lawn, seeing a huge billboard or a small bumber sticker that announces "The Goddess Is Alive and Magic Is Afoot" lets Pagans know that they are not alone. G2K showed it was possible to bring Goddess symbolism into the open and that the Goddess community is international in scope. Regardless of how big the project was or how many pieces of art were developed, it provided the Pagan community with a sense of its own presence and a form of legitimacy that comes from perceiving oneself to be part of an ongoing, productive, visible group.

While G2K is now part of contemporary Pagan history, it may serve as inspiration for further action. In an online discussion concerning the opening of England's first formally registered Goddess temple, a woman from Washington, D.C., wrote:

> I feel one of the reasons that (IMO) visibility of Goddess spirituality/religion is diminishing (compared to about a decade ago) is that there have been no "places" for those dedicated to the Goddess to meet. I believe this is a big reason many Goddess people have been subsumed into Pagan sects that are not woman-empowering and into various New Age nonsense, similarly nonfeminist. And certainly as some of us age and are not able to go to outdoor rituals because of various disabilities, this problem becomes even more pressing. You know Abby Willowroot's wonderful "Goddess on every block"—I'd like to see a (fully accessible) Goddess building (temple?) in every town. Well, ok, in the U.S. we can start with every state. (Miriam 2003)

Gendered Voices

Although G2K was created and guided by one woman, both women and men were involved as artists and participants in Goddess events. Studies demonstrate that a majority of Pagans are female (Adler 1986; Berger et al. 2003), but very few scholarly researchers in Paganism focus on gender specifically. Yet a careful examination suggests certain insights. For example, NightMare quotes a woman saying that the Internet:

> gives us a voice we never had before by presenting the number of Pagans no one would have believed existed in a medium that doesn't have morals like other forms of media. It is our words, uncensored and stripped of the Hollywood image. For the first time, our work, words, thoughts stand side by side with everyone else's with equal weight and without editorial comment. (NightMare 2001: 58)

The language quoted is strikingly familiar to anyone versed in the history of the American women's movement. In a process commonly referred to as women "finding our voice," feminists have long argued that self-expression and communication are intrinsic elements of women's liberation. Hence it was important to establish "safe" places where women could share their stories and experiences, such as the consciousness-raising (CR) groups in the 1960s and 1970s and Women's Studies classrooms today. Here women could escape the social conditioning and consequences that silence what Foucault (1984: 113) called "forbidden speech." In fact, it was in these early CR groups that the first feminist critiques of traditional religions led to the development of thealogy and of women's and feminist spirituality groups. In North America, feminism itself has had a tremendous impact on Paganism (Berger 1999; Griffin 2003). But although these early spiritual groups grew quickly, they were limited to those who knew someone or who had access to select books or a very few magazines (Griffin 2003). Clearly, this is no longer the case. As of 2000, women reportedly made up 50.4 percent of Web users in the United States (New York Times 2000), and many women are actively searching the Web for spiritual/ religious information (Pew Research Center 2003). This is significant because women's voices in traditional religions have been filtered through institutional restraints that have shaped, interpreted, translated, and even silenced them. As Youngs observes, "the circumstances within which women communicate are an essential part of understanding not only the limitations on how or what they communicate, but also their possibilities for imagining alternatives. There is a long history of feminist debate about the social locations of women and the ways in which these shape their power relations and possibilities in the world as well as their own consciousness about their lives" (Youngs 1999: 59). Just as NightMare's respondent pointed out regarding Pagans in general, the Web offers Goddess women the potential for a "safe place" where they cannot be censored or condemned for their ideas or judged intellectually or spiritually inadequate because of their gender by men. Given this safe space, the question then becomes: What are Goddess women talking about in this virtual room of their own?

The Community of Discourse

While much has been made of the disembodied quality of virtual voices and the potential anonymity of the Web that makes gender invisible, irrelevant, or even fluid (see, e.g., Youngs 1999), other researchers argue that users frequently give off gender cues in computer-mediated communication, often in very traditional, even stereotypical ways. Successful online gender-bending appears to be infrequent (see Herring 2001). This is important in the consideration of a gender-safe discussion group. While a participant in a women-only group may be judged, dismissed, criticized, and even flamed, it is extremely unlikely that this would happen because she is female. Thus she can expect to be freer to discover or exercise her "voice."

In order to examine this more closely, five distinct Goddess discussion groups were selected for study. A content analysis of communications resulted in five general types of discourse: Purpose, Activism, Shared Information, Thea/ology and Meaning, and what Lennie and colleagues (1999:161) call "a gendered discourse of care and connection."

A Discourse of Purpose

All five groups did extensive networking online. This involved such obvious things as announcing events (conferences, workshops, and Pagan celebrations), arranging to meet at conferences or when traveling, discussing how to get published, requesting the names of books for classes or sample syllabi, announcing the publication of one's own book, and looking for book reviewers. One author and lay scholar even sent "helpful" guidelines for people who might want to write a review of her new book.

> Since my brand new book has been released . . . it has become clear to me that my target audience (you!) might naturally not have the specialized academic foundation required for registering precisely the significant original contribution I am making in the fields of archaeology, history and even science. Ultimately this doesn't really matter, as you will (hopefully) just enjoy the book as a revolutionary treatise on women's history and simply a good read. But for anyone who plans to review the book, reccommend [sic] it to your lists, use it in a book-study group, college course, or perhaps discuss the contents on a radio or t.v. show—it will be helpful, I think, if you have an outline of the primary original points I am making (in between the lines, in many cases) throughout the book. For this reason I am attaching a formatted outline of points for printing out, and also pasting it into this email message for anyone who wants to quickly scan through the guidelines. (Shakti 2003)

A Discourse of Activism

A call to activism was prominent on three of the lists, although at one time or another, petitions appeared on all five. By far the greatest focus in this area was the war in Iraq, where there was strong support for protesters. This support ranged from regular reports forwarded to the Listserv from jailed protestors in Ireland's Limerick Prison to announcements of rallies in California of Witches for Peace.

Another example of activism involved preparing for March 8, International Women's Day. Three different lists forwarded daily postings from a project called Gather the Women. During the week leading up to March 8, members of these Listservs were asked to spend about an hour each day focusing on things like introspection, healing, and connecting. Purposeful action was very much a part of this message, which for Day Six read in part:

> Whatever issues touch your heart,
> educate yourself and brainstorm solutions.
> Start petitions or letter-writing campaigns.
> Write press releases.

Urge media to inform you accurately.
Inadequate response?
Make a list of products they advertise,
and tell the media source AND their sponsors
you will not buy their products until they comply—
THEN DO IT!
Frequent websites with conscientious information
and action resources.
Participate in vigils and peace marches.
Organize or join boycotts. (Magdalena 2003)

The other issues covered in this discourse were things like threats to the environment, breast cancer and AIDS walks, and petitions that dealt with women's issues.

A Discourse of Shared Information

This usually occurred when someone either asked for specific information or made a statement that another list participant believed was inaccurate and rushed to correct. For example, one participant asked: "Does anyone have a good source for information about Eostre? I've been reading some rabid Christian websites [*sic*] fulmination about the pagan origins of Easter. They claim Eostre is really Ishtar/Astarte, which sounds good to me, but I've also heard the name is related to Eos and that she's an Anglo-Saxon goddess" (Anne 2003). Conversely, in the latter category would fall a discussion on the dubious historicity of the "Burning Times"—a three-hundred-year period during which some Pagans believe nine million witches, primarily women, were put to death. This began on the NRSN list with an innocent comment about victimization and was met with multiple responses, including who came up with the name of the Burning Times, speculation on the origin of the number of women killed, reasons why the figure is inaccurate, discussion of the problems of "victim mentality," and, finally, a short article one of the list participants had published on the topic in an encyclopedia.

A Discourse of Thea/ology and Meaning

Discussions in this area had the potential to become arguments. This occurred primarily when people made assumptions about the uniformity of beliefs of other list participants. A prime example concerns the meaning of the work done by archeologist Marija Gimbutas.

Gimbutas (1974) argued for the existence in "Old Europe" of a prehistoric, peaceful, agrarian culture that was matrifocal and worshiped a primary female deity. This culture, she claimed, was invaded in a series of waves over a period of two thousand years by horseback-riding, patriarchal warriors, who brought with them their male-dominated religion. Although her work (especially her later work) has been criticized by many scholars (see Griffin 2003), the myth of the "Golden Age of Matriarchy" continues to be embraced by some practitioners of Goddess Spirituality, who draw inspiration from what they believe is long-denied human history. Although academic scholars are much more likely to critique her work than lay scholars in the field, not all academics find fault with her conclusions.

One academic who has been very vocal in her criticism is Cynthia Eller (2000). In October 2002, Eller spoke at a conference at Sonoma State University. The reaction to her critique of Gimbutas and the tone in which it was reportedly delivered was immediate. A participant on the GS listserv forwarded a twenty-page, single-spaced critique of Eller's argument written by Joan Marler, a critique later Web-published on the site of a production company organized by noted Witch and author Starhawk and Donna Reed, who are producing a film on the life of Gimbutas (www.belili.org/belili.html). The GS Listserv members who had attended the conference were bombarded with questions. Why was Eller invited? Who was responsible? The response by an attendee was that it was a conference on gender and archeology, and that the invitation was the responsibility of the "straight" women organizing the conference. However, when queried, it appeared that the word "straight" was used to refer to academic as opposed to lay scholars, and not heterosexual women. A posting by an academic member reminded everyone that there were academic scholars on the list and that some, but not all of them, had concerns about the belief in a prehistoric Golden Age. A request was made to post some of the concerns. While this was done, these concerns were never discussed and the topic was dropped. Seven months later, in the context of an entirely different discussion on Stonehenge, the following was posted:

> [We] have touched upon what I think is a very crucial question in goddess scholarship. How is it we know what we know? I find it entertaining, for instance, that Eller so confidently states that Stonehenge is phallic (last time I looked, penises weren't round, but oh well). To me one of the most interesting and possibly controversial aspects of Gimbutas's scholarship is that she dispensed with the "Rosetta stone" approach and argued that we can interpret unknown symbols by looking at the symbols themselves. Had she found proof of a worldwide, ageold [sic] patriarchy, I believe that her approach would have been welcomed and lauded. But she found something quite different, which has led her conclusions to be defamed while her methods are not, to me, sufficiently debated (Fiona 2003a).

And two days later, "there is a lot of reading-into Gimbutas. And also people thinking they are talking about her theories when they're talking about interpretations (sometimes projections) of/it into her theories" (Fiona 2003b).

The lack of argument among list members in this example may be because those who did not find their positions supported simply chose to not respond rather than openly disagree. Herring's (2001) research on gender and power in electronic communications found that (1) males and females tend to have different styles of communication online; and (2) women often appear to be aligned online, even when they disagree with each other. However, this apparent lack of disagreement did not occur on all the lists under study.

A rather surprising finding was that while the Listserv that included men (NRSN) was much more likely to be involved in disagreements in the Discourse of Thea/ology and Meaning, women on the list were among the most vocal and argumentative participants. This was evident, for example, in communications that either announced or implied that because of their spiritual beliefs, Pagans were vegetarians or pacifists. These statements were quickly met by Pagans who were hunters, by farmers who raised and slaughtered their own meat, or by Pagans in the military. This is the only list of the five where particularly belligerent members were removed by the list moderator. As this was the only list where disagreements grew heated, as well as the only list to which males posted, it might be inferred that the influence of gender was at play. Research has shown that the more numerous a gender is in an online group, the greater the influence it will have on shared discursive norms (Herring 2001). However, NRSN is roughly evenly divided between males and females, and at this point it is impossible to say with certainty if gender played a decisive role in this regard.

The women-only lists were much more prone to "I" statements regarding belief and meaning, rather than actual discussions in thea/ology. In the former category could be found descriptions of how a particular woman celebrated a Pagan holiday and the individual meaning it held for her, or a trip one took to an ancient ruin and how she felt about the place. This was true for both academic and lay scholars. However, even if they are not actively exploring thea/ology, women are exchanging information about the way traditional religious texts and traditions are being reinterpreted. For example, an article was posted from *The Hartford Courant* on the GS list. In part, it was an interview with Hartford Seminary Professor Miriam Therese Winter, a nun who has written extensively on women in the Bible. She referred to the passage in Genesis where Jacob blesses his sons. The article read, in part: "He [Jacob] invokes 'Shaddai,' a Hebrew word that has traditionally been translated as 'the almighty.' But 'shad' is a Hebrew word meaning breast. 'Shaddai' really means, 'God the breasted one,' Winter explains. In Genesis 49:25, Jacob says, 'By Shaddai who will bless you . . . with blessings of the breast and of the womb'" (Altimari 1998). The image of God the Breasted One was warmly received on the GS list, as it both presented the Divine as female and appeared to confirm the belief in a patriarchal cover-up of "true" Goddess history.

A Discourse of Care and Connection

Although this discussion included announcements such as academic degrees granted or deaths of respected Elders in the Pagan community, the responses these announcements generated place them in this category. Warm congratulations followed the granting of a degree, often with personal stories of the horrors involved in the dissertation process. News of an individual's death were met with personal anecdotes of the deceased person's life, how much his or her work meant to the "speaker," and an offering of blessings or prayers.

More unexpected on scholarly lists were the rare announcements from a participant that she had cancer or that she was afraid her abusive husband was likely to try for child custody because of her Paganism, or that her child's serious illness and the resulting demands on her resources forced her to remove herself from the list. These generated an outpouring of emotional support and advice. Women wrote in about their own brushes with cancer and abuse and suggested many potentially helpful resources. While some of this had little to do with spirituality, other messages were clearly focused on the kind of help only the Goddess community could offer. For example, one Los Angeles woman with cancer asked for very explicit help. She wrote:

> As I prepare for my surgery . . . I'm looking for a good Witch or two, specifically a Reiki master and/or Touch For Life practitioner. I'm looking for someone to come to my home . . . on Saturday, afternoon or evening, for a preoperative treatment and for someone to come to the . . . hospital on Wednesday or Thursday, for a postoperative treatment. I've been doing major visualizations to get that tumor outta there, and I know I'm being showered by people all over the U.S., but some hands-on work might also help. Will also help.
>
> If you can help me with this energetic work, can you please email me off-list? Many thanks (Patricia 2003).

A member of the list who met her qualifications responded and arranged hands-on healings for her, and the virtual relationship became a real-world one.

Conclusions

Goddess women read the online description of God with breast and womb, and it gives legitimacy to what they may already believe. Clearly, new readings of religious texts and a safe place to delve into them are helping women—and Pagans in general—to discover and explore their voices. In this way, the Web provides space for fragile but potentially productive zones of resistance to dominant religious ideologies. Older Goddess scholars as well as many Pagan practitioners were profoundly influenced by the feminist activism of the 1970s and 1980s, as was the early Goddess scholarship published during those decades (see Griffin 2003). However, the trend among today's participants appears to be more in terms of individual interpretations and spiritual self-fulfillment rather than the defiant feminist political challenges to religious orthodoxy more typical of earlier times (see Griffin, forthcoming; Lozano and Foltz 1990). This may explain Miriam's remarks about her perception of the diminished visibility of Goddess Spirituality and its becoming less feminist. Another example is G2K, which began as a global project partially in reaction to the attempted Christianization of the new millennium and ended up with small-scale, personalized Goddesses in gardens and on street corners.

It has been suggested that the tremendous amount of information available on religions, combined with an estrangement from traditional cultural institutions, makes this highly individualized spirituality possible (Roof 1999). Some of the resulting blend of Paganism and New Age spirituality was forseen as a logical outcome of modernity's shift from an external locus of control to an internal one (Heelas 1996; York 1995). Horsfall (2000) points out that even those who do not use the Web are affected by it because of its wide dissemination of ideas, and she even suggests we may be headed toward a "Personal Reformation" similar to the Protestant Reformation, as people develop their own ideas about theology. An example of this can be seen in the idiosyncratic blending within various Goddess traditions (Griffin 2003).

If the online communities are too transitory to be considered genuine communities, the Web certainly provides the opportunity for cohesion among the dispersed Pagan community of flesh and blood. Solitary Witches who practice alone can interact online with others in their area or in distant foreign countries; they can even join a virtual coven. The temporary nature of this kind of community is questionable when one takes into account claims such as McSherry's (2003), that one virtual coven founded in 1997 is still in existence. In addition, suggestions for readings, for rituals, and for Goddess art facilitate a certain measure of group cohesion. Pagans online do extensive networking, and sometimes this translates into personal relationships in the real world as a healer responds to a call, an isolated rural Pagan discovers another, or two Goddess scholars arrange to meet at a conference. Hence the Goddess Net may be understood as both the electronic activity that takes place online among Pagans and the interwoven connections that are made there and enacted in the real world.

The questions that remain are: With multiple understandings of Paganism available in the virtual marketplace and the current impulse toward self-fulfillment, individualized spirituality, and personal reformation, what will hold the members of this community together as time passes? How will the nature of Paganism be changed? And what role will women, who have been so important in the development of contemporary Paganism, play in these changes?

Notes

1. The unusual spelling of "magick" is used by some Pagans to indicate a spiritual practice and to differentiate it from slight-of-hand tricks.
2. In May 2003, this discussion group was combined with another and moderated for announcements only. I was informed that the change was for the moderator's convenience, and not for any other reason.
3. While the names of the discussion groups are genuine, I have provided pseudonyms for the members.
4. The language also suggested a reaction to the Christian celebrations of the new millennium.
5. Walking the dog one morning, I came upon a sidewalk chalk goddess in my neighborhood and, even with contacts made from doing research for fifteen years in the field, I was unable to discover the artist.

References

Adler, M. (1986). *Drawing Down the Moon: Witches, Druids, Goddess-Worshippers, and Other Pagans in America Today.* Boston: Beacon Press.

Altimari, D. (1998) "The Word of God, According to Female Biblical Scholars" *Hartford Courant,* September 29.

Anne. (2003). E-mail communication to GoddessScholars@yahoo.com, electronic discussion group, March 5.

Arthur, S. (2002). "Technophilia and Nature Religion: The Growth of A Paradox." *Religion*, (32): 1–12.

Berger, H. (1999). *A Community of Witches: Contemporary Neo-Paganism and Witchcraft in the United States*. Columbia, SC: University of South Carolina Press.

Berger, H. A., E. A., Leach, and L. S. Shaffer, (2003). *Voices from the Pagan Census: A National Survey of Witches and Neo-Pagans in the United States*. Columbia, SC: University of South Carolina Press.

Brasher, B.E. (1996). "Thoughts on the Status of the Cyborg: On Technological Socialization and Its Link to the Religious Function of Popular Culture." *Journal of the American Academy of Religion* 64(4): 809–830.

Brasher, B. E. (2001). *Give Me that Online Religion*. San Francisco: Jossey-Bass.

Dawson, L. L. (2002). "Religion and the Quest for Virtual Community." Paper presented to the annual meeting of the Association for the Sociology of Religion/American Sociological Association Chicago, August 16.

Eller, C. (2000). *The Myth of Matriarchal Prehistory: Why an Invented Past Won't Give Women a Future*. Boston: Beacon Press.

Fiona (2003a). E-mail communication to GoddessScholars@yahoogroups.com, electronic discussion group, July 14.

———. (2003b). E-mail communication to GoddessScholars@yahoogroups.com, electronic discussion group, July 16.

Foucault, M. (1984). "The Order of Discourse." In *Language and Politics*, ed. M. Shariro, Trans. I. McLeod, 108–138. Oxford, UK: Basil Blackwell.

Gimbutas, M. (1974). *The Gods and Goddesses of Old Europe: 7000 to 3500 BC: Myths, Legends and Cult Images*. Berkeley and Los Angeles: University of California Press.

Griffin, W. (1995). "The Embodied Goddess: Feminist Witchcraft and Female Divinity." *Sociology of Religion* (56) 1: 35–49.

———. (2003). "Goddess Spirituality and Wicca." In *Her Voice, Her Faith: Women Speak on World Religions*, ed. A. Sharma and K. Young, 243–282. Boulder, CO: Westview Press.

———. (forthcoming). "Webs of Women: Feminist Spiritualities in North America." In *Witchcraft and Magic in 20th Century America*, ed. H. Berger. Philadelphia: University of Pennsylvania Press

Hadden, J. K., and D. E. Cowan, (2000). "The Promised Land or Electronic Chaos? Toward Understanding Religion on the Internet." In *Religion on the Internet: Research Prospects and Promises*, ed. J. K. Hadden and D. E. Cowan, 3–21. London: JAI Press/Elsevier Science.

Heelas, P. (1996). *The New Age Movement: The Celebration of the Self and the Sacralization of Modernity*. Oxford, UK: Blackwell Publishers.

Herring, S. C. (2001). "Gender and Power in Online Communication." Center for Social Informatics. Indiana University–Bloomington. Retrieved from www.slis.indiana.edu/CSI/WP/WP01-05B.html, February 15, 2003.

Horsfall, S. (2000). "How Religious Organizations Use the Internet: A Preliminary Inquiry." In *Religion on the Internet: Research Prospects and Promises*, ed. J. K. Hadden and D. E. Cowan, 153-182. London: JAI Press /Elsevier Science.

Jorgensen, D., and S. Russell, (1999). "American Neopaganism: The Participants' Social Identities." *Journal for the Scientific Study of Religion*. 38 (3): 325–338.

Lennie, J., et al. (1999). "Empowering On-Line Conversations." In *women@internet*, ed. W. Harcourt, 184–196. London: Zed Books.

Long, A. (1997). The One or the Many: The Great Goddess Revisited. *Feminist Theology* 15: 13–29.

Lozano, W. G., and T. G. Foltz, (1990). "Into the Darkness: An Ethnographic Study of Witchcraft and Death," *Qualitative Sociology* 13 (3): 211–234.

Magdalena (2003). E-mail communication to feas2t@yahoogroups.com, electronic discussion group, March 6.

McSherry, L. (2002). "Choosing to Work Magick Online: A Guideline for Seekers." Retrieved from www.thevirtualpagan.org/Choosing.html, April 27, 2003.

———. (2003). "Virtual Covens." Retrieved from www.thevirtualpagan.org/information.html# Virtual, April 27, 2003.

Miriam (2003). E-mail communication to GoddessScholars@yahoogroups.com, electronic discussion group, June 24.

New York *Times*. "Technology Briefings." (2000). August 9. Retrieved from www.nytimes.com/library/tech/00/08/biztech/articles/09tbr.html, September 16, 2002.

NightMare, M. M. (2001). *Witchcraft and The Web: Weaving Pagan Traditions Online.* Toronto: ECW Press.

O'Leary, S. (1996). "Cyberspace as Sacred Space: Communicating Religion on Computer Networks." *Journal of the American Academy of Religion* 64 (4): 781–808.

Patricia (2003). E-mail communication to GoddessScholars@yahoogroups.com, electronic discussion group, July 3.

Pew Research Center (2000). *Internet and American Life Report: Tracking Online Life: How Women Use the Internet to Cultivate Relationships with Family and Friends.* Retrieved from www.pewinternet.org/reports, July 16, 2003.

———. (2003). *Pew Internet & American Life Project Tracking Surveys (March 2000–present).* Retrieved from www.pewinternet.org/reports, July 21, 2003.

Roof, W. C. (1999). *Spiritual Marketplace: Baby Boomers and the Remaking of American Religion.* Princeton, NJ: Princeton University Press.

Shakti (2003). E-mail communication to GoddessScholars@yahoogroups.com, electronic discussion group, July 18.

Willowroot, A. (1998). "Goddess 2000 Project." Retrieved from www.goddess2000.org/Info.html, February 15, 2000.

——— (1999). "'Dancing The Goddess Home' Ritual." Retrieved from www.goddess2000.org/G2000Ritual.html. February 15, 2000.

York, M. (1995). *The Emerging Network: A Sociology of the New Age and Neo-Pagan Movements.* Lanham, MD: Rowman and Littlefield.

———. (2000). "Defining Paganism." *The Pomegranate: A New Journal of Neopagan Thought* 11: 4–9.

Youngs, G. (1999). "Virtual Voices: Real Lives." In *women@internet,* ed. W. Harcourt, 55–69. London: Zed Books.

14

The House of Netjer: A New Religious Community Online

MARILYN C. KROGH AND BROOKE ASHLEY PILLIFANT

In 2001 about 28 million adult Americans, or 25 percent of all adult American Internet users, got religious or spiritual information online (Pew 2001: 2). These "religion surfers" overwhelmingly use the Internet as a giant reference library and as a way to contact people they already know rather than as a place to meet new people, take classes, or contribute money. Of these religion surfers, 84 percent are members of a congregation who in effect add an online channel to their existing offline relationships (Pew 2001: 4).

Nonetheless, 16 percent of religion surfers do not belong to a religious organization, and they are among the "most enthusiastic beneficiaries of the Internet" (Pew 2001: 19). Compared to members, nonmembers are more likely to use online than offline resources for information, conversation, worship, contact with clergy, and volunteering. For nonmembers, the Internet "provides resources for private practice and, to those who desire it, a safe place to explore reentering a community of faith" (Pew 2001: 21). Those communities include not only established religions but new religious movements (NRMs) as well (Pew 2001: 2).

In 1999, Dawson and Hennebry explored whether new religious movements were using the Internet to become visible in cyberspace or whether they were also using it to recruit new members. They found that most of the Web sites for NRMs simply posted reproductions of their print materials and urged interested people to visit the nearest temple or center. As a result, they ventured, "it is unlikely that it [the Internet] has intrinsically changed the capacity of NRMs to recruit new members" (Dawson and Hennebry 1999: 30).

Mayer echoed their skepticism a year later. "Scholars who do field research with various religious movements," he wrote, "have yet to report instances of person who changed their beliefs and joined a new religion though the Internet. It may be that the widespread use of the Internet is just too recent to have recorded systematic observations" (Mayer 2000: 252). Similarly, Bedell found that mainline Protestants were "eagerly adopting Internet solutions" for information and communication problems, but not forming new religious communities or supporting new spiritual practices online (Bedell 2000: 183).

In addition to lacking empirical evidence for religious recruitment online, researchers do not yet agree on whether an online community is even possible, and if it is, what it would look like (Dawson, this volume; Wellman and Gulia 1999). This aspect of the debate is rooted in two schools of sociological thought, one derived from Toennies ([1887] 1957), the other from Durkheim ([1912] 1995). Both saw communities as "aggregates of people who share common activities and/or beliefs and who are bound together principally by relations of affect, loyalty, common values, or personal concern" (Brint 2001: 9).

However, according to the tradition derived from Toennies, the word "community" should refer only to small groups of people who have strong, dense, and long-standing attachments to each other and to something they hold in common, such as a shared place, belief, or institution. In this view, relationships online are far too superficial, dispersed, and fleeting to merit the name of community; at best, they are only pseudocommunities. On the other hand, according to the tradition derived from Durkheim, "community" should refer to a "set of variable properties of human interaction that could be found not only among tradition-bound peasants of small villages, but also among the most sophisticated denizens of modern cities" (Brint 2001: 3).

Drawing on the Durkheimian tradition, Brint argues that relationships online might constitute one subtype of community, depending on the motivation, frequency, and priority of interaction among the participants (Brint 2001: 11). However, Brint does not define the volume or value of interaction that constitutes a community; instead he suggests that this judgment has to be made from comparative empirical studies. In summary, the available scholarship suggests the possibility of religious communities online but does not demonstrate the *reality* of religious communities online.

Now, just a few years after Dawson and Hennebry (1999), Mayer (2000), and Bedell (2000), we would like to present evidence that not only have Web sites for some NRMs become more interactive, but at least one new religious movement has grown from a small group of friends meeting face-to-face to a larger group functioning almost entirely online, to a group that is seeking to integrate life both online and off. Called Kemetic Orthodoxy, this new religious movement has reinvented aspects of ancient Egyptian religion and established both a temple and a seminary called the House of Netjer (The House of God).

Some of the first members of the House of Netjer created sites where Web visitors could learn about this faith, meet Kemetic believers, convert, and worship online. To date, most of the four hundred members of the House of Netjer have participated in this religion online. However, according to the founder, Tamara Siuda, they are not trying to create a virtual religious community; instead, they are using the Internet to reach enough people "to improve their offline connections" (personal interview with Pillifant, 2000).

Background

Understanding the House of Netjer requires bringing together what was known about NRMs in the era before the Internet and what we are learning about social life on the Internet. From Dawson's summaries of research on NRMs we highlight four conclusions. First, the social organization of NRMs varies from those that stress communal life and exclusive commitment to the group, such as the Unification Church and the International Society for Krishna Consciousness, to those that accept segmented and plural commitments, such as Theosophy and Transcendental Meditation (Dawson 1998: 9–10). These latter NRMs expect "individuals to live ordinary lives while engaging in a course of religious education" (Dawson 2000: 41).

Second, NRMs attract people who have a great desire "to live in a more coherent or at least more meaningful world" (Dawson 1998: 160), and such people are usually drawn to the group through "preexisting social networks" of family and friends (Dawson 1998: 79). Third, some of those people go on to join the group through intensive interaction with existing members (Dawson 1996: 147–149). And fourth, despite the fears of family members who believe they have lost a relative forever, most of the people who join NRMs leave voluntarily within two years. This makes the stability and longevity of NRMs problematic at best (Dawson 1998: 32, 92, 119).

Among other groups of people, from soap opera enthusiasts to medical doctors, researchers are accumulating evidence of significant social organization on the Internet, reporting online identities, roles, norms, conflicts, sanctions, and even some persistence over time. That is, as members of an online group work to keep interactions going and develop a sense of differentiation from nonmembers, some degree of communal life is sustained (Baym 1998; Fernback 1999; Fox and Roberts 1999; Liu 1999; Watson 1997).

An online group, however, can easily dissolve or fragment. With just a few keystrokes, members can drop out of a group, "kill" all messages from another group member, log in under a different name, or start another group. Although little research has examined the longevity of online groups, the evidence to date suggests that some face-to-face interaction is needed to sustain them over time. Kolko and Reid, for example, argue that "there must be multiple aspects to personae and multiple social connections between personae if a group is to survive" (1998: 219).

In light of what is known about NRMs and the Internet, Dawson speculates that an online religious community, like its offline counterpart, is "likely to be characterized by a moderate level of interaction and commitment with regard, in most cases, to a fairly specific set of concerns" (2000: 41). Moreover, he predicts that, "in the end, online communities are most likely to succeed, to truly affect people's lives, when they are paired with other offline involvements" (Dawson 2000: 41).

New Religious Movements Online

In the spring of 2002, we looked for evidence of online communities on the Web sites of new religious movements. We updated and enlarged Dawson's and Hennebry's (1999) survey by coding a range of technical and content features for each site and developed a typology of sites inductively. We identified five types: public relations sites, cyberhubs, seeker sites, joiner sites, and potential online communities.

Public relations sites provide basic information about the group but do not invite the reader into a relationship with the group and the material on the site appears static. Cyberhubs serve existing group members and feature timely news of interest to them. Seeker sites instruct individual inquirers and appear to be a contemporary form of surface mail correspondence courses. Joiner sites explain what membership (or training) entails and urge interested people to join the nearest offline class.

In our sample, very few groups have even attempted to create a community on the Internet, although some provide ways for existing and potential members to interact online. Only two groups instruct and initiate new members entirely online: the Movement for Spiritual Inner Awareness and the House of Netjer. Of these two, only the House of Netjer also holds worship services online. Consequently, the House of Netjer provides the most complete example in our sample of a potential online community.

The House of Netjer has two official Web sites, www.kemet.org and www.netjer.org. Established in 1996, kemet.org presents information about the faith, a glossary of Egyptian gods and goddesses, an image library, devotional writings, and a virtual ancestor shrine. Netjer.org, which went online in 1999, offers a photo gallery, classes in Kemetic Orthodoxy, and conversation and worship through both public and private Internet Relay Channel (IRC) chat rooms and message boards.

The House of Netjer

In this chapter, we ask three questions about the House of Netjer. First, and most important, does the House of Netjer constitute a community? Second, does the House of Netjer differ significantly from offline new religious movements? And finally, does it fulfill Dawson's expectations for a religious community online (Dawson 2000: 41)?

For our definition of community, we draw on Brint's interpretation of the Durkheimian tradition in sociology. We consider a community to be "aggregates of people who share common activities and/or beliefs and who are bound together principally by relations of affect, loyalty, common values, or personal concern" (Brint 2001: 9), where those relations are expressed in regular and valued interactions (Brint 2001: 11).

To answer these questions, we analyzed publicly available material from the House of Netjer's official Web sites, from phone and e-mail interviews with leaders and members conducted in 2002 and 2003, and from e-mail correspondence with the brother of a member who initiated contact with us through one of this book's editors, Douglas Cowan. As nonmembers, we were not allowed to observe any of the advanced classes, private forums, or worship services, although we read and were told about them by participants.

We also drew on material gathered during prior research with this group, specifically transcripts of IRC discussions that occurred during an online class, plus an in-person interview with the founder of Kemetic Orthodoxy and a phone interview with her assistant (see Krogh and Pillifant 2003). All this was preceded by informed consent of the leadership and the people directly involved. Except for the names of the founder, Tamara Siuda, and the Webmaster, Stephanie Cass, all the personal names used in the rest of this chapter are pseudonyms.

We begin by describing the origins of the House of Netjer and conclude with some reflections on the limitations of community. In between we use the nine design strategies from *Community Building on the Web* (Kim 2000) to present our material. This handbook for Webmasters provides online uses for well-known sociological principles, and we found those strategies to be a simple and coherent way to frame this presentation. However, members of the House of Netjer did not have access to this handbook when they began their sites, and we do not mean to imply that they were following Kim's instructions as they developed their sites.

The Origins of the House of Netjer

The House of Netjer did not begin online. It began with Tamara Siuda in Chicago in 1988. When Siuda was in a meditative trance, seeking contact with Pagan deities as part of her initiation as a Wiccan priestess, she felt contacted by Egyptian gods and goddesses who told her to revive their ancient forms of worship. Consequently, over the next four years, Siuda tried to recover as much as she could of ancient Egyptian religion, and was joined by a handful of college friends who met together for study and worship.

In 1992, Siuda met Robert, who was dissatisfied with contemporary religion and had been interested for years in ancient Egyptian philosophy, mythology, and religion. Robert believed that "they still had things to say and they still had vibrant lessons that applied to the modern age." As he recalled, "We both had similar leanings and [we realized] we actually could start to put this together and start to see if ancient lessons could work in modern life" (personal interview with Pillifant, 2000).

From 1994 to 1998, Siuda worked as an adviser and interfaith manager for the Spirituality Forum of America Online, as did Robert from 1995 to 1997. Other early members of the House were also active online. Consequently, according to

Cass, creating a religious community online felt like "a natural extension" of their face-to-face interaction (personal interview with Krogh, August 2002).

Today, the leadership still depends on the trust and understanding generated by their early face-to-face relationships, even though some of the original priests no longer live in the same city, and other priests from other places have joined them. The number of members has grown from a few people in 1988 to about sixty in 1999, to about four hundred in 2003. Of those four hundred, about three hundred are active members and about one hundred are inactive.

Strategies for Community-Building

Purpose, Places, and Profiles

According to Kim's first design principle, "a successful community serves a clear purpose in the lives of its members and meets the fundamental goals of its owners" (2000: 1). The purpose of www.netjer.org is reflected in its tag line, "Living Kemetic Orthodox Faith," and explained in a mission statement titled "About Kemetic Orthodoxy." It states: "Ancient Egyptian religion lives again within the Kemetic Orthodox Faith, a current-day practice of the traditional religion of Kemet (known today as Egypt). With Netjer's help and blessing, this most ancient tradition is honored anew by people in Egypt and beyond, returning the principles of Ma'at to a new world" (www.kemet.org/home.html).

Although this site is dedicated to a new religion, it looks rather ordinary. Across the top of the House of Netjer home page (www.netjer.org) are six photos of people smiling or hugging. The main colors on the page are teal and white, not unlike a number of Roman Catholic Marian devotional sites. Beyond the unfamiliar name of the group, the only hint of something unusual is the name of the Webmaster, Kai-Imakhu meryt-Bast.

According to the founder of the House of Netjer, her goal is not to create a virtual religion but to reach enough people online so that they can "improve their offline connections" (personal interview with Pillifant, 2000). Cass reports that they are moving steadily towards that goal (personal interview with Krogh, August 2002). Three or four years ago, the group functioned almost entirely online, but now they are blending life online and off. For instance, in 2003, www.kemet.org highlighted the openings of both a children's charity and a retreat house in Harbor County, Michigan.

Kim's second design principle states that communities need a gathering place. "On the Web," she writes, "a gathering place can be a mailing list, a discussion topic, a chat room, a multiplayer game, a virtual world, a web site, or some combination of these spaces" (Kim 2000: 27). The House of Netjer uses both public and password-protected message boards and chat rooms to create gathering places with graduated levels of privacy. These serve the public, inquirers, members, and priests, respectively. While the public discussion board looks fairly standard, a Kemetic flair is conveyed by greetings such as

Em hotep ("Welcome") and blessings such as *Ankh Udja Seneb* ("Life, Prosperity, and Health").

Discussion topics on the public boards include a range of religious issues. One popular thread concerns the personalities associated with different Kemetic gods and goddesses and the people who are dedicated to their worship. For example, one person wrote that she is a creator like her Kemetic father, and another wrote that his fascination with bones and scavenger animals comes from his Kemetic father, who is a mortuary deity. Another claimed that Wesir, the King and Judge of the Dead, is a sociable deity and as a result, "Wesir kids" like to talk a lot. Other threads discussed whether vegetarians should offer meat to the gods and goddesses, how to make *natron* (a substance used ritually to purify bathwater), and what to do about ritual accidents, such as mixing up the words to a prayer or knocking over a statue.

Introducing her third design strategy, Kim states, "People may come to your community for the content, but they'll stay for the relationships" (2000: 76). To develop relationships, participants often post personal profiles on discussion boards and in chat rooms. The profiles of active participants at netjer.org typically feature either a photo of the person or an Egyptian hieroglyph or icon. They often include the person's status in the group—inquirer, beginner, member, or priest—as well as his or her Kemetic name: *Taneferwesir* (The Goodness of Wesir), *Herumesueni* (Heru extends His hand to me), or *Imateninpu* (Yinepu's Kindness), for example.

We noted that when introducing themselves, participants tended to write more about their hobbies than their employment. Common interests included arts of all kinds, alternative medicine, and online gaming. Each participant is expected to have only one username and profile, however, and anyone who is caught using multiple identities without permission is subject to expulsion from the site by the priests.

Roles, Leadership, and Etiquette

Kim's fourth design strategy urges the founders of online communities to plan for a "membership life cycle" that allows people to progress from visitor to novice, to regular participant, to leader, to elder (2000: 117). As she suggests, the House of Netjer welcomes visitors, instructs novices, rewards regular members, empowers leaders, and honors elders. To welcome visitors, the House of Netjer offers a standard set of features, such as a list of Frequently Asked Questions (FAQ) and a guest book. To instruct novices, the House of Netjer encourages visitors to become registered users who can post to public message boards, such as one titled "Welcome in Peace." Currently the House of Netjer has about four hundred registered users.

More important, though, is that the House of Netjer instructs novices through Probationer's Groups, which convene online every three to four months and last for sixteen weeks. At the conclusion of a Probationer's Group, the participants may refrain from further involvement or become members of the House of Netjer, either as community associates or full converts. Over half of the people who have completed Probationer's Groups have gone on to become members. Members have access to personalized start pages, buddy lists, advanced classes, private chats and forums, and online worship services. While welcome to participate in some House activities, community associates can also maintain other religious beliefs or responsibilities. Converts, however, must dedicate themselves to the exclusive service of a particular Kemetic god or goddess.

Some members become informal or official leaders. For instance, on the message boards, some members make a special effort to greet newcomers and answer questions. Two converts have become "Ambassadors of Fellowship," who convene small offline gatherings of people in the southwest and northwest regions of the country, and ten converts have become priests who assist in the liturgies. Among these, four also have pastoral responsibilities, and one is the House of Netjer Webmaster. Siuda and her assistant, Robert, provide the priests with religious training, and Cass confers on them a clear identity and authority online. Priests have distinctive titles and they can delete posts from the message boards and control chat rooms used for classes or worship.

Siuda, the founder of Kemetic Orthodoxy, is more than an elder; she has a semi-divine status within the religion and is often referred to as "Her Holiness." She is active and visible, teaching, leading worship, counseling, and posting daily devotional messages. Most importantly, she is seen "as a physical and spiritual bridge between and the faithful Netjer" (www.kemet.org/kemexp5.html). Through ritual divination, she discerns the will of Netjer on particular matters and communicates it to Netjer's followers. For instance, when a person wants to convert, she undertakes divination to find that person's Parent Name. The Parent Name is the manifestation of deity associated with that person's birth, to which the person directs worship, and from which the person expects help.

In her fifth design strategy, Kim claims that "running an effective leadership program involves recognizing what your members are already doing, and helping them do it better" (2000: 159). She suggests promoting a few regular members into official volunteer leadership roles when they have already demonstrated commitment and enthusiasm for the site.

Although Siuda and Robert managed the first live chat meetings and Web sites for the House of Netjer on America Online servers in 1994, they soon found they could not handle all the demands on their time. Cass, who had been building personal Web pages, volunteered to take over the online responsibilities for the House of Netjer. Eventually, she bought a public domain and purchased InfoPop services for the House. Now the Web sites for the House cover several hundred pages, and Cass downloads about two gigabytes of data a month from the forum boards. The experience she gained with the House has led to a promotion at her job with an online gaming company.

Cass is assisted by a small team of volunteers with specific responsibilities such as maintaining mailing lists or monitoring forums. She uses instant messaging to keep in contact with her assistants throughout the day, since, as she observed, "Even the most likeable person can go a little crazy [with online abilities]." She looks forward to someday promoting one of her assistants into the position of Webmaster and retiring to an advisory role (personal interview with Krogh, August 2002).

In her sixth design strategy, Kim asserts that a Web community needs some written ground rules. "Along with visual and navigational cues, your ground rules mark the social (and legal) boundary between your community and the rest of the Net" (Kim 2000: 203). The House of Netjer has a policy statement at the top of the forums page that is similar to the WELL policy of "You own your own words" (www.netjer.org/forums/ubbthreads.php).

Like many other sites, the House of Netjer has had some trouble with "smerts," people who deliberately disrupt online conversations, as well as with unhappy or angry members who vent their feelings inappropriately. But Cass reports that, by and large, the site is "remarkably well behaved" and self-policing. When a member reads an offensive post, he or she is likely to respond by suggesting that the author rethink the message or apologize for it. This minimizes the need for an authority to intervene. Nonetheless, Cass and her assistants monitor the site closely. Between them, they read the forum boards three to four times a day, and all the priests and priests-in-training spend at least two hours a week participating in and monitoring the site (personal interview with Krogh, August 2002).

Events, Rituals, and Subgroups

Seventh, Kim states that "every long-lasting community is brought together by regular events: family dinners, weekly card games, monthly club meetings, annual celebrations" (2000: 233). More structured than mailing lists, message boards or chat rooms, an online event "occurs at a specific time and place, and has a beginning, middle and end" (Kim 2000: 234).

The central online events for the House of Netjer are the Probationer's Groups and other classes. Each week during the course, a priest e-mails the lesson to a group of fifteen to thirty people and then convenes a discussion about the lesson through an IRC session. Lessons in the Probationer's Group include an introduction to the cosmology, ritual cycle, hierarchy, and ethics of Kemetic Orthodoxy. Lessons for more advanced groups include further instruction on Kemetic language, beliefs, and ritual. The IRC discussions are supplemented by Listserv e-mail and postings on the private side of the Web site.

Conversations among people in the Probationer's Group concerned not only the lesson of the week, but also their personal lives. People who mentioned their birthdays or anniversaries were congratulated, and people who expressed their anxieties about exams, moves, or health problems received encouragement and promises of prayer support. People also circulated jokes and cartoons and exchanged tips on where to buy things online.

Online events are supplemented by offline events, such as weekend workshops at the retreat house and restaurant dinners, as well as trips to museum exhibitions on ancient Egypt and even to the Parliament of World Religions. Although not all members can participate in such events, our interviewees report that they strengthen the relationships among those who can.

In her eighth design strategy, Kim states: "From the mundane to the magical, rituals help guide us through the transitions of life . . . incorporating some familiar and time-tested rituals can help your members develop a sense of belonging and add power and depth to their community experience" (2000: 277, 279). Unlike most other Web communities, however, the House of Netjer is creating a new ritual cycle that includes daily temple liturgies and personal devotions, biweekly worship services, individual rites of passage, and annual community holidays. Although the daily liturgies and devotions are carried out only in the temple in Chicago and in people's homes, respectively, most of the other rituals are conducted simultaneously offline and online.

In the daily temple liturgy, a priest honors one of the Names of Netjer by purifying the room that serves as the temple, kneeling or prostrating on the floor before the temple shrine, pronouncing invocations, performing ritual gestures, and either offering incense and perfume or dressing and feeding an icon. A priest typically conducts this ritual in solitude. Similarly, individual members perform daily devotions, known as *Senut*, at a household shrine containing a table, a small lamp or candle, an incense burner, and a dish in which to place offerings. In addition to performing *Senut*, a worshipper may also venerate deceased ancestors, either offline at their household shrine or online at a Web page dedicated to their memory. Although these are solitary practices, during our interviews members said that they feel connected to others who are performing the same ritual, and the common practice provides a foundation for their conversations and friendships.

Most other rituals are observed simultaneously offline and online. Typically, a small group gathers at the temple in Chicago while a larger group assembles online through an Internet Relay Channel. One priest sits at a computer keyboard to communicate between the offline and online participants. This priest describes what people are saying and doing at the temple and then, at the relevant points in the service, instructs the online participants to say or do something themselves, such as performing a certain gesture or making an offering. The online participants then type back a confirmation that they have done it. In order to minimize disruptive or mistimed posts during these rituals, the priest at the keyboard controls who can post to the chat room.

The biweekly worship service is known as *Dua*, the Kemetic word for praise. The liturgy is presented in both English and Kemetic, and participants may wear ordinary Western clothes or Egyptian-style robes and headdresses, as well as ankh pendants or scarab rings. The service may include readings, prayers, chants, songs, music, dance, or drama.

At times, the *Dua* service incorporates a rite of passage for members of the House of Netjer. These include naming ceremonies for children, rites of initiation and ordination, as well as divination by oracle. For example, on May 30, 2001, forty-two people participated online in a *Dua* service that included a naming ceremony for the children of converts. Five children were given a Parent Name corresponding to the Name of Netjer related to the day of their birth and assigned a sponsor, or godparent, who also belongs to that Name of Netjer. This was the largest group yet assembled online for a *Dua* service.

Other Kemetic rituals include a rite of initiation in which an adult publicly dedicates him-or herself to the service of a particular Name of Netjer; a ritual of ordination to the priesthood; and oracular divination, known as *saq*, which is performed for spiritual guidance. *Saq* is a form of full-trance possession. During a *saq*, one of the possession-priests speaks as the mouthpiece of Netjer, giving messages and responding to questions posed by the people participating at the temple and online.

The House of Netjer organizes a large number of community holidays. The most important holiday is the New Year's Retreat, held every year since 1998 in Chicago during the first week of August. Many members save money throughout the year to pay for their transportation and lodging in order to attend this three-day observance. Other holidays include the Mysteries of Wesir, the Raising of the Djed Pillar, and the Festival of Purification. The holidays are observed with processions of icons and statues, prayer, special liturgies and sometimes ritual drama and a communal meal. These festivities are often commemorated online with essays and photos.

Sometimes, meeting face-to-face sparks new relationships that continue online; at other times, meeting face-to-face solidifies relationships that began and continue online. For instance, Phil recounted: "Aside from [my partner], my closest friends are Mark and Jennifer. They live in another state. I met them first at the retreat two years ago and we've always been close since. Usually we chit chat at *duas* and email back and forth to each other while I'm at work" (personal interview with Pillifant, February 2003).

In her interview, Lisa recalled the first time she met someone face-to-face after having known her online. "We manage to have the best conversations," she said. "I remember one time in particular we just sat around sipping coffee and talking about our youthful searches for religion (or lack thereof) and what brought us where we are and what we thought of it all, in light of our individual and respective lives" (personal interview with Pillifant, February 2003).

In her final design strategy, Kim advocates building subgroups within a larger community to maintain intimacy while managing growth (2000: 310). The House of Netjer encourages members to start their own mailing lists, chat rooms, forums, and Web rings. Cass says these are the "natural offspring" of their religious community, and the leaders are delighted to see them "bloom" as long as they are clearly identified as private ventures of the members (personal interview with Krogh, August 2002).

The other side of subgroups, however, is splinter groups, and the House has had a few of those as well. Some former members have established sites on the Web drawing on what they learned in the House of Netjer. While some of these sites are now defunct, Akhet Hwt-Hrw (www.hwt-hrw.com) remains somewhat active. Akhet Hwt-Hrw was founded by a man who left Kemetic Orthodoxy a short time before he would have been ordained as a priest. The site offers a free monthly newsletter by e-mail as well as a biweekly online discussion group led by a priest. It charges $120 for a ten-session course similar to the lessons in a Kemetic Orthodox Probationer's Group. Perhaps counterbalancing this fragmentation, the House of Netjer has become part of the newly formed International Network of Kemetics (www.inkemetic.org).

Limits of Community: Relationships In and Outside the Group

While the members report finding close friendships and spiritual fulfillment through the House of Netjer, they do not report major financial obligations to the group or to each other. According to Robert, although some members sponsor fund-raisers and donate the proceeds, and others make monthly pledges or occasional donations, most of the money to support the House comes from the priests. Members are required to make a contribution only once, in the token amount of $20, when they undergo divination to discover their Parent Name (personal interview with Pillifant, 2000).

When one young woman in a Probationer's Group said she could not afford to pay, this amount due to her health problems and low income, a few other participants offered to help her pay, while others told her to save a little "here and there" until she had what she needed. Although some other people in the group alluded to financial constraints, none of them asked the group for assistance, and there was no teaching about financial obligations to the House during the course.

Participants in the Probationer's Group as well as the people interviewed reported little conflict about this faith with their family or friends. Several women in the Probationer's Group reported that their partners took a "live and let live" approach to their religious searching. They commented, for example, "As long as he does not have to get involved, he tolerates my searching," and "In his own way he supports me, so long as he's not involved." Another woman observed, "My husband is respectful, but I don't think he truly understands. He has admitted, however, that he thinks Heru and Yinepu are pretty cool. ☺" (transcript of Probationer's Group conversation, Pillifant, 2000)

Some nonbelieving spouses take a tolerant, if skeptical, attitude toward this religion. For instance, when Brenda converted, she found enthusiastic support among her friends and parents and guarded support from her husband, who is a Reformed Jew. She explains that over the years: "He's become more accepting of it. He's been a really good sport about it, letting me build this library and this shrine outside and he pretty well lets me do whatever I want with it. I try not to let it intrude too much on my family life."

Brenda practices her shrine rites when her husband is at work or asleep and when her children are at school. She does not raise her children in Kemetic Orthodoxy, but they have asked her about it and are familiar with it. She and her husband believe that their children should make their own religious choices when they are adults (personal interview with Pillifant, 2001).

Like people in other religions, some members report that this faith has enabled them to understand themselves better and have better relationships with their families. For instance, in her interview, Tanya said that Kemetic Orthodoxy has:

> helped me to not be afraid of being myself anymore. . . . It has helped me to understand a little better about myself and how I see my world. It has given me the opportunity to have some very long talks with my parents and sister regarding philosophy and religion. I understand how I act and react to stimulus around me. It has allowed me to be more confident in who I am. It has brought me closer to my mom and dad and sisters. It has also allowed me to really talk with both of my children (ages twenty and eighteen). (Personal interview with Pillifant, 2001)

On the other hand, like other NRMs, the House of Netjer also creates divisions between members and their families. In at least one case, the family of a member was distressed because he was neglecting his relationships with them and with his girlfriend in order to spend most of his evenings in private at his attic shrine and computer keyboard. Once he attended a New Year's Retreat, and met other members face-to-face, his family felt he withdrew from them even more and became a very different person.

Conclusion

We conclude that The House of Netjer is a community, because its members share beliefs and activities that bind them together in relations of affect and personal concern, they interact regularly, and they value their relationships. However, the House of Netjer is not the egalitarian and democratic community expected by some Internet proponents. It is a hierarchical community reflecting a hierarchical religion. The leadership exercises control over all religious instruction and most interactions online.

This case study suggests that the Internet has not dramatically altered the development of an NRM. The House of Netjer online looks similar to other NRMs offline. It attracts people who join through intensive interaction with existing members and who practice this religion while continuing with their everyday lives. We do not know, however, how long people remain active with the House of Netjer and how this compares to other, similar NRMs.

Finally, the House of Netjer does fulfill Dawson's expectations for a religious community online. The members focus on individual spiritual, social, and emotional concerns rather than a broader range of issues and they show a moderate level of interaction with and commitment to each other. Perhaps most important is that the House of Netjer is not a virtual community sustained only by electronic communication among members. Instead the House of Netjer is a blend of offline and online relationships.

This preliminary sketch of the House of Netjer could be improved in several ways. We could more directly compare the level of interaction and commitment among members in the House of Netjer to other groups if we used a standardized measurement rather than our more subjective assessments. We would have a more complete view of the community if we observed members who disaffiliate rather than only those who are currently active. And if we were allowed access to the private classes, conversations, and worship, we would know something about the inner life of this community. This, however, seems unlikely, at least in the near future, as the House has expressed no willingness to let outsiders further in.

Finally, this study suggests that the lack of online recruitment to NRMs noted by other researchers may be a function of the lack of new religious communities online. For the next few years, it seems likely that the Internet will remain a valued source of information and means of communication for NRMs but not a typical place for community life.

References

Baym, N. K. (1998). "The Emergence of On-Line Community." In *Cybersociety 2.0: Revisiting Computer-Mediated Communication and Community*, ed. S. G. Jones. Thousand Oaks: Sage Publications.

Bedell, K. (2000). "Dispatches from the Electronic Frontier: Explorations of Mainline Protestant Uses of the Internet." In *Religion on the Internet: Research Prospects and Promises*, ed. J. K. Hadden and D. E. Cowan. London and Amsterdam: JAI Press/Elsevier Science.

Brint, S. (2001). "*Gemeinschaft* Revisited: A Critique and Reconstruction of the Community Concept." *Sociological Theory* 19 (1): 1–23.

Dawson, L. L. (1996). "Who Joins New Religious Movements and Why: Twenty Years of Research and What Have We Learned?" *Studies in Religion/Sciences Religieuses* 25: 193–213.

———. (1998). *Comprehending Cults: The Sociology of New Religious Movements.* New York: Oxford University Press.

———. (2000). "Researching Religion in Cyberspace: Issues and Strategies." In *Religion on the Internet: Research Prospects and Promises*, ed. J. K. Hadden and D. E. Cowan. London and Amsterdam: JAI Press/Elsevier Science.

———. (2002). "Religion and the Quest for Virtual Community." Paper presented at the Association for the Sociology of Religion Annual Conference, Chicago, August.

Dawson, L. L. and J. Hennebry, (1999). "New Religions and the Internet: Recruiting in a New Public Space." *Journal of Contemporary Religion,* 14: 17–39.

Durkheim, E. [1912] (1995). *The Elementary Forms of Religious Life*, trans. K. E. Fields. New York: Free Press.

Fernback, J. (1999). "There Is a There There: Notes toward a Definition of Cybercommunity." In *Doing Internet Research: Critical Issues and Methods for Examining the Net*, ed. S. Jones. Thousand Oaks: Sage Publications.

Fox, N., and C. Roberts, (1999). "GPs in Cyberspace: The Sociology of a 'Virtual Community.'" *Sociological Review*, 47: 643–671.

Kim, A. J. (2000). *Community Building on the Web: Secret Strategies for Successful Online Communities.* Berkeley, CA: Peachpit Press.

Kolko, B., and E. Reid, (1998). "Dissolution and Fragmentation: Problems in On-Line Communities." In *Cybersociety 2.0: Revisiting Computer-Mediated Communication and Community*, ed. S. G. Jones. Thousand Oaks: Sage Publications.

Krogh, M., and B. A. Pillifant (2004). "Kemetic Orthodoxy: Ancient Egyptian Religion on the Internet." *Sociology of Religion*, in press.

Liu, G. Z. (1999). "Virtual Community Presence in Internet Relay Chatting." *Journal of Computer Mediated Communication* 5 (1). Retrieved from www.ascusc.org/jcmc/vol5/issue1/liu.html, September 7, 2002.

Mayer, J-F. (2000). "Religious Movements and the Internet: The New Frontier of Cult Controversies." In *Religion on the Internet: Research Prospects and Promises*, ed, J. K. Hadden and D. E. Cowan. London and Amsterdam: JAI Press/Elsevier Science.

Pew Internet and American Life Project (2000). "Wired Churches, Wired Temples: Taking Congregations and Missions into Cyberspace." Retrieved from www.pewinternet.org/reports, January 15, 2002.

———. (2001). "CyberFaith: How AmericansPursue Religion Online." Retrieved from www.pewinternet.org/reports, January 15, 2002.

Powazek, D. M. (2002). *Design for Community: The Art of Connecting Real People in Virtual Places*. Indianapolis: New Riders.

Toennies, F. [1887] (1957). *Community and Society*, trans. Charles P. Loomis. New York: Harper.

Watson, N. (1997). "Why We Argue About Virtual Community: A Case Study of the Phish.Net Fan Community." In *Virtual Culture: Identity and Communication in Cybersociety*, ed. S. G. Jones. Thousand Oaks: Sage Publications.

Wellman, B., and M. Gulia, (1999). "Net-Surfers Don't Ride Alone: Virtual Communities as Communities." In *Networks in the Global Village*, ed. B. Wellman. Boulder, CO: Westview Press.

IV

Religious Quests and Contests in Cyberspace

15
Virtual Pilgrimage to Ireland's Croagh Patrick

MARK W. MACWILLIAMS

Introduction

One form of Net religious traffic that is increasingly popular is virtual pilgrimage. "Virtual pilgrimage" is an Internet neologism for a Web site where people can simulate a sacred journey for educational, economic, and spiritual purposes. Examples of virtual pilgrimages online abound. For instance, Beliefnet (http://beliefnet.com), a commercial Internet site combining marketing with online prayer circles, discussion groups, and timely articles on contemporary spirituality, had its own "Virtual *Hajj*" site for some time. Many of the major Christian pilgrimages of Western Europe have their own official and nonofficial virtual pilgrimages for e-travelers (e.g., the famous Lourdes shrine in France; www.lourdes-france.com). Numerous Holy Land virtual pilgrimages are also available on the Internet (e.g., the commercial nondenominational holylandnetwork.com).

But are these instances of true pilgrimage? An anthropologist and scholar of pilgrimages, Victor Turner, states that pilgrimages involve a "journey to a center out there." Is that what the Internet surfer does when she links to one of these sites? Do these sites take someone, virtually, beyond the confines of their home or office in an appropriate way?

Some would say, no! You cannot do the *Hajj* or the Holy Land pilgrimage without traveling to the "real"—meaning the actual, physical—sacred site. Turner himself argues that pilgrimage is a type of "extroverted mysticism" where "the pilgrim physically traverses a mystical way; the mystic sets forth on an interior spiritual pilgrimage" (Turner and Turner 1978: 33–34). Pilgrimage takes place "on foot or donkey or camel through rough country with danger of robbers and brigands, and not much in the way of food or shelter," or, at the very least, in the modern world, "by jet aircraft and stay in the best hotels." In either case, it is a physical journey. The pilgrim moves from a "familiar place" that is "secular, mundane, everyday, ordinary" to a "far place" this is "sacred, rare, often miraculous" (Turner 1974b: 305).

However such a view, as Alan Morinis has argued, overemphasizes the physical over the spiritual, the actual over the ideal dimensions of pilgrimage:

> Anthropologists tend to pay far more attention to actual ritual goings-forth on sacred journeys in geographical space, but the other sorts of venturing toward ideals undertaken by humans are equally pilgrimages. It is, indeed, questionable to distinguish between terrestrial and "metaphorical" pilgrimages. The distinction portrays the earthly journey as somehow more real, when, in fact, most cultures subsume physical journeys and other quests into one more inclusive category: the spiritual life is a pilgrimage, the ascetic learns to visit the sacred shrines in his own body, devotion is a journey to God. (Morinis 1992: 4)

Pilgrimage is as much an act of the mind as an act of the body. There can be "metaphorical" pilgrimages that are as spiritually powerful and meaningful to believers as actual ones. For example, one way to experience Christ's *via crucis*, the Way of the Cross, is to travel physically to the Holy Land. The Spanish nun Egeria, one of the first Christian pilgrims to Jerusalem, did so in 381 to 384. According to the seventh-century Galician monk Valerius, it was an arduous undertaking for the time: "In the strength of the glorious Lord she fearlessly set out on an immense journey to the other side of the world" (Wilkinson 1973: 175). But does one have actually to travel all those weary miles to do the Holy Land pilgrimage? In fact, many Roman Catholics do not. They do the journey virtually by means of the Stations of the Cross, popularized by the Franciscans in the late-medieval period. The fourteen Stations, symbolically represented by paintings or plaques depicting the key moments on Christ's way to the Cross, are typically displayed on the outer walls of a church. They function as a symbolic substitute for the real pilgrimage, known since the sixteenth century as the "Via Dolorosa." Circumambulating the stations, especially during Lent or Holy Week, is an act of piety for "pilgrims," who ritually experience the same Gospel story symbolized by the Stations that are in Jerusalem on Christ's "original" route to his Crucifixion. In effect, the Stations enable the faithful to imagine a virtual spiritual reality through what Jonathan Z. Smith calls their symbolic "relations of equivalence" with the actual sacred site (Smith 1987: 86–87). This symbolic substitution goes one more level of abstraction in the case of computer-mediated communication. When visitors log on to sites such as Franciscan Cyberspot's "Jerusalem—the Way of the Cross" (http://198.62.75.1/www1/jsc/TVCmenu.html) or holylandnetwork.com's "Jerusalem Via Dolorosa," virtual pilgrims gaze at the electronic walls of cyberspace instead of the real walls and stained glass of an actual church.

Virtual pilgrimages on the Internet are important for understanding new ways of being spiritual in the postmodern world. Whether strictly for informational purposes or for something more, these pilgrimages draw upon the symbolic relations of equivalence between their cyberspace sites and real-life sacred ones. In what follows, I argue that virtual pilgrimages have four key characteristics as forms of religious travel. First, they create a "mythscape," a dematerialized, highly symbolic, sacred geography based largely upon oral and historical narratives and Scripture. As such, they are usually conservative, exploiting the new technological possibilities of the Internet to reimagine the received tradition of sacred persons, stories, symbols, and temples and shrine buildings already associated with the real-life holy place. Second, they exist as an interactive visual-auditory medium for experiencing the numinous presence of the Divine. Third, they generate liminoid forms of entertainment for the traveler/viewer. Fourth, as a leisure activity for those "Net surfing" from their home or office computers, they can create "virtual traveling communities." Such virtual pilgrims and religious tourists occasionally describe their experience in terms that Turner called *communitas*—an experience of "generic bonding" of humankind or comradely harmony. Traveling to such Internet sites is an important means at the very least, to satisfy spiritual curiosity and at the very most to utilize a powerful new technology to secure a wide range of spiritual benefits—educational, ritual, and, for some people, interactive communication and communion with the sacred.

The Croagh Patrick Pilgrimage on the Web

Rather than surveying the broad range of virtual pilgrimage sites on the Internet, I have chosen to focus on one based upon the famous pilgrimage center of Croagh Patrick in Western Ireland. Croagh Patrick, also popularly called "the Reek," is an imposing mountain ridge rising 2,510 feet and capped by a spectacular quartzite cone towering above the seaside town of Westport in County Mayo and Clew Bay. Even the staid nineteenth-century English man of letters William Thackeray paid it the ultimate chauvinistic compliment when he described it as "Wonderful, wonderful! . . . It forms an event in one's life to have seen that place, so beautiful is it and so unlike all other beauties that I know of. Were such beauties lying upon English shores it would be the world's wonder" (Dunning and Dunning 2003: 2). Though a holy site from pre-Christian times (Watt 1995: 1), Croagh Patrick is so named because Ireland's national saint, Saint Patrick, fasted there in 441 for the forty days of Lent before he banished the venomous snakes from the island. For fifteen hundred years, the holy mountain, with the ruins of Patrick's primitive chapel, Teampall Phádraig, on its summit, has served as pilgrimage center of national and more recently international stature. Dr. John Healey, former archbishop of Tuam, summed up the feelings of many when he said: "We have come to love the Reek with a kind of personal love, not merely on account of its graceful symmetry and soaring pride, but also because it is Patrick's Holy Mountain—the scene of his penance and his passionate yearning and prayers for our fathers and us. It is to us, moreover, the symbol of Ireland's enduring faith" (Hughes 1991: 15).

Today's pilgrimage is largely the result of the tireless efforts of local clergy. Dr. Healey was a major catalyst for Croagh Patrick's revival. On August 16, 1903, special trains were organized for what was to become a national pilgrimage. In 1905, ten thousand pilgrims celebrated Mass at a new chapel built on the summit. In 1907, Dr. Healey changed the date of the national pilgrimage to

"Reek Sunday," the last Sunday in July—a time that coincided with the ancient harvest festival of Lughnasa (in honor of the god, Lugh), as well as the designated date of a special indulgence granted to pilgrim penitents by Pope Eugene IV in 1432 (Hughes 1991: 22–25). Today, devout pilgrims may secure the plenary indulgence granted in 1958 by ascending the mountain on Saint Patrick's Day or at any time from June though September and praying on the summit (Hughes 1991: 59). In 2000, over thirty thousand people climbed the mountain on Reek Sunday (Sugach 2001: 10).

Why do they go on the pilgrimage? The ecclesiastical rationale for pilgrimages was clearly stated by Dr. Healey; they "are for the purpose of visiting in the spirit of faith and penance holy places sanctified by the presence and by the labours of our Savior and his Saints" (Hughes 1991: 32). According to Turner, this rationale is the "fundamental signified" at Lough Derg and other Saints Patrick pilgrimages; the goal is for "personal sanctification through self sacrifice" as symbolized by the martyrdom of saints whose "annealing suffering" to atone for personal and collective sins is "the way to blessedness" (Turner and Turner 1978: 113, 131). Such a motivation is enacted ritually on the Reek when pilgrims walk in bare feet on the "jagged, ankle tearing stones" to the top. According to Archbishop Neary, "without this pain ingredient, without some hardship, the journey could become more of an outing or a holiday. Indeed the pain, undertaken at a time when we continually search for ease and convenience, may become a stimulus toward spiritual growth. Pain has always been written unto this reek pilgrimage" (2001: 2). Nevertheless, penitence is only one of a broad range of motivations for going on this pilgrimage. Many come simply to experience the beauty and majesty of the natural surroundings, finding in this scenic location "an opening to the sacred, a reflection of the God they are groping for" (Nolan and Nolan 1989: 45).

By typing in "Croagh Patrick" or "The Reek" on Google, one finds a number of Internet sites related to the holy mountain. First, there are informational sites. Some are officially tied to the pilgrimage, such as Teach na Miasa, the site of the Croagh Patrick Visitor Centre located in Murrisk at the base of the mountain (www.croagh-patrick.com/centre.html). Others are informational sites posted by people with some connection to Croagh Patrick, such as Croagh Patrick— Ireland's Holy Mountain (www.dunningspub.com/croagh_patrick.htm) of local pub owners Pat and Mary Dunning. Here one can get general information on the Reek, what is of historical interest, what there is to see and do, and what you need to know in order to do the pilgrimage, and also view galleries of photos of the holy mountain.

Second, there are many commercial sites offering special pilgrimages and tours to the Reek. For example, a local tour company advertises Croagh Patrick Walking Tours on the Web (www.walkingguideireland.com/pages/introduction.html). They will "guide you through a magnificent and mystical landscape" on treks such as their "Magical Mayo tour." Others reveal how the holy mountain has recently become a global pilgrimage center. Centered Yoga Retreats 2003 (www.centredyoga.com), for example, organized a tour led by Paul Dallaghan, a teacher from Mysore, India, who "grew up in Ireland" and "loves the land and feels it is a spiritual and open place." His seven-day trip, which included a stop at Croagh Patrick, involved "breathing in the air and vibration while doing yoga in different scenic parts of the country."

Third, there are autobiographical sites authored by people who have something to say or show about their journey to Croagh Patrick. Andrew Graziano's home page (www22.homepage.villanova.edu/andrew.graziano) is one example. He posted his story with pictures of his family trip to Western Ireland. Similar sites include "blogs," or online diaries such as the "North Atlantic Skyline" (www.monasette.com/blog/ja2002.htm), with its photomontage of the stations and pilgrims on the Reek, and sermons on experiences of pilgrims, such as "The Tea Kettle," posted by the minister of St. Mary's Episcopal Church, Cypress, Texas (www.stmaryscypress.org/worship/sermons/2000-07-23.htm). Most of these just provide information, are designed for instructional purposes, or are autobiographical accounts of particular trips to the holy mountain.

However, there is one Croagh Patrick site that merits the label "virtual pilgrimage." That is "Croagh Patrick—Ireland's Holy Mountain," designed by Joseph Rose, who lives in Ellensburg, Washington, and the local County Mayo Clew Bay Network (www.cbn.ie/reek). This site shows the variety of virtual pilgrimages available on the Web. Unlike www.holylandnetwork.com, it is not a commercial operation meant to attract a broad-based clientele, nor is it an official site, like www.lourdes-france.com, which is sponsored by the clergy in charge of the pilgrimages. Inspired by Rose's own intensely spiritual experience on the mountain in 1993, "Croagh Patrick— Ireland's Holy Mountain" displays the four key characteristics of a virtual pilgrimage.

A Sacred Center Out There/In There: The Mythscape of Croagh Patrick

Virtual pilgrimage to Croagh Patrick is an imaginative act that takes place when someone mentally traverses the online mythscape of the pilgrimage. Cyberpilgrims travel electronically through the same mythical *imaginare* that is architecturalized *in situ* in the "real" pilgrimages. This is so because cyberspace draws upon a similar "mental geography that has existed in the living mind of every culture, a collective memory or hallucination, an agreed-upon territory of mythical figures, symbols, rules and truths owned and traversable by all who learned the ways, and yet free of the bounds of physical space and time" (Benedikt 1991: 3).

Several scholars have noted how Christian pilgrimages, particularly to the Holy Land, take place in what Glenn Bowman has called a "mythscape"—a fusion of Christian symbols, ideals, narratives, and places in which sacred centers are "riveted to the ground of Christian scriptures" in pilgrims' minds. This can be seen in pilgrims' travel diaries, which typically draw correspondences between *loci* seen with the *topoi* read in Gospel narratives (Smith 1987: 86). In this respect, mythscapes reveal "the extent to which physical travel is largely an imaginative act, fictional in that the traveler sees what s/he expects to see which is often what was read" (Bowman 1992: 154–56).

Virtual pilgrimages are also based upon a mythscape that originates from the same sacred narratives, such as gospels, legends, and folk tales, as well as pilgrimage histories and travel literature; together, these form a mythscape for the virtual pilgrim-traveler. The Croagh Patrick pilgrimage is a case in point. One finds the mythscape in the act of the pilgrimage itself. It is ideally done in bare feet, the way Patrick himself climbed the Reek, which, of course, also follows the biblical model of Moses in the Book of Exodus (3:5), who removed his shoes on Mount Horeb, the mountain of God, since it was "holy ground." The path from the first station, Leacht Benain, to the summit, Casán Phádraig, has Christian cosmological associations. As a steep, rocky slope that is extremely treacherous for the climber, it is compared to Hell, the place where the penitents suffer until they reach Heaven, the summit itself, where they can be at rest close to God (Hughes 1991: 40). Croagh Patrick also has a rich sacred geography tied to both the archaic Celtic and Christian traditions. For example, the third station of the pilgrimage, Roilig Mhuire, called "Mary's Station" or the "Virgin's Cemetery," is a place associated with a pre-Christian fertility goddess. In the past, women who wanted to have children or have their children blessed came on the pilgrimage (Hughes 1991: 64).

But primarily, the Reek is Saint Patrick's holy mountain. It was Patrick who fought the "Devil's mother," Caorthannach or Corra, in a battle beginning on Croagh Patrick and ending at Lough Derg, where he killed the snake, eel, or dragon fiend with his crozier, a victory that allowed him to spread Christianity to the pagan Irish (Turner and Turner 1978: 123). When pilgrims walk in the saint's footsteps on the mountain, they can identify the *loci* along the route of Tóchar Phádraig, or "Patrick's causeway," with the *topoi* of Saint Patrick's ancient narratives and devotional literary traditions. These literary sources are the *Book of Armagh*, which includes the *Confession* that Saint Patrick supposedly wrote in his old age, Tírechán's memoir of his travels and fast on Croagh Patrick (ca. 670), Muirchu's life history of the saint, and the tenth-century *Tripartite Life of St. Patrick* (Hughes 1991: 12).

These texts have become contextualized as part of the mythscape of Croagh Patrick. This is clearly seen in the present-day configuration of the route. The path from Murrisk, which eventually links to Tóchar Phádraig, begins at Teach na Miasa, the Croagh Patrick Visitor Centre (opened in 2000) opposite the National Famine Monument (dedicated in 1997). The first symbol that greets the pilgrim's eyes is Saint Patrick's statue, erected by Fr. Patterson at the base of the mountain in 1928. The three traditional stations that follow are rich in their associations with Saint Patrick's own spiritual journey. The first station, Leacht Benáin, is a heap of stones associated with Bionnan, Saint Patrick's charioteer, who was buried there as well as Saint Benignus, the successor of Saint Patrick in the See of Armagh (Hughes 1991: 64). The second station on the summit of the mountain was, according to Aneas MacDonnell's description of 1820, a monument forty feet in diameter with loose stones where pilgrims knelt because it was said to be the place where Saint Patrick knelt before his own fast—a place called Gloon Phádraig, Saint Patrick's knee. Probably the same monument is today called Leaba Phádraig, or Saint Patrick's bed, and it is believed to be where the saint slept during his forty days' and nights, sojourn on the mountain. Nearby is also what little remains of the saint's little chapel, Teampall Phádraig, and the new chapel that replaced it, Saint Patrick's Oratory (built in 1905, with wings added in 1962). Except for the new visitor's center, a few signs, the statue, and the relatively new chapel on the summit, all the untutored person would see on the climb would be heaps of stones at the three stations. It is only through the rich mythical heritage that lives on there that the stones of "nature's cathedral" become filled with meaning and power.

As one would expect, Rose's "Croagh Patrick—Ireland's Holy Mountain" site draws upon this traditional mythscape. Rose's home page has pictures of the *Book of Armagh* that link to a history navigator of key events in Croagh Patrick's history, articles from the The Times of London and The *Irish Times* about the various archeological excavations carried out there in 1994, a picture of the statue of Saint Patrick that is at the beginning of the real pilgrimage, and links to Rose's own virtual pilgrimage. On his virtual pilgrimage page, Rose uses several images to mark the beginning of his pilgrimage that are exactly what the pilgrim would see on the real journey: the statue and a panoramic QuickTime movie of the holy mountain seen from Murrisk Abbey. Here, Rose draws upon the rich mythscape of the holy mountain with a description of Tobair Padraig or Patrick's well, "named for the natural spring nearby where Patrick baptized his first Irish converts." Included is a QuickTime movie of the stream with clouds moving rapidly over Croagh Patrick in the background. Like other online pilgrimages, Rose's is generally conservative, drawing on the traditional mythscape to create the "imagined and imaginary space" in which the personal narrative of his journey up the Reek unfolds.

Real Presence in a Virtual Medium

As we have seen, Rose's Croagh Patrick virtual pilgrimage is not only textual. The great advantage of computer-mediated communication is its visual power. It combines narrative with a "series of virtual images," a "chain of signs with one image leading to another" (Beaudoin 1998: 47). It is a "vision machine" and "through its myriad, unblinking video eyes, distant places and faces, real or unreal, actual or long gone can be summoned to presence" (Benedikt 1991: 1). Walter Ong has noted that this power of "telepresence" in electronic media marks a significantly new stage in human cultural evolution. Cyberspace is a kind of "second orality" in which "the divorce between word and image begun by print culture is reversed, so that the total sensorium again includes sight and sound, voice, image, and music" (O'Leary 1996: 785; also in this volume). According to Ong, this stage is a throwback to earlier primal societies whose oral traditions and ritual life evoked a "participatory mystique."

The ability of computer-mediated communication to create a "telepresence" is important for understanding the power of the virtual pilgrimage. At the center of most pilgrimages is an intensely visual experience—seeing the visible traces of saints and divine beings in the evocative power of the temple buildings and sacred objects, and in the powerful rituals that take place in the natural splendor of their setting. Computer-mediated communication is perfectly suited to evoke this sense of "real presence." What is striking about Rose's "Croagh Patrick—Ireland's Holy Mountain" site is its power to convey this telepresence. Part One opens with the lilting Christian hymn "Lord of all Hopefulness" and Rose's brief, poetic evocation of the ineffable power pervading the sacred mountain: "[It is] a mystical place of beauty and peace, where the surrounding glens, hills and mountains—like whales—seem to talk to each other. A stone church, weathered by storm and haunted by Ireland's prayers, waits at the summit. It is there where the people of Ireland flock and the descendents of emigrants return to kneel together in submission on the cold rock, asking for peace and giving thanks for their freedom" (Rose 1998).

Rose's site is filled with stunning photographs and QuickTime movies documenting his own climb up "the Reek." Users can also link to the "Sights and Sounds" gallery to get views of the Bay, sunsets in County Mayo, the fields below the mountain, and so on. They can also investigate the history, archeology, and geology pages to find more information.

Rose divides the pilgrimage itself into three parts: "First Steps," "Penance in the Mist," and "The Summit." "First Steps" includes a movie taken by a handheld camera at the base of the mountain as Rose began his ascent. The viewer is able to see step by step, as if through his own eyes, Rose's difficult, barefoot hike up the rocky trail to the summit. Part Two, "Penance in the Mist," begins with a photo of the author's feet, bloody from the sharp stones, which reveals the difficulty of undertaking this penitential part of the pilgrimage. You can also hear audio files of the "marrow-chilling wind" as you read the following passage from Rose's "Irish Journal": "I swear I heard a whisper in the air, a murmur mingling with the winds scream. It could have been God's voice. Hard to say. It was carried away before my mind and soul could make anything of it." Part Three, "The Summit," has a QuickTime movie of the summit as well as additional pictures and video clips of the view from the summit, accompanied by an explanatory text. The tour concludes with some good advice: "True to Ireland's mystic warmth, you can rest your sore body over a pint of Guinness or a cup of Irish coffee at a pub at the base of the mountain. Catching a ride back to Westport requires only a thumb and a passing car." What Rose's pages show is the power of computer-mediated communication to create a "total sensorium" of sight, sound, and even virtual touch, with his evocative descriptions of the difficult climb up the mountain.

How Rose's site evokes a participatory mystique for his cybervisitors is complex. In his analysis of the "rhetoric of the image," Roland Barthes (1977) argues that photographs and film evoke different perceptual responses in viewers. The photograph is perceived as a "recording," a natural rendering of an object despite the fact that the photographer has used artifice, selfconsciously choosing a certain speed, focus, distance, and composition to create the desired image. The photograph creates a revolutionary form of human consciousness, according to Barthes, "since it establishes not a consciousness of the *being-there* of the thing (which any copy can provoke) but an awareness of *having-been-there*. What we have is a new space-time category spatial immediacy and temporal anteriority" (1977: 44).

This is exactly how some people respond to Rose's photographically rich site. It allows them to take a trip down memory lane. For example, one virtual pilgrim, Leo Archer, writes in Rose's guest book, "As I took your virtual tour the innocent memories of my childhood have come flooding back." Archer was born and raised in Ireland and climbed Croagh Patrick when he was a young boy. Visiting this site on Saint Patrick's Day opened a treasure of happy memories of his childhood and a longing to return:

> I remember vividly how the slope turned to loose rock and appeared to drop off on either side into an abyss. Your description of the weather is exactly how I remember it. I felt very powerless against the force of the elements. I didn't make it to the top but remember coming back down to the bottom and how peaceful and tranquil it all seemed. I would love to return someday with my own kids to complete the journey. Most of all, though, I remember being struck by the simple devotion of my grandfather. It was apparent even to a boy. Both my grandparents are gone now but your page has helped me remember that and many more happy times I spent with them. It has reminded me of home and its richness of heritage and faith. It has made this St. Patrick's Day even better (Rose 1998).

Others, however, experience the Reek very differently. Perhaps they have not had the opportunity to climb it themselves, but they feel they have experienced "being" at Croagh Patrick through the movies, text, and sounds of Rose's site. Lisa Duncan, for example, writes, "Hi! I really enjoyed your Web page. Oddly enough, it did make me feel like I was there."

In *The Power of Images: Studies in the History and Theories of Response*, David Freedberg has studied this religio-aesthetic response in the history of Western art. Paintings and statues of the Greek gods and, with the rise of Christianity, of Christ, the Virgin, and various saints are often experienced, even by contemporary viewer-worshippers, as fully alive and real—the "living embodiment" of their prototype. They perspire, move their arms, legs, and eyes, bleed when struck, exude healing oils and milk, speak, and so on. Their vitality goes far beyond mere "caricatural simulation." Freedberg argues that even if one were willing to grant that viewers only respond as if the image were alive, one must grant that such responses "provide proof of the constructive power of metaphorical and metonymical thought and of the way in which all perception elides representation of reality" (1989: 30).

Freedberg suggests that this experience of immanence is a universal human psychosensual response to the "power of images." In particular, this response often occurs for worshippers before enshrined images at pilgrimage sites. But it is not only iconic. As Duncan's experience of "being there" suggests, images of the site itself can evoke a sense of real presence. This experience is intensified by the many movies on Rose's site. As Barthes has suggested, in film the "spectatorial consciousness" of photography is replaced with a more projective, magical, fictional consciousness in viewers, "where the *having-been-there* gives way to the *being-there* of the thing" (1977: 45). In the case of Croagh Patrick and other virtual pilgrimages like it, the panoply of images—photographs, video clips, and, at some sites, real-video—can evoke in the pilgrim/viewer either as something present to memory or "really present" now on the screen.

Rose's site shows the difficulties of drawing a hard-and-fast distinction between the virtual and real. The very phrase "virtual reality," according to Shawn Wilbur, "attests to the possibility that seeming and being might be confused, and that this confusion might not matter in the end" (1997: 9). In this case, "virtual" does not mean illusory, intangible, or the opposite of real. Virtual comes from the Medieval Latin *virtualis* meaning "strength" or "power," and in scholastic philosophy it refers to something that exists potentially rather than actually (Levy 1999: 22–23). I argue that Rose's site is virtual in this way because, it has the potential for some viewers to evoke a feeling of spiritual presence and power.

Virtual Pilgrimage as a Liminoid Phenomenon

Turner's major theoretical contribution to pilgrimage studies lies in his characterization of it as a "liminoid phenomenon." By "liminoid" Turner means that pilgrimage has an initiatory structure like a rite of passage. The journey itself marks the liminal stage, a transitional state "betwixt and between." Only by traveling to the sacred center out there, on the periphery of where they live their lives ordinarily, can pilgrims temporarily escape from the usual social roles and realities that define who they are. At the sacred site, with its dense symbolism of icons, temple architecture, and rituals, pilgrims can intensely focus on the central values and mystical knowledge of their religion. This liminoid experience can be transformative existentially by giving them a new depth of understanding of their lives.

According to Turner, as a liminoid phenomenon pilgrimage has four characteristics. First, unlike a rite of passage, it is usually a voluntary devotion rather than an obligatory rite. Pilgrimage continues to thrive because it appeals to the modern/postmodern view that being religious means participating not only in the collective rituals of a tribe, church, or sect but also in the spiritual activities of the solitary person. This "idealistic mysticism," as Ernst Troeltsch originally labeled it, is a form of radical individualism where association "is based on a 'parallelism of spontaneous religious personalities'" (McGuire 1992: 134). Second, pilgrimage is ludic. It is as much a pleasurable leisure-time activity (such as sightseeing and tourism) as a solemn rite. Third, rather than functioning as a means of transforming one's social position (e.g., a wedding transforms one from single person to a married person), it fosters personal autonomy, freeing the pilgrim from his ordinary social roles and expectations for more demo-cratic and nonhierarchical forms of association. Fourth, pilgrimage can create *communitas*, a special bonding based on a common experience of humanity.

Does Turner's model apply to pilgrimage on the Internet? Turner was aware of the new ways technology had transformed religion. He noted that a new type of pilgrimage had emerged in the past two centuries that was "frankly technolog-ical" (1987: 330). What he had in mind was the powerful impact that automo-biles, airplanes, and new electronic information sources had in the "dramatic resurgence" of pilgrimage in the modern world. Turner also noted that moder-nity had created many "liminoid specialized performative genres" in the leisure sphere beyond traditional religion. These secular forms of entertainment, such as theater, film, and television can substitute for "the orchestrated religious *gestalt* that once constituted ritual." In particular, Turner saw film as "the dominant form of public liminality in electronically advanced societies" (Tomas 1991: 34).

Since Turner's time, computer-mediated communication has replaced movies as the newest technological medium for experiencing liminality. Like the darkness of a movie theater, the electronic void of computers is a "betwixt and between," a heterogeneous place apart from the quotidian places of home and office (Stenger 1991: 53–54). It can be emancipatory—an "unshackling from RL constraints"—liberating people temporarily from the normal flow of everyday experiences (Wilbur 1992: 11). The fact that the Internet is a place for experiencing liminality has important implications for being religious online.

What about in the case of virtual pilgrimage? Instead of buses, trains, and airplanes, to get there a pilgrim uses "virtual devices for traversing vast hybrid hypermedia spaces that have both active links and dynamic nodes" (Novak 1991: 230). By initiating a search with a navigator, for example, by typing in "pilgrimage Ireland," the user travels to a list of hypertext links that open portals in cyberspace. In this case, the journey metaphor is used to describe how the "virtual traveler" reaches a Web site like Croagh Patrick. The liminoid character of the journey is also reinforced by the very structure of Rose's multimedia pre-sentation, which is divided into three parts that Turner, following van Gennep (1909), has defined as typical of rites of passage: an initial stage that symbolically separates us from our past and profane existence, followed by a stage that secludes us from life and brings us into contact with the sacred, and a final stage that reintegrates our transformed selves into normal life.

What about the specifics? Like "real pilgrims," virtual ones choose voluntarily to go on a pilgnimage. Each has his own reasons for going. In the Croagh Patrick guest book, for example, ordinary people of various ages and gender offer many reasons for visiting the site. Some experience it nostalgically: the site moves Leo Archer because it helps him recall his childhood. Some, such as Pat Mills, find it enlightens them about their Irish heritage: "Thank you for this wonderful tour. I shall visit it again and again to be sure I haven't missed a thing. You enlighten my heritage and the thought of climbing Croagh Patrick on the Holy Days would certainly strengthen my faith in our Holy God. It's the top of the world. Thanks!" Others are simply tourists searching for an interesting holiday trek in Ireland. Still others talk about their deep religious experiences. Courtney Bayne writes: "I too experienced the sensations you speak of: an overwhelming sense of being close to God and of voices of the past."

In all these cases, personal choice is key. Pilgrims choose to visit Croagh Patrick online. Their modems release them from their everyday lives for a trip to an "awe-inspiring" sacred place. And, like the "real" thing, this is best described as a leisure activity, as the metaphor "net surfing" suggests. This is seen in Courtney Bayne's and her husband's visit, who "just happened by [the] Web page while looking about real estate in Galway." Archer did it on Saint Patrick's Day, a time to celebrate what it means to be Irish. People log on to this site for fun: to be entertained by the amusing format, to reminisce about the past, and to satisfy their curiosity—all forms of leisure activity.

Nevertheless, virtual pilgrimage is not the same as "the real thing." First, it is almost instantaneous—travel to the site is a click of the button away. Second, it takes place figuratively, not literally. The arduous journey to a distant place, the ascetical practices that are so important in penitential pilgrimages, do not exist virtually. The virtual journey is a disembodied act of the imagination that cannot fully simulate the physical rigors of the RL original. On the Croagh Patrick Web site we can look at the picture of Rose's bloody feet, but the pain he felt walking barefoot up the cold, rough rock—like the Irish poet Patrick Kavanagh. "physically weary, spiritually exhilarated"—cannot be simulated fully on the Internet, at least not yet (Hughes 1991: 51). On this point, virtual pilgrimage does not fulfill the ecclesiastical vision of pilgrimage as a penitential ascetic practice for the renewal of the spirit of lay people (Turner and Turner 1978: 128).

Virtual Pilgrims' Communities and *Communitas*

The final characteristic of pilgrimage is the experience of *communitas*, which Turner defines as an undifferentiated sense of community or "even communion of equal individuals" who are bound together by the "generic bond" of humankind or comradely harmony (1969: 131–33). Turner believes the special community created on the journey when social boundaries of class, race, gender, and status break down and pilgrims share a common sense of brother- or sisterhood. Can virtual pilgrimages offer a similar experience of *communitas*?

As Wertheim (1999) points out, cyberenthusiasts often argue that this experience is the greatest promise of the computer mediated communication, one that realizes technologically what the great religions through the ages have indicated is the goal of humanity's spiritual quest:

> As with Christianity, cyberspace too is potentially open to everyone: male and female. First World and Third, North and South, East and West. Just as the New Jerusalem is open to all who follow the way of Christ, so cyberspace is open to anyone who can afford a personal computer and a monthly Internet access fee. . . . Like the Heavenly City, cyberspace is a place where in theory people of all nations can mix together. (1999: 23)

A degree of virtual *communitas* does form inside the guest book of Croagh Patrick. In the nonplace of cyberspace, just as in real physical space, "communities of meaning" unite over sets of symbols and texts that people share (Bellah et al. 1985: 52–55). Although disembedded from their ordinary social relations in physical space, members of these cybercommunities have a highly articulated symbolic arena on their shared Web sites. In the case of Croagh Patrick, writing in the guest book and reading what others have said creates a web of personal relationships. It offers virtual guests shared symbols—Saint Patrick, the beauty of Ireland, Guinness Stout—to help them overcome their personal idiosyncrasies.

In this respect, it is interesting to note that many of Rose's guests-pilgrims are linked by a common Irish heritage or by their own deep spiritual experiences of climbing "the Reek." Rose's site continues the modern tendency of the Croagh Patrick pilgrimage to reinforce Irish nationalist sentiments. As Archbishop Neary has pointed out, the "place is holy, but not just because it is associated with St. Patrick, but because it bears the imprints of the feet of our ancestors who climbed this mountain in search of God or to seek his forgiveness of sin in their lives" (Neary 2001: 1). And, like Rose himself, most of the people in the guest book are expatriates living in America and returning to Croagh Patrick not through special package cruises from America on the Cunard line but through the magic of the Internet (Hughes 1991: 74).

Besides this, the guest book pilgrims share something else—a non-hierarchical and nonclerical nature. Catholic church rituals, doctrines, and ecclesiastical authority are never mentioned. This reveals the Internet's power to foster new possibilities of communion through online communication, with a lay community that forms on the Internet outside clerical lines of spiritual authority. It also supports Rheingold's contention that "because we cannot see one another in cyberspace, gender, age, national origin are not apparent unless a person wants to make these characteristic public" (1993: 26). The anonymity of Internet guest books, chat rooms, MUDs, and so on is ideal for what Turner calls "spontaneous *communitas*," a form of community that characterizes the immediate, ever-changing circumstances in which modern Americans find themselves" (Healy 1997: 57).

But the Croagh Patrick guest book also reveals that Turner's model may be deficient for understanding virtual communities. Some critics argue that computer-mediated communication fosters a monadic individualism since, after all, "all of its users exist as individuals extending their selves through the computer network but isolated by the necessary mediation of the cathode ray tube and keyboard" (Foster 1997: 26). To be sure, virtual pilgrims can "meet" at the Croagh Patrick site, but all that they have before them are the letters in the guest book. Their interconnectedness, therefore, is limited by the technology that binds them together, mainly textually. What sense of *communitas* they have, therefore, must lack the intensity of the real-life pilgrimage, with its direct face to face physical contact. As yet, computer-mediated communication cannot provide the sights, sounds, and feelings of circumambulating the Ka'ba with thousands of other *hajjis* or the feeling of the piercingly cold wind of the Reek on your cheeks as you climb the mountain with thirty thousand other people. Moreover, some pilgrimage theorists would argue that Turner is wrong about *communitas*. Real pilgrimages are often acts of individual piety rather than a collective act, something that is privately meaningful instead of a publically shared religious experience (Morinis 1992: 8; see also Aziz 1987). The notes in the Croagh Patrick guest book support this interpretation; each letter tells how the pilgrimage affects the individual writer. Even when they discuss how the Reek symbolizes their common Irish heritage, it is always done in deeply personal terms. Perhaps virtual pilgrimage appeals to the individual who reaches out in cyberspace in his solitariness to find some form of spiritual communion through communication.

References

Aziz, B. N. (1987). "Personal Dimensions of the Sacred Journey: What Pilgrims Say." *Religious Studies* 23: 247–261.
Barthes, R. (1977). *Image, Music, Text*, trans. Stephen Heath. New York: Noonday Press.
Beaudoin, T. (1987). *Virtual Faith: The Irreverent Spiritual Quest of Generation X*. San Francisco: Jossey-Bass Publishers.
Bellah, R., et al. (1985). *Habits of the Heart: Individualism and Commitment in American Life*. New York: Harper and Row.
Benedikt, M. (1991). "Introduction." In *Cyberspace: First Steps*, ed. M. Benedikt, 1–25. Cambridge, MA: MIT Press.
Bowman, G. (1992). "Pilgrimage Narratives of Jerusalem and the Holy Land: A Study in Ideological Distortion." In *Sacred Journeys: The Anthropology of Pilgrimage*, ed. A. Morinis, 149–168. New York: Greenwood Press.
Dunning, P., and M. Dunning, (n.d.) "Croagh Patrick—Ireland's Holy Mountain." Retrieved from www.dunningspub.com/croagh_patrick.htm, July 17, 2003.
Foster, D. (1997). "Community and Identity in the Electronic Village." In *Internet Culture*, ed. David Porter, 23–37. London: Routledge.
Freedberg, D. (1989). *The Power of Images: Studies in the History and Theory of Response*. Chicago: University of Chicago Press.
Healy, D. (1997). "Cyberspace and Place: The Internet as Middle Landscape on the Electronic Frontier." In *Internet Culture*, ed. D. Porter, 55–72. London: Routledge.
Hughes, H. (1991). *Croagh Patrick (Cruach Phádraig—the Reek) An Ancient Mountain Pilgrimage*. Westport, Ireland: Harry Hughes.
Levy, P. (1998). *Becoming Virtual: Reality in the Digital Age*. New York: Plenum Press.
McGuire, M. (1992). *Religion: The Social Context*, 3rd ed. Belmont, CA: Wadsworth.

Morinis, A., ed. (1992). *Sacred Journeys: The Anthropology of Pilgrimage*. New York: Greenwood Press.

Neary, M. "Homily for National Pilgrimage to Croagh Patrick." Retrieved from www.catholiccommunications.ie/Pressrel/27-july-2001.html, July 7, 2003.

Nolan, M. L., and S. Nolan (1989). *Christian Pilgrimage in Modern Western Europe*. Chapel Hill, NC: University of North Carolina Press.

Novak, M. (1991). "Liquid Architecture in Cyberspace." In *Cyberspace: First Steps*, ed. M. Benedikt, 226–254. Cambridge, MA: MIT Press.

O'Leary, S. D. (1996). "Cyberspace as Sacred Space: Communicating Religion on Computer Networks." *Journal of the American Academy of Religion*, 64: 781–808.

Rheingold, H. (1993). *The Virtual Community: Homesteading on the Electronic Frontier*. Reading, MA: Addison-Wesley.

Rose, J. (1998). "Croagh Patrick: Ireland's Holy Mountain." Retrieved from www.cbn.ie/reek, July 11, 2003.

Smith, J. Z. (1987). *To Take Place: Toward a Theory of Ritual*. Chicago: University of Chicago Press.

Stenger, N. (1991). "Mind Is a Leaking Rainbow." In *Cyberspace: First Steps*, ed. M. Benedikt, 49–58. Cambridge MA: MIT Press.

Sugach, M. (2001). "Returning to Athea." *Limerick Leader* (March 10). Retrieved www.limerick-leader.ie/issues/20010310/seoighe.html, July 11, 2003.

Tomas, D. (1991). "Old Rituals for New Space: Rites de Passage and William Gibson's Cultural Model of Cyberspace." In *Cyberspace: First Steps*, ed. M. Benedikt, 31–48. Cambridge, MA: MIT Press.

Turner, V. (1969). *The Ritual Process: Structure and Antistructure*. Ithaca, NY: Cornell University Press.

———. (1974a). *Dramas, Fields, and Metaphors; Symbolic Action in Human Society*. Ithaca, NY: Cornell University Press.

———. (1974b). "Pilgrimage and *Communitas*." *Studia Missionalia* 23: 305–327.

Turner, V., and E. Turner, (1978). *Image and Pilgrimage in Christian Culture: Anthropological Perspectives*. New York: Columbia University Press.

van. Gennep, A. (1909). *The Rites of Passage*, trans. M. B. Vizedom and G. L. Caffee. London: Routledge and Kegan Paul.

Watt, N. (1995). "Pre-Christian Remains Found on Ireland's Holy Mountain," *Times (London)* (September 27). Retrieved from www.cbn.ie/reek, July 7, 2003.

Wertheim, M. (1999). *The Pearly Gates of Cyberspace: A History of Space from Dante to the Internet*. London: Virago Press.

Wilbur, S. (1997). "An Archaeology of Cyberspaces: Virtuality, Community, Identity." In *Internet Culture*, ed. D. Porter, 5–22. London: Routledge.

Wilkinson, J., trans. (1973). *Egeria's Travels*. London: S.P.C.K.

16
Searching for the Apocalypse in Cyberspace

ROBERT A. CAMPBELL

A Google search using the keyword "apocalypse" yields more than 1.2 million returns; a more precise search for "the apocalypse" results in just under half that number. One observation that can be made from these numbers is that interest in predictions or revelations about our future is widespread within popular culture (see Easterbrook 2003). Certainly, the anticipation of the millennium (Y2K) and its uneventful passing (see Cowan, 2003), the aftershock of the September 11, 2001, terrorist attacks on the World Trade Center and the Pentagon, as well as the recent war in Iraq have gone a long way towards sustaining this interest. Beyond that, however, it is difficult to say very much. Our knowledge of how exactly the apocalypse is discussed on the Internet, by whom, and for what purpose is cursory at best (see Dawson 2000: 28). Consequently, one of the primary objectives of this chapter is an analysis of a small sample of Web sites devoted to discussions of the apocalypse in order to begin to answer some of these fundamental questions. Further, I hope to demonstrate some ways in which the nature of apocalyptic discourse has changed as a result of the existence of the Internet. However, first, it is necessary to understand some of the terminology and issues associated with apocalypticism, particularly as it manifests itself in the American context that dominates the World Wide Web.

Apocalypticism: Its Nature and Appeal and the Internet

In his excellent exploration of apocalypticism in America, Daniel Wojcik (1997: 11–12) points out that the word *apocalypse* was originally associated with Jewish and Christian prophetic (and often quite cryptic and highly symbolic) literature that contained predictions about the end of time and the establishment of a new world. Linked particularly to the Book of Revelation by Christian theologians, *apocalypse* came to mean revelations by a supernatural being involving the defeat of evil, the judgment of the world, and the creation of this new world under divine rule. In more popular parlance, without any specific reference to divine revelation, the notion of apocalypse has become synonymous with any sort of disaster and doom—the end of the world as we know it. However, for the purposes of this chapter, I follow Wojcik's use of the term to mean "the catastrophic destruction of the world or current society, whether attributed to supernatural forces, natural forces, or human action" (1997: 12).

Speculation about end-times is often referred to as eschatology, with *individual* eschatology meaning the existence of the soul and an afterlife, while cosmic eschatology treats the destiny of humanity, the world, and the created universe more generally. Hence we might expect apocalyptic predictions about the end of the world to include some ideas on what will happen afterwards. As Wojcik (1997: 14) points out, because they contain concepts of redemption and the potential for a new and better world, traditional approaches to eschatology are generally optimistic. However, in the last century or so, belief in a meaningless or unredemptive end, one that stands outside religious belief systems, has developed and given rise to what Warren Wagar (1982) calls a secular eschatology characterized by anxiety and pessimism. Such attitudes have been fostered by the threat of nuclear annihilation and the breakdown of values and institutions associated with the collapse of modernity (Beck 1999).

Wojcik (1997: 14–17) explains that the apocalyptic tradition has persisted largely through myths and folkways outside official church-sanctioned beliefs and usually in the hands of visionaries and prophets, who rely more on their own charisma and on the content of the messages that have been revealed to them than on some official status as trained theologians or as representatives of a religious institution (see Boyer 1992: 304–311). Teachings and ideas are spread through popular books, pamphlets, audio and video cassettes, and on television—all forms of communication that are more consistent with the experience of lay consumers rather than more scholarly or ecclesiastical forms associated with academic writers and church doctrinalists. These "subliterary forms" of expression (Dorson 1977) not only help to give the messages their popular appeal but provide a more familiar conduit through which people are likely to express their feelings, concerns, and hopes. Further, because they come directly into people's homes, these technologies have contributed to the privatization or personalization of religion, allowing people to deal with the materials and ideas on their own terms and at their own pace while at the same time providing a way for them to be part of a much larger phenomenon (Helland 2000).

Fatalism, the notion that future events are "inevitable, determined by external forces, and unalterable by human will or effort" (Wojcik 1997: 18), is a fundamental aspect of American apocalypticism. However, because it provides meaning and order to what appear as otherwise senseless events, the idea of inevitability has an unexpectedly positive aspect to it (Doob 1988). In other words, apocalypticism provides a framework within which to interpret events that might otherwise appear random or incomprehensible. For many people, linking events that are beyond their control with the fulfillment of God's will provides a much greater sense of meaning and comfort than simply thinking that the world will end either in an abrupt nuclear holocaust or more slowly through the spread of disease or the destruction of the ozone layer. Irrespective of how this inevitability is conceived, one of the key points that Wojcik (1997: 6) makes is that Americans are fascinated with apocalypticism, that apocalyptic ideas are "as American as the hot dog" (Nelson 1982: 179), and that the preoccupation with the millennium "has become, even more than baseball, America's favorite pastime" (Sweet 1979: 531).

Paul Boyer (1992: 293–324) indicates that the persistence of apocalyptic or prophetic thought in America is related to the high level of Christian evangelical faith and practice found here. He suggests that the appeal of apocalypticism lies in the resolution of certain psychic tensions felt by evangelicals. An understanding of some of these tensions helps elucidate the special appeal of the Internet as a means of expressing apocalyptic views. First, apocalypticism serves to reinforce the evangelical emphasis on the Bible as the key to understanding the past, present, and future. Matching the predictions of Scripture with world events, for example, serves as a sort of quasi-empirical validation of evangelical faith. Second, belief in prophecy provides an acceptable balance between free will and determinism. That is, while the overall course of history is seen as foreordained by God, an element of individual choice ensures that people can act in ways that fit with their destiny. Third, apocalyptic beliefs clarify the social responsibilities of evangelicals. Their task as Christians is not to change the world nor to build a just society here on earth—both pointless in the face of an imminent eschaton. Rather, their righteous obligation is limited to preparing for the Second Coming of Christ and "warning" people of the need to repent and convert so that they may escape the wrath of God. Fourth, apocalyptic thought in America also reflects a "theology of the people," part of a long tradition of American religious populism and anti-intellectualism. The truth, evangelicals assert, is simple and open to all. In these circumstances it is common for institutional dogma to be replaced by more diverse and particularistic interpretations of the Word of God. Fifth, apocalypticism provides a more comprehensive framework within which events that might otherwise be regarded as distinctly separate are linked as part of a holistic divine plan. This understanding reassures evangelicals that they are soon to be compensated for physical woe, social strife, and economic inequality they have experienced, and they are to be rewarded for their humility with eternal bliss.

It should not be surprising that apocalypticism appears to be receiving a great deal of attention on the Internet. The evangelical's primary duty is to spread the Word of God, and, at least in the technologized West, the Internet is the first form of mass media in which a large segment of the population can participate as contributors. By comparison with newspapers, radio, or television, the costs are minimal, while the potential exposure is global. No one vets the material uploaded to the Internet. In the West, neither religious nor civil authorities can successfully suppress idiosyncratic or allegedly heretical interpretations of the Bible or the prophecies people claim to have received from

God (though see Cowan, this volume). It is a public forum dominated by a culture of liberalism, and Internet enthusiasts take pride in the near anarchistic character of cyberspace.

But are there other, more subtle indications of a special affinity between the Internet as a medium of communication and apocalypticism as a type of thought? James Slevin's discussion (2000) of the "empowering" aspects of the Internet as a means of "cultural transmission" indicates some links to explore. Slevin also reveals, however, how the Internet can be a double-edged sword that may work to soften instead of sharpen the apocalyptic fervor of some believers. First, Slevin argues, use of the Internet tends to encourage and reinforce our sense of individual agency: "Probably more than with any other medium, individuals using [the Internet] have to actively negotiate mediated experience and endow it with structures of relevance to the self" (2000: 175). Second, since it allows lay people readily to access seemingly "expert" information, the Internet facilitates increased control over certain kinds of knowledge and skills. Likewise, it allows people to "compare and assess claims made by rival authorities," to "bypass certain intermediaries or gatekeepers who once managed and limited their access to information" (2000: 177). Third, by bringing people into contact with a greater diversity of cultures and social groups, the Internet compels users to be more articulate about their individual commitments, while offering "a great many opportunities for forging new alliances [and] entering into new social engagements" (2000: 178). It expands the horizons of interaction by which the user can develop and promote an ideological or religious agenda; and as the social and material conditions in a person's offline context (and the world in general) change, it presents opportunities for shifting alliances and commitments. Fourth, while the Internet can expose individuals to conflicts and risks that challenge their own day-to-day routines, it can also teach users how to cope with and even transcend these problems through dialogue and the acquisition of more useful information. Obversely, of course, the Internet allows people to build networks of like-minded individuals across vast distances and have a rich social interaction that systematically excludes all contrary or disturbing sources of information.

The Internet is a medium ideally suited in some regards to the populist, emotional, eclectic, and assertive style of the American tradition of apocalyptic prophecy. It should allow this tradition to spread and diversify, boosting the confidence of those fatalistically fascinated with the approaching "end of the world as we know it." As the following survey of only a handful of sites suggests, it unleashes a vast creative potential for finding and announcing new proofs of God's intent. Yet it also places those seeking insight into the apocalypse into direct and easy contact with a disconcerting variety of views, including overtly skeptical ones. This exposure may serve to chasten budding apocalypticists by undermining the simple assumptions of so much apocalyptic rhetoric. It also reveals how apocalyptic thought is increasingly coming adrift from its religious origins and sources. The idea of the apocalypse is being secularized by some people and in some instances even turned into a source of popular entertainment. These trends certainly predate the Internet (Boyer 1992; Wojcik 1997), and Hollywood has long exploited the box office appeal of apocalyptic themes, as exemplified by the highly successful *Mad Max* (I, II, and III) and *Terminator* (I, II, and III) movies and numerous others. In cyberspace the biblical and the popular, even the commercial visions of the end become confused, as genres are even more readily blended in this multi-media environment where seemingly anything goes. Few Christians could have anticipated a site like "Apocamon" (www.e-sheep.com/apocamon/), for example, where the Book of Revelation has been reproduced as a comic strip with characters that mimic the Japanese Pokemon cartoons so popular with children all over North America in the 1990s.

Apocalypse on the Net

The Web sites described in this section were selected from among many that contained references to "the apocalypse." Table 16.1 provides a listing of some terms commonly associated with apocalypticism that could form the basis for building an alternate sample, along with the number of returns generated by the Google search engine. (Note that these returns do not indicate individual, separate Web sites.)

Here I discuss seven different Web sites, picked to show the range of sites available and the relevance of some of the themes discussed above. The first site demonstrates that the media are keenly aware of the importance of this aspect of American culture. The second and third offer different critiques of apocalypticism. The fourth site provides a decidedly secular view of the end of the world, with an emphasis on surviving whatever catastrophe might take place. The fifth and sixth offer evangelical Christian perspectives on the apocalypse.

Table 16.1 Results of a Google Search for Terms related to Apocalypticism (June 8, 2003).

Term	Number of Returns
Antichrist	366,000
Armageddon	16,600
Book of Revelation	101,000
Dispensationalism	15,300
Doomsday	239,000
End times	182,000
Eschatology	101,000
Fatalism	55,900
Millennialism	12,400
The Rapture	124,000

And finally, I have included one site that suggests an alternative religious context (Baha'i) as the culmination of Christian apocalypticism.

Apocalypse (www.pbs.org/wgbh/pages/frontline/shows/apocalypse)

This site was produced in November 1999 to accompany a two-hour television documentary, "Apocalypse! The Evolution of Apocalyptic Belief and How It Shaped the Western World," that had aired two months earlier on the PBS series *Frontline.* While the fact that apocalypticism received this level of attention was almost certainly related to the Y2K phenomenon, that was only a small part of the material covered. The show was divided into two parts; the first hour focused on the origins of apocalyptic ideas, particularly in the Book of Revelation, while the second hour explored the influence of these ideas in Western history. The Web site parallels this presentation and includes video excerpts, transcripts of interviews, essays, and scholarly articles, comments from viewers, links to related sites, a glossary of terms, and directions for ordering tapes of the show and transcripts.

The history of apocalypticism is traced from its literary origins in Jewish prophetic writings, through the Book of Revelation, and historically from the Crusades to the Reformation and the rise of Marxism and Nazism. Apocalypticism in America proceeds from Christopher Columbus, through the Puritans, the American Revolution, the evangelical "doom industry" (with an emphasis on the writings of Hal Lindsey, e.g., 1974, 1983, 1995; cf. Wojcik, 1997: 37–59), and the so-called "doomsday cult" phenomenon. The final sections highlight the resiliency of apocalyptic beliefs, the influence of the year 2000, signs of the end-times, and the influence of the apocalyptic worldview. The Book of Revelation and the figure of the Antichrist, both of which are seen as the key elements of evangelical Christian apocalypticism, receive lengthy treatment in dedicated sections on the site.

The interactive nature of the Web is also an important element of this site. A roundtable discussion between six scholars who have written extensively on apocalyptic matters—Michael Barkun (1974), Paul Boyer (1992) Richard Lande (2000), Stephen O'Leary (1994), and Catherine Wessinger (2000)—and which was carried out via e-mail over several weeks demonstrates the efforts of the producers of this site to provide a solid academic footing for their material. Each scholar offered an assessment of apocalypticism and its relation to the American psyche, along with some predictions on what might happen after the year 2000. There is also an Antichrist quiz in which visitors are asked to guess which individuals from a list of given personalities (e.g., Adolf Hitler, Bill Clinton, and Saddam Hussein) have been identified as the Antichrist in their time. Further, the site provides an opportunity for viewers to join the discussion, with comments from over eighty people who watched the show.

While the producers of this site are not espousing a particular view of the apocalypse, they are reinforcing the view that apocalypticism is an important factor in history and current affairs, especially in America. Furthermore, by creating this site and inviting participation from the public, they have become active partners in propagating and shaping apocalyptic discourse.

A Brief History of the Apocalypse (www.abhota.info)

Created in 1999 by Chris Nelson, this site is designed "to debunk end-time prophecy by listing hundreds of failed doomsday predictions, allay the fears spread by end-time preachers, and demonstrate that doomcrying is nothing new. I also hope you will derive amusement from some of the bizarre prophecies."

The site is organized into seven main areas, each reflecting a range of predicted dates for the end of the world (2800 B.C.–1700 A.D.; 1701–1970; 1971–1997; 1998–1999; 2000 to the present; the future; and "SOON!"). In each case the author indicates the predicted date, the person or group responsible for the prediction, details of the circumstances surrounding the prediction, and the source of his information. In only a very small number of cases are there links to other Web pages where more information can be found on any of the predictions. Nelson does, however, provide links to a small number of other pages that contain doomsday time lines.

Basically, the author has compiled his information from about twenty-five books on apocalypticism (including Wojcik 1997). The examples provided in each section cover a broad range of secular and religious sources, and the author's primary message appears to be that there are as many different predictions of imminent doom as there are people to make them. Nowhere does he indicate whether he believes that there will or will not be an apocalypse. Rather, based on inductive reasoning, he demonstrates a significant level of skepticism about our ability to predict when such an event might occur. He does not cover contemporary issues, nor does he attempt to link events, past or present, to any notion of the apocalypse. He provides no form of analysis or systematic commentary on the content or context of the predictions he lists. As a consequence, it is difficult to determine in any depth the author's motivation for constructing this site or what exactly the visitor to the site is to take away.

On this last point, the "SOON!" section of the site is quite interesting in that it contains a number of predictions with no specific dates attached. On the one hand, Nelson mentions the first-century Roman philosopher Seneca, who thought that the world as he knew it would "soon" be consumed by fire (leading to the establishment of a new world), and on the other hand, he includes the present-day Aetherius Society, which predicts that the Great Avatar will appear "soon" by spaceship to usher in a new world. The difficulty with these predictions is that there is no point at which the skeptic can say "I told you so" when the predictions fail to come to fruition.

Nelson also uses this site for more general personal items: favorite links; pictures and Web logs of his travels around the world; Chinese philosophical resources; and a guide to things to do in Iowa (at one time the author's home state). We might infer from his inclusion of these links that he sees apocalypticism as just another normal part of American culture and as a form of entertainment or amusement. However, the fact that he has exerted so much effort to read through and summarize a large volume of written material suggests that he is not trivializing the apocalypse. Rather, he demonstrates to others how a critical and informed approach to certain phenomena provides a mechanism for interpreting events as part of everyday experience, thus limiting their potential as external sources of control over your life.

Surfing the Apocalypse (www.surfingtheapocalypse.com)

Established in 2001, this site is designed and maintained by Theresa de Veto (also called Theresa Durbin), who, because of her difficult life, makes several emotional appeals to readers for donations so that she can devote her time to maintaining and updating the site. She states:

> On these pages you will find much thought provoking and "unusual" ideas and theories, but as you weave the pieces together, somehow they all seem to connect and make some sort of strange sense! Could it be that the "end of the world" that is so much talked about is but an end to the ignorance and darkness that for too long mankind has stumbled about in? Could this be the time of awakening, a time of lifting the veil that for so long has blinded us to the workings and wonders of the universe and its Creator? The Internet has provided a powerful new way to exchange these sometimes revolutionary and yes, even wacky ideas. Here you will find a road map to some of the places, people, and ideas that are unique unto this time. Some of the sites you will find listed here are Universal conversations and some, you will get the feeling are just talking to themselves. It is not the purpose of the creators of this site to endorse or promote any of these ideas over another. This site has been created to serve as a mirror to the times. It is our personal belief that it is important to focus on the positive aspects of knowledge and life. It is also our viewpoint that it is important to know the other or darker side of the stream of things in order to strike the balance that is wholeness. One cannot hide away from those things that do not agree with personal belief systems. Information is power and knowledge is wisdom. The time of standing with our heads in the sand is over. It is important to "Know Thyself," it is also important to "Know Thine Enemy."

This rather long quotation demonstrates a number of important points, one of which is the clear recognition on de Veto's part of the power of the Internet as a means of disseminating information. Further, she appears to be suggesting that the imminent apocalypse is really an awakening, a form of enlightenment, a liberation from ignorance. Like many late modern conspiracists, for her, the significant signs of this shift are found in a wide variety of diverse and often bizarre "facts"—some of which are just "coming to light"—that relate to almost every aspect of our lives. Similarly, she suggests that we are now coming to understand that a great deal of information has been kept from us or purposely distorted by governments and other large institutions.

The site's main page is divided into three panels, with the left and middle panels containing links to news and current event items, and the right panel providing links to related thematic areas, including Health/SARS, Politics/ Economics, Military/Iraq, Technology Takeover, Privacy, History, Science, Religion, UFOs, and Space. Many of the items are replicated from online versions of American and British newspapers as well as Internet news services. Consider the following three examples: "Food processors have been caught on video boasting that they have developed undetectable methods of adulterating the chicken that goes into British hospitals, schools and restaurants with cheap beef waste and water" (from www.smh.com.au/articles/2003/05/21/ 1053196641965.html); "without any contact with the subject, Remote Neural Monitoring can map out electrical activity from the visual cortex of a subject's brain and show images from the subject's brain on a video monitor. NSA operatives see what the surveillance subject's eyes are seeing" (from www.cyberspaceorbit.com/ SigintInfo.htm); and "Vulcan is the distant, yet to be observed, dark star companion of our Sun. It has flavored the human spirit, aided in the manifestation of avatars like Christ and Buddha, and stimulated quasi-periodic bombardment of Earth by comet strikes re-directing the course of human civilization" (www.barrywarmkessel.com).

Items from the right panel include links to other conspiracy theory sites and thousands of sites indexed by key words related to the stories in the two other panels, including crop circles, earth changes, the Holy Grail, Mars anomalies, sacred geometry, and weird science. One site is "The Universal Seduction" (www.theuniversalseduction.com), which contains "a collection of knowledge from experiencers and scholars exposing All that has been suppressed from the masses for a very long time." The author also highlights an extensive interview with John Maynard, a former American army intelligence officer, who indicates, for example, that "there are certain government installations (military and/or civilian), where daily UFOs and Alien contact was, and is, a normal event of the day. "

Unlike the author of the previous site, who takes a more casual and measured approach to the topic, de Veto exhibits missionary zeal. She is desperate to keep people informed, even to the point of asking visitors to her site for financial help so that she can continue to be of service to them. At the same time, like Chris Nelson, she advises caution. The following quotation, attributed to Buddha, which appears at the bottom of the site's main page, provides an excellent précis of de Veto's main message: "Believe nothing, no matter where you read it, or who said it, no matter if I have said it, unless it agrees with your own reason and your common sense."

Surviving the Apocalypse (www.survivingtheapocalypse.com)

While there does not appear to be a clear articulation of the objectives of this site, the authors (who do not identify themselves) make the following statement:

> As Thomas Jefferson so elegantly put it, "The price of freedom is eternal vigilance. . . . Let the eye of vigilance never be closed." Recent developments in the tracking of asteroid threats, the proliferation of environmental watchdog

agencies, and continued international cooperation in biohazard identification and containment, are all very encouraging examples of such observational efforts. And these efforts may be the most important of any—after all, the success of any survival plan, personal or planetary, hinges on perceiving the threat while there is still time enough to act. (www.survivingtheapocalypse.com)

Following this, the main point of the authors of this site is that observation of current events while there is still time to act leads to an increased readiness and enhanced ability to meet threats to our existence when time has run out.

The site is divided into four main areas, only three of which were operational during the period of research for this chapter. The first deals with apocalyptic themes, including postapocalyptic utopianism, apocalyptic cinema, reports on past predictions that have not come to pass, and links to pages with apocalyptic content. The second reports on the results of a large number of ongoing opinion polls run that are on the site and that deal with various aspects of apocalypticism. One poll, for example, called "Hole in the Pole" asks how concerned visitors are in terms of the following scenario: "In late August of 2000, reports were released that indicate ice formations in the northern polar regions are melting quickly enough to raise sea levels. This discovery opened up a global debate about whether it is a sign of global warming, or part of a natural cycle. Are you concerned by these reports?" (www.survivingtheapocalypse.com/opinions/polehole.shtml). A number of other polls deal with environmental issues, overpopulation, natural terrestrial disasters, and apocalypse by asteroid.

While the "Discussions" page was not functioning, the fourth area of the site—"Outfitters"—contains information on suppliers of survival, camping, and wilderness gear, homesteading equipment, long-term food storage containers, as well as natural toilet, composting, and water purification systems.

This site has a more practical focus than the two previous sites, in that the authors are concerned with helping others prepare for the eschatological aftermath. It also differs in as much as it provides numerous opportunities for visitors to participate through the various polls and surveys in the construction of the knowledge and opinions being expressed on the site. Further, the authors appear to be advocating a highly practical rather than ideological approach to the apocalypse. In other words, they seem to be saying that it does not really matter what you believe or think; without a roof over your head and a source of food and water, you are not going to make it anyway.

Apocalypse Soon (www.apocalypsesoon.org)
This site was established in 1997 by Pietro Arnese, who left the Word Faith Movement when he began to believe that God had provided great insight through Scripture into the state of the Church prior to His return. The author, who indicates that he worked for the largest Christian television network in North America, now believes that most Christian churches, particularly Evangelical and Pentecostal groups, have gone astray and that people need to

turn to the Bible to understand what is going on in the world and how the events that are unfolding point clearly to the apocalypse. "This website is not associated with any particular denomination," he states, "but it is intended as a service to the Body of Christ and as an information medium to those outside the Body. The objective of Apocalypse Soon is to provide information concerning Christianity in various languages, with a particular focus upon the End Times prophecies. The English page functions as the central hub of the site, hosting articles and updates which are then translated into other languages." At present the site is available in English, Spanish, Italian, and Esperanto, with the non-English versions containing only portions of the material found on the main site.

Arnese addresses a number of different audiences on his site. Christians, for example, are encouraged to strengthen the Church by criticizing the way that money is wasted on missions. Jews are welcomed and encouraged both to read the Bible and to understand that "real" Christians have a positive attitude towards them. Finally, Gentiles (anyone who is neither Christian nor Jewish) are encouraged to read the site materials and come to the realization that the best thing they can do for themselves is to convert to Christianity.

The author makes it clear that he believes the apocalypse is imminent and that the information provided on his page is meant to help people "choose their destiny in light of current and upcoming events." Visitors are encouraged to question social institutions and scientific knowledge, judging for themselves the truth of the Bible, which Arnese believes has been distorted by the churches. The unification and strengthening of Europe, unrest in the Middle East, and the growth of technology—particularly technology used to collect and distribute personal data—are seen as the most important signs of impending doom. According to Arnese, the destruction of the powerful nations of the world, as outlined in Ezekiel 38 and 39, will bring "the end to Islam's expansion, (today easily the fastest growing religion) and to Arab bloody fundamentalism. (I will go one step further and say that this will be the end of Islam)," and "Israel will become the most influential nation on earth. Only after this will Israel be able to build the Temple and experience a spiritual awakening, a prelude to her final conversion to the Lord Jesus Christ." Finally, links are provided to a number of related sites that "reflect a sound, time-tested orthodoxy."

The author of this site is advocating a move away from the beliefs and practices of established Christian churches, particularly as reflected in their efforts to spread their message, toward what he regards as a purer biblical interpretation of the apocalypse. At the same time, however, he offers visitors his own highly individualistic interpretation of current affairs in light of biblical prophecy. In an effort to legitimize his position, he confesses to having been an active participant in the organizations he is now criticizing and offers a testimony of his own awakening and realization of the truth.

Endtimes (www.endtimes.org)

This site was established in 1997 by Mark Esposito, Les Fleetwood, and Jack Brooks, all of whom are associated with Evangelical churches in the southern United States and who claim that they have "no special secret knowledge, or new revelation, but only what can be learned from a literal, grammatical-historical reading of the Bible." The authors are followers of premillennial dispensationalism (see Wojcik 1997: 35–39; Howard 2000), the belief that we are now in a time of turmoil and injustice that necessarily precedes the rise and defeat of the Antichrist, the Second Coming of Jesus, and the establishment of a thousand-year reign of peace on Earth under Christ. They continue:

> Our objective is to give Christians a well-documented foundation for understanding prophecy and Endtimes events. It just so happens that the conclusions will indeed give us confidence in our future. Hopefully, the result will be a reason to share the Gospel–The Good News of the Person and work of Jesus Christ, and to thank the Lord daily for new life we have in Christ, the promised life to come, and finally to help keep our eyes focused on His coming. (www.endtimes.org)

The site is divided into seven sections, the last two of which provide commentaries on recent events and links to related Web sites. All contain extensive citations from Scripture as well as keys to "proper" doctrine and "proper" interpretation of biblical texts. Section I describes the lives and intentions of the authors in greater detail as well as providing answers to what the authors regard as fundamental questions: How do I get to heaven? Who is Jesus really? Section II provides a theological rationale for reading Scripture the way they do, including detailed discussions of hermeneutics (interpretation), biblical inspiration, progressive revelation, dispensationalism, and covenants. Section III is devoted to the Old Testament, with an emphasis on the succession of covenants from Abraham to Jesus and a synopsis of the Book of Daniel (a key apocalyptic text), while Section IV on the New Testament discusses the Rapture (the salvation and rescue of the faithful prior to the destruction of the world), and the Book of Revelation. The final section considers the millennial kingdom and the eternal state that are to come.

Unlike Arnese, the authors of this site clearly attempt to identify themselves as advocates and upholders of a particular institutional view of the apocalypse. They make it clear that "the content of their message is not new but that the Internet offers a new, highly effective means for spreading it.

The Baha'is: Christians of the Second Advent
(www.angelfire.com/mo/baha/christians.html)

This site contains a lengthy article (135 pages) reflecting the personal views and opinions of Darrick T. Evenson, who does not claim to be representing an official position of the Baha'i faith. As he describes it:

> This article reveals the Truth about the Second Coming of Christ as "a thief in the night" and "in the glory of His Father" and "in the clouds of heaven," the

Mark of the Beast", the number of the Beast ("666"), the "Image of the Beast," the Red Dragon, the meaning of Jesus' Parable of the Lord of the Vineyard, the Great Tribulation, the Rapture, the Antichrist, the False Prophet, the New World Order, Muhammed and Islam, Islamic terrorism, the Three Wise Men, Armageddon, the 7-Bowl Judgment, the 144,000, the Third Woe, the Millennial Kingdom, and the City of New Jerusalem.

Evenson's objective is to demonstrate that the coming of the Baha'i faith's founder, Baha'u'llah (1817–1892) was in fact the Second Coming of Christ. Readers are encouraged to make copies of the article and make it available to Christian seekers. The primary message of this site is that a new millennium has already begun and that Christians can stop looking for the return of their Savior, for in fact he has arrived. On a technical level, this site is one of the least sophisticated I examined inasmuch as it uses the Internet as a means of distributing one large document that people are asked to print out and read. From an ideological point of view, however, it is quite sophisticated in its effort to present Baha'i faith as the logical continuation of the Christian apocalyptic message.

Concluding Remarks

As the above examination of Web sites demonstrates, some authors are quite forthcoming with their personal identities, institutional affiliations, objectives, and opinions. In other cases, any or all of these elements are less obvious; in some they are completely hidden. The sheer diversity and volume of apocalyptic discourse on the Web means that it is difficult to refer to "the apocalypse" and assume that there will be some level of common understanding about what that might mean. However, it seems clear that the nature of apocalyptic discourse—as well as those who are now able to participate in it—has changed as a result of the Internet and the World Wide Web.

First, the Web has provided an opportunity for more individuals and groups to become involved in defining and critiquing what constitutes the apocalyptic message. This contributes to a breakdown of both individual (e.g., experts, professionals) and institutional (e.g., churches) authority with respect to the production and dissemination of cultural knowledge about the apocalypse. Second, the nature of what counts as relevant information and as legitimate sources of that information has changed. Scriptural prophecy, scientific predictions, political events around the globe, and natural disasters can all be offered as evidence. Similarly, the Bible, the local newspaper, as well as the late-night musings of some unidentified person can all be presented as equally valid sources of such evidence on the unvetted Internet. Third, as a consequence of these, the distinction between the sacred and secular becomes blurred. It is no longer clear how or whether it is even important to distinguish among notions of the end that are divine, human, or natural. The Internet is helping to foster a more generic apocalyptic discourse, adapted to the more pluralistic and secular public consciousness of late-modern societies, particularly in the

North American context. As might be anticipated, not everyone will view these changes as positive—whether they are believers or not.

Ironically, as Douglas Cowan (2003) indicates, both computers and the Internet are often viewed by many Christian dispensationalists as tools of the Antichrist, as the means of world destruction. They will be used by the Antichrist to corrupt and enslave humanity. This view is reiterated to some extent on the "Surfing the Apocalypse" and "Apocalypse Soon" sites. Hence believers may be unwittingly abetting the forces of evil in relying on this modern and invasive technology in the first place. But equally, the irony may lie in how the righteous are using the Internet to subvert the evil intent of some of its managers by raising awareness of the need to resist and to prepare for the final struggle. In this direct sense, the medium itself appears to be a neutral agent in the larger spiritual confrontation. Indirectly, however, the Internet may also be contributing to the trivialization of apocalyptic thought by functioning "as a dialectic partner in the transformation of late modern societies" (Dawson, 2000: 45–47). By its nature the medium may be extending social trends toward increased individualism, detraditionalization, commercialism, and institutionalized reflexivity (Beck 1999; Giddens 1990; Heelas, Lash, and Morrris 1996) that are antithetical to the simple faith and solidarity so characteristic of the worldview underlying the evangelical apocalyptic vision.

References

Barkun, M. (1974). *Disaster and the Millennium*. New Haven, CT: Yale University Press.

Beck, U. (1999). *World Risk Society*. Oxford, UK: Blackwell.

Boyer, P. (1992). *When Time Shall Be No More: Prophecy Belief in Modern American Culture*. Cambridge, MA: Belknap Press of Harvard University Press.

Cowan, D. E. (2003). "Confronting the Failed Failure: Y2K and Christian Eschatology in Light of the Passed Millennium." *Nova Religio: The Journal of New and Emergent Religions*, 7(2): 71–85.

Dawson, L. L. (2000). "Researching Religion in Cyberspace: Issues and Strategies." In *Religion on the Internet: Research Prospects and Promises*, ed. J. K. Hadden and D. E. Cowan, 25–54. London: JAI Press/Elsevier Science.

Doob, L. W. (1988). *Inevitability: Determinism, Fatalism, and Destiny*. New York: Greenwood Press.

Dorson, R. M. (1977). *American Folklore*. Chicago: University of Chicago Press.

Easterbrook, G. (2003). "We're All Gonna Die!" *Wired* 11 (7):150–157.

Giddens, A. (1990). *The Consequences of Modernity*. Cambridge, UK: Polity Press.

Heelas, P., S. Lash, and P. Morris, eds. (1996). *Detraditionalization: Critical Reflections on Authority and Identity*. Oxford, UK: Blackwell.

Helland, C. (2000). "Online Religion/Religion Online and Virtual Communitas." In *Religion on the Internet: Research Prospects and Promises*, ed. J. K. Hadden and D. E. Cowan, 205–223. London: JAI Press/Elsevier Science.

Howard, R. G. (2000). "On-Line Ethnography of Dispensationalist Discourse: Revealed versus Negotiated Truth." In *Religion on the Internet: Research Prospects and Promises*, ed. J. K. Hadden and D. E. Cowan, 225–246. London: JAI Press/Elsevier Science.

Landes, R., ed. (2000). *Encyclopedia of Millenialism and Millennial Movements*. New York: Routledge.

Lindsey, H. (1974). *The Liberation of Planet Earth*. Grand Rapids, MI: Zondervan.

——. (1983). *The Rapture: Truth or Consequences*. New York: Bantam Books.

——. (1995). *The Final Battle*. Palos Verdes, CA: Western Front.

Nelson, J. W. (1982). "The Apocalyptic Vision in American Culture." In *The Apocalyptic Vision in America: Interdisciplinary Essays on Myth and Culture*, ed. L. P. Zamora, 154–182. Bowling Green, OH: Bowling Green University Popular Press.

O'Leary, S. D. (1994). *Arguing the Apocalypse: A Theory of Millennial Rhetoric.* New York: Oxford University Press.

Slevin, J. (2000). *The Internet and Society.* Cambridge, UK: Polity Press.

Sweet, L. (1979). "Millennialism in America: Recent Studies." *Theological Studies* 40: 510–531.

Wagar, W. W. (1982). *Terminal Vision: The Literature of Last Things.* Bloomington, IN: Indiana University Press.

Wessinger, C. (2000). *How the Millennium Comes Violently: From Jonestown to Heaven's Gate.* New York: Seven Bridges Press.

Wojcik, D. (1997). *The End of the World as We Know It: Faith, Fatalism, and Apocalypse in America.* New York: New York University Press.

17

Contested Spaces: Movement, Countermovement, and E-Space Propaganda

DOUGLAS E. COWAN

To deny a religious group the right to protect its esoteric knowledge, indeed its most sacred texts, runs contrary to history and the American experience. It constitutes a denial to that group the protection of the Free Exercise clause of the First Amendment of the Constitution of the United States

—Jeffrey K. Hadden

One of the perspectives from which the social history of religious development can be written is that of the clash between movements and countermovements. Much can be learned from examining the kinds of opposition various religious groups provoke in the societies of which they are a part and how that opposition expresses itself in countervailing social action. That is, how are groups targeted and how do they respond? Looking at the dialectic of movement and countermovement, we can see how these contests have often contributed significantly to the shifting patterns of dominance and marginalization in different social contexts. In some cases, countermovement takes the form of official state regulation—some religious groups are permitted, others are simply prohibited or suppressed (see, for example, Gualtieri 1989 on Ahmadi Muslims in Pakistan). In other cases, culturally dominant religious traditions—such as Christianity in the religiously plural West—maintain a measure of social ascendance because they benefit unofficially in ways that are not available to less dominant groups (see Durham 1996). Few Americans, for example, would argue that "In God We Trust" on U.S. currency is meant to refer to any deity other than the Christian God.

Whatever other aspects it may embrace, at a very basic level countermovement is a process of information assembly, management, and dissemination. In the history of the Christian Church, for example, even such rigorous measures of social control as the great campaigns against heretics, the Spanish Inquisition, and the various witch hunts across Europe depended fundamentally on the careful organization and presentation of relevant information: the conceptualization of target groups or individuals, accusations and testimony provided by plaintiffs, investigators, and witnesses, and the relative conformation of suspects to those data in the course of either religious or secular tribunals.

Even the public punishment of convicted transgressors served an informative as well as a punitive purpose. When these more stringent control mechanisms are not available—as they are not in our late-modern North American context of religious pluralism and relative religious tolerance—other countermovement processes emerge, processes that come to rely more and more on the authoritative enclosure and carefully managed dissemination of information about suspect religious groups.

Consider the secular anticult and evangelical countercult movements, those groups that have responded most negatively and most proactively to the rise of new religious movements in North America. While predicated on different conceptualizations of "the cult problem"—the secular anticult views new religious movements as a problem of human rights, while the evangelical countercult regards them as dangerous theological imposters (see Cowan 2002, 2003)—each has based much of its respective campaign against these new and often controversial religious groups on particular manipulations of information about the groups in question and on specific constructions of reality about the social threat they are alleged to present. Before the advent of the Internet and the World Wide Web, members of both the anticult and countercult movements had rather limited options in terms of direct action against suspect groups. Whereas in the 1970s and early 1980s, members of the anticult movement often attempted to kidnap and "deprogram" adherents of these movements (see Shupe and Darnell 2000), countercult evangelicals frequently picketed so-called "cult" institutions such as Latter-day Saints temples or Church of Scientology centers. More commonly, though, both movements have resorted to indirect action based on the dissemination of information that "exposes" the group in question, its practices, and/or its leader(s), and have subsequently sought to curtail the group's expansion in a particular social space. Prior to the Internet, disseminating either the anticult or the countercult message depended for the most part on the willingness of commercial publishers to release the material or else took the decidedly less attractive (and less prestigious) route of self-publication.

As a platform for religious countermovement, no other technological innovation has allowed for the expanded dissemination of information—and the subsequent expansion of countermovement groups themselves—as has ready access to the Internet and easily manipulated Web authoring tools. Now anyone with a Web design program, access to a server on which a page may be hosted, and the (relatively) simple skills required to design and publish a Web site can make the claim to authority in the countermovement worlds of the anticult and the countercult. In the latter especially, this development has generated something of an e-space cottage industry in the ongoing "war against the cults." Men and women with little or no formal theological education or academic training in the study of new religious movements, but who have often credentialed themselves as "cult experts" simply by virtue of their status as ex-members or outraged onlookers are designing Web sites, some of which have a very professional appearance, in an effort to contribute to the countercult enterprise.

Although the Internet represents in many ways an emerging democratization of both information and access, this expansion results in a projection of authority by Web site operators that may or may not be warranted. As Hadden and I have noted elsewhere, "in e-space, there is no authoritative peer-review process, no editorial chain up which a potential article or book must be sold, no reliable mechanism by which information is vetted" (Hadden and Cowan 2000: 6). Put simply, given the colloquial fetishization of the printed word (exemplified in such comments as "They wouldn't be allowed to print it if it wasn't true"), how do we evaluate the information with which we are presented on the Web? In addition, the metatechnology of the Internet has a multiplier effect on much of the information posted on it, in terms of both the information itself and the relative prestige of the site operator or author. In many cases, the more often a Web site operator is cited in the context of a particular topic—regardless of whether or not he or she is the actual author of the relevant material—the more authority is attributed to that operator. As the technological threshold of Web participation lowers, as the ability to produce a basic Web site no longer depends on purchasing Web design software (some Internet service providers now offer the basic programming and graphics materials online), more and more people will look upon the Internet as a chance to indulge various countermovement interests.

Rather than simply survey the uses made of the Internet by countermovement groups such as the anticult and the countercult movements, in this chapter I would like to use some of the recent struggles of one controversial group, the Church of Scientology (CoS), to explore deeper issues of cyberspace as contested space. This will allow me to address how the Internet is used as a platform for the projection of both authority and a self-limiting construction of reality, and how the Web is used as a communications medium in which countermovements flourish largely because the statutory controls (e.g., the peer-review process or international copyright laws) in force in real life are either virtually absent or practically unenforceable in e-space. It is important to note, however, that this contested space is not solely or even principally electronic. Rather, cyberspace is simply one more venue in which struggles for dominance and authority in the real world are carried out.

Two principal means exist by which movements and countermovements can exercise control in the online environment. First, they can try to dominate both the offline and the online mechanisms by which information is disseminated across the Web. In response to negative postings on the newsgroup alt.religion.scientology, for example, critics and other observers contend that CoS officials urged its members to overload the newsgroup with postings, effectively eliminating the bandwidth available for messages critical of the Church (Garcia 1994; Grossman 1995, 1997; Holmes 1995; Lippard and Jacobsen

1995a; Peckham 1998). A more rigorous attempt employed "cancelbots," programs that automatically delete newsgroup messages that contain specific words or phrases (Grossman 1995, 1997; Lippard and Jacobsen 1995a; Peckham 1998). In Scientology's case, these "cancelbots" declared that the messages had been removed for reasons of copyright infringement—an issue to which we will return. Offline, the Church sought legal injunctions in various countries to prevent Internet remailers (the basic store-and-forward servers by which Internet communication occurs) from reposting messages from particular discussion groups. Most seriously, though, some critics of Scientology have been sued by the Church and have had computer equipment and data confiscated, actions which, among other things, physically prevent access to the Web (see Grossman 1995, 1997; Lippard and Jacobsen 1995a; Lyons 2000; Peckham 1998).

Second, and far more common, movements and countermovements attempt to control the kind of information that is being circulated and to establish what appears to Internet visitors as an authoritative voice about the topic under discussion. However effective it might have been, physical control of Internet bandwidth through spamming or legal intervention into the operations of service providers is a rather artless way to suppress information when compared to the subtle—and often not-so-subtle—means by which the information about particular groups can itself be managed, manipulated, and disseminated online. In this we encounter the Internet and the World Wide Web as a metatechnological paradox: there is more information available more quickly than ever before in human history but with fewer controls on the quality, accuracy, and propriety of that information. I would like to suggest that the Web is becoming an often unrestrained venue for movement/countermovement *propaganda*, a mediative space where dominance is measured in terms of the symbolic resources over which one exercises (or appears to exercise) control and the authority granted that exercise by the audience for whom such information is intended (cf. Dawson 2001).

What We Mean by "Propaganda"
While different colloquial understandings of propaganda abound in society, most of them gather under two rather broad rubrics: fabrication and foreclosure. On the one hand, some believe that propaganda is information which is, by definition, untrue; propaganda is quite simply a lie. Certainly there are circumstances in which this is the case. In many other instances, however, (indeed, I would argue *most* instances), propaganda is less often the invention of outright falsehoods than it is the politic management of carefully selected truths, half-truths, and untruths. That is, rather than lies and altogether spurious disinformation, propaganda is more usefully understood as communication that is organized and manipulated in very particular ways for presentation to specific audiences. Deceit, then, is not the objective of propaganda but rather

one of the mechanisms by which propaganda's goal is realized. Second, there is the belief that "propaganda" is simply the word one uses to label in some pejorative manner information, arguments, or opinions of which one disapproves. Used thus, there is no need to engage the information at all, to determine what is accurate from what is not, and to make a decision about what is useful and what ought be discarded. Rather, dismissing something by calling it "propaganda" obviates the need to consider the material seriously at all.

Scholarly use of propaganda theory as an analytic tool has been plagued in recent decades by an inability to come to terms with a useful definition of the process. Indeed, as I have argued elsewhere (Cowan 1999), this inability accounts in large measure for the relative disuse into which propaganda as an analytic concept has fallen. While a variety of solutions to the problem of definition have been proposed since the end of World War One, when the study of "propaganda" gained considerable currency, none has proved satisfactory. A number of theorists sought to make either an implicit or explicit distinction based on "good" propaganda versus "bad," "enemy" versus "allied," or "black" versus "white" (to which some even add the category "grey"). Bearing in mind the historical use made of the word and drawing on various aspects of its development, the definition of propaganda that underpins this essay is:

> Propaganda is a systematic, ideologically driven, action-oriented manipulation and dissemination of information, which is (a) designed for a specific target audience, and (b) intended to influence the beliefs and behaviors of that audience in a manner consonant with the aims and objectives of the propagandist. (Cf. Cowan 1999: 161–170)

Regardless of its target audience or stated objectives, regardless of the particular mechanisms employed, successful propaganda is predicated on four basic, interdependent principles that function within the context of this definition. These are: affinity, repetition, consistency, and simplicity (Cowan 1999: 181–187). If any one of these principles is not in place, the relative effectiveness of a propaganda program will be reduced. Put propositionally—and recognizing that this is not an ordinal list but rather a mutually reinforcing array—successful propaganda:

- Presents an affinitive message, one that resonates with prejudices extant in the target audience
- Repeats the message constantly
- Frames relevant issues in a consistent manner and
- Deploys a simplified analysis of the problem and the proposed resolution

Since propaganda is aimed at specific target audiences, whatever particular mechanisms are in play, if a communication does not resonate with the established prejudices of that audience, if it is not sufficiently repeated, if it is not consistent in its message, and if it is not simple enough to be grasped quickly, then it will be less effective in motivating members of the target audience toward the goal defined by the propagandist.

Although there are many offline consequences to the battles which take place online (see, e.g., Grossman 1995, 1997; Lazlow 2003; Lippard and Jacobsen 1995a), the online battle centers primarily around the struggle for authority, control over dominant conceptions of target groups, and the ability to motivate behavior based on that authority and those conceptions. To illustrate this struggle I will consider two specific issues: (1) use of the Internet and its special qualities of replication and freedom from peer-review to augment the constant offline portrayal by anticult and countercult activists of CoS as a clear and present social danger; and (2) the conflict over relatively unrestricted Internet publication of esoteric Scientological teachings by non-Scientologists as a tactical countermove against the Church. Each of these demonstrates how the propagandistic manipulation of information and the enclosure of information spaces contribute to the Internet as an ideal countermovement venue.

A Clear and Present Danger?

According to its official Web site, Scientology is an "applied religious philosophy" and "the fastest growing religious movement on earth" (www.scientology.org). While some might question the accuracy of the latter claim, few would dispute that many of the social reform movements instituted by Scientology as well as the beliefs and practices of CoS itself have drawn significant criticism from a wide range of sources. Under the About-Picard Law, for example, its recently enacted "antisect legislation," France has declared Scientology a dangerous sect. In Germany, the Church was for a time labeled *verfassungsfeindlich*, a threat to the constitution (Hexham and Poewe 1999), and, among other things, Scientologists have been banned from membership in the ruling Christian Democratic Union Party, were unable to secure contracts with government agencies, and were subject to police surveillance (Agence France Presse 1996a, 1996b, 1997, 2002; Browne 1998: 197; Horwitz 1997: 123). In Spain, senior Church officials were charged with a variety of criminal offences ranging from threats and coercion to "inducement to suicide" (Lippard and Jacobsen 1995a).

While German courts ultimately struck down many of proscriptions against Scientology and reversed the Church's status as *verfassungsfeindlich* (on this, see Hexham and Poewe 1999; Richardson and Introvigne 2001; Schöen 2001), and the Spanish court dismissed all charges against Church officials (Agence France Presse 2001), these circumstances clearly illustrate the tension with which Scientology often exists.

Like other controversial new religious movements, former members, as well as interested and outraged others, have written putative exposés (Atack 1990; Corydon 1992; Miller 1987; Moos 1995; Wakefield 1991) and some now maintain elaborate Web sites dedicated to debunking the Church and what many regard as its hyperbolic claims. Unfortunately, though, for all its importance as a new religious movement, while Scientology has been the subject of some scholarly attention (cf. Bainbridge 1980, 1987; Beckford 1980; Bednarowski 1995; Berglie 1996; Black 1996; Bromley and Bracey 1998; Bryant 1994; Chidester, n.d.; Dericquebourg 1995; Flinn 1983; Frigerio 1996; Heino 1995; Kelly [1980] 1996; Kent 1999a, 1999b, 1999c; Melton 2000, 2001; Pentikainen and Pentikainen 1996; Ross 1988; Sabbatucci 1983; F. Sawada 1996; H.M.a.S. Sawada 1996; Siverstev 1995; Wallis 1973, 1976; Whitehead 1974, 1987), I maintain that the research has not been nearly as sustained and comprehensive as its prominence as a new religion warrants. In terms of the Internet as a contested meaning space, though, and because it is on the Internet that some of Scientology's most significant battles over public perception are being fought, the CoS is an important example of competing propagandas that struggle for authority and control both online and off.

"The Church of Scientology is a commercial enterprise that masquerades as a religion," writes Dutch evangelical Anton Hein, operator of the "Apologetics Index" Web site, and is an enterprise "that increasingly acts like a hate group" (www.apologeticsindex.org/s04aa.html). Andreas Heldal-Lund, owner of the anti-Scientology site "Operation Clambake" (www.clambake.org; www.xenu.net), echoes Hein, declaring that "the Church of Scientology is a vicious and dangerous cult that masquerades as a religion" (www.xenu.net/roland-intro.html). Even the name of Heldal-Lund's "www.xenu.net" site is provocative because it is meant to caricature one of the principal actors in the esoteric Scientological cosmogony. This particular situation illustrates one of the dilemmas encountered in researching new religious movements. As a scholar, I do not want to further abuse the wish of Scientology to keep its esoteric literature and practices appropriately confidential. But when some of this esoterica constitutes the domain name of a prominent anti-Scientology Web site that is central to the discussion of the topic of this chapter, I have no choice. Tilman Hausherr is even less ambiguous in his evaluation than Heldal-Lund: "Scientology is evil; its techniques evil; its practice a serious threat to the community, medically, morally, and socially" (http://home.snafu.de/tilman/#cos). His French colleague, Roger Gonnet, who often signs his communiqués "Le Secticide," defines Scientology simply as "the cult of homicides and suicides" (www.antisectes.net/defs.htm). While numerous other anti-Scientology sites exist—altreligionscientology.org links to more than one hundred of them in ten different languages—these few will serve to illustrate the principles of propaganda in e-space.

Despite considerable differences in design sophistication and appearance, each site frames its material on Scientology in a very similar fashion. In an effort to demonstrate that the CoS lacks any redeeming social value, each serves as an e-space host for a wide range of allegations and speculations about the authenticity of Scientology as a religion (Rashleigh-Berry n.d.), the church's ongoing Internet battles (http://home.snafu.de/tilman/prolinks/index.html), its tactics when dealing with critics (www.apologeticsindex.org/s04f.html), the career of L. Ron Hubbard (www.xs4all.nl/~kspaink/cos/LRH-bio), the nature of Scientology's emerging scriptures (www.xenu.net/archive/secret.html), the costs of Scientological training (www.xenu.netarchive/CoS_prices.html), and occasional demands for government investigations of accusations of criminal activities (West n.d.) Each of these sites, however, presents little in the way of original research that has been conducted by the owner. Rather, they hyperlink to a plethora of media reports, a few more detailed articles both scholarly and popular, court reports and transcripts, out-of-print exposés that have been for-matted for online use (e.g., Miller 1987), and ex-member accounts of life in CoS.

Most important, however, is that they link to other sites that themselves pres-ent essentially the same information. Hence, while the appearance is that there is an enormous amount of anti-Scientology material available, the actual pool is considerably smaller than the large number of sites that link to it might suggest. When some new resource appears, numerous sites either link to it or host a version of it. Hence, rather than deepen the pool of these resources by contributing original research and material, countermovement sites simply broaden it by repli-cating that which is available. For example, while fifty different Web pages may link to online copies of Wakefield's *The Road to Xenu* (1991), the reality is that this is but one example of apostate testimony, not fifty. This may seem a rather obvi-ous point, but in the often confusing welter of hyperlinks countermovement pages contain and Internet search engines generate, it is a point easily lost.

This process of replication is one of the more significant advantages of the Internet as a platform for the dissemination of countermovement propaganda and one of the main problems encountered by CoS in its battle to keep certain material out of the public domain. Since Web site operators are under neither obligation nor expectation to generate original material, the intellectual thresh-old for participation in countermovement propaganda lowers significantly. Cut-copy-and-paste Web sites abound. And while CoS may be able to keep a number of these sites under scrutiny (if not control), this lower participation threshold means that information placed on the Web has the potential to replicate exponentially.

This ongoing replication allows countermovement Web sites to present a consistent message that is repeated over and over, a consistency that contributes in no small measure to the self-limiting construction of reality that informs such material. Although some countermovement sites do link to official Scien-tology pages, there is very little variation in the material, and one looks in vain for more positive evaluations of Scientology such as testimonials from happy, healthy Scientologists. Why? Because Scientologists are not the target audience. These are Web sites designed not for supporters or adherents, but for those who are already predisposed to regard Scientology negatively. The subtitle on Heldal-Lund's "Operation Clambake" site makes its purpose clear: "The Fight Against the Church of Scientology on the Net." Hausherr declares that Church "adherents are sadly deluded and often mentally ill"—hardly candidates for his brand of countermovement propaganda. And while Scientology is not the only controversial religious movement discussed on Hein's massive site, Hein is very clear that his primary audience consists of evangelical Christians who are looking for countermovement resources. He recognizes that non-Christians may find and use the information on his site, but they are not his target audience. Similarly, for Heldal-Lund, if Scientologists visit Operation Clambake, well and good. The audience for whom the site is designed, however, comprises those who will hopefully join him in his fight against CoS. That is, in keeping with the fundamental principles of propaganda outlined above, the message that is presented repeatedly and consistently is one for which the target audience already has some basic affinity.

The self-limiting construction of reality that emerges when the Internet is the vehicle by which propaganda is replicated is reinforced by the often over-simplified and decontextualized nature of the information presented. In recent years CoS has adopted many of the trappings of mainline North American religion: its clergy are referred to as ordained ministers and chaplains; Church services include sermons, prayers, and hymns; official teachings are called a catechism; and Hubbard's own voluminous writings are revered as sacred scripture. Countermovement critics, however, universally refer to the CoS as a "cult," always deploying the most negative cultural stereotypes associated with the term. Indeed, Hein goes even further and classifies Scientology "as a hate group," though his working definition of the term tends more towards a text-book example of propagandistic oversimplification than it does a useful descriptor. In the introduction to his section on Scientology, he states that CoS "increasingly acts like a hate group" (www.apologeticsindex.org/s04aa.html). In his "Religion News Blog," a digest of world news reports related to new religious movements which he posts regularly to his Web site, items on Scien-tology are always listed as "[Hate Groups: Scientology]."

Into many of these reports Hein inserts his own commentary and links to relevant pages on the Apologetics Index site. For example, in a May 2003 article discussing the CoS's Citizen's Commission on Human Rights (CCHR), when the visitor mouses over the CCHR name, the following box appears: "Browsing Tip: This hate group is one of Scientology's many fronts. It employs the cult's usual unethical behavior." Following Hein's link to a definition of "hate groups" one not surprisingly finds the Ku Klux Klan, Aryan Nations, and Christian Identity. With regard to Scientology, however, he states that while it does not "*primarily* focus on hatred," "through deceitful propaganda and misinformation ... harassment of critics, and 'dead agenting' practices [i.e, spreading lies and malicious information about Church critics] they nevertheless create an atmosphere in which hatred thrives virtually unchecked" (www.apologeticsindex.org/h21.html). The important point here is that Hein does not say precisely how responding to critics—in whatever fashion— actually substantiates his claim that the CoS is a "hate group." Such evidence is largely unnecessary, however, because his target audience is already predisposed to believe the worst about Scientology.

The Online Battle for Offline Esoterica

One of the mechanisms by which religious groups establish and maintain essential social boundaries is the organization of sacred teachings into categories of *exoterica* and *esoterica*—that is, those that are publicly available and those that are reserved for institutional elites or devotees. The obvious print examples of Scientological exoterica are Hubbard's *Dianetics* ([1950] 1990), which has never been allowed to go out of print and for which the CoS claims a singular best-seller status, or the CoS International's introductory text, *What is Scientology?* (1998b). On the street and on the Web, Scientology is commonly encountered in the form of its two-hundred-question "Oxford Capacity Analysis" test, which serves as a primary recruiting tool for the organization and which provides the basis for initial auditing sessions.

Esoterica, on the other hand, are available only to those who have demonstrated a more significant level of commitment to the organization, its principles, and its spiritual and therapeutic product–what the Church calls its "technology" (or "tech"). While the exoteric teachings are designed to bring participants to the first level of organizational status, known as "clear" (see Bainbridge 1980; Hubbard [1950] 1990; Wallis 1976), the "tech" contained in levels above "clear"—what CoS calls the "Operating Thetan" or OT levels—are considered esoterica. Among other things, at these levels Scientologists become acquainted with teachings that serve as the cosmogonic underpinning of all Scientological theory and practice, and it is for the right to enclose or disclose this information that an Internet battle is being fought.

Though the more complex catachetical elements of the cosmogony are part of Scientology's carefully guarded OT esoterica, for more than a decade various details have been disseminated across a number of venues, both print and electronic, including exposés and critiques (Atack n.d., 1990; Wakefield 1991), magazine articles (Lippard and Jacobsen 1995a), scholarly studies (Melton 2001), and legal reviews and litigation documents (Browne 1998; Fishman 1993; Horwitz 1997). Indeed, the story came to Internet prominence as a result of litigation. In 1993 Steven Fishman included it in a court declaration that was part of his defense in *Church of Scientology International v. Fishman and Geertz*. Three years earlier Fishman was convicted of mail fraud. He claimed during his trial that he had been brainwashed by CoS and had committed the acts to pay for his sessions with the Church. This defense was rejected by the court and Fishman was later sued by the Church for libel. The civil litigation resulted in the cosmogonic elements of what has become known in anti-Scientology lore as "The Fishman Declaration" being posted to the alt.religion.scientology discussion list and they have remained on the Internet ever since. Even the Church itself, when faced with such widespread and unregulated distribution, realized it could not deny the existence of Hubbard's cosmogony and issued brief statements on each of the eight OT levels through its Religious Technology Center (the organization directly responsible for the maintenance of Scientological orthodoxy). "It is in our interests," reads the one-page press release, "to broadly disseminate the truth of these levels rather than allow suppressives to distort and misuse this information for their own purposes" (Project: Bridge Info n.d.).

Which is, of course, precisely the point. Countermovement critics *do* "distort and misuse this information" in their efforts to enclose and control information about the Church, and the specific qualities of the Internet—especially replication and nonregulation—contribute to this ongoing distortion.

All told, these events precipitated something of an e-space battle for control over Scientology's esoteric teachings. Not unreasonably, CoS contends that it has the absolute right to its own esoteric material and that any breach of that right—especially in the form of unauthorized reproduction and distribution—is an attack on its freedom of belief and practice and its free exercise of religion. It has sought to protect these teachings through an aggressive program of copyright enclosure facilitated through the Religious Technology Center (cf. Brill and Packard 1997; Frankel 1996; Fraser 1998; Grossman 1995, 1997; Lyons 2000; Peckham 1998). Anti-Scientologists, on the other hand, maintain three interrelated positions: (1) a loosely construed constitutional right to freedom of speech (recognizing, however, that not all countries share equally in this concept); (2) a quasi-anarchist notion that on the Internet any and all information should be freely available and free from restriction, regulation, or control; and (3) the contention of critics bent on "exposing" the Church that publication of Scientological esoterica is warranted on the grounds that anyone considering Scientology has the right to full and fair disclosure about what they are getting themselves into. Addressing the issue of copyright, one critic declares unapologetically; "I, Andreas Heldal-Lund, have reviewed the secret materials of Scientology and after careful consideration have concluded that these materials are being kept secret in order to withhold information from the public with the sole purpose of deceiving the public as to the true nature of Scientology" (www.xenu.net/copyright.html). The impressive presentation of material on the Operation Clambake sites masks the obvious question of why Heldal-Lund, who admits he has never been a Scientologist and has training in neither religious studies nor theology, believes he is qualified to make these kinds of evaluations.

While obviously important, who owns the copyright to various material, esoteric or otherwise, is not the only issue in this discussion. Nor is it simply whether CoS has a right to keep its esoteric teachings private, despite the argument of Church critics that it is precisely these teachings that lay the foundation for seeing Scientology as a devious cult. The real question is: Why expose secret teachings at all? For anti-Scientologists, what purpose is served by constantly republishing this esoteric Scientological material, no matter how it came into the public domain? Those who contend that in a free society it is their right to present this material argue that the very fact of religious teachings that are not available to all only proves their more general suspicions about the dangerous character of Scientology. After all, if they have nothing to hide, why keep this material hidden? This position, however, while compelling perhaps for the anti-Scientologists' target audience, fundamentally misunderstands (and misrepresents) the function of esoterica in the framework of religious organizations. As Hadden made clear in an affidavit filed in support of an *amicus curiae* brief in the Fishman case, "secrecy functions to protect the internal integrity of a group" (Hadden 1994: 2); that is, it defines one of the principal boundaries between group insiders and outsiders. In one sense it separates "we who know" from "you who do not." Hence, the unauthorized distribution of these teachings disrupts not only the normative functioning of the group but also the organizational and catechistic integrity to which these teachings contribute.

On the other hand, if the intent of reproducing Scientology's esoteric material is simply to demonstrate the allegedly fanciful nature of the cosmogonic myth itself or its derivative *heilsgeschichte* and thereby discredit the organization, then one could as easily point to similarly fanciful creation stories and salvation histories in Christianity—for example, an *ex nihilo* creation in six literal days, or the miracles and physical resurrection of Christ. Online replication of this material also contributes to the public ridicule of Scientology offline. For the last few years, for example, Church critics have traveled to various locations in both North America and Europe to picket Scientology centers. Many of the photographs from these events are posted on countermovement Web sites and feature stereotypical "alien" dolls which are alleged to represent characters in the Scientological cosmogony. By presenting these beliefs as patently ridiculous and opening the Church up to public derision on that basis, opponents hope to weaken Scientology's ability to present itself as a credible religion. Once again, however, there are any number of other religious mythologies that would appear equally ridiculous to nonbelievers. (Witness one non-Christian student of mine who was astonished to learn that Easter was *not* a ritual during which Christians worship bunnies!)

Favoring the Critic: The Internet as a Delivery System for Countermovement Propaganda

If, as I and other scholars have noted (e.g., Cowan 2000; Introvigne 2000; Mayer 2000), countermovement use of the Internet is in many ways a propaganda war, whom does the Web favor in that conflict? Peckham's analysis of the countermovement struggle over Scientology suggests that the Internet needs to be reconceptualized as a delivery system for "virtual resources," which "have no intrinsic value and little meaning outside the context of on-line activity, yet are highly valued by Internet users" (1998: 322). He concludes that the most important of these "virtual resources" are bandwidth and anonymity. In point of fact, though, the Internet does not provide anything particularly new or innovative in terms of the ability of a countermovement to prosecute its argument. Bandwidth, for example, is less important when one operates a countermovement Web site and one does not rely on postings to alt.-type discussion lists. As well, none of Scientology's most trenchant Internet critics operate anonymously; for the most part, they are very clear about who they are and why they do what they do. While Peckham's "virtual resources"are not unimportant in some venues, I would like to suggest that the Net favors the countermovement for very different reasons.

Taken together, the Internet and the World Wide Web constitute a more efficient technological platform for a contest that has been ongoing in the real world for millennia: the control, manipulation, and, most significantly, replication of symbolic resources. Four factors converge in this replication as it contributes to the concept of propaganda: (1) the breadth and architecture of the Internet; (2) the perception of credibility and authority conferred on widely replicated material; (3) the predisposition of the target audience; and (4) the limited organizational resources available to contest countermovement propaganda.

First is the fact of replication itself, in which the (mis)information provided assumes something of a life of its own. The real value of the Internet as a venue for countermovement propaganda is its amorphous breadth and the difficulty faced by any group in policing that which is propagated on the Web. That is, since the Internet is designed specifically to route data from one node to another by whatever means are available, it interprets attempts at censorship and control as instances of systemic failure. Blocked on one route, the Internet looks for another. The CoS might very well secure copyright injunctions on behalf of its esoteric teachings, but the Internet itself will not recognize them. Proscribed material that is removed from one anonymous server reappears on a different server; attempts at suppression actually force the migration of their material further and further out onto the Internet; and data that are prevented from routing along one address path simply find their way along a different path.

Second, such replication often confers the semblance of authority on those believed to be the originators of the material. For example, countermovement sites regularly refer to the operators of similar sites as "experts" and "authorities," evaluations by which casual Internet visitors may easily be swayed. This propensity is especially prevalent in the evangelical countercult movement (Cowan 2003).

Third is the predisposition of the target audience for whom propaganda is constructed. The manner in which replication occurs online—material produced by putative authorities is then reappropriated and reloaded on other sites—can result in what I have called elsewhere "a progressively deteriorating epistemic loop, the intellectual rigor of which will continue to degrade over time" (Cowan 2003: 209). Original sources and research become lost in the replication, and the oversimplified portrait of the group under attack comes to represent far more a caricature than an analysis. Since a countermovement's target audience is unlikely to question the simplistic nature of the presentation, however, this does not matter.

Finally, the Web also favors the countermovement because for most religious organizations, if they engage in it at all, answering criticism and misrepresentation online is at best a secondary agenda. Few groups have shown themselves willing to go to the lengths employed by CoS when responding to Internet brickbats. If religious movements such as CoS, the Local Church, the Latter-Day Saints, Jehovah's Witnesses, or any of the other religious groups attacked online by members of the evangelical countercult, the secular anticult, or other countermovements are considered as systems containing a particular, finite amount of organizational energy, the more energy that is expended responding to countermovement propaganda, the less that remains available for the prosecution of one's primary religious mission. Propagation of (mis)information, on the other hand, *is* the primary agenda of countermovement Web sites, the goal toward which all organizational energy is directed, a goal that is well served in a number of ways by the Internet and the World Wide Web.

References

Agence France Presse (1996a). "Kohl Party Decides to Ban Scientologists from German Public Service" (October 21).
Agence France Presse (1996b). "Scientologists Banned from Public Service in Bavaria from Friday" (October 29).
Agence France Presse (1997). "German States Seek to Outlaw the Church of Scientology" (April 17).
Agence France Presse (2001). "Spanish Court Acquits Scientology Members Accused of Conspiracy" (December 3).
Agence France Presse (2002). "Scientologists File Complaint Against Germany at UN" (October 2).
Atack, J. (n.d.). "The Total Freedom Trap." Retrieved from www.clambake.org/archive/books/ttft, April 13, 2003.
Atack, J. (1990). *A Piece of Blue Sky: Scientology, Dianetics and L. Ron Hubbard Exposed.* New York: Lyle Stuart Books.
Bainbridge, W. S. (1980). "Scientology: To Be Perfectly Clear." *Sociological Analysis* 41: 128–136.
Bainbridge, W. S. (1987). "Science and Religion: The Case of Scientology." In *The Future of New Religious Movements*, ed. D. G. Bromley and P. E. Hammond. Macon, GA: Mercer University Press.
Beckford, J. A. (1980). "Scientology, Social Science and the Definition of Religion." Los Angeles: Freedom Publishing.
Bednarowski, M. F. (1995). "The Church of Scientology: Lightning Rod for Cultural Boundary Conflicts." In *America's Alternative Religions*, ed. T. Miller. Albany, NY: State University of New York Press.
Benkler, Y. (1999). "Free as the Air to Common Use: First Amendment Constraints on Enclosure of the Public Domain." *New York University Law Review* 74: 354–446.
Berger, P., and T. Luckmann (1966). *The Social Construction of Reality: A Treatise on the Sociology of Knowledge.* London: Penguin Books.
Berglie, P-A. (1996). "Scientology: A Comparison with Religions of the East and West." Los Angeles: Freedom Publishing.
Black, A. W. (1996). "Is Scientology a Religion?" Los Angeles: Freedom Publishing.
Brill, A., and A. Packard, (1997). "Silencing Scientology's Critics on the Internet: A Mission Impossible?" *Communications and the Law* 19 (4): 1–23.

Bromley, D. G., and M. L. Bracey (1998). "The Church of Scientology: A Quasi-Religion." In *Sects, Cults, and Spiritual Communities: A Sociological Analysis*, ed. W. W. Zellner and M. Petrowsky. Westport, CT: Praeger Publishers.

Browne, M. (1998). "Should Germany Stop Worrying and Love the Octopus? Freedom of Religion and the Church of Scientology in Germany and the United States." *Indiana International & Comparative Law Review* 9: 155–202.

Bryant, M. D. (1994). "Scientology: A New Religion." Los Angeles: Freedom Publishing.

Chidester, D. (n.d.). "Scientology: A Religion in South Africa." Los Angeles: Freedom Publishing.

Church of Scientology (n.d.). "Response to Lyons." *Rutgers Journal of Law and Religion* 2 (1), retrieved from http://camlaw.rutgers.edu/publications/law-religion/response.pdf, April 20, 2003.

Church of Scientology International (1998a). *Scientology: Theology & Practice of a Contemporary Religion.* Los Angeles: Bridge Publications.

Church of Scientology (1998b). *What is Scientology?* Los Angeles: Bridge Publications.

Corydon, B. (1992). *L. Ron Hubbard: Messiah or Madman?* rev. ed. Fort Lee, NJ: Barricade Books.

Cowan, D. E. (1999). "Bearing False Witness: Propaganda, Reality-Maintenance, and Christian Anti-Cult Apologetics." Ph.D. dissertation, University of Calgary.

Cowan D. E. (2000). "Religion, Rhetoric, and Scholarship: Managing Vested Interest in E-Space." In *Religion on the Internet: Research Prospects and Promises*, ed. J. K. Hadden and D. E. Cowan. Amsterdam and London: JAI Press/Elsevier Science.

Cowan, D. E. (2002). "Exits and Migrations: Foregrounding the Christian Counter-cult." *Journal of Contemporary Religion* 17 (3): 339–354.

Cowan, D. E. (2003). *Bearing False Witness? An Introduction to the Christian Countercult.* Westport, CT: Praeger Publishers.

Dawson, L. L. (2001). "New Religions in Cyberspace: The Promise and Perils of a New Public Space." In *Chercheurs de Dieux dans l'Espace Public/Frontier Religions in Public Space*, ed. P. Côte. Ottawa, Ont.: University of Ottawa Press.

Dericquebourg, R. (1995). "Scientology." Los Angeles: Freedom Publishing.

Durham, W. C. (1996). "Perspectives on Religious Liberty: A Comparative Framework." In *Religious Human Rights in Global Perspective: Legal Perspectives*, ed. J. D. van der Vyver and J. Witte, Jr. The Hague and Boston: M. Nijhoff Publishers.

Fisher, M. (1995). "Church in Cyberspace; Its Sacred Writ is on the Net. Its Lawyers are on the Case." *The Washington Post* (August 19): C01.

Fishman, S. (1993). "Declaration of Steven Fishman," *Church of Scientology International v. Fishman and Geertz*, retrieved from www.xs4all.nl/~kspaink/fishman/home.html, May 2, 2003.

Flinn, F. K. (1983). "Scientology as Technological Buddhism." In *Alternatives to American Mainline Churches*, ed. J. H. Fichter. Barrytown, NY: Unification Theological Seminary.

Frankel, A. (1996). "Making Law, Making Enemies." *The American Lawyer* (March): 68.

Fraser, F. (1998). "The Conflict Between the First Amendment and Copyright Law and Its Impact on the Internet." *Cardozo Arts & Entertainment Law Journal* 16(1): 1–52.

Fraser, F. (1994). "Scientology: Marks of a Religion." Los Angeles: Freedom Publishing.

Frigerio, A. (1996). "Scientology and Contemporary Definitions of Religion in the Social Sciences." Los Angeles: Freedom Publishing.

Garcia, W. (1994). "A Battle of Beliefs Waged in Megabytes." *St. Petersburg Times* (August 3): 1A.

Grossman, W. M. (1995). "alt.scientology.war." *Wired* 3 (12), retrieved from www.wired.com/wired/archive/3.12/alt.scientology.war_pr.html, April 20, 2003.

Grossman, W. M. (1997). *Net.Wars.* New York: New York University Press.

Gualtieri, A. R. (1989). *Conscience and Coercion: Ahmadi Muslims and Orthodoxy in Pakistan.* Montreal: Guernica.

Hadden, J. K. (1994). "Declaration of Jeffrey K. Hadden." Photocopy of typescript.

Hadden, J. K., and D. E. Cowan, (2000). "The Promised Land or Electronic Chaos? Toward Understanding Religion on the Internet." In *Religion on the Internet: Research Prospects and Promises*, ed. J. K. Hadden and D. E. Cowan. Amsterdam and London: JAI Press/Elsevier Science.

Heino, H. (1995). "Scientology: Its True Nature." Los Angeles: Freedom Publishing.

Hexham, I., and K. Poewe (1999). "'Verfassungsfeindlich': Church, State, and New Religions in Germany." *Nova Religio* 2 (2): 208–227.

Horwitz, P. (1997). "Scientology in Court: A Comparative Analysis and Some Thoughts on Selected Issues in Law and Religion." *DePaul Law Review* 47: 85–154.

Hubbard, L. R. [1950] (1990). *Dianetics: The Modern Science of Mental Health.* Los Angeles: Bridge Publications.

Introvigne, M. (2000). "'So Many Evil Things': Anti-Cult Terrorism via the Internet." In *Religion on the Internet: Research Prospects and Promises*, ed. J. K. Hadden and D. E. Cowan. Amsterdam and London: JAI Press/Elsevier Science.

Kelley, D. M. [1980] (1996). "Is Scientology a Religion?" Updated ed. Los Angeles: Freedom Publishing.

Kent, S. A. (1999a). "The Creation of 'Religious' Scientology." *Religious Studies and Theology* 18 (2): 97–126.

Kent S. A. (1999b). "The Globalization of Scientology: Influence, Control and Opposition in Transnational Markets." *Religion* 29: 147–69.

Kent S. A. (1999c). "Scientology—Is this a Religion?" *Marburg Journal of Religion* 4 (1), retrieved from www.uni-marburg.de/religionswissenschaft/journal/mjr/kent.html, April 25, 2003.

Lazlow. (2003). "Online Treachery." *Playboy* (March): 93, 142.

Levy, S. (1997). "Blaming the Web." *Newsweek*, April 7: 46.

Lippard, J., and J. Jacobsen (1995a). "Scientology v. the Internet: Free Speech & Copyright Infringement on the Information Super-Highway." *Skeptic* 3 (3): 35–41, available at www.skeptic.com, accessed April 20, 2003.

Lippard, J., and J. Jacobsen (1995b). "Scientology Loses Judgment in Internet Case." *Skeptic* 3 (4): 18–19, available at www.skeptic.com, accessed April 20, 2003.

Lyons, T. A. (2000). "Scientology or Censorship: You Decide: An Examination of the Church of Scientology, Its Recent Battles with Individual Internet Users Service Providers, the Digital Millennium Copyright Act, and the Implications for Free Speech on the Web." *Rutgers Journal of Law and Religion* 2 (1), retrieved from http://camlaw.rutgers. edu/publications/law-religion/scientology.pdf, April 20, 2003.

Mayer, J-F. (2000). "Religious Movements and the Internet: The New Frontier of Religious Controversies." In *Religion on the Internet: Research Prospects and Promises*, ed. J. K. Hadden and D. E. Cowan. Amsterdam and London: JAI Press/Elsevier Science.

Melton, J. G. (2000). *The Church of Scientology*. Torino, Italy: Signature Books.

Melton, J. G. (2001). "The Sea Org: A Report of Research on a Contemporary Ordered Religious Community." Paper presented at the International Conference of CESNUR, London, England.

Miller, R. (1987). *Bare-Faced Messiah: The True Story of L. Ron Hubbard*. Toronto, Ont.: Key Porter Books.

Moos, K. (1995). *A Chronological View of L. Ron Hubbard and Scientology*. Silkeborg, Denmark: Seagull Productions.

Peckham, M. (1998). "New Dimensions of Social Movement/Countermovement Interaction: The Case of Scientology and Its Scientology Critics." *Canadian Journal of Sociology/Cahiers Canadiens de Sociologie* 23 (4): 317–347.

Pentikainen, J., and M. Pentikainen, (1996). "The Church of Scientology." Los Angeles: Freedom Publishing.

Project: Bridge Info. (n.d.). "OT LEVELS (For Immediate Release)." Press release. Religious Technology Center.

Rashleigh-Berry, R. (N.d.). "What is Scientology?" retrieved from www.xenu.net/rolandintro. html, November 26, 2003.

Richardson, J. T., and M. Introvigne (2001). "'Brainwashing' Theories in European Parliamentary and Administrative Reports Reports on 'Cults' and 'Sects,'" *Journal for the Scientific Study of Religion* 40 (2): 143–168.

Ross, M. W. (1988). "Effects of Membership in Scientology on Personality: An Exploratory Study." *Journal for the Scientific Study of Religion* 27: 630–636.

Sabbatucci, D. (1983). "Scientology: Its Historical-Morphological Frame." Los Angeles: Freedom Publishing.

Sawada, F. (1996). "The Relationship Between Scientology and Other Religions." Los Angeles: Freedom Publishing.

Sawada, H. M. a. S. (1996). "Scientology and Islam: An Analogous Study." Los Angeles: Freedom Publishing.

Schöen, B. (2001). "New Religions in Germany: The Publicity of the Public Square," *Nova Religio* 4 · (2): 266–274.

Shupe, A. D., and S. E. Darnell (2000). "CAN, We Hardly Knew Ye: Sex, Drugs, Deprogrammers Kickbacks, and Corporate Crime in the (Old) Cult Awareness Network." Paper presented to the annual meeting of the Society for the Scientific Study of Religion, Houston, Texas.

Sivertsev, M. A. (1995). "Scientology: A Way of Spiritual Self-Identification." Los Angeles: Freedom Publishing.

Stark, R., and W.S. Bainbridge (1985). *The Future of Religion: Secularization, Revival, and Cult Formation.* Berkeley and Los Angeles: University of California Press.

Tepper, M. (1997). "Usenet Communities and the Cultural Politics of Information." In *Internet Culture*, ed. D. Porter. New York: Routledge.

Wakefield, M. (1991). *The Road to Xenu: A Narrative Account of Life in Scientology*, retrieved from www-2.cs.cmu.edu/~dst/Library/Shelf/xenu/xenu.pdf, January 10, 2003.

Wallis, R. (1973). "A Comparative Analysis of Problems and Processes of Change in Two Manipulationist Movements: Christian Science and Scientology." In *The Contemporary Metamorphosis of Religion.* Lille, France: Edition du Secrétariat.

Wallis, R. (1976). *The Road to Total Freedom: A Sociological Analysis of Scientology.* London: Heinemann Educational.

West, C. D. (n.d.) "Demand For Investigation of The Church of Scientology," retrieved from www.petitiononline.com/cofs1/petition.html, November 26, 2003.

Whitehead, H. (1974). "Reasonably Fantastic: Some Perspectives on Scientology, Science Fiction, and Occultism." In *Religious Movements in Contemporary America*, ed. I. I. Zaretsky and M. P. Leone. Princeton, NJ: Princeton University Press.

Whitehead, H. (1987). *Renunciation and Reformulation: A Study of Conversion in an American Sect.* Ithaca, NY: Cornell University Press.

Contributors

Helen A. Berger is Professor of Sociology at West Chester University. She is the author of *A Community of Witches: Contemporary Witches and Neo-Pagans in the United States* and primary author (with Evan Leach and Leigh Shaffer) of *Voices from the Pagan Census: A National Survey of Withces and Neo-Pagans in the United States*, both published by the University of South Carolina Press.

Gary R. Bunt is a Lecturer in the Department of Theology, Religious Studies and Islamic Studies, University of Wales, Lampeter, United Kingdom. He has published two books on Islam and the Internet: *Virtually Islamic: Computer-Mediated Communication and Cyber Islamic Environments* (University of Wales Press) and *Islam in the Digital Age: E-Jihad, Online Fatwas and Cyber Islamic Environments* (Pluto Press).

Heidi Campbell is a Research Fellow with the Institute for Advanced Studies in the Humanities at the University of Edinburgh (Scotland). She is the author of several publications including "A Review of Religious Computer-Mediated Communication Research" in *Mediating Religion: Conversations in Media, Culture and Religion*, and a forthcoming text, *Exploring Religious Community: We Are One in the Network* (Peter Lang Publishers).

Robert A. Campbell is Associate Principal–Academic Resources, at the University of Toronto at Scarborough, where he also teaches courses on world religions. His publications are on the sociology of science, the interaction of Science and religion, and other aspects of the study of religion.

Douglas E. Cowan is Assistant Professor of Religious Studies and Sociology at the University of Missouri-Kansas City. He is the author or editor of several books, including *The Remnant Spirit: Conservative Reform in Mainline Protestantism* (Praeger Publishers) and *Cyberhenge: Magic, Metatechnology, and the Neopagan Internet* (Routledge).

Lorne L. Dawson is an Associate Professor of Sociology and Chair of the Department of Religious Studies at the University of Waterloo, Waterloo, Ontario, Canada. He has published several articles and book chapters on religion and the Internet and is the author of *Comprehending Cults: The Sociology of New Religious Movements* (Oxford University Press) and editor of *Cults and New Religious Movements: A Reader* (Blackwell).

Douglas Ezzy (Ph.D.) is a Senior Lecturer in Sociology at the University of Tasmania, Australia. He has also published *Qualitative Analysis: Practice and Innovation* (Routledge) and *Practising the Witch's Craft* (Allen & Unwin).

Wendy Griffin is a Professor of Women's Studies at California State University, Long Beach, and has been doing research into Goddess Spirituality since 1988. Her most recent publications include "Goddess Spirituality and Wicca" in *Her Voice, Her Faith: Women Speak on World Religions* (Westview Press), and *Daughters of the Goddess: Studies of Healing, Identity and Empowerment* (AltaMira Press).

Christopher Helland is a Ph.D. candidate in the Sociology of Religion at the University of Toronto, Centre for the Study of Religion. His publications on religion and the Internet include the book chapter "Online Religion/Religion Online and Virtual Communitas" (JAI) Press and the article "Surfing for Salvation," in the journal Religion.

Jenna Hennebry is a Ph.D. candidate in the Department of Scoiology at the University of Western Ontario in Canada. Her primary research interest is the representation of migration, development, and globalization in academic discourse and popular media.

Marilyn C. Krogh is an Assistant Professor in the Department of Sociology and Anthropology at Loyola University, Chicago. Her primary research is in Urban Sociology and inequality in labor markets.

Elena Larsen spent three years as a Research Fellow with the Pew Internet and American Life Project. She researched and published several reports on the intersection of the Internet with religion and government in the lives of Americans. Her work on religion has included general population surveys, use of the Internet by religious congregations, and pursuit of methodologies for surveying religious minorities in the United States. She has also participated in studies conducted by the University of Pennsylvania and the State University of New York on the 2000 and 2002 elections as manifested on the Internet.

Mia Lövheim is a doctoral candidate in the Sociology of Religion at the Faculty of Theology at Uppsala University, Sweden. Her research focuses on the construction of religious identity among young men and women in contemporary Sweden, primarily in relation to the Internet. She is currently finishing her dissertation, "Intersecting Identities: Young People, Religious Identities, and Interaction on the Internet."

Mark W. Macwilliams is an Associate Professor at St. Lawrence University and the author of a number articles on religion and the Internet.

Stephen O'Leary is Associate Professor in the Annenberg School of Communication at the University of Southern California. He is the author of Arguing the Apacalyse (Oxford University Press 1994), and his current research focuses on religion, rhetoric, technology, and communication ethics.

Brooke Ashley Pillifant graduated with an MA in Sociology from Loyola University of Chicago. She is currently leading a research team for Louisiana State University Health Science Center and Xavier University of Louisiana investigating the utilization of pharmacists to deliver a brief motivational intervention in order to reduce alcohol levels in low-income minority populations.

Charles S. Prebish is Professor of Religious Studies at the Pennsylvania State University. He is the author or editor of fifteen books, the most recent of which are *Westward Dharma: Buddhism beyond Asia and Buddhism in the Modern World: Adaptations of an Ancient Tradition*. He is also a founding Coeditor of the *Journal of Buddhist Ethics* and the *Journal of Global Buddhism*.

Glenn Young is an interdisciplinary Ph.D. candidate in Religious Studies and English at the University of Missouri–Kansas City.

Index

UNDERSTANDING
THE CONTEMPORARY
MIDDLE EAST

UNDERSTANDING

Introductions to the States and Regions of the Contemporary World
Donald L. Gordon, series editor

Understanding Contemporary Africa, 3rd edition
edited by April A. Gordon and Donald L. Gordon

Understanding the Contemporary Caribbean
edited by Richard S. Hillman and Thomas J. D'Agostino

Understanding Contemporary China, 2nd edition
edited by Robert E. Gamer

Understanding Contemporary India
edited by Sumit Ganguly and Neil DeVotta

Understanding Contemporary Latin America, 2nd edition
edited by Richard S. Hillman

Understanding the Contemporary Middle East, 2nd edition
edited by Deborah J. Gerner and Jillian Schwedler

DATE DUE